D0940238

Privacy in America

Interdisciplinary Perspectives

Edited by
William Aspray
Philip Doty

THE SCARECROW PRESS, INC.
Lanham • Toronto • Plymouth, UK
2011

Published by Scarecrow Press, Inc.
A wholly owned subsidiary of The Rowman & Littlefield Publishing Group, Inc.
4501 Forbes Boulevard, Suite 200, Lanham, Maryland 20706
http://www.scarecrowpress.com

Estover Road, Plymouth PL6 7PY, United Kingdom

British Library Cataloguing in Publication Information Available

Library of Congress Cataloging-in-Publication Data

Privacy in America : interdisciplinary perspectives / edited by William Aspray, Philip
Doty.
       p. cm.
    "This book originated in a series of conversations . . . at the School of Information at
the University of Texas at Austin" — Introduction.
    Includes bibliographical references and index.
    ISBN 978-0-8108-8110-5 (pbk. : alk. paper) — ISBN 978-0-8108-8111-2 (ebook)
    1. Privacy, Right of—United States—Congresses. 2. Data protection—Law and
legislation—United States—Congresses. I. Aspray, William. II. Doty, Philip.
    KF1262.A75P754 2011
    342.7308'58—dc22   2011004376

Printed in the United States of America

Contents

Introduction

Philip Doty and William Aspray
University of Texas at Austin

This book originated in a series of conversations that we had in 2009 about the research and teaching of privacy at the School of Information at the University of Texas at Austin. One of us (Bill Aspray) had recently come from Indiana University at Bloomington and had some research funds he wanted to dedicate to a series of meetings of prominent researchers about breaking research fronts. The second meeting, which resulted in this book, focused on privacy and convened in December 2009.

We wanted to invite a small but heterogeneous group of privacy scholars, each known and respected in his or her own right, but a group in which even the most senior of the invitees knew no more than two or three of the other participants. The most important goal of the meeting was for these scholars, from many disciplines and at various stages of their careers, to share their newest research about privacy and to critique each other's work in progress. For us, it was essential that the widest range of high-quality research work in privacy would be represented at the meeting.

Over three days, each author or group of authors of the eighteen invited presented a working draft of a paper, followed by lively discussion of every paper, from all quarters of the room. Learning from the informative discussion of the papers in progress at the workshop, the authors revised their papers in the spring and summer of 2010, participants in the workshop and other privacy experts reviewed the papers anonymously, and the authors submitted a second round of papers. This book is the collection of those revised papers. While some of the workshop participants could not contribute to this collection (Ami Pedahzur and Arie Perliger, David Phillips, and Lance Hayden), the others did. In addition, Anita Allen, a leading legal-studies privacy scholar who could not attend the workshop because of circumstances beyond her control, was able to contribute a chapter to the current volume, reprinted through the generous permission of *California Law Review*, the original publisher. We want to thank Anita and all the participants in the workshop for their willingness to share their works in progress and to help others by their comments and suggestions.

CREATING PRIVACY

Political concepts such as privacy are created in a number of ways and by a number of actors. Social mores; formal policy instruments such as statutes and case law; cultural traditions and norms; popular cultural expression of all kinds, including television shows featuring entertainment and political news and commentaries, newspapers, and blogs; and many other cultural products help us to construct political concepts. These means all help us to understand what we mean when we use terms like *liberty*, *compromise*, and *rights* by providing context and examples to such abstractions. Another means of constructing important political concepts is the work of academic researchers. Like other elements of what we might broadly consider information and communication policy, discussion of the concept of privacy is no longer limited to experts in the three academic disciplines that dominated conversations about political matters in the Western tradition for millennia: political science, political history, and law. Instead, we have a much richer and complex mosaic of academic study in which privacy and related concepts are considered, discussed, and created in multiple ways. The twenty scholars who participated in the workshop represent a multitude of disciplines in several ways: the terminal degrees they hold, their teaching and research affiliations, and the literatures and research traditions they use in their work. These disciplines include public policy, law, computer science, political science and government, feminist studies, history, sociology, gender studies, American studies, engineering, history, international affairs, science and technology studies, communication and media studies, and philosophy, as well as information studies.

Privacy is an especially rich and complex concept that merits study from a wide number of academic perspectives. As the invited scholars engaging the variety of disciplines listed above submitted their draft papers, the editors began to recognize that a common and substantial theme of all of the papers, whether implicit or explicit, was engagement of an important question. How do privacy scholars create or construct privacy in their research? In particular, how do researchers create privacy in the modes of argumentation they use, the questions they engage, the evidence they invoke, and the work of other researchers whom they cite and rely on? Privacy, like other areas in public policy with wide implications for many audiences and communities, is constructed—literally made, in part, by the scholars who investigate what it is. These scholarly conceptions, in turn, help other researchers, policy makers, and people more generally to frame and understand privacy. In large part, this book is a demonstration of how leading researchers create privacy in their scholarship from a variety of perspectives. As Frazer and Lacey (1993) and others remind us, how we talk (our shared discourses) and the concepts we use to understand and describe our shared lives help to create those lives. The authors of the chapters in this book give us insight into many of the various ways that we constitute privacy through our questions, terminologies, and concepts.

The primary goal of this collection is to share this original and interdisciplinary work in privacy with scholars, practitioners, and students in information science, library science, information systems, information policy studies, and other subdisciplines of information studies. In particular, the book's intended audiences are these: researchers and faculty members in information studies, especially in library and information science programs; researchers and faculty members in cognate academic units, e.g., policy studies, communication, American studies, sociology, and law; graduate students, particularly PhD students, in information studies and other programs; administrators of institutions of cultural memory, including libraries, archives, museums, research institutes, and schools—all of them institutions that have particular concerns with privacy; policy makers, members of their staffs, and administrators and staff members of nonprofit and for-profit organizations with special interests and expertise in privacy; and advanced undergraduates with an interest in privacy studies. All of these groups and others will benefit from the book's broad and deep look at how privacy is made in the research of privacy scholars across multiple disciplines, in part because none of the chapters requires any special expertise to read. Yet, because the authors are recognized authorities and writing about their latest work in privacy studies, experts in many disciplines will also likely find the chapters useful.

THEMES IN THE BOOK

The study of privacy has evolved considerably since Alan Westin (1967) and others generated discussions about privacy in the 1950s and 1960s. Research in privacy has changed even more since Samuel D. Warren and Louis D. Brandeis introduced the modern concept of privacy into American policy and cultural discussions with their 1890 paper "The Right to Privacy," which famously called privacy "the right to be let alone," citing Judge Thomas M. Cooley (1888, 29). Among these changes in the study of privacy have been these (see, e.g., Agre 1997; Bennett 2008; Braman 2006; Doty 2001; Foucault 1977; Lyon 2006a and 2006b; McGaw 1989):

- The increased commodification of personally and group-identifiable information of many kinds by commercial actors of many kinds
- The unprecedented growth of the kinds of digital information and communication technologies (ICTs) and of the number and kinds of people using these technologies
- The increased amount of information shared using these ICTs among governmental, private sector, and other organizations
- The flourishing of scholarly and popular literature about privacy, especially in light of the proliferation of digital information technologies
- Erosion of the former hegemony of the panopticon as the dominant metaphor for surveillance by metaphors such as assemblages
- The deepened and broadened engagement with privacy among a much wider variety of disciplines, e.g., the wide variety of disciplines represented by the authors of the chapters in this collection
- Investigation of how gender and social class implicate privacy and how privacy in turn affects them and similar social typologies, e.g., ethnicity
- Changing conceptions of what constitutes privacy and what constitutes unacceptable intrusions; these changes are especially important across generations and in various personal contexts, e.g., social networking websites
- The establishment of federal, state, and other governmental task forces and other groups to investigate the various roles of privacy in citizens' interactions with the increasingly informatized state
- The growth of professional associations' policy study and advocacy groups engaged in public conversations about what privacy means and how it can be given appropriate forms of recognition, e.g., task forces of the National Academy of Sciences and public policy divisions of groups such as the Association for Computing Machinery and the American Medical Association
- The mushrooming of advocacy groups, conferences, websites, and other nonprofit venues for engaging the public interest in privacy; examples include organizations represented by authors in this collection, e.g., James Harper of the CATO Institute and Alissa Cooper of the Center for Democracy and Technology

One way of answering the question about how scholars create privacy is to consider how the chapters in this collection reflect these and other changes in the making of privacy. These chapters engage some overarching, recurring themes. One of the most important is how governmental and private-sector actors work cooperatively to develop and deploy technologies that can pose serious compromises to privacy of many individuals and groups while at the same time offering many social and political benefits. The chapters by James Harper, Alissa Cooper, Andrew Harris et al., Gary Marx, Shimon Modi and Eugene Spafford, Andrew Clement, and those by the editors (Gesse Stark-Smith et al. and Philip Doty) provide rich and specific examples of such cooperation and its threats to privacy.

Another major overarching theme is how information and communication system designs pose systemic threats to privacy; see, e.g., the chapters by Cooper, Harper, Harris et al., Modi and Spafford, Marx, and Doty. The concern with the systemic takes another specifically nontechnical turn in the chapters by Patricia Boling and Andrew Clement, in which they engage the question of how we manage in various polities to recognize what are generally thought to be private concerns (child care, job leave, and identity) as public issues amenable to political action and shared awareness. Stark-Smith et al.'s chapter on privacy and war, as well as Doty's on copyright and privacy, echo this concern with how commonly presumed private, highly individualized concerns (e.g., the privacy of the mails and of our reading) are matters for public discussion and policy intervention.

Another persistent theme involves power; more specifically, the fundamental asymmetry of power that exists between individuals and small groups on the one hand and large governmental and corporate entities on the other. This theme of asymmetry is closely related to the theme of systems' threats to privacy noted above, but it involves a more explicit awareness of social and political power. Whether in Stark-Smith et al. about privacy and war, Marx on developing a framework for analyzing personal information, Harris et al. about the relative impotence of users of integrated financial services online, Cooper on Internet service providers' (ISPs) intrusion through deep packet inspection, Modi and Spafford about demands for biometric identifications, Clement on identification and organizational decision making, or Doty on surveillance under the guise of copyright protection, the chapters abound with examples of what this asymmetry of power can be like and why it matters. This theme is, perhaps, one of the most enduring in privacy studies generally, but it continues to grow in importance as networked information systems proliferate and grow more influential in ordinary people's lives.

Another theme the chapters engage concerns the temporal relationship between the development of information technologies and the development of governmental and corporate policy instruments (and social mores related to those technologies). The chapters by Modi and Spafford and Harris et al.

argue persuasively that the rate of technological change outpaces the rate of policy formation, most especially by the U.S. federal government. At the same time, however, the chapters by Harper and Doty provide substantial support for how policy formation can lead technological development as well. Trying to understand this mutually defining relationship is a theme of growing importance in privacy studies generally, whether in the United States or beyond, and the chapters in this book reflect the complexity of that conversation.

Perhaps fittingly, the last of the overarching themes of this collection of essays to consider here is history. By that we mean how it is that we can learn from what has come before in order to understand the political, social, and technical character of privacy in contemporary life. Previous scholars, policy makers, ordinary citizens, social institutions, and others have all made important decisions about privacy that can inform our own understanding and decisions. Too often, contemporary conversations about privacy are ahistorical; for example, asserting that questions about privacy are artifacts only of the latest digital technologies and services or of current failures of policy making. Stark et al., Clement, Boling, Marx, Doty, and Harper all demonstrate in their chapters the value of historical analysis in understanding and protecting privacy.

While these themes (public and private Information Technology [IT] development and deployment, making private concerns matters for policy discussions, asymmetry of power, IT and policy change, and history) are not the only ones expressed in this book, they are a good indication of how the authors of these chapters move our understanding of privacy forward while reflecting major elements in the ever-expanding privacy literature.

ORGANIZATION OF THE BOOK

The book has three parts, and the first focuses on Law and Policy. Patricia Boling's "Deprived, Protected, Empowered: Privacy's Roles in Public Life" begins the collection by engagement with how it is that formerly private concerns related to work leave and same-sex marriage became important matters of public policy in the United States, Japan, and Germany. Anita Allen's "Privacy Torts: Unreliable Remedies for LGBT Plaintiffs" follows, exploring the mixed record of lesbian, gay, bisexual, and transgendered plaintiffs in using privacy rights in the United States to protect their intimate and political lives. "Toward Identity Rights beyond Privacy" by Andrew Clement, with extended examples from Canadian public policy, provides a close analysis of how expanding privacy concerns to a wider understanding of identity can be useful in addressing what many regard as intractable concerns about privacy. James Harper's paper on "Privacy-Invasive Technologies and Their Origins" concludes this opening part by examining some of the most important of technologies that we regard as threats to privacy in contemporary life, finding their origins in the close cooperation of government and the private sector.

Information Technology is the focus of the second section of the book, and it includes three chapters. Alissa Cooper's "Doing the DPI Dance: Assessing the Privacy Impact of Deep Packet Inspection" considers the technologies and motivations behind deep packet inspection by Internet service providers and the threats such inspection poses to Internet users. "Future Biometric Systems and Privacy" by Shimon Modi and Eugene Spafford catalogues some of the most important failures of information systems that rely on biometric methods of identification and how such systems are becoming important means to compromise privacy. The chapter by Andrew Harris, Frank Park, Seymour Goodman, and Patrick Traynor, "Emerging Privacy and Security Concerns for Digital Wallet Deployment," is a comprehensive consideration of the technologies of near-field communication and cell phones generally and the major public policy concerns related to how these technologies combine in the emerging technology of the digital wallet.

The third part of the book focuses on Other Perspectives: Information Studies, History, and Sociology. The section begins with Philip Doty's "Privacy, Reading, and Trying Out Identity: The Digital Millennium Copyright Act and Technological Determinism," which considers how the surveillance of users of digital files demanded by the Digital Millennium Copyright Act undermines the privacy of reading and thus undermines the formation of identity through the Act's technological determinism. Gesse Stark-Smith, Craig Blaha, and William Aspray give a historical review of some of the most important ways that governments and other actors have tried to control and share information in "Privacy in Time of American War." The last chapter in the collection, Gary Marx's "Turtles, Firewalls, Scarlet Letters, and Vacuum Cleaners: Rules about Personal Information," is a metaconsideration of strategies, themes, policy instruments, social mores, and other means used in reference to personal information. The taxonomy that Marx offers is a good way to conclude this book of essays that attempt to reflect the many ways that we create privacy in America and elsewhere in our world.

REFERENCES

Agre, Philip E. 1997. Introduction. In *Technology and privacy: The new landscape*, ed. Philip E. Agre and Marc Rotenberg, 1–28. Cambridge, MA: MIT Press.

Bennett, Colin J. 2008. *The privacy advocates: Resisting the spread of surveillance.* Cambridge, MA: MIT Press.

Braman, Sandra. 2006. *Change of state: Information, policy, and power.* Cambridge, MA: MIT Press.

Cooley, Thomas M. 1888. *A treatise on the law of torts, or the wrongs which arise independent of contract*, 2nd ed. Chicago: Callaghan.

Doty, Philip. 2001. Digital privacy: Toward a new politics and discursive practice. In *Annual review of information science and technology*, ed. Martha E. Williams, vol. 36, 115–245. Medford, NJ: Information Today.

Foucault, Michel. 1977. *Discipline and punish: The birth of the prison*, trans. Alan Sheridan. New York: Pantheon Books.

Frazer, Elizabeth, and Nicola Lacey. 1993. *The politics of community: A feminist critique of the liberal-communitarian debate.* New York: Harvester Wheatsheaf.

Lyon, David. 2006a. The search for surveillance theories. In *Theorizing surveillance: The panopticon and beyond*, ed. David Lyon, 3–20. Portland, OR: Willan.

———, ed. 2006b. *Theorizing surveillance: The panopticon and beyond.* Portland, OR: Willan.

McGaw, Judith. 1989. No passive victims, no separate spheres: A feminist perspective on technology's history. In *In context: History and the history of technology*, ed. Stephen Cutcliffe and Robert Post, 172–91. Bethlehem, PA: Lehigh University Press.

Warren, Samuel D., and Louis D. Brandeis. 1890. The right to privacy. *Harvard Law Review* IV, 5: 193–220.

Westin, Alan F. 1967. *Privacy and freedom.* New York: Atheneum.

1

LAW AND POLICY

1

Deprived, Protected, Empowered

Privacy's Roles in Public Life

Patricia Boling
Purdue University

This chapter takes a conceptual approach to privacy, contrasting it with what is public, has broad impact, or is political. Matters we call "private" can be important and protected, or they can seem to be merely private, unworthy of public recognition or remedy. I examine several contentious social issues (same-sex marriage and parental leaves in the United States, the introduction of generous work-family policies in Germany and Japan) in terms of privacy protections and processes of translating practices that occur in the privacies of families, homes, and intimate relationships into political issues. I propose that studying how easily countries can articulate the public importance of private matters—a crucial step toward effective policy responses—could be a valuable way to compare welfare regimes. At both the level of U.S. domestic policy and cross-national comparative work, it is crucial to translate issues located in intimate life into properly political claims and actions and to transform private sufferers into citizens.

I take a conceptual approach to privacy, distinguishing different meanings and valences of privacy and noting the different contrasts we draw to "private." Reflecting on different senses in which something can be private can help us be clear about what we are claiming when we demand that others respect our privacy or when we assert a right to privacy. Any conceptual clarity we gain may be an especially useful contribution to a book of essays that address technologies that threaten interests in informational or communicative privacy or undermine control over one's identity.

After identifying distinct senses of privacy and considering some common contrasts to privacy, I consider three contested issues that revolve around public-private distinctions. The first issue concerns claims to decisional privacy or individual autonomy with respect to decisions like abortion or choice of sexual partner. Until recently, most states considered abortion and sodomy to be appropriate matters for regulation under criminal law. But the U.S. Supreme Court recognized and expanded a constitutional right to privacy that was used to strike down state criminal abortion statutes in *Roe v. Wade* (1973) and state sodomy laws in *Lawrence v. Texas* (2003). Now the conversation has shifted to whether the federal or state constitutions require that same-sex couples be allowed to marry on the grounds that all couples deserve access to the privileges and perquisites of marriage, regardless of their sexual orientation.[1] While privacy was the engine for decriminalizing intimate and profoundly important decisions, current discussion is pushing for public, civil recognition of same-sex intimacy using arguments about equality and community. The second example is the struggle to pass family leave legislation in the United States, an instance of translating responsibility for childrearing and caring for ill family members from being purely a private, familial responsibility to requiring that employers give job-protected leaves to parents of new babies or workers with serious illnesses in the family. The third example moves beyond the United States to a cross-national comparative approach that examines how readily different welfare regimes are able to articulate the public significance of work-family reconciliation policies like parental leave.

SENSES OF PRIVACY

We often use privacy in a protective sense, to indicate a zone into which others may not intrude without our permission. Consider, for example, signs that say "Posted: Private property, no trespassing," or documents from our credit card company or medical care providers that promise not to disclose information about us to others without our permission. We expect to be able to exclude strangers or uninvited persons from our homes, belongings, personal conversations, or from viewing highly personal or confidential information about us. Indeed, American courts have articulated clear protections under the Fourth Amendment against unwarranted searches and seizures, albeit somewhat frayed after 9-11 and antiterror laws that permit surveillance and wiretaps under certain circumstances. Protections from such intrusions into our privacy, especially as related to relatively new technologies involving information exchange and storage, surveillance, and identity theft, form the core of many of the essays in this book; we might broadly refer to such concerns as ones about *informational privacy*.

If freedom from intrusion into personal spaces such as the home and safeguards on sensitive information are central to the protective sense of privacy, so too is privacy as a zone of *decisional autonomy*. For example, we expect to be able to raise our children and educate them as we see fit, absent intrusion or regulation from the state (although some intrusions—vaccinations, truancy laws—are deemed acceptable). When we make decisions that fundamentally affect our futures, we sometimes assert that they are private matters into which others (including the state) cannot intrude, at least not to the point of prohibiting us from deciding as we see fit, for example, to terminate a pregnancy or to choose someone to be our sexual partner, so long as he or she is a competent and consenting adult.

If one sense of "privacy" designates information, spaces, decisions, or activities that should be protected or privileged under the law, another conceptual strand relates to matters or persons that are *deprived* of public status or importance. For example, a private in the army is a soldier without rank, or what is limited in impact or occurs in settings like the home or the family may seem to be "merely" private, not properly a matter for public concern or consideration. Thus the housewife who is asked at a party, "What do you do?" and answers "I'm just a housewife" is an example of this sense of lacking public status or importance; so is the now outdated practice of patrol cops waiting to respond to domestic disputes to see if the fights would blow over, believing that they were not properly matters for police intervention. Like the housewife who feels like the work she does is not really a job or legitimate status in the world, many people feel that their problems are personal, idiosyncratic, and private, not patterned or often repeated in many people's lives in ways that invite a more public, systemic understanding of the difficulty. For example, a working mother may feel that her work responsibilities and family ones are spiraling out of control, leaving her no option but to step off the career track for a while—a set of conflicts and pressures that she identifies as private troubles rather than shared ones, even though many working mothers feel this way and find their choices structured by understandings of gendered responsibility for work inside the home that are commonly accepted and constrain many or most people's choices (Stone 2007, discusses the "opt out" revolution at length).

When we consider common contrasts or opposites, private is opposed to public, of course, but it is useful to consider the different dimensions of such oppositions: limited as opposed to broad or universal impact; what is secret or known only to a few versus what is broadly publicized or known; that which we only want to communicate or display to our intimates or family members versus that which we articulate or "dress up" to take out in public (for example, uninhibited jokes, stories, or opining that are meant for only the few who know us best versus the way we present ourselves in a public meeting).

Although much of this book is devoted to privacy concerns rooted in controlling access to oneself (who can see, phone, or contact us via email or Facebook, and the like) or information about oneself, such as medical records, credit card purchases, photographs, lab results, PINs, passwords, or biometric characteristics, our concerns with privacy go beyond avoiding unwanted contact or scrutiny and protecting informational privacy. Privacy also extends to decisional privacy or autonomy, the freedom to make decisions about crucial life-changing matters without state prohibition. When we consider privacy in the sense of being deprived of public importance or status, being *merely* private, we may need to attend to how the private individual or sufferer can come to see that his or her experiences are shared and common, even perhaps amenable to public policy interventions that might address matters that may commonly be viewed as entirely personal, familial, and private, such as domestic abuse or work-family tensions. Let us turn to a more detailed consideration of privacy issues related to decisional autonomy and translating problems long deemed to be private into publicly negotiable ones that might be amenable to public discussion and policy solutions.

SAME-SEX INTIMACY AND MARRIAGE: PRIVACY PROTECTIONS AND PUBLIC RECOGNITION

Same-sex intimacy and marriage have called forth a variety of constitutional arguments from the U.S. and state supreme courts that aim to protect fundamentally important choices about sexual and marriage partners, including U.S. Supreme Court (*Bowers v. Hardwick*, 1986; *Lawrence v. Texas*, 2003) and state supreme court decisions (Hawaii's *Baehr v. Lewin,* 1993; *Baker v. Vermont*, 1999; Massachusetts' *Goodridge v. Department of Public Health*, 2003; Connecticut's *Kerrigan v. Commissioner of Public Health*, 2008; and Iowa's *Varnum et al. v. Brien*, 2009) and several referenda and legislative actions on same-sex unions that have limited or reversed judicial/constitutional holdings favorable to same-sex marriage.[2] I show how decisions about sexual and intimate partners were protected under the right-to-privacy rubric and then were extended to include access to civil marriage via arguments about discrimination and community membership.

In its 1986 decision in *Bowers v. Hardwick,* the U.S. Supreme Court upheld Georgia's sodomy law against challenges that it violated the right of two men to engage in consensual sex in the privacy of their bedroom. Justice White wrote for the Court in *Bowers* that:

This case does not require a judgment on whether laws against sodomy between consenting adults in general, or between homosexuals in particular, are wise or desirable. It raises no question about the right or propriety of state legislative decisions to repeal their laws that criminalize homosexual sodomy, or of state-court decisions invalidating those laws on state constitutional grounds. The issue presented is whether the Federal Constitution confers a fundamental right upon homosexuals to engage in sodomy and hence invalidates the laws of the many States that still make such conduct illegal and have done so for a very long time. (186, 190)

After explaining that the Court of Appeals (which had struck down the Georgia law in question) had misconstrued the relevant precedents establishing a right to privacy in areas related to childrearing, education, family relationships, marriage, contraception, and abortion, the majority continued:

We think it evident that none of the rights announced in those cases bears any resemblance to the claimed constitutional right of homosexuals to engage in acts of sodomy that is asserted in this case. No connection between family, marriage, or procreation on the one hand and homosexual activity on the other has been demonstrated, either by the Court of Appeals or by respondent. Moreover, any claim that these cases nevertheless stand for the proposition that any kind of private sexual conduct between consenting adults is constitutionally insulated from state proscription is unsupportable. (186)

In explaining why the Court was bound to refuse to extend privacy protections to consensual adult homosexual activity in the home, Justice White recounted the existence of numerous and long-standing state laws against sodomy and public moral condemnation of homosexuality. He rejected the privacy challenges brought against Georgia's law prohibiting sodomy, arguing that privacy protections should not be extended to behavior that had long been regarded as abhorrent and deviant. Four other justices, with four in dissent, joined White's opinion.

Upon revisiting *Bowers* in its 2003 decision, *Lawrence v. Texas*, the majority switched, with a four justices joining Justice Kennedy's decision to strike down Texas's sodomy law on right-to-privacy grounds. In addition, Justice O'Connor concurred, and justices Scalia, Rehnquist, and Thomas dissented. The Court began its opinion by characterizing the interests at stake:

Liberty protects the person from unwarranted government intrusions into a dwelling or other private places. In our tradition the State is not omnipresent in the home. And there are other spheres of our lives and existence, outside the home, where the State should not be a dominant presence. Freedom extends beyond spatial bounds. Liberty presumes an autonomy of self that includes freedom of thought, belief, expression, and certain intimate conduct. The instant case involves liberty of the person both in its spatial and more transcendent dimensions. (562)

Referring to Justice White's characterization of the issue presented in *Bowers* as "whether the Federal Constitution confers a fundamental right upon homosexuals to engage in sodomy," the majority wrote:

> To say that the issue in *Bowers* was simply the right to engage in certain sexual conduct demeans the claim the individual put forward, just as it would demean a married couple were it to be said marriage is simply about the right to have sexual intercourse. The laws involved in *Bowers* and here are, to be sure, statutes that purport to do no more than prohibit a particular sexual act. Their penalties and purposes, though, have more far-reaching consequences, touching upon the most private human conduct, sexual behavior, and in the most private of places, the home. The statutes do seek to control a personal relationship that, whether or not entitled to formal recognition in the law, is within the liberty of persons to choose without being punished as criminals. . . . It suffices for us to acknowledge that adults may choose to enter upon this relationship in the confines of their homes and their own private lives and still retain their dignity as free persons. When sexuality finds overt expression in intimate conduct with another person, the conduct can be but one element in a personal bond that is more enduring. The liberty protected by the Constitution allows homosexual persons the right to make this choice. (567)

With respect to the argument that homosexual conduct has been broadly viewed as immoral, the majority acknowledged that for many "these are not trivial concerns but profound and deep convictions accepted as ethical and moral principles to which they aspire and which thus determine the course of their lives." Nevertheless, the issue presented here:

> is whether the majority may use the power of the State to enforce these views on the whole society through operation of the criminal law. "Our obligation is to define the liberty of all, not to mandate our own moral code." . . . In all events we think that our laws and traditions in the past half century are of most relevance here. These references show an emerging awareness that liberty gives substantial protection to adult persons in deciding how to conduct their private lives in matters pertaining to sex. "History and tradition are the starting point but not in all cases the ending point of the substantive due process inquiry." (571–72)

In explaining why it reversed *Bowers,* the majority opinion in *Lawrence* cited two pivotal cases decided since 1986, *Planned Parenthood of Southeastern Pennsylvania v. Casey* (1992) and *Romer v. Evans* (1996).

The first of these has been taken to settle the line of cases dealing with the right-to-privacy protections for abortion by upholding the core of *Roe v. Wade,* which had been under attack for nearly twenty years when *Casey* was decided. The *Lawrence* court relied on the *Casey* decision to explain why the

relationships and sexual activities it had to adjudicate, like those at issue in
Roe and *Casey*, were of central importance:

> These matters, involving the most intimate and personal choices a person may
> make in a lifetime, choices central to personal dignity and autonomy, are central
> to the liberty protected by the Fourteenth Amendment. At the heart of liberty is
> the right to define one's own concept of existence, of meaning, of the universe,
> and of the mystery of human life. Beliefs about these matters could not define
> the attributes of personhood were they formed under compulsion of the State.
> (*Lawrence v. Texas*, 2003, 574, quoting from *Planned Parenthood v. Casey*)

The Court relied on the decision in *Romer* to reach a different issue, discrimination on the basis of animosity to homosexuals. Just as the *Romer* "Court
struck down class-based legislation directed at homosexuals as a violation of
the Equal Protection Clause," the majority in *Lawrence* concluded that the
Texas sodomy law "was 'born of animosity toward the class of persons affected'" and insupportable on equal protection grounds (2003, 574).

The change in argument and tone between *Bowers* and *Lawrence* is dramatic: whereas the only public, political concern addressed in *Bowers* was
the right of the state to criminalize homosexual sodomy, the Court's opinion
in *Lawrence* eloquently argues that respecting the privacy of intimate sexual
relationships is central to the right to define one's own notion of the meaning
of life, and it recasts decisions about personal bonds with intimate partners
as being on a par with marriage. The suggestion from *Romer* that discriminating on the basis of sexual orientation raises equal protection concerns is
also significant: in addition to arguing for privacy—the constitutional and
conceptual rubric for protecting the individual's autonomy with respect to
decisions related to one's self-definition from state criminal regulation—the
Court also argues that lesbians and homosexuals are a discrete and insular
minority subject to discrimination and social opprobrium and that regulations
that target them as a group should be subject to analysis under the Fourteenth
Amendment to the Constitution. Privacy is enlisted in progressive battles
against the state's interest in regulating and normalizing sexual behavior; it
provides a doctrinal tool for saying "thou shalt not" to state regulation that
intrudes on fundamentally important decisions about who one is to be—and
who one can love—in the world. *Lawrence* articulates a public (and constitutionally protected) value or right of privacy as freedom from state laws
criminalizing sodomy.

The state court decisions regarding same-sex unions and marriage from
Vermont, Massachusetts, Connecticut, and Iowa make varied constitutional
arguments for striking down laws that permit only heterosexual couples to
marry. In *Baker v. Vermont* (1999) the Vermont Supreme Court held that

under the Common Benefits Clause of the Vermont Constitution "the State is constitutionally required to extend to same-sex couples the common benefits and protections that flow from marriage under Vermont law" (1999, 197). Noting that government is "instituted for the common benefit, protection, and security of the people, nation, [and] community," the Court held that "plaintiffs may not be deprived of the statutory benefits and protections afforded persons of the opposite sex who choose to marry" (197). The Vermont court also relied on the U.S. Supreme Court's decision in *Loving v. Virginia* (1967), which struck down Virginia's antimiscegenation law, to support the notion that "'the freedom to marry has long been recognized as one of the vital personal rights,' [and] access to a civil marriage license and the multitude of legal benefits, protections, and obligations that flow from it significantly enhance the quality of life in our society" (1999, 220).[3]

Massachusetts relied on two core arguments in *Goodridge v. Department of Public Health* (2003), both founded in the Massachusetts Constitution: first, the notion that marriage is a deeply personal commitment and a fundamental right, related to the dignity and autonomy of all; and second, the central value of equality for all citizens. Relying on several U.S. Supreme Court decisions (*Lawrence v. Texas, Loving v. Virginia*, and *Zablocki v. Redhail*), the court in *Goodridge* argued that the state law allowing only heterosexuals to marry "deprives individuals of access to an institution of fundamental legal, personal, and social significance—the institution of marriage—because of a single trait: skin color in *Loving*, sexual orientation here" (328). The discrimination is invidious and insupportable under Massachusetts' protections for equality and due process, and the personal liberty at stake here—the right to marry the partner of one's choice free from government incursion—is of fundamental importance. The Massachusetts Supreme Judicial Court also noted that the Massachusetts Constitution is in some instances more protective of individual liberty than is the federal Constitution, an argument that almost every state supreme court decision mentioned in explaining why they found unconstitutional state laws permitting only heterosexuals to marry.

The Connecticut and Iowa Supreme Court decisions striking down their states' marriage laws, *Kerrigan v. Commissioner of Public Health* (2008) and *Varnum et al. v. Brien* (2009), both develop the argument that discrimination on the basis of sexual orientation must be reviewed with heightened scrutiny because sexual orientation is an immutable characteristic that has nothing to do with a person's ability to contribute to society but which is associated with invidious discrimination and political disability. Therefore, any law that discriminates on the basis of sexual orientation should be subjected to heightened or intermediate scrutiny. Using this approach, both courts held that their states do not meet the high standard that laws must meet under intermediate scrutiny. In addition to these equal protection arguments, both the Connecticut and Iowa decisions also made the right to and the fundamental importance of being able to marry the partner of one's choice a linchpin of their arguments.

Being able to marry the partner of one's choice is central to one's deepest values and way of being in the world, and each of the state supreme court opinions gets at that argument in explaining the injustice of denying this choice to homosexuals. Most explicitly analogize the situation of gays and lesbians who are prevented from marrying the person they wish on the basis of their sexual orientation to the antimiscegenation law found unconstitutional in *Loving v. Virginia* (1967), seeing both race and sexual orientation as arbitrary and unfair ways to decide who should have access to this fundamental right.

The fact that state supreme courts in several states are writing opinions that strike down laws limiting marriage to heterosexual couples is not altogether surprising. State supreme court justices are expected to write well-reasoned arguments responding to disputes that arise under their states' laws and constitutions, not to run for reelection. They can afford to lead public opinion on this issue, and the fact that two states, Maine and California, have passed referenda to overturn court decisions mandating gay marriage suggests that the judges are sometimes pushing the issue harder and faster than average citizens would. Unlike legislatures, courts do not have to build broad coalitions to get laws passed or worry about bringing along diverse groups of supporters and placating interests who are opposed to their views. If they can persuade a majority of justices to sign the opinion, that is enough. Furthermore, since courts have long seen themselves as the champions of insular minorities who are likely to be disfavored by the conventional political processes, it makes sense that many are construing state constitutional law to protect the rights of gays and lesbians to equal civil rights.

Summing up the same-sex intimacy and marriage cases, a powerful U.S. Supreme Court opinion in *Lawrence v. Texas* (2003) provided a basis for declaring state antisodomy laws in violation of the right to privacy and staking out a zone of decisional and emotional autonomy. In doing so, *Lawrence* expanded on the reasoning in *Roe v. Wade* (1973) and set a range of behaviors that some elected majorities have found repugnant beyond state criminal prohibition. It also set the stage for state courts (and perhaps eventually the U.S. Supreme Court itself) to articulate arguments based on the guarantee of equal protection under the law banning discrimination against discrete minorities, the fundamental importance of marriage, and community arguments about the contours of the public sphere and who must be admitted to its privileges and protections.

PARENTAL LEAVES: MOVING FROM PRIVATE TO PUBLIC

Here I address how we translate concerns rooted in private life into political demands that can be discussed and negotiated with one's fellow citizens. One still often hears the claim that "the personal is political," a slogan that has long given me misgivings because of the way it equates personal and political life, ignoring the task of articulating concerns rooted in intimate life in such a way that their public and political claims are manifest. But the point of the slogan was consciousness raising; that is, helping women see that the unfairness, inequality, and lack of power experienced in the family and their most intimate relationships could be a source of empowerment and change if women came to see them as structural issues that could be addressed through collective action—not just as individual, personal problems that are not amenable to change. This move spurs personal, social, legal, and political change in the United States and elsewhere, as recognition of injustice in family life fuels movement building and cultural change.

Such changes in perception transform the woman who suffers in private into a citizen who perceives injustices and can act collectively to change them, fighting for policies and changes that will make a difference for working mothers or gay or lesbian couples, for example. Translating a personal trouble into a political issue goes along with transforming a private sufferer into a citizen whose participation in public life matters. Such transformations are crucial to getting one's fellow citizens and representatives to listen to new grievances, to getting new issues on the public policy agenda by recognizing them as legitimate public problems to which there are feasible solutions, and to taking advantage of or producing a political and cultural environment where legislative action is possible.

An instance of this kind of transformation from private to political occurred with the emergence of conflicts over maternity and parental leave laws in the 1980s. The United States had long been a standout among wealthy, postindustrial countries for not providing any guaranteed job leave for workers with new babies, and parental leaves reached the agenda-setting stage at a propitious time, as economic growth boomed and broad coalitions formed in support of such laws.

In *The Moderation Dilemma* (2001), Anya Bernstein's detailed analysis of the evolution of leave policies at the state and national levels tells the story of how the issue was introduced and fared in several different political opportunity structures. She studied two liberal New England states, Connecticut and Massachusetts; two conservative southern states, Tennessee and North Carolina; and the efforts to pass the national Family and Medical Leave Act (FMLA) in those states. Eventually, leave laws passed at the national level and in Connecticut and Tennessee, but they failed in Massachusetts and North Carolina. Bernstein was especially interested in understanding the role of compromise and coalition building in the policy process, but her book also illuminates how the issue came to be understood as an appropriate focus for political action, not simply a personal matter.

One of the biggest obstacles to passing leave legislation was the perception that laws requiring employers to give employees job-protected parental leaves would be an unreasonable intrusion of government into employer-employee relations (Bernstein 2001). Employers resisted the notion that government could require companies to grant leaves to employees; they preferred to treat this question as a private matter, subject to voluntary or discretionary adoption of parental leave policies on a company-by-company basis. Their resistance to such policies was mitigated by compromises over the length and coverage of proposed leaves. Thus, Tennessee's law covered businesses with one hundred or more employees, Connecticut's applied to employers with seventy-five plus employees, and the national law applied to companies with fifty plus employees. These limitations meant that the Tennessee and Connecticut laws covered only tiny minorities of workers, and the national law covered only 55 percent of employees (Bernstein 2001, 54, 73). Another measure adopted to reduce business opposition to leave laws was to make the leaves brief: four months in Tennessee, sixteen weeks in Connecticut, and twelve weeks nationally.

Other compromises that aimed to make leave laws more acceptable to conservative supporters included making the law a *maternity* leave in Tennessee, which made the law seem more consistent with traditional family values and gender expectations. But note that the FMLA and Connecticut leave laws were gender neutral, a matter of importance to the coalitions that pushed for passage because of feminist concerns about not reinforcing gendered expectations about childrearing and consequently gender discrimination in hiring, promotions, and firing. Also crucial to the credibility and feasibility of leave proposals was the early decision not to insist on *paid* leaves. Thus Bernstein remarks that pushing for paid leaves is one of the reasons why the Massachusetts bill failed to pass, and several people who were involved in insider strategizing and negotiations indicated that, if they had insisted on making the leave a paid one, no one would have taken the legislation seriously.[4]

Bernstein focuses on advocates' strategies for insuring that their proposed legislation would be taken seriously, distinguishing between the approaches taken in successful and unsuccessful efforts. One key strategy was to frame leaves as a family-values concern rather than a feminist or economic one. Grouping such bills with other profamily legislation made them more acceptable to conservative supporters and defused potential opposition from groups that would be hostile to feminist values. Bernstein notes that:

> Family and medical leave was a government mandate and reflected societal acceptance of the fact that many women work outside the home. On the other hand, it was also a bill that encouraged families to spend more time with each other and was supported by a number of prominent socially conservative legislators. (103)

The compromises necessary to gain support kept the parental leave laws that passed from being as generous or feminist as many wished for, but they garnered broad support from across the political spectrum for laws that were regarded as helping beleaguered families.

One of the most interesting themes to emerge from the politics of passing parental leave laws is the importance of legitimizing parental leave as a public policy issue and not merely a private concern to be negotiated between employers and employees. People had to be convinced that the state should be involved in parental leave, that it was properly a matter for public action. Bernstein notes that:

> One tenet of the women's movement is "consciousness raising," whereby women (and men) learn to associate formerly private concerns with public problems and solutions. Introducing legislation is one way of raising consciousness, as the legislative process itself involves identifying and publicizing an issue as a public problem demanding a public solution. Thus one can argue that introducing and publicizing family and medical leave might have led members of the public to consider their own situation and perhaps to see the work-family problems they were experiencing as worthy of public response. It follows that introducing a paid family and medical leave might encourage people, for the first time, to imagine that they could have access to wage replacement when they needed to take family and medical leaves. Over time, an expanded public imagination might catalyze further policy development, just as enacted policies sometimes feed back and lead to other policies. (64)

But in order for such consciousness raising to occur, bills have to be taken seriously enough to engender public discussion and publicity. In states where sponsors could not muster adequate legislative support to establish their bills as having a good chance of passing, these discussions did not occur, and the benefits of passing parental leave laws never got a hearing. This loss in turn meant less support and momentum for the cultural changes that had to occur if a family- or parental-leave bill were to have a chance of passing, such as taking for granted that mothers work for pay outside the home and expecting men to take responsibility for childrearing. Although Bernstein recognizes that FMLA fell far short of what proponents of parental leave wanted (it provides twelve weeks of unpaid job-protected leave for workers employed by companies with fifty or more employees and can be taken for the birth or adoption of a baby or for serious medical conditions affecting oneself or a relative), she thinks that it succeeded in fostering "recognition that work-family issues are public problems worthy of public solutions and . . . the development of a national sense that there is a social responsibility to help families balance their work and family lives" (132).

Bernstein's study of the nuts-and-bolts of passing parental leave laws in the 1980s and 1990s focuses on political opportunity structures, credible sponsors, effective advocacy coalitions, issue framing, and the political strategy of accepting less than advocates wanted in order to succeed in passing at least some kind of leave law, what she calls the "moderation dilemma." I believe the mechanics of coalition building and issue framing are the story of articulating political claims in ways that resonate for a broad range of citizens and political actors. Women's movement ideological purists who completely "got" the idea that parental leave is crucial for working mothers to have continuous careers and not suffer enormous motherhood penalties had to articulate arguments for leave policies that women and men with more traditional views about gender roles and government-business relations would find convincing. So the issue got framed in terms of facilitating time to connect with new babies and care for gravely ill family members, tapping into a family-values discourse that resonated with both political and social conservatives and older people.

The prolonged conflict over family leave suggests that the move from private to public is a slow, messy business, composed in equal parts of consciousness raising, social movement activism, and astute, insider efforts to work the political opportunity structures via strategic compromises. At the end of the struggle, the FMLA did not cover workers employed in small (less than fifty employees in a regional zone) companies, nor was it of much use to those who could not afford to take twelve weeks off from work without pay. As a case study of how personal, familial responsibility for caring for infants and sick family members came to be understood as a public responsibility, the effort to pass parental leave highlights the structural problems with the political process in the United States. Diffuse access and veto points, weak progressive and labor groups (and the lack of a left-labor political party that embraces their interests), and the prominence of "culture wars" involving conservatives and powerful business interests are components of a system in which overcoming opposition to controversial, ideological measures required policy advocates to trade away the coverage and generosity that would have made parental leave accessible and usable in order to pass any legislation at all.

Using the example of parental leave, I have argued that the move from personal to political is important as a shift in perspective that enables individuals to see problems as collective and shared, rather than as personal troubles or failings. Because it is so common to view problems as private and matters of individual volition in liberal welfare states with expansive private spheres, like the United States, translating them into issues of public significance about which people can make political claims is vital. To take another example, a woman working at a job that requires her to work sixty hours a week might decide that things were not working out once a first or second baby came along—stress levels were too high, the kids could not get enough attention, the compromises between work and family were too frequent and difficult—and that her best course of action was to quit and stay home full time with her children. Adopting the language and thought pattern of choice, she tells a story about her situation that is individuated and personal and finds herself cut off from language that could help her see her situation as rooted in structures and expectations that presume the availability of workers who can put in long hours and mothers who can devote themselves to childrearing (Williams 2000, chapter two; Stone 2007). But when she approaches her situation as the product of a power structure that assumes inflexible work patterns and career ladders and reinforces gendered divisions of labor in which women interrupt their work lives in order to do most of the unpaid care work, she is more likely to see her situation as shared and patterned and to ask for accommodations from her employer or from the government that would ease the work-family tensions she encounters, e.g., reduced and flexible hours while her children are young, paid parental leave, and affordable, high-quality childcare. She is transformed from individual sufferer to citizen, approaching her fellow citizens and voicing claims for support that are comprehensible and negotiable—and this is important even if, as will often be the case, she does not prevail in policy conflicts.[5]

Articulating the public dimensions of practices that arise from the private spheres of intimate life or market relations can be tricky, because such practices are usually regarded as off-limits to public scrutiny or intervention. Practices like childrearing, housework, and domestic abuse fit this pattern of "privacy-as-privation," because respecting privacy often obscures the fact that they have widespread impact and are rooted in institutions and social structures that reinforce inequality, injustice, or oppression. Finding ways to articulate such practices as properly matters of public concern is of critical importance, especially in liberal welfare states where the private realms of family and market are accorded enormous respect and are viewed as off-limits to most kinds of state intervention.

Protective notions of privacy are also common in the United States, where one commonly asserts rights to privacy as a way of protecting individual autonomy in crucial areas of human life. There are places and realms of experience that are generally considered off-limits to scrutiny or interference by others, and there is a public discourse about the need to protect such privacy interests and rights. But the public policy conflict over gay marriage extends beyond freedom from interference to claims about entitlement to enter into a public status—marriage—that affords numerous legal benefits and affirms one's long-term commitment to one's spouse. Although the state court decisions cite and build on arguments about privacy rights that have evolved through a long line of privacy cases (*Griswold v. Connecticut*, 1965; *Eisenstadt v. Baird*, 1972; *Roe v. Wade*, 1973; *Planned Parenthood of SE Pennsylvania v. Casey*, 1992; and *Lawrence v. Texas*, 2003), they also articulate fundamental rights to human dignity and access to key forms of recognition that are more about personhood and equality than privacy.

So far we have examined two cases that illustrate differing valences of privacy, depending on whether we are concerned with practices that we value and want to protect or problems that have long been kept in the obscurity of private life that we want to publicize and attempt to remedy through policies that can address patterned inequalities and injustices. In the United States, a country where privacy is a protean idea, both of these notions are common and present us with contrasting political tasks. For some issues, we want to articulate the public character of responsibilities and practices that have long been taken for granted and seen as part of private, familial life. For others, we use a rich, evocative notion of privacy to protect diverse choices about fundamentally important matters that majorities might want to regulate or criminalize.[6]

EVALUATING WELFARE REGIMES ACCORDING TO THEIR ABILITY TO TRANSLATE PRIVATE TO PUBLIC

In this section I move from the protective and privative senses of privacy in social policy contexts within the United States to focusing on private-to-public transitions as a way to compare welfare regimes cross-nationally. Moving beyond the borders of the United States and the particular liberal connotations of "public" and "private" that make sense here, I consider how private-to-public transitions work in other welfare states and the relative ease with which different welfare states move from private to public as they expand state responsibilities. We are, of course, revisiting the theme of private-to-public translations we explored with respect to efforts to promote family leave laws in the United States, but now the focus is on comparing how different welfare states legitimize or justify shifts from private to public.

Several historians, sociologists, and political scientists have contrasted the public-private mix, or more specifically the degree of reliance on states, markets, and families in different welfare regimes.[7] Many accept the three worlds of welfare capitalism typology that divides welfare states into liberal, conservative, and social democratic regimes (Esping-Andersen 1990). Liberal welfare regimes (the United States, Canada, the United Kingdom, Ireland, New Zealand, and Australia) stand out for having few universal public programs and relying heavily on welfare provision through employment and the market. While less reliant on markets than liberal states, conservative continental regimes (Germany, Italy, France, Austria, the Netherlands, and Belgium) are more likely to rely on family provision of care and to be guided by the principle of subsidiarity, the idea that citizens should exhaust all possible personal and community resources before the state steps in to offer assistance. In social democratic welfare regimes (Sweden, Denmark, Norway, Finland, and Iceland), universal provision by the state for paid parental leaves, childcare, early childhood education, and direct expenditures is common.

However, two conservative states that had always expected families to take care of core welfare functions, relying on women to provide care without pay in the home, have begun to shift from deeply held cultural norms of personal responsibility and intensive mothering to public responsibility and provision of services via generous work-family policies. Germany and Japan have both started this shift with respect to work-family policies like parental leave, a striking change from long-held policies that relied on mother care for children under the age of three and part-time kindergarten for preschoolers, policies that many believe have contributed to very low fertility rates in both countries. The ability to shift from thinking of care for infants and toddlers as mother's work to thinking of the state playing an active role in easing work-family tensions in order to make it easier for women to work while raising children suggests that even states deeply committed to private approaches to welfare can shift their commitments and find ways to justify public responsibility for mandating job-protected leaves and childcare.

Germany and Japan have both initiated active, generous work-family policies in recent years. Germany passed a dramatically expanded parental leave law in 2007 after years of studies and recommendations urging the adoption of policies that would address the high opportunity costs German women faced should they decide to have children. For many years women faced with stark trade-offs between kids and careers had been deciding to work and have fewer children, and the German total fertility rate (TFR) had gradually fallen into the 1.3 to 1.4 range, among the lowest in the world. The new law gives parents twelve months off work paid at 67 percent of one's usual salary, up to a cap of €1800 ($2,528) per month, with two months of designated paid "partner" leave aimed at getting fathers to participate in childrearing responsibilities. This contrasts to the parental leave policy in existence up until that time that gave parents a twenty-four-month leave paid at a flat rate of €300 ($421) a month. The law was passed at a moment when a grand coalition government had taken power (the Social Democratic Party, Christian Democrats, and Christian Socialists took power in 2005), and the government had succeeded in jawboning the Länder and municipalities into expanding the availability of kindergarten and childcare spaces in return for the federal government's taking responsibility for administering and financing the revamped, high-reimbursement-level parental leave program. This is a remarkable change in public responsibility to address work-family tensions; German family policies prior to 2007 reinforced long separations from the labor force for mothers and did little to provide care for children under age three. The policy is also a giant step toward challenging a commonplace stereotype that working mothers are "Rabenmütter," expressing a harsh, blaming stereotype of mothers who work instead of staying home with their children being like raven mothers who flap off to take care of themselves, leaving their chicks in the nest forlornly cheeping. Passage of the new leave and childcare laws was possible because concerns about very low fertility coincided with the recommendations of feminist research commissions and the election of a coalition government that provided the political muscle to pass the law and browbeat the Länder and local governments into going along with expanding childcare and kindergarten spaces (Henninger et al. 2008).

Japan's public-to-private transition dates back to government deliberative councils that met and recommended fundamental reforms in the early 1990s in response to the perceived crisis occasioned by the "1.57 scare" of the late 1980s (when total fertility rates first fell below the level of the year of the fiery horse, an especially unlucky astrological sign that caused people to have far fewer children than usual) and the overall sense that Japan was becoming an aging, low-fertility country that was losing its economic dynamism. Responding to the recommendations of the councils, experts from the Ministry of Health and Welfare and associated think tanks, the government adopted a set of five-year plans known as the "Angel Plan" (and the new Angel Plan, and the new Angel Plan) that set about to expand childcare spaces, require employers to give workers a one-year childrearing leave at 40 percent of their pay, and expand family allowances for families with small children (Boling 2007). The impact of these reform plans has been minimal, as total fertility rates have trended stubbornly downward to the 1.3 range. Yukio Hatoyama, the Democratic Party of Japan prime minister who was elected in a stunning victory that unseated the Liberal Democratic Party in August 2009, proposed dramatic increases in spending to encourage women to have more children, including a birth bonus of $6,000, further improvements in childcare, and a plan to pay high school tuition for children, a major expense for Japanese families.[8]

In sum, both Germany and Japan, which have traditionally left core welfare functions like childrearing (and in Japan care of the elderly) up to families, have begun to shift from deeply held cultural norms of intensive mother care to public responsibility and provision of services like parental leaves and childcare. Both have recognized that they can no longer rely with impunity on women's unpaid work to raise children and care for sick or old relatives now that women are better educated, expect to work for pay, and tend to judge the opportunity costs of taking time off from work to raise kids to be unacceptably high, causing total fertility rates to plummet to levels that are viewed as constituting a public crisis.

How should we make sense of this policy shift in terms of public-private divides? First, the shift from seeing childrearing as mother's work to believing that the state ought to adopt policies to ease work-family tensions suggests that even states deeply committed to private responsibility for care and welfare can find ways to justify public responsibility for mandating job-protected leaves and childcare. If countries like Germany and Japan can find ways to make urgent the public stakes of supporting working mothers, then perhaps such arguments could also be made in other countries that are primarily committed to private approaches to caring for young children and taking time off around births and adoptions, including the United States. On this view, Germany and Japan are role models because they show us that even regimes that were long committed to private familial provisions of welfare can change their minds when a looming public crisis exists to drive policy change. Understanding how these two conservative welfare regimes developed persuasive arguments to change government policies and voters' minds might provide lessons for policy makers and citizens in other countries about how to translate private problems into political ones.

But a second interpretation of the move toward policies to support working mothers would note that historically, neither Japan nor Germany has had any problem adopting pronatalist policies or celebrating and reinforcing women's role in the home as part of state policy and rhetoric. As the traditional family has failed and women have refused to have children, both countries have found it relatively easy to move from private to public. Conservative, statist welfare regimes like Germany and Japan take subsidiarity seriously: they want to leave welfare functions like childrearing up to the family. But if families fail, and fail at crisis levels, then obviously the state should intervene.

The same easy move from private to public is *not* what one would antici-pate in liberal welfare regimes like the United States. In the United States, the state does not oppose or encourage working mothers: working is simply a matter of personal taste and choice, and services to make it easier to deal with work-family tensions are best provided by employers or the market, perhaps with some tax write-offs from the state. Justifying state intervention—making the transition from private to public—is harder than in Japan or Germany. But by the same token, Americans also draw on rich, protective notions of privacy to map out zones of protected activities and choices; an ideology of Kinder, Küche, and Kirche (children, kitchen, church) never took hold here the way it did in Germany.

And if the United States *were* to make a transition from private to public with respect to the state assuming more of the burden of providing care for preschool-age children and paid parental leaves, it would not do so the same way that Germany or Japan has. Very low total fertility rates are not likely to be the crisis that provokes the United States to take more public responsibil-ity for work-family reconciliation policies, nor is it very likely to embrace explicitly pronatalist policy rationales. If the United States were to take greater public responsibility for work-family policies, its reasons for doing so might revolve around a cost-benefit analysis of universal high-quality early childhood education and daycare. Even though such educational systems are costly, some researchers have argued that their long-term impact (children so educated become reliable workers with good jobs who pay their taxes and are less likely to commit crimes and be incarcerated) will lead to a net savings for the government (the Danish government did such a projection, reported in Esping-Andersen 2009, 109). Furthermore, the recent passage of health care reform in the United States after many failed attempts suggests that given adequate leadership, focusing events, and shifts in political power, even social policies that have long been provided privately through employers or purchased on the market can be discussed and understood in terms of the need to take public responsibility to ensure universal care at adequate levels.

In short, some welfare states are more likely than others to adopt public, state-sponsored programs to assist working parents, and furthermore, that the triggers for such policies vary enormously among countries and over time—for example, contemporary Japanese share a sense of national crisis due to declining birthrates and population aging, while many Americans are concerned about all children getting a good start in life and helping at-risk kids avoid the fast track to prison or poverty. Some countries may never see work-family concerns as requiring public intervention or action or may re-main deeply committed to nongovernmental approaches to providing welfare services. The point is that it may be useful for comparative scholars to pay attention to how readily different welfare regimes translate private familial and market responsibility for welfare into demands for public action. Such an approach might also call attention to the enormous variability in the mix of how states, markets, and families contribute to caring for children, the infirm, and the elderly (see O'Connor et al. 1999) and help analysts focus on the political and rhetorical strategies activists and states use as they argue for greater or lesser public responsibility for providing for welfare needs.

Using private-to-public transitions as a conceptual tool for comparing how readily welfare states embrace public provisions to support working families is not likely to replace approaches to analyzing policy outcomes across welfare regimes that focus explicitly on political resources and historical explanations.[9] But as a complement to more conventional approaches, studies that attend to how readily states can articulate arguments for treating care work as a public responsibility can help us better understand the interaction among core political values, institutional structures, and the policies that each country has inherited that affect what states can hope to accomplish in the near future.

To conclude, the conceptual discussion of privacy undertaken in this chapter focused on two case studies of contested social policy issues in the United States, same-sex marriage and parental leave. In the former, the U.S. Supreme Court used privacy in its protective mode to articulate same-sex intimacy between consenting adults as a fundamentally important activity that should not be criminalized by state sodomy laws, and state supreme courts have expanded on that basic protection in manifold ways as they have articulated constitutional bases for same-sex marriage. In the latter, state legislatures and the U.S. Congress argued that childrearing and other care activities that had long been regarded as private responsibilities should be publicly supported by family leave laws. Expanding on the notion that activities rooted in intimate life need to be translated into political claims if governments or businesses are to enact policies to support working parents, I then looked briefly at recent policy changes in Germany and Japan and argued that studying how readily countries articulate the public importance of private matters could be a valuable way to compare welfare regimes. Whether our focus is U.S. domestic policy or transnational comparisons of welfare regimes, thinking clearly about privacy can provide us with insight and inspire new approaches both to protecting privacy interests and to translating private matters into political claims.

NOTES

1. Shortly prior to the final revision of this chapter, the federal district court in San Francisco declared Proposition 8 unconstitutional in a decision that relied on equal

protection arguments, and it is likely to make its way to the U.S. Supreme Court within the next two years. While I am not able to fully discuss *Perry v. Schwarzenegger*, 2010 U.S. Dist. LEXIS 32499, decided August 4, 2010, I think the decision underlines the arguments I make in the text.

2. These include Hawaii's 1998 constitutional amendment outlawing gay marriage; California's Proposition 8, a referendum that overturned gay marriage in November 2008; Maine's 2009 referendum overturning gay marriage; and the New York State Senate's 2009 vote to turn down gay marriage. The federal district court in San Francisco recently declared Prop 8 unconstitutional, and appeals in that case are ongoing, with some likelihood that the U.S. Supreme Court will be asked to resolve the issue.

3. *Baker v. Vermont* did not strike down Vermont's marriage law but required the legislature to act either to amend the marriage law to include homosexuals or to pass a law establishing civil unions that would afford the same legal rights as marriage for same-sex couples. The legislature took the latter course, but the Vermont legislature eventually did adopt a gay marriage law in April 2009.

4. Paid parental leaves have been passed in three states, California, New Jersey, and Washington, but they have also been attacked during the recent economic downturn, and Washington had suspended implementation of its program as of 2009 (Fass 2009).

5. Such transformations have been central to feminist theoretical discussions of citizenship and the move from private to public. See Dietz 1985; Pitkin 1981; Phillips 1991; Boling 1996; Young 2000.

6. Note that I am making the distinction artificially cleaner and starker than it works in real life. One might draw on both senses of privacy at the same time; for example, some gay activists argue for abolishing the closet and also fighting to overturn sodomy laws.

7. For example, Rein and Rainwater 1986; Esping-Andersen 1990, 2009; Orloff 1993; O'Connor, Orloff, and Shaver 1999; Hacker 2002.

8. It is unclear where these recommendations are headed now that Hatoyama has stepped down and been replaced by Naoto Kan.

9. Tried-and-true approaches to studying welfare states most commonly focus on power resources (e.g., left parties, labor unions, social movements), institutional arrangements, or path dependency. See for example Pierson 2001; Huber and Stephens 2001; Esping-Andersen 1990; and Hacker 2002.

REFERENCES

Baehr v. Lewin, 74 Haw. 645 (Supreme Court of Hawaii, 1993).

Baker v. State of Vermont, 170 VT 194 (Vermont Supreme Court, 1999).

Bernstein, Anya. 2001. *The moderation dilemma.* Pittsburgh: University of Pittsburgh Press.

Boling, Patricia. 1996. *Privacy and the politics of intimate life.* Ithaca, NY: Cornell University Press.

Boling, Patricia. 2007. Policies to support working mothers and children in Japan. In *The political economy of Japan's low fertility*, ed. Frances McCall Rosenbluth, 131–54. Stanford, CA: Stanford University Press.

Bowers v. Hardwick, 478 U.S. 186 (U.S. Supreme Court, 1986).

Dietz, Mary G. 1985. Citizenship with a feminist face: The problem with maternal thinking. *Political Theory* 13, no. 1: 19–37.

Eisenstadt v. Baird, 405 U.S. 438 (1972).

Esping-Andersen, Gøsta. 1990. *The three worlds of welfare capitalism.* Princeton, NJ: Princeton University Press.

———. 2009. *Incomplete revolution: Adapting welfare states to women's new roles.* Cambridge, UK: Polity Press.

Fass, Sarah. 2009. Paid leave in the states: A critical support for low-wage workers and their families. Brief from the National Center for Children in Poverty. http://www.nccp.org/publications/pub_864.html

Goodridge v. Department of Public Health, 440 Mass. 309 (Supreme Judicial Court of Massachusetts, 2003).

Griswold v. Connecticut, 381 U.S. 479 (1965).

Hacker, Jacob S. 2002. *The divided welfare state: The battle over public and private social benefits in the United States.* New York: Cambridge University Press.

Henninger, Annette, Christine Wimbauer, and Rosine Dombrowski. 2008. Demography as a push toward gender equality? Current reforms of German family policy. *Social Politics: International Studies in Gender, State & Society* 15, no. 3: 287–314.

Huber, Evelyne, and John D. Stephens. 2001. *Development and crisis of the welfare state: Parties and policies in global markets.* Chicago: University of Chicago Press.

Kerrigan v. Commissioner of Public Health, 289 Conn. 135 (Supreme Court of Connecticut, 2008).

Lawrence v. Texas, 539 U.S. 558 (2003).

Loving v. Virginia, 388 US 1 (1967).

O'Connor, Julia S., Ann Shola Orloff, and Sheila Shaver. 1999. *States, markets, families: Gender, liberalism and social policy in Australia, Canada, Great Britain and the United States.* New York: Cambridge University Press.

Orloff, Ann Shola. 1993. Gender and the social rights of citizenship: The comparative analysis of gender relations and welfare states. *American Sociological Review* 58, no. 3: 303–28.

Phillips, Anne. 1991. *Engendering democracy.* University Park, PA: Pennsylvania State University Press.

Pierson, Paul, ed. 2001. *The new politics of the welfare state.* New York: Oxford University Press.

Pitkin, Hanna. 1981. Justice: On relating private and public. *Political Theory* 9, no. 3: 327–52.

Planned Parenthood of Southeastern Pennsylvania v. Casey, 505 U.S. 833 (1992).

Rein, Martin, and Lee Rainwater, ed. 1986. *Public/private interplay in social protection.* Armonk, NY: M.E. Sharpe.

Roe v. Wade, 410 U.S. 113 (1973).

Romer v. Evans, 517 U.S. 620 (1996).

Stone, Pamela. 2007. *Opting out? Why women really quit careers and head home.* Berkeley, CA: University of California Press.

Varnum et al. v. Brien, 763 N.W.2d 862 (Supreme Court of Iowa, 2009).

Williams, Joan. 2000. *Unbending gender: Why family and work conflict and what to do about it.* New York: Oxford University Press.

Young, Iris Marion. 2000. *Inclusion and democracy.* New York: Oxford University Press.

Zablocki v. Redhail, 434 U.S. 374 (1978).

2

Privacy Torts
Unreliable Remedies for LGBT Plaintiffs

Anita L. Allen, JD, PhD
University of Pennsylvania

In the United States, both constitutional law and tort law recognize the right to privacy, understood as legal entitlement to an intimate life of one's own free from undue interference by others and the state.[1] Lesbian, gay, bisexual, and transgender (LGBT) persons have defended their interests in dignity, equality, autonomy, and intimate relationships in the courts by appealing to that right.

In the constitutional arena, LGBT Americans have claimed the protection of state and federal privacy rights with a modicum of well-known success.[2] Holding that homosexuals have the same right to sexual privacy as heterosexuals, *Lawrence v. Texas* symbolizes the possibility of victory in the courts for LGBT Americans seeking privacy in intimate life. "Liberty," wrote Justice Anthony Kennedy in *Lawrence*, "presumes an autonomy of self that includes freedom of thought, belief, expression, and certain intimate conduct."[3] In another important decision, *Goodridge v. Massachusetts Department of Public Health*, the Massachusetts Supreme Judicial Court held that state prohibitions on same-sex marriage lacked a rational basis and violated the state constitution's affirmation of "the dignity and equality of all individuals," with a concurring justice explaining that the "right to marry is not a privilege conferred by the State, but a fundamental right that is protected against unwarranted State interference."[4]

In the U.S. tort arena, as in the state and federal constitutional arenas, LGBT plaintiffs have claimed violations of their privacy rights and have sometimes won.[5] In common law privacy tort cases, the defendants charged

---

This chapter was previously published in the *California Law Review*, vol. 98, no. 6 (2010).

with privacy violations typically have included private-sector employers,[6] the professional media,[7] retailers,[8] or private individuals.[9] As detailed throughout this chapter, LGBT plaintiffs have accused such defendants of prying, spying, insulting, or harassing them, or disclosing their birth sex, sexual orientation, or medical information without authorization. Lawsuits have framed the violations experienced by LGBT claimants as one or more of the four privacy torts Dean William L. Prosser distinguished[10] and subsequently enshrined in the American Law Institute's Second Restatement of Torts.[11] Several authors have argued that the invasion of privacy torts, especially Prosser's "unreasonable publicity given to the other's private life," are potentially useful remedies for LGBT plaintiffs.[12] But LGBT plaintiffs relying on Prosser's common law tort remedies have not been as successful as some would have predicted based on a general understanding of the torts and their superficial appeal. The common law of torts has yet to generate its *Goodridge* or *Lawrence*.

In this chapter I analyze about three dozen cases, mostly published appellate cases, in which LGBT plaintiffs have alleged one or more of Prosser's four common law privacy tort offenses on facts that expressly involve their sexual orientations or gender identities.[13] The aims of my analysis are twofold.

First, I wish to contribute to the understanding of the legacy of Prosser's four-fold taxonomy of privacy tort claims—intrusion, appropriation, publication of private fact, and false light publication. As noted, the taxonomy appeared in Prosser's 1960 article.[14] Serving as its lead reporter, Prosser later incorporated his taxonomy into the Restatement (Second) of Torts.[15] I argue that although most courts adopting the Restatement have not questioned the accuracy of Prosser's distinctive formal taxonomy,[16] plaintiffs' lawyers in LGBT issues-related cases implicitly challenge the taxonomy by alleging that a single encounter with defendants resulted in violations encompassing two, three, or all four of Prosser's invasion of privacy torts. I conclude that the frequent practice of characterizing a single privacy invasion as an instance of multiple privacy torts calls into question the integrity of Prosser's framework of formal categories. Although I do not claim that LGBT issues-related cases strain Prosser's taxonomy any more than other privacy tort cases, I do believe this body of cases exposes the limitations of Prosser's distinctions on particularly poignant and compelling facts.

Second, I wish to assess the efficacy of existing privacy tort remedies for persons alleging wrongs tied to sexual orientation and gender identity. In this regard, I maintain that the theoretically promising invasion of privacy torts have too often been practical disappointments for LGBT plaintiffs in the courts.[17] To provide real, consistent remedies for LGBT plaintiffs, courts must refashion their understandings of how critical elements of privacy torts can be met and withstand defenses.

The post-1960 cases tentatively support three main conclusions about the efficacy of privacy tort remedies. First, in the past half century, the invasion of privacy tort has not been especially useful to LGBT plaintiffs seeking monetary and injunctive relief in cases related to their sexual orientations or identities. Second, as applied, the invasion of privacy tort has not reliably vindicated the complex interest LGBT plaintiffs understandably assert in what I term "selective disclosure" of their sexual orientations or identities. Third, recent success in the LGBT population's historic quest for equality and inclusion potentially undercuts the already tenuous practical utility of the invasion of privacy tort. Courts may fail to discern that sexual orientation and sexual identity-related privacy protection is warranted for LGBT individuals if, on the societal level, there has been a significant reduction in violence, social stigma, and discrimination associated with open LGBT status. Wins in *Lawrence* and *Goodridge* signal such a reduction, as does pending legislation to abolish the nation's policy against homosexuals in the military.[18]

This first part of this chapter briefly recites the history and background of the invasion of privacy tort, an indispensable highlight of which is the seminal 1890 *Harvard Law Review* article by Samuel D. Warren and Louis D. Brandeis. I then organize my substantive analysis to mirror the structure of Prosser's classic 1960 article. Prosser's article devoted separate sections to each of the four torts comprising his descriptive taxonomy of privacy claims. The second part of the chapter examines LGBT plaintiffs' "intrusion" claims. I group plaintiffs' intrusion claims into subcategories Prosser did not identify and suggest why even seemingly strong intrusion claims brought by LGBT parties have failed. The third part examines LGBT plaintiffs' "public disclosure of private facts" claims. I explain why courts are unreceptive to the notion that a person should be legally entitled to disclose selectively—that is, disclose in some contexts to some persons but not others—sexual orientation, same-sex relationships, and birth sex. The fourth part assesses false light publication claims by LGBT plaintiffs and persons inaccurately depicted as such. Plaintiffs alleging they are not LGBT but that they have been publicly described as such appear to have an easier time with the false light tort than plaintiffs who are LGBT alleging that their lives and identities have been wrongfully distorted due to prejudice and intolerance. The fifth part examines LGBT plaintiffs' commercial appropriation claims and the doctrinal reasons they generally fail, unrelated to sexual orientation, gender, or birth sex. Tort doctrines afford remarkable freedom to those who make unauthorized use of photographs in "newsworthy" and other publications. The case law illustrates that implications of this doctrinal latitude are especially serious for LGBT people.

After defending his descriptive taxonomy, Prosser devoted the final sections of his article to "common features,"[19] "public figures and public interest,"[20] "limitations,"[21] and "defenses."[22] These sections reflected skepticism about the privacy tort and revealed concerns that unbridled expansion of the privacy torts could interfere with First Amendment freedoms of speech and press and crowd the proper domains of the defamation and infliction of emotional distress torts. Responding with hindsight to some of these jurisprudential concerns, the sixth part notes judicial observations about the interplay and possible redundancy of privacy invasion and defamation remedies. Rounding out my account of the experience of LGBT privacy plaintiffs, I conclude with an assessment of the fate of intentional infliction of emotional distress claims brought alongside LGBT plaintiffs' privacy claims.

HISTORY AND BACKGROUND OF THE PRIVACY TORT

The privacy tort is a modern cause of action that has been recognized in most states.[23] The concept of a common law right to privacy took flight in 1890. The prominent lawyer and affluent businessman Samuel D. Warren was unhappy about attention the press paid to his lavish social life.[24] Warren pressured his reluctant friend and law partner Louis D. Brandeis into coauthoring a law review article urging recognition of an invasion of privacy tort.[25] The tort would deter and redress publication in newspapers of gossip and photographs that "invaded the sacred precincts of private and domestic life" and thereby injured "inviolate personality."[26] A rhetorical tour de force, the article inspired the judiciary. Courts soon began citing the article with approval, eventually expanding the understanding of the kinds of litigable privacy wrongs to include violations of modesty and genteel refinement.[27] In 1906, relying on natural law to bypass the limitations of positive law that kept New York's Court of Appeals from recognizing a privacy right in a famous 1902 decision,[28] the Supreme Court of Georgia became the first state high court to allow a plaintiff to sue under the privacy tort theory.[29] According to the unanimous opinion by Justice Cobb, "The right of privacy has its foundation in the instincts of nature."[30] The victim of a privacy invasion is "in reality a slave, without hope of freedom, held to service by a merciless master."[31] Other courts followed Georgia's lead, and tort actions premised on invasion of privacy soon proliferated.[32]

Prosser's Influential Taxonomy

Prosser's historic 1960 article assessing the proliferation of privacy tort actions had a major impact on subsequent scholarly understanding of the early history of the invasion of privacy tort. Moreover, Prosser's descriptive taxonomy of a half century of cases would govern the subsequent doctrinal development of the invasion of privacy tort in the courts.

Prosser framed his article as an original analysis of about three hundred published court opinions in privacy-related tort cases.[33] Prosser's thesis was that the invasion of privacy tort, then recognized by what he called an "overwhelming" majority of state courts, was in reality four distinct torts.[34] Prosser labeled them: (1) intrusion; (2) public disclosure of private fact; (3) false light in the public eye; and (4) appropriation.[35] To defend his thesis, Prosser cited numerous cases illustrating each of the four categories of his four-part taxonomy.[36]

Prosser did not stop with a bare taxonomy. He also outlined the critical elements of proof courts required for each of the four torts. For example, Prosser observed that proof of conduct "which would be offensive or objectionable to a reasonable man" was required in the case of intrusion;[37] and proof of publication or broadcast to more than a few persons was required in the case of public disclosure.[38] In addition, Prosser ventured to characterize the different interests at stake in the recognition of each tort. He associated mental repose with intrusion, good reputation with false light in the public eye, and property with appropriation.[39] Prosser further noted common features of the torts, such as the "personal" nature of the rights conferred[40] and the availability of typical tort damages.[41] Recognizing a "head-on collision with the constitutional guaranty of freedom of the press,"[42] Prosser argued that liability and recovery in invasion of privacy cases were significantly affected by the plaintiffs' celebrity or public office and the news interest in the plaintiffs' lives.[43] Finally, Prosser identified common defenses to invasion of privacy claims, starting with consent.[44]

In the conclusion to his article, Prosser distilled an array of skeptical concerns about the privacy tort. It troubled him, first, that the courts had created so complex a series of four torts from the "use of a single word"[45] in the Warren and Brandeis article; second, that the right's existence narrows the constitutional freedoms of speech and press; and, third, that privacy actions crowd the established territory of other, more limited tort actions—chiefly, infliction of emotional distress and defamation.[46] He was also troubled that the privacy torts were unbounded enough to encourage suits over trivialities or intrusions brought on oneself: "A lady who insists upon sun-bathing in the nude in her own back yard" invites "neighbors [to] examine her with appreciation and binoculars."[47]

As Reporter for the American Law Institute's Restatement (Second) of Torts, Prosser enshrined his descriptive taxonomy as positive law.[48] The same four invasion of privacy torts Prosser identified in the 1960 article were included in the Restatement. Through the Restatement, Prosser may have achieved the ultimate aim of his landmark 1960 article: he made it more likely the bar and bench would "realize what we are doing, and give some consideration to the question of where, if anywhere, we are to call a halt."[49] In the fifty years since Prosser's article, additional state high courts have embraced the invasion of privacy tort. A few, however, have heeded Prosser's cautions and declined to embrace privacy actions premised on publication of private facts or false light, citing First Amendment limitations[50] or citing the adequacy of remedies in defamation and other torts.[51]

LGBT Issues in Privacy Tort Litigation

Prosser has been described as "antigay."[52] Yet there is nothing in principle "antigay" about the privacy torts he helped mold. Indeed, relying on the promise of the Prosser's four privacy torts, LGBT claimants and their attorneys have sought monetary and injunctive relief. As the cases I discuss here will reveal, LGBT plaintiffs have brought privacy claims because they were spied on, insulted, disparaged, and whispered about. They have alleged that the tortious publication of their sexual orientation has destroyed their jobs, professions, businesses, families, and intimate personal relationships. The proliferation of public lawsuits exposing the private lives of LGBT individuals has illuminated the unfortunate reality that members of the LGBT community do not fully benefit in everyday life from the rules of "deference and demeanor" that otherwise govern civil relationships.[53]

For example, common private places are not reliably private for the LGBT community. Neither a restroom stall[54] nor a bedroom[55] is free from intrusion. Members of a society that once told gays and lesbians to closet themselves have, in effect, crept into the closet with them to peep at and punish what goes on inside.[56] Straight husbands and wives have publicized their gay, lesbian, or bisexual spouses' sexual orientation,[57] sometimes hoping to prevail in a child custody battle.[58] Even more unfortunate, the cases surveyed in this chapter reveal that the history of the privacy tort is not a simple "us versus them" story. The LGBT community has invaded the privacy of its own members. For instance, in 2002 a gay model sued a well-meaning gay lifestyles magazine for using his photographs to illustrate a story about the dangers of unprotected sex and excessive drug use in a narrow segment of gay culture to which the model did not belong.[59] In 1997, a closeted gay man sued his vindictive ex-lover who had revealed his sexual orientation to his employer, mother, and neighbors.[60]

In the following four parts below, I examine privacy tort suits brought by LGBT plaintiffs (and by persons accurately or inaccurately characterized as LGBT by others). These plaintiffs have been willing to bring lawsuits, knowing that litigation would render hidden details of their personal lives more public. Like most privacy tort plaintiffs, LGBT plaintiffs ironically suffer publicity in order to use the tort system to remedy perceived invasions of their privacy. Occasionally, privacy plaintiffs manage to sue anonymously,[61] but most file publicly available lawsuits under their own names alleging one or more of Prosser's four torts: intrusion, publication of private fact, false light, and appropriation. I begin with LGBT intrusion cases.

INTRUSION

"Intrusion" is the name Prosser gave to the first of the four invasion of privacy torts discussed in his 1960 article.[62] "It appears obvious," Prosser wrote, "that the interest protected by this branch of the tort is primarily a mental one."[63] The intrusion tort has arisen, he stated vaguely, "chiefly to fill in the gaps left by trespass, nuisance, the intentional infliction of mental distress, and whatever remedies there may be for the invasion of constitutional rights."[64] According to Prosser, physical trespass into private domains is the paradigm of intrusion, but nontrespassory wiretapping and harassing debt-collection phone calls can be privacy intrusions, too.[65] Prosser pointed out that courts had found attempts to access private documents, such as bank records or work papers, to constitute intrusion.[66] But Prosser detected reluctance on the part of the courts to view either noise nuisances or insulting words and gestures as intrusions.[67] Moreover, "[o]n the public street, or in any other public place, the plaintiff has no right to be alone."[68] It is "clear that the intrusion must be something which would be offensive or objectionable to a reasonable man."[69]

This part of the chapter examines these aspects of the intrusion tort and concludes that, in operation, the tort has proven to be an unreliable remedy for LGBT plaintiffs. This part also identifies what I describe as four different categories or types of intrusion offenses that LGBT intrusion tort plaintiffs have alleged: (1) physical intrusion and surveillance; (2) verbal intrusion and prying; (3) verbal insult and disparagement; and (4) intrusive publication of private fact. Non-LGBT plaintiffs could theoretically experience—and have in fact experienced—all four categories of intrusion offenses. But the facts behind the case law suggest that an LGBT sexual orientation or identity can provoke especially thoughtless and egregious intrusion offenses, reflective of a social context of prejudice, homophobia, and discrimination.

Physical Intrusion and Surveillance

Given its surface potential, the intrusion tort has been surprisingly unhelpful to several LGBT plaintiffs in the years since Prosser's 1960 article defined its parameters. In cases of physical intrusion and surveillance of LGBT persons, courts have all too often deemed the defendants' conduct reasonable.

In *Elmore v. Atlantic Zayre, Inc.*,[70] the plaintiff-appellant unsuccessfully appealed a summary judgment order entered on behalf of a retail store at which he was arrested and charged with sodomy. Following a customer's complaint that homosexual activity was taking place in a restroom, store employees peeked through a crack in the restroom ceiling and observed Mr. Elmore in a toilet stall.[71] Elmore filed a complaint for intrusion upon seclusion, alleging that the defendants spied on him "in a private place."[72] Plaintiff-appellant Elmore argued that private citizens do not have the right to spy and should leave law enforcement surveillance to the police.[73] Elmore also denied that he was engaged in sodomy. The trial court granted summary judgment in favor of the retail defendants; the Court of Appeals of Georgia affirmed.[74]

The Court of Appeals found that "[a]n individual clearly has an interest in privacy within a toilet stall."[75] However, the court found the defendants' intrusion reasonable—not highly offensive to a reasonable person as the tort requires. The right to privacy in a public restroom stall is not absolute, the court stressed.[76] The restroom in question was for the use of customers, and the defendant had a duty to keep its restrooms free of crime.[77] Moreover, the spying activity was ignited by the store's loss-prevention manager's observation and complaint of "highly suspicious"[78] activity in the restroom.

Although a typical restroom open to the general public of all ages in a department store is not an appropriate place for sexual activity, the conduct of the defendants was reprehensible. Measures to abate sexual activity in toilet stalls do not have to include peeping at individuals through concealed openings. The defendant employees easily could have investigated their suspicions of merchandise theft or of sexual activity in a way that respected the privacy and dignity of persons inside the stall. If suspicious activity seemed to be occurring, for instance, they might have knocked on the door of the stall and asked anyone inside to come out. Instead, they engaged in surreptitious peeping, which, on these facts, a reasonable person could view as intrusion.

Carlos Ball has argued, with respect to the Supreme Court, that "the Court's geographization of sexual liberty has resulted in the protection of sexual conduct that takes place in the home (and, presumably, in analogous sites such as hotel rooms) while leaving unprotected sexual conduct that occurs in public sites" such as restrooms.[79] However, gays, lesbians, and bisexuals have a problem whether sexual liberty is formally "geographized" or not. The geographization of sexual liberty alone cannot ensure adequate legal protection for the compliant LGBT population that discretely limits sex to approved domestic and similar sites. The holding of *Lawrence v. Texas* leaves lower courts free to refuse the protection of the intrusion tort to lovers who are members of the same sex even when their consensual adult sexual activity has occurred in a private bedroom.[80]

Plaxico v. Michael illustrates that the private home is not a sanctuary for intimate sex for LGBT individuals where courts view homosexual relationships as illicit.[81] Glenn Michael was divorced, and his ex-wife had custody of their six-year-old daughter.[82] Michael learned his ex-wife was involved in a lesbian relationship with Rita Plaxico.[83] Michael drove to his ex-wife's cabin, crept up to a window, peered inside, and watched the couple having sex.[84] He returned to his vehicle, retrieved a camera, and photographed Plaxico half-naked on the bed.[85] Michael then filed for a modification of child custody, using the surreptitiously snapped photos of Plaxico during the trial.[86] The court granted him custody of his minor child.[87] Subsequently, Plaxico filed suit for intrusion upon her seclusion and solitude.[88] The Circuit Court of Tippah County rejected the suit, and the Mississippi Supreme Court affirmed.[89]

Like the plaintiff in *Elmore*, Plaxico lost because the court found secret, illegal surveillance of suspected homosexual activity justified due to the suspected activity's illicit and possibly illegal character.[90] The majority held that Plaxico failed to prove that Michael's actions were "highly offensive to the ordinary person."[91] Although he spied and photographed sexual intimacies, he was prompted to do so to protect his daughter from exposure to an "illicit lesbian sexual relationship."[92] The court concluded that most people would find the purpose of the defendant's spying "justified."[93]

The court emphasized, curiously and perhaps disingenuously, that it was not Michael's ex-wife's homosexuality that made her a suspect custodial parent. According to the court, the result in Plaxico's case would have been the same if the ex-wife had had an "illicit" affair with a man.[94] The court did not define "illicit." It left it to readers of its opinion to speculate about what would make a particular affair illicit. The court may have been alluding to the fact that certain heterosexual sex acts were illegal or had legal implications (e.g., sex with a married person, sex with an animal, sex with a minor, sex with a first-degree relative, oral sex, or anal sex), but the court neglected to provide explicit clarification.

A dissenting judge agreed with Rita Plaxico that "peeping into the bedroom window of another is a gross invasion of privacy" and that the end did not justify the means.[95] A second dissenting opinion described defendant Michael's act as "voyeuristic"[96] and suggested that because Plaxico was not party to the custody dispute, Michael did not have a right to take her picture. His ex-wife's picture might have been sufficient. One could argue, though, that on the facts of the case Michael's ex-wife would have had an intrusion claim as strong as her lover's.

Verbal Intrusion, Prying

Asking inappropriate personal questions and demanding personal information are common forms of what I call "verbal intrusion." Asking invasive
questions about sex and sexual orientation can amount to offensive verbal intrusion. Given the history of employment discrimination and violence targeting LGBT persons, a gay or lesbian employee could be expected to find even
casual inquiries about sexual orientation in the workplace "highly offensive."
By contrast, a heterosexual employee might be offended by intrusive questions but would not expect to risk injury or lose his or her job or social status
for providing truthful answers.[97]

In *Madsen v. Erwin*, Christine Madsen was fired from her writing post at
the church-affiliated *Christian Science Monitor* when her lesbian sexual orientation became public.[98] Madsen had no luck persuading some members of
the Massachusetts high court that her supervisor tortiously intruded into her
privacy by asking about her sexual orientation.[99] Madsen sued the supervisor, the newspaper, the church, and several key officials in the church in a
complaint alleging wrongful discharge, defamation, invasion of privacy, intentional infliction of mental distress, and other claims.[100] Among her privacy
claims, Madsen argued that the defendants disclosed information about her
personal life to the public and placed her in a false light.[101]

The *Christian Science Monitor* defendants lost their motion to dismiss and
summary judgment motions, but the Supreme Judicial Court of Massachusetts reversed in their favor on a key issue. The main question presented in
the case was whether the First Amendment free exercise principle allowed
the Christian Science Church to terminate Madsen's employment on account
of her sexual orientation.[102] The court held that the church had a right of religious freedom under both federal and state constitutions to discharge Madsen.[103] Yet, while the court noted that Madsen's allegations in her complaint
"do not survive attack by motion to dismiss," it allowed the plaintiff to amend
her complaint with regard to the tort claims.[104] The court did not fully discuss
the merits of those claims. In his separate opinion, Justice Francis Patrick
O'Connor hinted that her privacy claims were likely to fail on privacy tort
theories. The justice reasoned that since the church could lawfully discharge
the plaintiff because of her sexual orientation, by implication it could also
question her about her sexual orientation.[105]

In another verbal intrusion case, *Morenz v. Progressive Casualty Insurance Co.*, an employee similarly argued that being asked about his homosexual identity at work was intrusive.[106] However, a co-worker rather than a
supervisor asked plaintiff Ralph Morenz about his sexual orientation, and the
alleged prying was not accompanied by the threat of termination. Soon after
Morenz's company transferred him to a new office, a fellow employee there

asked him whether he was gay.[107] The co-worker apparently asked the question because he wanted to make sure that Morenz knew his sexual orientation would not be a problem on the job.[108]

In his suit Morenz complained of intrusion, isolation, and emotional distress due to his employer's cruel lack of responsiveness to his inability to cope with gruesome aspects of his responsibilities as an accident claims adjuster.[109] The court concluded that under the circumstances of the case the question, "Are you gay?" was not "highly offensive to a reasonable person, and indeed, not offensive at all."[110]

The conclusion that the question is not offensive at all cuts off fact-finding and analysis concerning whether nonmaliciously intended questions about sexual orientation could be offensive to a reasonable person. They might be highly offensive to a reasonable person because they are personal, patronizing, or presumptuous. They may be highly offensive because they enable potentially sensitive data to be shared with others in the workplace who may be less open-minded and well-intended than the person who first posed the question. Unless courts consider factors such as gossip and discrimination vital to understanding the full context of the LGBT workplace experience, they will continue to conclude—often erroneously—that verbal intrusions against LGBT individuals are not "highly offensive to a reasonable person."

Verbal Insult and Disparagement

Courts have often asserted that the privacy torts protect feelings and sensibilities.[111] Plaintiffs have brought intrusion claims because they have felt insulted or disparaged by the use of unkind words.

In *Logan v. Sears*, for example, a gay salon owner was speaking to a Sears employee by telephone when he overheard her describing him as "queer as a three-dollar bill."[112] Because the offensive language came to him over his own private phone line, he felt the unkindness constituted an intrusion.[113] The court agreed that the statement made by Sears's representative "was an intrusion upon Logan's solitude or seclusion"[114] but found that it was not so extreme or outrageous as to offend an ordinary person. The word *queer*, according to the court, has been used for a longer time than the new term *gay*.[115] Thus, the use of the word *queer* could not be described as "atrocious and intolerable in civilized society."[116] The court concluded that, because the plaintiff was truly gay, the use of the word *queer*, even though discouraged by the homosexual community at the time, did not cause humiliation.[117] The court opined that in order to create a cause of action, the tortious conduct needed to cause mental suffering, shame, or humiliation to a reasonable person, "not [be] conduct which would be considered unacceptable merely by homosexuals."[118]

It is unclear and never explained why the perspectives of a "reasonable" homosexual should be discounted in applying the standard "highly offensive to a reasonable person."

Unkind epithets have a greater chance of leading to actionable tort claims—either emotional distress claims or privacy invasion claims—when the epithets are combined with unlawful deeds. In *Leibert v. Transworld Systems*, a California man disparaged as "effeminate" and "a fag" alleged that he was discharged because of his homosexual orientation.[119] The court concluded that his suit stated a claim for intentional infliction of emotional distress when viewed in the context of a pattern of workplace harassment and loss of employment in violation of state law.[120] Similarly, but under privacy theories, a lesbian businesswoman successfully alleged in *Simpson v. Burrows* that "Concerned Citizens of Christmas Valley" intentionally destroyed her business and personal life by distributing threatening and false antilesbian diatribes, including a letter attacking her as a "fag."[121] It is doubtful Simpson would have prevailed on a privacy theory had she complained of being called a fag but had not also lost her partner and livelihood.

Intrusive Publication of Private Facts

To establish a prima facie case of "intrusion," plaintiffs must allege a highly offensive intrusion that may or may not lead to a publication of any information obtained as a consequence of intrusion. To establish a prima facie case of "publication of private fact," plaintiffs must allege that defendants disseminated private facts to others, whether orally or in writing. Intrusion claims have sometimes been accompanied by claims for publication of private fact. Blurring the distinction between two of Prosser's torts, LGBT plaintiffs experience unwanted publicity as a kind of intrusion. We might call the offense "intrusive publication of private facts." The essence of these cases in not an allegation of physical intrusion, prying, or disparagement, but instead an allegation that it is intrusion into private life for others to reveal one's secrets or to dredge up embarrassments.

Secrets Revealed. On his intrusion claim, the court determined that Prince did not have an objective expectation of seclusion or solitude at the party he had attended because the public at large had been invited to purchase a ticket by phone, at the door, or from the club, and approximately one thousand people attended the party.[122] If a person can be unlawfully stalked or sexually harassed in a crowded public place,[123] it is unclear why a person cannot be a victim of a privacy intrusion while at a party. The courts could easily construe the targeting of a person in a public place for a photograph intended for publication without his consent as an unwelcome intrusion, as indeed they have in the past.[124] But arguably the relevant intrusion at issue was the magazine's interference with the plaintiff's partially secret personal life through the inadvertent "outing" and potential character distortion.

Embarrassments Dredged Up. The memorable "Boys of Boise" case, *Uranga v. Federated Publications*, commenced when plaintiff Fred Uranga sued an Idaho newspaper for privacy invasion (including intrusion) and infliction of emotional distress. The *Idaho Statesman* published a photographic copy of a forty-year-old statement made to authorities by a man named Melvin Dir, who implicated Uranga in homosexual activities. Mr. Dir had been prosecuted for sex felonies, including forcing teenager Frank Jones to submit to oral sex. Dir claimed the sex was consensual and that Jones had led him to believe he had had earlier homosexual encounters with his cousin Fred Uranga and a high school classmate.[125]

Uranga's failed claim of intrusion was modeled on claims made in what are generally considered "private fact" cases such as *Melvin v. Reid* and *Briscoe v. Reader's Digest*.[126] But there was a difference: Uranga did not admit to the dredged-up embarrassing (to him) ascription of homosexuality, whereas Melvin admitted prostitution and criminal prosecution, and Briscoe admitted to hijacking.[127] The court noted Uranga's claim for intrusion but said it had not been clearly articulated in the lawsuit.[128] Attempting to make sense of it, the court speculated that the only possible intrusion at issue was an "intrusion" into public court records that related to the plaintiff.[129] Following the precedent of two landmark Supreme Court cases, *Florida Star v. B.J.F.* and *Cox Broadcasting Corp. v. Cohn*,[130] the *Uranga* court held that neither the examination of public records nor their publication could be the basis for an intrusion claim.[131]

And yet publication of allegations about one's past sex life that one regards as embarrassments can certainly feel like what in colloquial terms we could describe as an intrusion. *Uranga* and *Prince* reflect a gap between the broad, ordinary, informal conceptions of intrusion and the narrow, formal, legal conception of the intrusion tort. The design of formal doctrine precluded hybrid "intrusive publication" claims by Fred Uranga and Tony Sabin Prince. These plaintiffs were forced separately to plead intrusion upon seclusion and publication of private fact, losing on both causes of action.

Limited Utility

Overall, LGBT plaintiffs have not had much luck with the intrusion tort, whether alleging surveillance, prying, insult, disparagement, or publicly revealing partly hidden aspects of private life. Rita Plaxico's memorable case against Glenn Michael is illustrative. Ms. Plaxico's case did not survive a motion to dismiss despite the fact that Mr. Michael had driven his truck to the secluded cabin where she lived with his ex-wife, watched her through a window having sex with his ex-wife, and photographed her partly nude and seated on her bed.[132] The appeals court found that this egregious invasion was not "highly offensive to a reasonable person" since "a reasonable person would not feel Michael's interference with Plaxico's seclusion was a substantial one that would rise to the required level of gross offensiveness."[133] Along with Plaxico, other disappointed privacy tort plaintiffs were Prince, Uranga, Logan, Madsen, Morenz, and Elmore.

Based on the cases I analyzed, the intrusion tort has not been, nor promises to be, a useful a remedy for LGBT plaintiffs seeking monetary or injunctive relief. One would draw a different conclusion upon discovery of a cache of intrusion claims favorably settled by LGBT plaintiffs prior to pretrial motions, judgments, and appeals. One would also draw a different conclusion with strong empirical evidence of the intrusion tort's deterrent effect. But in the absence of evidence either of a strong deterrent effect or a history of favorable settlements, I conclude based on the available evidence that the intrusion tort is a tort of minimal practical utility to LGBT plaintiffs.

PUBLICATION OF PRIVATE FACT

Prosser's publication of private fact tort[134] is a favorite with privacy litigants. Ill-fated publication actions have even been brought on behalf of the dead.[135] New technologies and contemporary lifestyles add to the avenues through which actionable publication offenses can occur. In a recent case, a lesbian sued the popular online movie-rental company Netflix, alleging that it collected information on subscribers' rental histories from which their sexual orientations could be inferred and disclosed.[136]

The LGBT community has had mixed luck with the publication of private tort. On its face, a doctrine of civil liability for disclosures of private facts could deter and redress unwanted revelations and "outings." The tort has served well several plaintiffs whose closeted gender traits, sexual orientation, or birth sex were revealed to the public without their consent.[137] But it failed to provide a remedy for others.[138] In many cases, plaintiffs' failure to establish a "publication" or "private fact" to the satisfaction of the court precluded recovery. Instead or in addition, the First Amendment precluded a tort remedy in some cases, effectively privileging media defendants eager to construe nearly everything that preoccupies or vexes daily life as matters of legitimate public interest.[139]

When Prosser addressed the public disclosure tort fifty years ago, he volunteered no sidebar on how a public facts tort could deter or remedy unwanted attention to the fact that someone is homosexual, bisexual, or transgender. But Prosser did reference *Cason v. Baskin*,[140] a noteworthy public disclosure of private fact case in which a woman sued a writer whose best-selling memoir portrayed her as having a striking mix of masculine and feminine traits.[141] Although Prosser mentioned in passing the celebrated *Cross Creek*[142] case and seemed to grasp that it concerned unwanted attention to unconventional, culturally transgressive gender traits and sex roles, he nowhere noted a distinct feature of the body of case law that included and surrounded it: gender norms played a role in the development of the right to privacy and its recognition by the courts.[143] In its first decades, the right to privacy was often asserted by women—and on women's behalf—to vindicate the women's perceived interest in modesty, seclusion, propriety, and genteel refinement.[144] *Cason v. Baskin* fits the pattern of privacy suits brought to vindicate female character: "You have made a hussy out of me" was the plaintiff's accusation to her defendant.[145]

Public Attention to Unconventional Gender Traits and Sex Roles

In *Cason v. Baskin*, quaintly designated "feme sole" Zelma Cason, a rural Alachua County social worker and census-taker, sued to recover $100,000 from her friend and neighbor, the Pulitzer Prize–winning author Marjorie Kinnan Baskin (pen name Marjorie Kinnan Rawlings).[146] In 1942, Baskin published *Cross Creek*, an autobiographical work containing character portraits of her friends and neighbors, including her friend Zelma Cason.[147] One chapter of the memoir recounted Baskin's observations as she accompanied Cason on horseback on her census-taking duties in Florida's backwoods. Baskin depicted Cason colorfully as "an ageless spinster resembling an angry and efficient canary."[148] She described her as competent in the management of her orange groves, nurturing, and at ease among Negros.[149] "I cannot decide whether she should have been a man or a mother [as she] combines the more violent characteristics of both,"[150] Baskin wrote. Never using her subject's surname, Baskin quoted Cason's use of salty expressions such as "sons of [bitches]," "those [bastards]," and "It's a [goddamn] blessing."[151]

Cason denied the accuracy of Baskin's portrayal and alleged defamation as well as privacy invasion. The court framed Cason's complaint as one about the defendant's publication of sensitive private facts, even though Baskin's "vivid and intimate character sketch" did not reveal much of anything about Cason that was not already generally known or believed true in her community.[152] As weak as her privacy claim may have been, Cason's libel claims

were weaker. Trial witnesses affirmed that Cason had a temper, cursed frequently, and generously provided charitable succor to the poor, as Baskin described.[153] Moreover, "It was hard to ignore Zelma's masculine leanings."[154]

Cason won at trial. On appeal, the Florida Supreme Court held that "in spite
of the fact that the publication complained of, considered as a whole, portrays
the plaintiff as a fine and attractive personality," Cason had stated a cause
of action potentially worthy of at least nominal damages for invasion of her
private life.[155] The court speculated that Cason might be one of those people
who "do not want their acts of charity publicized" in a book's "vivid and intimate character sketch."[156] The Florida high court pointed to Cason's "acts of
charity"[157] as the facts she preferred to downplay, bringing to mind *Schuyler
v. Curtis*.[158] By contrast, Prosser stressed Cason's "masculine characteristics"
as the private facts she had wished to downplay. Prosser summarized Cason's
injury as publication of "embarrassing details of a woman's masculine characteristics, her domineering tendencies, her habits of profanity, and incidents
of her personal conduct towards friends and neighbors."[159] Prosser got closer
to the truth than the Florida court. Cason reportedly felt angry and betrayed
by a friend rather than embarrassed about any specific public disclosures.[160]
Cason was furious when she read what Baskin wrote about her.[161] When they
met after the book's publication, Cason accused Baskin of making a "hussy"
out of her.[162] Cason, who sat knitting demurely throughout her trial,[163] was
offended that by writing about her as she did, her friend Baskin portrayed her
as a cultural abomination, a morally transgressing female.[164]

Gay, Straight, or Bisexual: Public Attention to Sexual Orientation

Efforts to reinforce gender norms are a recognized dimension of privacy
case law, including the publication of private fact cases of which *Cason* is an
especially interesting early example. What of sexual-orientation- and sexual-
identity-related norms? Has the privacy tort been deployed to reinforce them
as well? The answer is that to an extent LGBT plaintiffs (of both sexes) have
sought through the publication of private fact tort to preserve the problematic
convention of lives sheltered in layers of inaccessibility and reserve. Courts
have sometimes gone along, asserting that sexual orientation is private in
nature, as in *Borquez v. Ozer*.[165]

Robert P. Borquez was a successful associate in a law firm, terminated
after informing his employer that his male partner had recently received an
HIV-positive diagnosis.[166] Before the disclosure Borquez hid his homosexual
orientation at work.[167] After losing his job, he sued for wrongful discharge
and for wrongful publication of his sexual orientation and possible HIV
status.[168] The jury awarded $30,841 in lost wages for wrongful discharge,

$20,000 for embarrassment on the publication of private facts claim, and $40,000 in exemplary damages.[169] The appellate court affirmed,[170] holding that sexual orientation and exposure to HIV are private matters.[171] Disclosing these details is offensive to a reasonable person because both homosexuality and AIDS are stigmatized.[172] Further, the court held that disclosing information regarding HIV was not in this instance disclosure of a matter of legitimate concern to the public.[173]

Courts have not been uniform in their willingness to allow a tort recovery when information or allegations about sexual orientation have come out.[174] For example, in *Crumrine v. Harte-Hanks Television* the court held that even if homosexual identity is a private matter, the plaintiff policeman's homosexual identity and HIV-positive status did not remain so once revealed during judicial proceedings, such as a child custody proceeding.[175]

A similar outcome greeted a gay priest in an earlier case, *Cinel v. Connick*.[176] Authorities found homosexual pornography in the residence of Dino Cinel, a Roman Catholic priest, along with a videotape of him engaging in consensual homosexual sex with two adult men.[177] The defendants in the case included several state officials, who released the videotape to a reporter and a television network. The television network broadcasted excerpts from the tape.[178] Plaintiff Cinel subsequently brought a Section 1983 claim against the state officials for violating his constitutional privacy rights by disclosing the names of the people who were taped having sex with him; by revealing their identities to unrelated third parties; and by releasing the materials to private litigants, including the church and the other participants in the sex acts.[179] The court rejected the claim, stating that the identities of the people and their addresses were not part of the plaintiff's private life.[180] In addition, the church and the participants in the sex acts had previous knowledge about the materials, so the information was not private as to them.[181] The state officials were similarly shielded from liability as they acted lawfully in disclosing materials pursuant to a valid subpoena.[182]

Plaintiff Cinel also claimed a publication of private facts tort under Louisiana Civil Code.[183] The trial court rejected this claim, finding that the materials were a matter of legitimate public concern since sodomy was a crime at the time.[184] In addition, the court concluded that identification of the participants by state officials was a matter that needed to be reviewed by the public.[185] This public need was strengthened by the fact that plaintiff Cinel had engaged in the private activity while he was a priest.[186] Finally, the court rejected the plaintiff's claim that broadcasting the videotape added no value to the story, even if it was not newsworthy.[187] According to the court, it may have been insensitive to publish the videotape, but the judiciary could not make decisions for the media as to what should be published.[188]

The *Uranga* case introduced in the second part is reintroduced here alongside *Crumrine* and *Cinel* as another example of the failure of a publication of private fact tort claim where concealments have come to light as a consequence of public records and media reports.[189] Fred Uranga brought an action against the publisher of the *Idaho Statesman* daily newspaper.[190] The newspaper published an article accompanied by a photograph of a handwritten statement by an accused sex offender implicating Uranga in youthful homosexual activity.[191]

Uranga filed a complaint for intrusion, publication of private facts, false light, and intentional and/or reckless infliction of emotional distress.[192] The trial court granted a motion to dismiss in favor of the newspaper.[193] The court of appeals affirmed. The Supreme Court of Idaho vacated the judgment of the trial court, but upon the newspaper's petition for rehearing, the court reversed itself.[194] The court dismissed the publication of private facts claim on the ground that the offending statement was on public record.[195] The court held that a statement implicating an individual in homosexual activity that happened forty years earlier is not a private fact because the statement was part of a court record available to the press.[196]

In distinguishing his claim from *Cox Broadcasting Corp. v. Cohn*,[197] Uranga argued that in *Cox* the information concerned a current criminal prosecution, while the statement to which he was objecting had been made to police forty years earlier.[198] The court rejected this distinction, stating that freedom of speech does not have a time line.[199] Uranga also argued that his name was not newsworthy.[200] The court rejected this argument as well, citing the Supreme Court decision in *Smith v. Daily Mail Publishing Co.*,[201] which held that determination of whether a publication is a matter of public concern is based upon an examination of the publication as a whole.[202] Even if Uranga's name was not newsworthy, the article about the Boys of Boise scandal was newsworthy for First Amendment purposes.[203] The dismissal of Uranga's intentional infliction of emotional stress claim was affirmed because the newspaper enjoyed First Amendment protection.[204]

While the above cases show that the private fact theory has not guaranteed victory for closeted homosexuals,[205] they also show that courts are prepared to voice the ideal that sexual orientation is prima facie private. *Simpson v. Burrows*, though its facts are extreme, reveals the possibility of complete victory for a gay woman relying on the public disclosure or privacy fact tort.[206] Jo Anne Simpson brought claims of intimidation, intentional infliction of emotional distress, invasion of privacy, and libel against the defendant couple Howard and Jean Burrows.[207] Ms. Simpson and her female partner moved to the small town of Christmas Valley, Oregon, where they purchased a restaurant.[208] Soon after their arrival and purchase of the restaurant, threatening and offensive letters warning people against the lesbian couple were circulated around town.[209] Letters were sent to Simpson and her partner with threatening content, such as "NO FAGS IN C.V. [Christmas Valley]" and "IT'S YOUR TURN TO GO[,] HEAD FIRST OR FEET FIRST."[210] Letters were also sent to other people and business owners in the town.[211] They called on citizens to boycott the restaurant due to the "perverts" who owned it, and they threatened that the restaurant would turn into "a mecca for Queers, Lesbians, Perverts & other degenerates."[212] The Burrows' letters had a greatly adverse effect on Simpson's life[213] and were among the principal reasons Simpson's partner left her and fled Christmas Valley.[214] Simpson testified that she felt threatened and lost trust in people, and even bought a gun for protection.[215] In support of her claim for economic damages, Simpson pointed out that as soon as the letter distribution commenced, fewer people patronized her restaurant business and she was forced to sell it at a loss.[216]

After finding the Burrowses responsible for sending the hateful letters that ruined Simpson's personal life and destroyed her livelihood,[217] the court held in favor for Simpson on her claims of intentional infliction of emotional distress, intimidation, and publication of private facts. The court concluded that the defendants intended to cause the plaintiff emotional distress and that their behavior was virtually criminal.[218] Though the Burrowses had the constitutional right to dislike homosexuality and to express their views, those rights did not grant them immunity from liability for direct threats.[219]

With respect to the disclosure of private facts claim, the court found that sexual orientation is a private fact that the defendants publicized to a large number of people.[220] The disclosure contained in the letters was "extremely outrageous" and thus was of the "highly objectionable kind."[221] Based on her valid privacy claims the court awarded Simpson $200,000 in noneconomic damages, $52,500 in economic damages, and $5,000 in punitive damages.[222]

The *Burrows* case illustrates that privacy invasions are actionable not only when unknown secrets are disclosed but also when information is moved without consent from one social network into another. The case thus represents Professor Lior Strahilevitz's theory in action:[223] facts can be private, not merely because they are secrets, but also because they are sensitive and have been released into new social networks with malicious intent. The *Burrows* court therefore implicitly endorsed an important point of view other courts have not—that LGBT persons have a right to selective disclosure of their sexual orientations.

Publication of Birth Sex of Transgender Persons

In an important California case in the tradition of *Melvin v. Reid*,[224] the court in *Diaz v. Oakland Tribune, Inc.*, reasoned that a transgender person's birth sex is a private matter and not newsworthy per se, even if she has become a public figure.[225] Plaintiff-respondent Toni Diaz was a transgender woman born as a biological male.[226] She underwent a sex-corrective procedure in 1975.[227] The surgery was a success, and society perceived Diaz as a woman. She kept her former sex a secret, except to her immediate family and closest friends.[228] Selective disclosure to a small group enabled her to break with the past, avoid constant scrutiny, and move on to enjoy a new life. She legally changed her name, social security card, and driver's license.[229] After the surgery, Diaz enrolled in the College of Alameda and was eventually elected as the student body president.[230] She was the first woman to hold this office.[231]

Diaz did not reveal her birth sex to the student body at College of Alameda.[232] A columnist from the *Oakland Tribune* found out about her gender reassignment surgery from confidential sources.[233] In the process of seeking to verify facts provided by those sources, the columnist discovered that before surgery Diaz had been arrested as a male for soliciting an undercover policeman but was never convicted of the crime.[234] With proof of Diaz's birth sex in hand, the columnist published a mocking article revealing that Diaz had been born a male.[235]

Diaz brought an action for publication of private facts.[236] Diaz maintained that the publication caused her depression, interrupted her college education, and led to insomnia, nightmares, and memory lapses.[237] The jury found that the defendant newspaper and columnist who disclosed the plaintiff's transsexual identity had publicly disclosed private facts, that the facts were private and not newsworthy, that the disclosure was highly offensive to a reasonable person, that the defendants knew the disclosure was highly offensive, and that the disclosure caused injury to the plaintiff.[238] The jury awarded Diaz $250,000 in compensatory damages and $525,000 in punitive damages.[239]

The defendants appealed, challenging the jury's findings that the plaintiff's birth sex was a private fact and not newsworthy.[240] The appeals court reversed and ordered a new trial on two grounds: instructional error and failure to meet the burden of proof of newsworthiness.[241] While the trial court instructed the jury that the defendant needed to present a "compelling public need" in order to abridge the plaintiff's privacy right,[242] it should have instructed that the defendant needed to show "legitimate interest" in exposing the private facts.[243] In addition, the trial court improperly instructed the jury that the burden of proof was on the defendant to prove newsworthiness, when it was actually the plaintiff who needed to prove that the publication was not privileged.[244]

Although the appellate court ordered a new trial, it reflected on the merits of the arguments and sided with plaintiff Diaz. This court, like the Oregon court in the *Simpson* case, implicitly endorsed an interest in selective disclosure. The court found that Diaz's "sexual identity," meaning her birth sex and transgender status, was a private matter even though it was not a complete secret. The court distinguished its determination from the Supreme Court ruling in *Cox Broadcasting Corp. v. Cohn.*[245] In *Cox*, the Supreme Court ruled that the father of a deceased rape victim could not file a publication of private facts tort claim against the media outlets that disclosed his daughter's name in connection with the incident.[246] The Supreme Court mainly based its decision on the fact that the daughter's name already appeared in the indictment.[247] In contrast, the court in *Diaz* found that the plaintiff's birth information was not part of the public record.[248] Diaz took affirmative steps to alter the public record to indicate her female identity.[249] According to the public record of her life, she was a female.[250] The police record concerning the solicitation of an officer did not even mention Diaz's new female name[251]—the journalist made the connection based on confidential sources rather than public records.[252] The court reasoned that even if the plaintiff's original birth certificate could be viewed as a public record, the defendants had not seen it before the article published.[253]

The court then rejected the defendants' argument that since plaintiff Diaz was a public figure as the first female student body president of a public college, the article they wrote and published was newsworthy.[254] While the court conceded that, as a matter of law, a person who seeks out a public position waives his or her right to privacy, the court held that Diaz was at best a "limited-purpose" public figure who did not abandon all privacy interests.[255] The plaintiff's status as the first female student body president did not mean she was not entitled to keep her "domestic activities and sexual relations private."[256] And the court found the plaintiff's gender transformation would not affect her honesty or judgment so as to render her publicly accountable for her private life.[257] Finally, the court rejected the defendant's argument that the case was newsworthy because it reflected a change in women's positions in society.[258] In the court's view, the columnist had no academic news intent. Rather, his clear attempt to mock the plaintiff undercut any claim that he was trying to educate the public.[259]

The court also rejected the argument that awarding punitive damages was improper because the plaintiff did not prove that the defendant acted with malice or intent to injure.[260] The court held that the defendant did not just publish the article but had exacerbated Diaz's injury by making her the "brunt of a joke."[261] The columnist did not even bother to ask Diaz for her consent prior to publishing the article (despite the lack of a deadline) but instead threw his energies into efforts to acquire sensitive information about her.[262] A reasonable jury could have taken this disparity of effort as evidence of malice.[263] The court also found the newspaper liable for punitive damages because it approved and published the columnist's article.[264]

The court rejected the argument that the compensatory damages awarded were excessive.[265] The defendants argued that the special damages presented by Diaz were only $800 for psychotherapy.[266] The court concluded that the damages were not limited to out-of-pocket losses but included personal suffering and humiliation.[267] The court also ruled that the damages were not easy to evaluate and should be left for the jury to decide.[268] The *Diaz* case sends a message that invading the privacy of a transgender woman is a serious offense that can lead to liability in the form of substantial compensatory and punitive damages.

In stark contrast to Diaz's broad success with the merits of her privacy claims, another court was less willing to view information dredged up about a transgender person's birth sex as private and not newsworthy. In *Schuler v. McGraw-Hill Cos.*, the plaintiff Eleanor Schuler, the CEO of Printron, Inc., was a male-to-female transgender woman.[269] Schuler sued the publisher of *Business Week* and its employees for publishing an article that allegedly defamed her, interfered with her business relations, invaded her privacy, and caused her emotional distress.[270] Published in 1994, the article criticized the American Stock Exchange (AMEX) for failing to examine the registration statements of Printron and other Emerging Company Marketplace firms.[271] The article referred to Schuler's status as a transgender woman and mentioned a lawsuit that had been filed against her when she was still a man.[272] According to Schuler, the article implied that she had "changed her sex in order to conceal an SEC filing rather than to cure her gender dysphoria syndrome."[273] Schuler's complaint alleged several torts, three of which were from Prosser's four categories: publication of private fact, intrusion, and false light.[274] The court granted *Business Week's* motion to dismiss on all counts. Without strongly siding with Schuler, it bears pointing out that her suit was not without a tinge of merit.

The *Diaz* court and the *Schuler* court reached dramatically different assessments of the merits of the private fact claims of their respective plaintiffs. Although both cases involve a private fact claim brought by a transgender woman, the primary difference between the two cases was the degree of secrecy the women accorded to their birth sex. Diaz, the woman elected class president, had not made her transgender status public to the world at large, but Schuler had. Rejecting Schuler's publication of private facts claim, the court appropriately pointed out that in the 1970s she had given interviews to the *Washington Post* and *People Magazine* recounting her sex change, making the facts a matter of public record.[275] It could be argued, however, that those interviews had lapsed into practical obscurity.[276]

Schuler's intrusion claim, which the court rejected, struck the court as pro forma because all Schuler had done to support it was to restate the same facts and arguments used to support her weak publication of private facts tort claim.[277] Unsurprisingly, the court held that Schuler failed to state a claim for intrusion.[278]

The court held that the references to Schuler's transsexual status were not false or defamatory.[279] In doing so, it dealt inadequately with whether the article placed her in a false light. With regard to defamation, the court analyzed twenty-eight sentences in the *Business Week* article, some of them pointing to the plaintiff's sex change.[280] The court concluded that the article raised the legitimate question of whether the sex change was an advantage for Schuler, because AMEX did not realize that a lawsuit filed against the plaintiff under her male surname (Huminik) was a suit against her. The plaintiff argued that statements such as the "Schuler/Huminik affair," "the next Huminik/Schuler exploit," and the "Huminik/Schuler matter" suggested that she either had a multiple personality disorder or was "involved in a game of hide and seek."[281] In response, the court held that these phrases are not false statements of facts and not defamatory in the context of the article.[282] If, however, the *Business Week* story could have been fairly read as implying that Schuler changed her sex to escape recognition as the person the business world knew as Mr. Huminik, she arguably would have had a plausible false light action. It is one thing to point out that a sex change can have career advantages but something else to imply that a sex change was prompted by an unethical and perhaps pathological desire to gain those advantages.

Finally, Schuler's intentional infliction of emotional distress claim was rejected on the ground that there was nothing outrageous in *Business Week* magazine's conduct.[283] Furthermore, the court found Schuler's transsexual status was relevant to the article—a new sex and a new name meant that some individuals in the business community did not know that when dealing with Schuler they were dealing with a person who was already known to them as Huminik. But there are several questions of fact the court did not give Schuler a chance to prove to a jury.[284] These questions include whether the article implied that she changed her sex for success in the business world, whether publishing the implication was outrageous, and whether Schuler experienced severe emotional distress as a result of the defendant's outrageous conduct. Imagine that Schuler produced evidence of a psychiatric diagnosis of gender dysphoria dating back to adolescence and evidence of years of therapy and medical treatments, culminating in surgical sex reassignment. A fact finder might well have concluded that it was outrageous for a magazine to suggest blithely that Schuler would have changed her sex merely to advance her career.

Problems of Selective Disclosure

In addressing wrongful publication of private fact claims, courts have not always grappled with the important question of what might be termed LGBT "selective disclosure rights." Is there a right to maintain secrecy with respect to sexual orientation in some contexts, despite freely disclosing sexual orientation in other contexts? Should there be a legal right to be "out" for some purposes and "in" for others? What are the psychological, social, and political dimensions of LGBT Americans' need to control the flow of information about sexual orientation?

These questions are implicit in cases in which courts must decide whether unwanted disclosure to a small group constitutes "publication." In *Borquez*[285] and *Greenwood v. Taft*[286] employment cases, the courts answered the question in the affirmative. The workplace in each case was a law firm. The court in *Borquez* held that the publication private fact claim's secrecy element could be satisfied by limited disclosure to a discrete segment of the public, such as fellow employees in a workplace.[287]

In *Greenwood v. Taft*, plaintiff Scott Greenwood argued that the defendant law firm Taft, Stettinius & Hollister fired him because he was gay.[288] The trial court granted a summary judgment in favor of the defendant.[289] The appellate court affirmed the rejection of Mr. Greenwood's wrongful discharge claim because Ohio offered no defense to LGBT people in its antidiscrimination law.[290] However, the court reversed the dismissal of Greenwood's publication of private fact claim.[291] Greenwood argued that when he amended his benefits forms to include his male partner as the recipient of his pension, staff within the law firm disclosed the information to other people to whom the information was irrelevant.[292] The court concluded that a reasonable person who has disclosed his sexual orientation for some employment-related purposes might nonetheless have been offended by being more generally "outed."[293] The court emphasized that the plaintiff shared the information with people to whom the information was irrelevant and that the information did not stay within the law firm, implying that the requirement of public disclosure could potentially be established at trial.[294] However, the court ultimately held that whether the defendant publicly disclosed the information was a question of fact that needed to be examined by the trial court.[295]

Few cases better highlight the problem of selective disclosure than *Sipple v. Chronicle Publishing*,[296] a case in which a bid for selective disclosure rights was rejected on dramatic facts. Oliver W. Sipple, a gay ex-marine, prevented the assassination of President Gerald Ford by foiling Sara Jane Moore's attempt to shoot Mr. Ford.[297] Following the incident, Sipple became a hero and received significant publicity.[298] Subsequently, several newspapers published articles describing Sipple as a gay activist and as a friend of Harvey Milk,[299] a famous gay political figure. Sipple's heroism and military service history challenged the once pervasive stereotype of homosexual men as weak and timid. The public speculated whether the White House's failure to display gratitude toward Sipple stemmed from the administration's bias toward homosexuals.[300]

Sipple found press reports of his homosexuality offensive and filed a complaint for publication of private facts.[301] He argued that press reports exposed his sexual orientation to close relatives, his employer, and other people who previously did not know about it.[302] As a consequence his family abandoned him, and Sipple suffered embarrassment and mental anguish.[303]

Mr. Sipple appealed a trial court's summary judgment order in favor of the defendants, who consisted of several publishers, a newspaper, and a columnist.[304] The appellate court upheld the dismissal of Sipple's complaint, finding that Sipple's sexual orientation was not a private fact and the publication was newsworthy and thus protected by the First Amendment.[305] The court stated that Sipple was a known gay figure in San Francisco who had marched in gay parades and who gay magazines mentioned as a close friend of Milk.[306] Moreover, when asked about his sexual orientation, Sipple himself admitted that he was gay.[307] Therefore, the court concluded that the articles disclosed a fact that was not private but already publicly known.[308] In addition, the court held that the publication was newsworthy and did not reveal a fact that met the requisite level of offensiveness.[309]

While Sipple's bid for selective disclosure rights met with understandable failure, the failure of other LGBT plaintiffs' bids for selective disclosure raises concern. In *Merriwether v. Shorr*, substantively a public disclosure case brought under New York's commercial appropriation statute,[310] a court found that a picture of a lesbian couple taken at their commitment ceremony and published years later in a magazine was newsworthy because gay couples' commitment ceremonies are a reflection of the progress of society.[311] Yet the abatement of stigma and discrimination on a societal level should not mean the end of individuals' entitlement to keep their relationships out of the press.

Plaintiffs Valerie Merriwether and Rosetta Fords, a lesbian couple, took part in a religious commitment ceremony in which one plaintiff was dressed in a bridal gown and the other a tuxedo, thereby appearing as a traditional bride and groom.[312] Defendant Kathy Shorr was a professional photographer and also served as their limousine driver on the day of the ceremony.[313] In the limousine she took the plaintiffs' pictures with their permission.[314] She asked for the plaintiffs' written consent to use the photographs for commercial purposes, but the plaintiffs refused.[315] Six years later, defendant magazine *Popular Photography* published an article on Ms. Shorr's work, accompanied by a montage of her pictures, including one of the plaintiffs' pictures with the caption: "LESBIAN COUPLE . . . two women on their way to a commitment ceremony in a church in Greenwich Village."[316] The plaintiffs filed a complaint claiming invasion of privacy and infliction of emotional distress.[317] The plaintiffs sought monetary and injunctive relief,[318] not denying they were gay but arguing that they always kept their sexual orientation private and discreet.

They also contended that they never disclosed this information to their co-workers and that the publication caused them embarrassment and distress.[319]

The court dismissed the privacy claim against the magazine on the ground that intimate homosexual ceremonies are a reflection of the progress of society and are thus newsworthy.[320] The court rejected the couple's emotional distress claim, too. The court stated that the defendants' conduct did not reach the level of outrage required for establishing this tort.[321] According to the court, the picture did not present the plaintiffs in a sensational manner or make the gay wedding event appear foolish.[322] Furthermore, the wedding was held in a public venue and the festivities took place in several locations.[323] In reaching these conclusions about public and private, the court ignored the potential relevance of the vast size and effective anonymity of New York City and the couple's likely knowledge of how to avoid "running into" workplace colleagues.

The dismissal of the privacy and emotional distress claims ignored the importance to a gay couple of controlling the flow of information regarding sexual orientation from limited groups to the broad public.[324] The dismissal entails a rejection of selective disclosure rights, and even more, reflects a policy of subordinating the personal desire of LGBT individuals for privacy to the public need for keeping pace with LGBT lifestyles.

Many LGBT Americans have sought to live lives in which their sex, sexuality, or sexual orientation remains undisclosed in some social networks—perhaps those including parents or co-workers—but is disclosed in other social spheres. Yet appellate courts often take what might be called a simplistic "once out, always out" point of view.[325] If tort doctrine currently demands this point of view, the doctrine and the tort require rethinking and redesign to accommodate the reasonable privacy preferences of some members of the LGBT population.

FALSE LIGHT IN THE PUBLIC EYE

The false light tort is among the four recognized in Prosser's 1960 article and later incorporated into the Second Restatement of Torts under his influence.[326] The cause of action serves to vindicate interests in both mental repose and reputation. According to Prosser, the roots of the "false light in the public eye" tort were deep in the ground before the Warren and Brandeis article.[327] Prosser traced the origins of this tort to an 1816 suit brought by the poet Lord Byron "enjoining the circulation of a spurious and inferior poem attributed to his pen."[328] Prosser identified three categories of false light in the public eye cases: (1) inaccurate attribution cases (like Byron's); (2) misleading use of photographs cases; and (3) imputation of criminality cases.[329] Prosser wrote that "[t]he false light cases obviously differ from those of intrusion, or disclosure of private facts" in that the interest protected is reputation as in defamation.[330] But as previously emphasized, plaintiffs alleging invasion of privacy after 1960 also commonly allege two or more of Prosser's torts. The contemporary false light case—whether involving inaccurate attribution, misleading photographs, and/or implied immorality or criminality—is also likely to be an intrusion case and/or a disclosure of private fact case. For example, LGBT plaintiffs or plaintiffs claiming not to be LGBT who bring suits alleging false light commonly also allege intrusion, publication of private facts, and even appropriation claims. If false light is normatively akin to defamation, then defamation is normatively akin to the invasion of privacy tort generally.

Misattribution of Sexual Orientation

In several cases alleging false light, the plaintiffs argued that they were not gay, lesbian, or transgender but were falsely portrayed as such and sought recovery. In *D.C. v. Harvard-Westlake School*, the parents of a high school boy filed an action against his secondary school. The school allegedly allowed or assisted students and the school newspaper to depict falsely the youth as gay and to belittle him as a "faggot."[331] In another case, *Langford v. Sessions*, a man's photograph was used in a flier that promoted a gay club and portrayed him as gay.[332] In *Douglass v. Hustler Magazine, Inc.*, a heterosexual woman alleged that nude photographs of her posing with another woman published in *Hustler Magazine* falsely portrayed her as a lesbian.[333] In *Geissler v. Petrocelli*, a woman claimed a book authored by a former colleague falsely depicted her as transgender.[334] Finally, in *Tina Thompson v. John Doe*, a female "exotic dancer" filed a false light claim against a male entertainer known as "Shawty Shawty" who frequented Pleasers, the Atlanta club at which she worked.[335] Shawty Shawty posted on his Twitter account: "Pass this on. There is a nigga dancing at Pleasures. His name is Nairobi and it looks female. Ass and titties and pussy! Be careful!"[336]

The false light tort does not require proof on the part of plaintiffs that a defendant has published an untruth. It requires that the defendant has published words or images that depict the plaintiff in a false or misleading light. Plaintiffs need not be prepared to characterize defendants as liars. However, courts struggle with how to distinguish false light actions from defamation actions.[337] Some courts will dismiss false light actions if the plaintiff's claim is that attributions of LGBT status are flatly untrue. Thus in *Nazeri v. Missouri Valley College*, the court found that a state school system employee condemned by a college vice president as incompetent and a "fag" would have to seek recovery through a defamation claim.[338] In *Albright v. Morton*, a straight man alleged privacy invasion following the publication of a book in which a gay man's photograph appeared alongside a caption bearing his name.[339] Plaintiffs James Albright, a former bodyguard and the ex-lover of the pop star Madonna, and his ex-employer Amrak Productions sued defendants Andrew Morton, Michael O'Mara Books, St. Martin's Press, and Newsgroup Newspapers for allegedly falsely portraying Albright as a homosexual in their book.[340] The court held that Albright's false light claim was actually a defamation claim because "he objects to the making of a *false* statement, not the revelation of private information."[341] *Albright* was an especially far-fetched, even silly false light claim litigated by a straight man.[342] However, the Massachusetts court took advantage of the case as an opportunity to advance large claims about the modern significance of stating that a person is a homosexual: it can be defamatory to assert falsely that someone is homosexual, but it is no longer inherently highly offensive or defamatory per se to assert that someone is a homosexual.

The defendants purchased from Albright the rights to publish information about his romantic relationship with Madonna and later published it in an internationally distributed book.[343] The book contained a picture of Madonna walking beside her ex-employee, Jose Guitierez.[344] Guitierez was outspoken about his sexual orientation and represented "his homosexual ideology in what many would refer to as sometimes graphic and offensive detail."[345] According to the complaint, Guitierez was well known because he appeared in a documentary about Madonna and performed on stage with her.[346] The caption accompanying the picture of Guitierez read "Jim Albright (with Madonna in 1993) told Morton he felt 'overwhelming love' for her."[347] Albright in turn argued that the picture portrayed him as gay.[348]

The plaintiffs filed a complaint for defamation, among other claims, but the court held that the photograph contained nothing to imply that Albright was gay.[349] Furthermore, the book described Albright as having had a long heterosexual relationship with Madonna.[350] The court also stated that, even if the picture implied that Albright was gay, to identify someone as gay is not a defamatory act per se, and such a holding would "legitimize relegating homosexuals to second-class status."[351] The court discussed several developments in law, including the Massachusetts Supreme Judicial Court's decision in favor of same-sex marriage, as indicating that the law cannot support a discriminatory view of gays.

Misattribution of Lifestyle or Character

Sometimes LGBT individuals resort to the privacy tort, not to complain that someone has revealed their sexual orientation but that someone has distorted or degraded their characters in a way connected to their sexual orientation.

Andrea Dworkin's false light claim against *Hustler Magazine* can be understood in this light.[352] In another case, a former employee sued Sun Microsystems alleging that his supervisor depicted him in a false light by telling others he had "hit on" co-workers, turning him into a perpetrator of sexual harassment.[353] The *Schuler v. McGraw-Hill Cos.*[354] court, as discussed earlier, rejected the false light claim of a transgender businesswoman who argued that the article implied she "changed her sex in order to conceal an SEC filing rather than to cure her gender dysphoria syndrome."[355] The court held that the article "raise[d] the legitimate issue of whether Plaintiff's sex change worked to her advantage by concealing part of her past."[356] The court stated that a false light claim required proof of a false statement of fact, which in this case the plaintiff did not establish.[357] Schuler also did not prove that the article placed her under false light.[358]

In *Whitaker v. A&E Television Networks*, defendant-appellant A&E Television Networks broadcasted a picture of the plaintiff in its documentary, "The History of Sex," that suggested the plaintiff was gay, HIV positive, and a drug user.[359] According to the court,

The narrator state[d]: "AIDS had exacted a deadly toll on gay men and [intravenous] drug users as well as hundreds of thousands of heterosexuals in Africa and Haiti. But it wasn't publicly acknowledged by [President] Ronald Reagan until well after Rock Hudson died of the disease in 1985. . . ." Just before the narrator [stated] "users," the documentary shows a picture of [plaintiff-respondent Miles] Whitaker on the street at night shaking what appears to be a cup and nodding at people walking by.[360]

The documentary neither mentioned Whitaker's name nor mentioned he was HIV positive, a drug user, or homosexual.[361] Nonetheless, the plaintiff argued that the documentary inaccurately portrayed him as a gay drug user living with HIV.[362] The plaintiff filed a complaint for defamation, false light, and intentional infliction of emotional distress, and he sought injunctive relief.[363] The defendant moved to strike, arguing the causes of action arose from First Amendment–protected activity.[364] The trial court denied the motion, and the defendant appealed.

Affirming the trial court's decision, the appellate court held that, while the subject matter of the documentary was a matter of public concern, the plaintiff was not a public figure, and whether he was a drug user or HIV carrier was not a matter of public concern.[365] The defendants argued that the documentary did not disclose the plaintiff's name, and his appearance was brief.[366] The court rejected this argument, stating that the relevant question was whether the documentary implied that the plaintiff belonged to one of the groups mentioned: gays, drug users, or HIV carriers.[367]

False Light and Beyond: Privacy Invasions Excused for the Greater Good

Individuals who have sued under any privacy tort theory alleging that their actions, opinions, or beliefs were portrayed in a false and misleading light have often lost these suits.[368] In *Dominick v. Index Journal Co.*,[369] the defendant newspaper, *Index Journal*, published a pro-gay letter and attributed it to the plaintiff. The plaintiff denied writing it. The letter preached tolerance toward same-sex marriage, arguing against the "'close-minded opinions' of a lot of local citizens . . . towards the gay and lesbian celebrations" in the area, and calling for the "need to expand our horizons on prejudice."[370] The plaintiff was gay and argued that the article exposed his "private affairs," although it was not clear if he argued that his homosexual identity was exposed or just his view on gay marriage.[371] Among the privacy torts, a false light claim would have been better suited to the facts, but the tort is not favored in South Carolina and may not be available at all.[372] Dominick filed a complaint for negligence, libel, invasion of privacy, and intentional infliction of emotional distress.[373] The trial court granted the media defendant's motion for summary judgment as to all counts except negligence.

On appeal, the court held that Dominick failed to establish a libel claim because the publication did not adversely affect the plaintiff or his reputation in the community.[374] The court also denied the publication of private fact claim because the plaintiff did not establish that the defendant intentionally gave publicity to private fact or had knowledge that adverse results were likely to follow.[375] As to the intentional infliction of emotional distress claim, the court determined that the plaintiff could not establish that the defendant's "conduct was so extreme or outrageous that [it] exceeded all possible bounds of decency."[376] Finally, the court dismissed the negligence cause of action because the plaintiff's libel claim had been denied, and the court did not want the plaintiff to use the negligence claim to "sneak into the courthouse through the back door."[377] Since the libel claim provides some constitutional protections that do not exist in negligence, the court expressed concern that allowing the plaintiff to plead negligence would undermine the media's First Amendment protection and defeat the purposes of libel law.[378]

Of special interest, the court seemed unwilling to punish the media for publishing a letter discussing a matter of public interest. The court observed that the "letter discussed two major public events, one of which occurred in South Carolina and was the subject of two news articles in the *Index Journal* the month preceding the publication of the letter."[379] Moreover the "letter called for community tolerance and promoted constitutional values."[380]

In *Dominick*, as in other cases, the national importance of the LGBT population's historic quest for equality and inclusion undercuts the practical utility of the invasion of privacy tort and perhaps the defamation tort as well. Recall the Massachusetts judge in *Albright* arguing that the lessening of stigma and discrimination in his state, which recognized same-sex marriage in 2003 in *Goodridge*, means it can no longer be considered defamatory to gossip that someone is a homosexual.[381] In the words of another judge: "Several legal authorities have suggested that one's identity as a homosexual—even though it is in essence a private matter—is inherently a matter of public concern because it 'necessarily and ineluctably' involves that person in the ongoing public debate regarding the rights of homosexuals."[382] In *Prince*, the gay model lost on his privacy claims against *Out* magazine because photographs of him selected for the magazine had been taken in a "public place" and illustrated a newsworthy public health story.[383] It did not seem to matter to the court that the model whose photographs *Out* had appropriated had not yet come out to his family and did not live the reckless life of excessive illegal drug use and unprotected sex described in the article.[384] Although information about sexual orientation can be highly sensitive, courts have deemed the conduct and experiences of members of the LGBT population broadly "public," "newsworthy," and "of legitimate public concern" even when individual members of the group have not.[385]

APPROPRIATION

A plaintiff's prima face case of appropriation will typically allege a nonconsensual use of the name, moniker, or photographic likeness of the plaintiff in an advertisement or in connection with a business or commercial product such as a book, magazine, newspaper, or film. The first state court to recognize the existence of a freestanding invasion of privacy cause of action did so in the context of an "appropriation" case.[386]

Prosser identified "appropriation" as among the four extant privacy torts and included it in his formulation of the tort for the Second Restatement.[387] Prosser did not think commercially appropriating attributes of personal identity, intrusion upon seclusion, or false light were the kind of offenses Warren and Brandeis had in mind for their new tort action to address, and he seems to have been correct.[388] But common law courts citing Warren and Brandeis nonetheless came to regard these offenses, along with publication of private fact, as actionable "invasions of privacy."[389] Upon reflection, it should not be surprising that courts would regard using a person's name, picture, or likeness in circulated materials as a wrong in the same general category of tort as prying into that same person's private life or publishing the details of her private life. Commercial appropriation and publication of private fact are both ways of paying attention and calling attention to someone who might prefer to be let alone.

Tort Winners

Appropriation claims by those portrayed as homosexual are occasionally successful, as in *Langford v. Sessions*.[390] Plaintiff Marcus Langford was an amateur bodybuilder who alleged that the defendants, a nightclub and flier-design company, impermissibly used his photograph on a flier to promote a gay party.[391] The flier was also posted on a website.[392] Langford argued that the flier wrongfully portrayed him as gay, and as a result, he allegedly suffered emotional damage. Based on his religious background and beliefs, a gay lifestyle was intolerable.[393] He argued that since the publication, more gays approached him in the gym, and he had to explain to friends that he was not gay.[394] He also contended that after the flier was distributed, the website Gay.com started using his photograph as a profile picture.[395] In addition to punitive damages, Langford filed a complaint for misappropriation, false light, intentional infliction of emotional distress, negligence, and defamation.[396] The court found Langford entitled to compensatory damages for counts of misappropriation, false light, and negligence and awarded him $70,000.[397]

The court found that the defendants appropriated Langford's photograph for their benefit.[398] This holding is consistent with Prosser's description of the appropriation tort as effective for plaintiffs who show that a defendant has pirated the plaintiff's identity for some advantage of his own.[399] The *Langford* court also held that the use of the photograph placed the plaintiff in false light because it portrayed him as something he was not, and he had a right to portray himself in that context in a manner of his choosing.[400] The court thus found the defendant liable for negligence because reasonable care would have included asking for the plaintiff's permission to use his photograph.[401]

The court rejected Langford's intentional infliction of emotional distress claim because he had not shown he asked the defendants to stop using the photograph.[402] In addition, the defendants' conduct was not so extreme and the plaintiff did not prove he suffered emotional damage "so acute a nature that harmful physical consequences might be not unlikely to result."[403] The court also dismissed the claim for punitive damages, finding that the defendants' conduct was not outrageous and that they did not act in malice, did not risk harm to others, did not physically or economically harm the plaintiff, and did not repeat the tortious act.[404] Rejecting the claim for defamation, the court held that the plaintiff did not prove that claiming someone is homosexual is a defamatory act.[405]

Albright v. Morton, cited by the *Langford* court to support the notion that "an allegation of homosexuality is defamatory does not have an initial plausibility or appeal,"[406] rejected an appropriation claim brought by

Madonna's ex-bodyguard and lover.[407] In *Albright* the court stated that for plaintiffs to prevail in an appropriation case, they need to prove that the appropriation's purpose is to take advantage of their reputation or prestige.[408] The court held that, even though the defendant used Albright's picture to sell more books, since the picture was also published in a newspaper article, it did not use the reputation of Albright or make commercial use of Albright's name.[409]

Tort Losers

As in *Albright*, appropriation claims by those wrongly portrayed as homosexual are sometimes unsuccessful. *Raymen v. United Senior Ass'n, Inc.*, is another, less palatable, example.[410] In *Raymen*, a newspaper photographer shot a picture of the plaintiffs, a same-sex couple, kissing while waiting their turn to marry.[411] The photograph was published in the newspaper and on its website and later used without permission as part of an advertisement for a nonprofit organization, United Senior Association (USA Next).[412] USA Next challenged the positions taken by the American Association of Retired Persons (AARP).[413] The advertisement contained two pictures: one of the plaintiffs kissing with a green checkmark over it and a second picture of an American soldier, presumably in Iraq, with a red X over it.[414] Under the photograph there was a caption: "The Real AARP Agenda," suggesting that AARP opposes the United States' wars abroad and supports gay lifestyle.[415] The plaintiffs argued that the advertisement portrayed them as against American troops and unpatriotic.[416] They allegedly suffered embarrassment and extreme emotional distress in consequence and filed a complaint for libel, false light, appropriation of their likeness, and intentional infliction of emotional distress.[417]

The court rejected the men's appropriation claim, stating that the advertisement was noncommercial.[418] The photograph had been used by a nonprofit organization and was not for commercial use.[419] The court then characterized the publication as newsworthy and thus protected by the First Amendment.[420] The court held that the campaign used the photograph to address matters of legitimate public concern—same-sex marriage and support for the military.[421] The court also dismissed libel, false light, and intentional infliction of emotional distress claims.[422]

In *Prince*, the court held that the misappropriation claim was not actionable because the photograph accompanied an article on a gay lifestyle that was an "element of popular culture" and thus newsworthy.[423] The contention that a matter is newsworthy merely because it relates to the amorphous beast "popular culture" threatens to gut the right to privacy entirely.

INTENTIONAL INFLICTION OF EMOTIONAL DISTRESS

Prosser was skeptical of the privacy tort. He feared the tort—the four torts—would be overly generous to plaintiffs with trivial or self-inflicted wounds.[424] He also feared the tort would be duplicative of other actions with the same gist: "Taking intrusion [e.g.], the gist of the wrong is clearly the intentional infliction of mental distress, which is now in itself a recognized basis of tort liability."[425] He could not have known that fifty years later lawyers would survey the privacy tort case law and find duplication (1) among the four privacy torts; and (2) between the privacy torts and defamation, and the privacy torts and intentional infliction of emotional distress, and—not examined here—between the privacy torts and the right to publicity[426] and confidentiality.[427] The privacy torts have been additive and duplicative, but not in ways that appear to have made a difference in the justice of outcomes.

There may be duplication and even cannibalization, but LGBT cases suggest that the invasion of privacy tort and the infliction of emotional distress torts function more as friends than competitors. The intentional infliction of emotional distress tort commonly accompanies the invasion of privacy torts in lawsuits alleging wrongs of intrusion, publicity, and appropriation, with the latter two more or less standing or falling together. In *Simpson*, for example, the court held that the sending of threatening and intimidating letters to a lesbian couple invaded privacy and caused extreme emotional distress, driving them to sell their newly acquired restaurant business and leave town.[428] The repetition of the letters and the death threats supported the emotional distress claim.[429] Meanwhile, the act of publicizing the plaintiff's sexual orientation in disparaging letters mailed to the community supported a privacy invasion claim.[430] The court acknowledged that the defendants had the right to believe that homosexuality "is at odds with the teachings of the bible," but it found that the defendants' behavior "constituted an extraordinary transgression of the bounds of socially tolerable conduct" and enjoyed no immunity.[431]

However, in many other cases, the plaintiffs' emotional distress did not make the grade.[432] Courts in these cases have ruled that wrongdoings did not amount to extreme and outrageous conduct, which is either intentional or reckless and which causes the plaintiff severe emotional distress.

Templeton is a good illustration of privacy and emotional distress claims meeting the same doomed fate.[433] Plaintiff Doe and a friend permitted the defendant Templeton, a professional skateboarder, to take their photograph after he had misrepresented himself as world-renowned professional skateboarder Tony Hawk.[434] Defendant Toy Machine used the photograph to advertise a videotape describing the company's skateboard team.[435] The advertisement, with the plaintiff's picture, instructed those who wanted the videotape to "[w]rite to:

I am gay in a happy way not a sexual one" at a specific address.[436] Doe, who was gay, argued that the advertisement drew attention to and disclosed her sexual identity.[437] She filed a complaint for violation of the Illinois Right of Publicity Act, publication of private facts, intentional infliction of emotional distress, and negligence.[438] The plaintiff, who worked as a teacher, had to discuss the advertisement with her employer but did not expose her sexual orientation during the conversation.[439]

The court granted summary judgment in favor of the defendants on the counts of publication of private facts and intentional infliction of emotional distress. As to the publication of private facts count, the court held that the plaintiff did not establish the necessary elements of the tort because the advertisement did not disclose that she was gay but at most "disclosed what plaintiff looked like on that particular day in June 2002," and the defendants did not know that the plaintiff was gay and therefore could not intentionally reveal any private fact.[440] In so holding, the court stated for the record that a plaintiff's sexual orientation is not a legitimate public concern, and its disclosure could be highly offensive to a reasonable person in an appropriate case.[441]

For similar reasons, the court also denied the intentional infliction of emotional distress claim. For one, the defendants' behavior was not extreme or outrageous.[442] Second, they did not intend to cause emotional distress to the plaintiff, as they did not know about the plaintiff's sexual identity.[443] Third, the plaintiff failed to introduce compelling evidence to demonstrate severe emotional distress. Her claims of stress, weight loss, and eczema were insufficient.[444] The claim for punitive damages was denied because the plaintiff did not establish that the defendants' conduct was "similar to that found in a crime."[445] Jane Doe's privacy and emotional distress actions thus stood and fell together.

CONCLUSION

Although there have been victories worth mention, the invasion of privacy tort has not proven especially useful to lesbian, gay, bisexual, and transgender plaintiffs. Despite the apparent limited success by LGBT plaintiffs in the cases examined here, one must acknowledge the theoretical possibility that the invasion of privacy tort has been a powerful deterrent to privacy invasions targeting the LGBT population. It is also possible that many invasion of privacy suits have been filed and either successfully settled out of court or litigated and won without appeal. Nonetheless, published appellate court opinions paint a troubling picture, suggesting that privacy tort litigation may not be worth the bother.

American society seems to be moving toward a more socially tolerant future. One day, sexual orientation and sex change will cease to warrant special notice. People will stop threatening, mocking, and discriminating. Although we are not there yet, some courts have prematurely declared that LGBT persons have achieved sufficient equality—that what is whispered in the closets can now be shouted from the rooftops.[446] That to be known as queers or fags or simply as LGBT is no longer to be vulnerable or despised. Courts deciding whether a privacy claim should withstand summary judgment, a motion to dismiss, or an appeal should be cautious in adopting what may be overly expansive, optimistic assumptions about what is appropriately privileged, public, and newsworthy. I make this point not to cling to the false security of the closet on behalf of LGBT Americans or to encourage hypersensitivity about their orientation, identity, and relationships but firmly to decline the invitation to assume an inherent lack of merit or wisdom in privacy seeking in everyday life after *Lawrence* and *Goodridge*.

The enduring legacy of Prosser's article is beyond dispute. However, several questions must be asked. First, did Prosser acknowledge all of the categories and subcategories of "privacy" torts?[447] The LGBT cases suggest that Prosser missed or oversimplified cases or categories that ought to have been included in his purportedly comprehensive analysis of privacy case law. Second, did Prosser exaggerate the distinctiveness with which his four torts were imminent in the case law? Edward Bloustein famously argued that the four privacy torts have an important commonality: the concept of dignity.[448] In fairness, Prosser neither affirms nor denies that there is a common value that justifies recognition of all four invasions of privacy torts. Yet stressing, as he did, the severability of the tort into four discrete categories can obscure the unifying fact that defendants have affronted plaintiffs in a way that leaves plaintiffs feeling—to borrow an image from the Georgia opinion *Pavesich v. New England Life Insurance*—like slaves to a merciless master.[449]

The cases examined reveal that a gap has developed between the formalities of pleading that can be credited to Prosser's enormous influence and the actual experiences of LGBT plaintiffs. LGBT plaintiffs often allege in their complaints that a single injurious episode has given rise to multiple privacy causes of action. Indeed, LGBT plaintiffs often allege, as a formal matter, that defendants in a single action violated two, three, or all four of Prosser's privacy subtorts, plus the defamation and emotional distress torts.[450] This allegation of multiple torts is an undisputable fact about pleading, a function of responsible lawyering within the taxonomic framework of the positive law Prosser shaped. But as Prosser's critics note, the four torts have in common a singular normative foundation of respect for human dignity and inviolate personhood.[451] Thus, while LGBT plaintiffs typically allege that a single wrongful encounter with disrespectful defendants has affronted their basic desire to be left alone, their attorneys formally divide these encounters into multiple causes of action. People want to be let alone; leave it to lawyers and analytic philosophers to tell them they want to be let alone in four or more distinguishable senses.

In principle, LGBT individuals, like everyone else, can recover for highly offensive wrongful acts of intrusion, publication, or appropriation. But on the evidence of the tort cases cited in this chapter, I reluctantly conclude that recovery for invasion of privacy is unlikely where the "reasonable person" and the "reasonable LGBT" person part ways. What is offensive to LGBT persons struggling for liberty, equality, dignity, and intimacy is not always offensive to the judiciary's hypothetical everyman. Homosexuality, gender unorthodoxy, and sex change were once considered morally illicit, dangerous, and potentially criminal. Secrecy and selective self-disclosure are needs that arose in a time of intolerance and discrimination. As long as intolerance and discrimination against LGBT individuals remain, the need for seclusion, secrecy, and selective self-disclosure will remain as well.[452]

*   *   *

I would like to thank Mr. Erez Aloni, LLM, for invaluable research assistance.

NOTES

1. The right to privacy is also recognized by federal statutes. *See, e.g.*, Privacy Act of 1974, 5 U.S.C. § 552a (2006). *See generally* Anita L. Allen, *Privacy Law and Society* (2007) (textbook of common law, constitutional, and statutory privacy and data protection law, including chapters that focus on federal Internet, communications, and surveillance statutes). Federal statutes whose bare titles do not suggest privacy protection nonetheless function to create medical, financial, and other privacy rights federal agencies are empowered to enforce. Implicated in a recent controversy concerning LGBT youth, the Federal Trade Commission Act is an apt example. In a July 1, 2010, letter, David Vladek, Director of the Federal Trade Commission's Bureau of Consumer Protection, warned that plans pursuant to a bankruptcy proceeding to sell personal information of defunct *XY Magazine* subscribers and XY.com site users (as an asset belonging to magazine and site founder Peter Ian Cummings) could violate the Federal Trade Commission Act's prohibition against "unfair or deceptive acts or practices." *See* Letter from David C. Vladek, Director of the Bureau of Consumer Protection, U.S. Federal Trade Commission, to Peter Larson and Martin E. Shmagin (July 1, 2010), *available at* http://www.ftc.gov/os/closings/100712xy.pdf. XY.com had expressly promised privacy and anonymity to its site users, most of whom were teenagers interested in gay lifestyles and issues. *Id.* Mr. Vladek requested that "to avoid the possibility that this highly sensitive data" revealing the sexual orientation of young men and teens "fall into the wrong hands," the data " be destroyed (along with any credit card data still being retained) as soon as possible." *Id.*

2. *See Lawrence v. Texas*, 539 U.S. 558 (2003) (striking down laws criminalizing consensual sexual acts between same-sex adults); *see also Goodridge v. Dep't. of Pub. Health*, 798 N.E.2d 941 (Mass. 2003) (recognizing the right to same-sex marriage in the Commonwealth of Massachusetts).

3. *Lawrence*, 539 U.S. at 562.

4. *Goodridge*, 798 N.E. 2d at 948.

5. *See, e.g., Simpson v. Burrows*, 90 F. Supp. 2d 1108 (D. Or. 2000) (lesbian businesswoman alleging locals invaded her common law privacy rights, inflicted emotional distress, and defamed her in a concerted campaign to oust her and her partner from Christmas Valley community).

6. *See, e.g., Greenwood v. Taft, Stettinius & Hollister*, 663 N.E.2d 1030, 1034 (Ohio Ct. App. 1995) (whether a law firm invaded a gay employee's privacy by disclosing his sexual orientation within the firm after he named his male partner as his pension beneficiary was a question of fact for a trial court).

7. *See, e.g., Prince v. Out Publ'g*, No. B140475, 2002 WL 7999 (Cal. Ct. App. January 3, 2002) (gay lifestyle magazine not liable for invasion of privacy for having acquired and published photographs of partly closeted gay model without his consent).

8. *See, e.g., Elmore v. Atl. Zayre, Inc.*, 341 S.E.2d 905, 905 (Ga. Ct. App. 1986) (plaintiff not entitled to recover for privacy invasion where retail store employees called police after peeping through a ceiling crack to view him in a toilet stall, where he was allegedly engaging in "sodomy").

9. *See, e.g., Plaxico v. Michael*, 735 So. 2d 1036, 1038 (Miss. 1999) (lesbian plaintiff not entitled to recover for privacy invasion after lover's ex-husband spied on her, photographed her partially nude in her bedroom, and then distributed photographs to gain advantage in a child custody dispute).

10. William L. Prosser, *Privacy*, 48 Calif. L. Rev. 383, 423 (1960).

11. The Restatement (Second) of Torts provides that the right of privacy is invaded by "(a) unreasonable intrusion upon the seclusion of another . . . or (b) appropriation of the other's name or likeness . . . ; or (c) unreasonable publicity given to the other's private life . . . ; or (d) publicity that unreasonably places the other in a false light before the public. . . ." Restatement (Second) of Torts § 652A(2) (1977).

12. *See, e.g.*, Barbara Moretti, "Outing: Justifiable or Unwarranted Invasion of Privacy? The Private Facts Tort as a Remedy for Disclosures of Sexual Orientation," 11 Cardozo Arts & Ent. L.J. 857, 896–98 (1993) (the private facts tort should be available as a remedy for persons whose sexual orientation is exposed without consent by others seeking to combat AIDS, identify secret homosexuals, or provide homosexual role models); Eric K. M. Yatar, "Defamation, Privacy, and the Changing Social Status of Homosexuality: Re-Thinking Supreme Court Gay Rights Jurisprudence," 12 Tul J.L. & Sexuality 119, 127 (2003) (the private facts tort offers a potential "route to recovery for the individual who is accused of or revealed as being a homosexual"); cf. Keith J. Hilzendeger, Comment, "Unreasonable Publicity: How Well Does Tort Law Protect the Unwarranted Disclosure of a Person's HIV-Positive Status?," 35 Ariz. St. L.J. 187, 188 (2003) (courts should offer a broader protection to plaintiffs suing under privacy facts torts than the Restatement of Torts currently calls for); Ronald F. Wick,

"Out of the Closet and Into the Headlines: 'Outing' and the Private Facts Tort," 80 Geo. L.J. 413, 427 (1991) (same).

13. For this chapter, I attempted to gather all of the reported privacy tort cases to date in which plaintiffs self-identified as lesbian, gay, bisexual, or transsexual or transgender. (In the attempt I uncovered a number of pending and unpublished LGBT-plaintiff privacy tort cases, along with cases in which persons have sued under privacy tort theories for misattribution of gender-nonconforming traits, *see Cason v. Baskin*, 20 So. 2d 243 [Fla. 1944], homosexuality or being transgender. I have incorporated all of these interesting cases into the chapter.) Extrapolating from my findings and the empirical results reported by William McLauchlan, see William McLauchlan, "Why People Litigate: An Examination of Privacy Tort Cases" (April 3, 2008) (paper presented at the annual meeting of the Midwest Political Sci. Ass'n Annual Nat'l Conference, Palmer House Hotel, Hilton, Chicago, IL), *available at* http://www.allacademic.com/meta/p266091_index.html. I estimate that reported appellate cases brought by LGBT persons alleging LGBT-related offenses probably account for no more than 3 percent of the total number of appellate privacy cases decided since 1906. McLauchlan offers 350 as the total number of appellate privacy tort cases decided in forty-seven states between 1906 and the year 2000. *Id.* at 27.

14. Prosser, *supra* note 10.

15. Restatement (Second) of Torts § 652A(2) (1977).

16. Even the courts that have rejected the false light tort or the private fact tort have not done so on the ground that the taxonomy itself is flawed. *See generally* James B. Lake, "Restraining False Light: Constitutional and Common Law Limits on a 'Troublesome Tort,'" 61 Fed. Comm. L.J. 625, 639–48 (2009) (stating courts reject false light tort because they believe it overlaps the defamation tort and the publication of private fact tort because they believe it impairs freedom of speech).

17. *Cf.* Hilary E. Ware, Note, "Celebrity Privacy Rights and Free Speech: Recalibrating Tort Remedies for 'Outed' Celebrities," 32 Harv. C.R.-C.L. L. Rev. 449, 468, 488 (1997) (arguing that privacy torts are "unpromising" remedies against unwanted disclosure of homosexuality and need to be "reconceptualiz[ed]"). My broader contention is that the torts are unpromising remedies against not only unwanted disclosure but also against unwanted intrusion, false light publicity, and appropriation.

18. *See* National Defense Authorization Act for Fiscal Year 2011, H.R.5136, 111th Cong. (2010) (received and read twice in the Senate, June 28, 2010); *see also Log Cabin Republicans v. United States*, No. CV 04-08425-VAP EX, 2010 WL 3960791 (C.D. Cal. October 12, 2010) (holding Don't Ask Don't Tell [DADT] unconstitutional and issuing an injunction to stop the enforcement of the policy); *accord, Witt v. U.S. Dept. of the Air Force*, No. 06-5195RBL, 2010 WL 3732189 (W.D. Wash. September 24, 2010) (holding that the application of DADT violated the plaintiff's due process rights and ordered restoring her military service).

19. Prosser, *supra* note 10, at 407.

20. *Id.* at 410.

21. *Id.* at 415.

22. *Id.* at 419.

23. The first use of the word *privacy* in a state court case may have been in *State v. Mann*, 13 N.C. (2 Dev.) 263 (1829), where the court declined to consider punishment for battery against a slave "by reasons of its privacy"—a privacy that permits the master to exact "bloody vengeance" in response to unruly disloyalty. *Id.* at 267; *see also* Frederick S. Lane, *American Privacy: The 400-Year History of Our Most Contested Right*, 59 (2009). The term cropped up again in 1830 and 1868 in the voices of judges describing the proper realm of women (privacy life) and the rationale for the authority of husbands to physically discipline their spouses (domestic privacy). *Id.* at 60. The state of Washington in 1889 became the first to "explicitly codify a right to privacy in its state constitution: 'No person shall be disturbed in his private affairs, or his home invaded, without authority of law.'" *Id.* (citation omitted).

24. *See generally* Melvin I. Urofsky, *Louis D. Brandeis: A Life*, 46–104 (2009). In his influential article on privacy, Dean Prosser stated that the invasion of privacy tort was "a most marvelous tree to grow from the wedding of the daughter of Mr. Samuel D. Warren." Prosser, *supra* note 10, at 423. But it is doubtful that Warren had a daughter of marriageable age in 1890, a mere seven years after his own marriage. Warren married his wife Mabel Bayard in 1883, a wedding from which the bride banned the groom's best friend, Louis D. Brandeis, because he was Jewish. *See* Urofsky, *supra* note 24, at 97.

25. Urofsky, *supra* note 24, at 98. ("Naturally the penny press of the era wanted to report on the doings of [Warren's circle of family and friends] . . . men and women who seemed to party constantly, had homes in the city and the country, rode to the hounds, sailed, and had money to support such a lifestyle. For reasons not altogether clear, at some point Sam began to resent what he saw as press intrusion into his private life, and turned to Louis. Brandeis did not really want to get involved [he said he would have preferred to write on the duty of publicity than on the right to privacy] but, at his friend's importuning, agreed to look into the issue.")

26. Samuel D. Warren & Louis D. Brandeis, *The Right to Privacy*, 4 Harv. L. Rev. 193, 195, 205 (1890).

27. *See, e.g., Union Pac. R.R. Co. v. Botsford*, 141 U.S. 250, 252 (1891) (holding that a female plaintiff could not be forced to undergo a medical examination and thereby "lay bare the body," citing "[t]he inviolability of the person" and the right "to be let alone," and thus echoing Warren and Brandeis); *Schuyler v. Curtis*, 15 N.Y.S. 787, 788 (N.Y. Sup. Ct. 1891) (family of deceased women could block the erection of a bust in her honor, on the ground that she was not a "public character" but "a woman of great refinement and cultivation" who preferred privacy and had a right to it).

28. *See Roberson v. Rochester Folding Box Co.*, 64 N.E. 442, 442 (N.Y. 1902) (holding that the right to privacy tort had not yet been adopted and therefore could not provide a remedy for a woman whose photograph had been used on packaging for baking flour without her consent).

29. *Pavesich v. New England Life Ins. Co.*, 50 S.E. 68, 80–81 (Ga. 1905) ("So thoroughly satisfied are we that the law recognizes within proper limits, as a legal right, the right of privacy, and that the publication of one's picture without his consent by another as an advertisement, for the mere purpose of increasing the profits and gains of the advertiser, is an invasion of this right, that we venture to predict that

the day will come that the American bar will marvel that a contrary view was ever entertained by judges of eminence and ability. . . .").

30. *Id.* at 69.

31. *Id.* at 80.

32. In his 1960 article, Prosser comprehensively cited and sorted the cases spawned by *Pavesich*, notable examples of which are *Sidis v. F-R Publishing*, 113 F.2d 806 (2d Cir. 1940) (New York was not liable for publishing an unflattering story about a former child prodigy); *Melvin v. Reid*, 297 P. 91 (Cal. Ct. App. 1931) (privacy of ex-prostitute and acquitted murder defendant was invaded by an unauthorized film about her life); and *Cason v. Baskin*, 20 So. 2d 243 (Fla. 1944) (memoir writer liable to woman repelled by portrayal of her as a woman with masculine virtues).

See also McLauchlan, *supra* note 13. According to McLauchlan, about ten privacy tort cases are decided each year on appeal in the United States (excluding Alaska, Hawaii, and Utah), and there have been a total of about 350 such cases through the year 2000, most losses for their plaintiffs. *Id.* at 25, 27 fig. 1. He places the odds of winning a privacy appeal as no better than three to one. *Id.* at 28 fig. 2. He speculates that people litigate privacy wrongs due to an emotional attachment to their claims. *Id.* at 25.

33. Prosser, *supra* note 10, at 388.

34. *Id.* at 386.

35. *Id.* at 389.

36. Although it would become the most influential, the 1960 article was not the first to introduce Prosser's taxonomy. Prosser may have debuted it in articles written in the mid-1930s. *See* Neil M. Richards & Daniel J. Solove, *Prosser's Privacy Law: A Mixed Legacy,* 98 Calif. L. Rev. (forthcoming 2010). Suggestive of his influence even before 1960, the taxonomy appears, minus the false light tort, in the 1956 case *Housh v. Peth*, in which the state of Ohio first recognized the right to privacy. *Housh v. Peth*, 133 N.E.2d 340, 343 (Ohio 1956). There the court distinguished three causes of action: (1) "the unwarranted appropriation or exploitation of one's personality"; (2) "the publicizing of one's private affairs with which the public has no legitimate concern"; and (3) wrongful intrusion into one's private activities." *Id.* at 341.

37. Prosser, *supra* note 10, at 391.

38. *Id.* at 393–94.

39. *Id.* at 392.

40. *Id.* at 408.

41. *Id.* at 408–09.

42. *Id.* at 410.

43. *Id.* at 410–15.

44. *Id.* at 419.

45. *Id.* at 422.

46. *Id.*

47. *Id.* A real-life version of this scenario unfolded in 2002 when television celebrity Jennifer Aniston sued and eventually settled with various media defendants who published photographs of her sunbathing at her home with her breasts exposed.

The photographs were taken by professional paparazzi. *See* "Aniston Snaps Case 'Is Settled,'" *Birmingham Post*, July 4, 2002, at 9.

48. *See* Restatement (Second) of Torts § 652A(2) (1977).

49. Prosser, *supra* note 10, at 423.

50. *See, e.g., Hall v. Post*, 372 S.E.2d 711 (N.C. 1988) (rejecting public disclosure of private facts tort on constitutional free speech grounds).

51. *See, e.g., Denver Publ'g Co. v. Bueno*, 54 P. 3d 893 (Colo. 2002); *Lake v. Wal-Mart Stores*, 582 N.W.2d 231 (Minn. 1998); *Cain v. Hearst Corp.*, 878 S.W.2d 577 (Tex. 1994) (all rejecting the false light tort as duplicative of the older defamation tort).

52. Professor Stephen Sugarman, "Opening Remarks at the California Law Review Symposium: Prosser's *Privacy* at 50" (January 29, 2010), *available at* http://www.californialawreview.org/information/prosser-info.

53. Erving Goffman, "The Nature of Deference and Demeanor," 58 *Am. Anthropologist* 473, 475–99 (1956). According to Goffman,

In all societies rules of conduct tend to be organized into codes which guarantee that everyone acts appropriately and receives his due. In our society the code which governs substantive rules and substantive expressions comprises our law, morality, and ethics, while the code which governs ceremonial rules and ceremonial expressions is incorporated in what we call etiquette. *Id.* at 476–77.

Nor do persons perceived as belonging to the LGBT population get the benefits of civility. *See* Complaint for Libel, False Light, Intentional Interference with Business Relations, Intentional Infliction of Emotional Distress, and Injunctive Relief, *Thompson v. Doe*, No. 2010CV183037 (Ga. Super. Ct. March 19, 2010) [hereinafter Complaint for Thompson] (An Atlanta adult entertainment dancer "Nairobi" sued rapper/comedian whose derogatory Twitter message suggested she was a man in drag.).

54. *See Elmore v. Atl. Zayre, Inc.*, 341 S.E.2d 905, 905 (Ga. Ct. App. 1986).

55. *See Plaxico v. Michael*, 735 So. 2d 1036, 1038 (Miss. 1999) (lesbian photographed partially nude by lover's Peeping Tom ex-husband).

56. *See Elmore*, 341 S.E.2d 905.

57. Ex-husbands have also uncloseted ex-wives. *See, e.g., Weaver v. Nebo Sch. Dist.*, 29 F. Supp. 2d 1279, 1284 (D. Utah 1998) (holding that a school district's restrictions on a lesbian teacher's right to express her sexual orientation outside the classroom impermissibly infringed upon the teacher's First Amendment rights in a case in which the schoolteacher's ex-husband revealed her lesbian sexual orientation to others); *see also Crumrine v. Harte-Hanks Television, Inc.*, 37 S.W.3d 124 (Tex. App. 2001) (affirming a summary judgment in favor of a television station on the First Amendment grounds that the publication of private fact was of "legitimate public concern" in the case in which a gay, HIV-positive father and police officer in a custody battle with his ex-wife revealed his status to the media).

58. *See Plaxico*, 735 So. 2d 1036.

59. *Prince v. Out Publ'g*, No. B140475, 2002 WL 7999 (Cal. Ct. App. January 3, 2002).

60. *Doe v. S.B.M.*, 488 S.E.2d 878, 880 (S.C. Ct. App. 1997).

61. *See, e.g., Doe v. Templeton*, No. 03 C 5076, 2004 WL 1882436 (N.D. Ill. August 6, 2004) (A lesbian plaintiff who was tricked into being photographed with

an imposter posing as the famous skateboarder Tony Hawk sued the publication over a photograph with the caption she believed revealed to others her sexual orientation for the first time).

62. *See* Prosser, *supra* note 10, at 389. The rule is stated in the Restatement (Second) of Torts as "[o]ne who intentionally intrudes, physically or otherwise, upon the solitude or seclusion of another or his private affairs or concerns, is subject to liability to the other for invasion of his privacy, if the intrusion would be highly offensive to a reasonable person." Restatement (Second) of Torts § 652B (1977).

63. Prosser, supra note 10, at 392.

64. *Id.* at 392.

65. *Id.* at 389–90.

66. *Id.* at 390.

67. *Id.*

68. *Id.* at 391.

69. *Id.* at 390–91.

70. 341 S.E.2d 905, 905 (Ga. Ct. App. 1986).

71. *Id.*

72. *Id.*

73. *Id.* at 906.

74. *Id.* at 907.

75. *Id.* at 906.

76. *Id.* (citing *Pavesich v. New England Life Ins. Co.*, 50 S.E. 68 [Ga. 1906]); *see also* Anita L. Allen, *Driven into Society: Philosophies of Surveillance Take to the Streets of New York*, Amsterdam L. F. (2009), *available at* ojs.ubvu.vu.nl/alf/article/download/92/157 (noting that there is a privacy interest in conduct in public places that has limits and is not absolute).

77. *Elmore*, 341 S.E.2d at 906.

78. *Id.* at 905.

79. Carlos A. Ball, "Privacy, Property, and Public Sex," 18 Colum. J. Gender & L. 1, 4 (2008). *Lawrence v. Texas*, 539 U.S. 558 (2003), and *Griswold v. Connecticut*, 381 U.S. 479 (1965), indeed tie sexual privacy to the bedroom. *But see Katz v. United States*, 389 U.S. 347 (1967) (holding that a man engaged in illegal activities in a phone booth on a public street has a legitimate expectation of privacy for Fourth Amendment purposes).

80. *Lawrence* struck down criminal prohibitions on gay sex. It does not dictate that private intrusions into the bedrooms of gay persons must be ruled "highly offensive to a reasonable person" in state court tort actions. Restatement (Second) Torts § 652B (1977).

81. 735 So. 2d 1036 (Miss. 1999).

82. *Id.* at 1038.

83. *Id.*

84. *Id.*

85. *Id.*

86. *Id.*

87. *Id.*

88. *Id.*

89. *Id.* at 1040.

90. Prior to *Lawrence v. Texas*, oral sex and anal sex could be criminalized. Many states kept on the books rarely enforced laws criminalizing these acts when performed by heterosexuals and/or homosexuals. *See Lawrence v. Texas*, 539 U.S. 558, 573 (2003) ("In those States where sodomy is still proscribed, whether for same-sex or heterosexual conduct, there is a pattern of nonenforcement with respect to consenting adults acting in private.").

91. *Plaxico*, 735 So. 2d at 1040.

92. *Id.* at 1039.

93. *Id.* at 1040.

94. *Id.* at 1040.

95. *Id.* at 1040 (Banks, J., dissenting).

96. *Id.* at 1041 (McRae, J., dissenting).

97. *Cf. Phillips v. Smalley Maint. Servs., Inc.*, 711 F.2d 1524 (11th Cir. 1983). (A heterosexual married woman lost her job after refusing to provide oral sex and answers to an employer's intrusive questions about her sex life.)

98. *Madsen v. Erwin*, 481 N.E.2d 1160 (Mass. 1985).

99. *Id.* at 1167.

100. *Id.* at 1161.

101. *Id.* at 1172.

102. *Id.* at 1163–66; *cf. Gunn v. Mariners Church*, 84 Cal. Rptr. 3d 1, 7 (Cal. Ct. App. 2008) (holding that "the ministerial exception . . . bars courts from reviewing employment decisions by religious organizations affecting employees who have religious duties of ministers").

103. *Madsen*, 481 N.E.2d at 1165–66.

104. Id. at 1167.

105. Id. at 1172.

106. *Morenz v. Progressive Cas. Ins. Co.*, No. 79979, 2002 Ohio App. LEXIS 2474 (Ohio Ct. App. May 23, 2002).

107. *Id.* at 5.

108. *Id.* at 5.

109. *Id.* at 11–12. Morenz did not like his new post, which required him to handle insurance claims stemming from very serious accidents. *Id.* at 4–5. His employer was unresponsive to his requests for reassignment, and Morenz experienced symptoms of post-traumatic stress disorder. *Id.* at 5.

110. *Id.* at 5.

111. Hence courts have repeatedly held that corporations, as fictitious entities without feelings and sensibilities, can have no common law right to privacy. *See* Restatement (Second) of Torts § 652I cmt. c (1977). *See generally* Anita L. Allen, *Rethinking the Rule against Corporate Privacy Rights: Some Conceptual Quandaries for the Common Law*, 20 J. Marshall L. Rev. 607 (1987).

112. *Logan v. Sears, Roebuck & Co.*, 466 So. 2d 121, 122 (Ala. 1985).

113. *Id.* at 123.

114. *Id.*

115. *Id.* at 123–24.

116. *Id.* at 123.

117. *Id.* at 124.

118. *Id.*

119. *Leibert v. Transworld Sys., Inc.*, 39 Cal. Rptr. 2d 65, 66 (Cal. Ct. App. 1995) (appellant alleged that he suffered discrimination based on his sexual orientation, violations of privacy rights protected under California's state constitution, and intentional infliction of emotional distress).

120. *Id.* at 73. ("Employment discrimination, whether based upon sex, race, religion or sexual orientation, is invidious and violates a fundamental public policy of this state. . . . We conclude that he stated viable claims for wrongful discharge in violation of public policy and intentional infliction of emotional distress.")

121. *Simpson v. Burrows*, 90 F. Supp. 2d 1108 (D. Or. 2000).

122. *Id.* at 8.

123. *Cf. Galella v. Onassis*, 487 F.2d 986 (2d Cir. 1973) (popular former First Lady Jacqueline Kennedy Onassis sought and obtained an injunction requiring a photographer to keep a safe distance from her and her children John and Caroline Kennedy).

124. *See, e.g., Id.*

125. *Uranga v. Federated Publ'ns, Inc.*, 67 P.3d 29, 31 (Idaho 2003) (aftermath of infamous scandal in which hundreds of people were suspected of involvement in soliciting homosexual activity from minors associated with the YMCA in Boise, Idaho).

126. *Melvin v. Reid*, 297 P. 91 (Cal. Ct. App. 1931); *Briscoe v. Reader's Digest Ass'n*, 483 P.2d 34 (Cal. 1971).

127. *Cf.* Paul M. Schwartz, "From Victorian Secrets to Cyberspace Shaming," 76 U. Chi. L.Rev. 1407, 1414 (2009) (quoting Lawrence Friedman, *Guarding Life's Dark Secrets: Legal and Social Controls over Reputation, Propriety, and Privacy* 218 [2009] [claiming that Melvin may have been an active prostitute at the time she sued those responsible for calling attention to her history of homicide acquittal and prostitution]).

128. *Uranga*, 67 P.3d at 32.

129. *Id.* at 32–33.

130. *Fla. Star v. B.J.F.*, 491 U.S. 524 (1989) (holding that the First Amendment bars press liability in a case where, in violation of state law, a newspaper published the name of woman who survived a rape after an inexperienced reporter copied her name from police reports inadvertently made available to the press); *Cox Broad. Corp. v. Cohn*, 420 U.S. 469 (1975) (holding that the First Amendment bars media liability in a case where, in violation of state law, a television station broadcasts the name of a murdered rape victim obtained from police records). The court also cited *Baker v. Burlington Northern, Inc.*, 587 P.2d 829 (Idaho 1978), where the court found no privacy invasion where defendant has accessed court records. *Uranga*, 67 P.3d at 32.

131. *Uranga*, 67 P.3d at 35.

132. *Plaxico v. Michael*, 735 So. 2d 1036, 1037 (Miss. 1999).

133. *Id.* at 1039.

134. The Restatement (Second) of Torts provides "Publicity Given to Private Life: One who gives publicity to a matter concerning the private life of another is subject to liability to the other for invasion of his privacy, if the matter publicized is of a kind that (a) would be highly offensive to a reasonable person, and (b) is not of legitimate concern to the public."—§ 652D (1977).

135. *See, e.g., Justice v. Belo Broad. Corp.*, 472 F. Supp. 145 (N.D. Tex 1979) (parents' publication of a private fact suit against a media defendant who reported that their murdered son had had a homosexual affair with his employer was dismissed). The general common law rule applicable to all of the privacy torts is that right to privacy actions survive death, but new privacy claims for postdeath offenses are not actionable. *See, e.g., Flynn v. Higham*, 197 Cal. Rptr. 145 (Cal. Ct. App. 1983) (adult children's false light privacy suit against a media defendant who reported that their deceased father was a homosexual and Nazi spy was dismissed).

136. *Valdez-Marquez v. Netflix Inc.*, No. C09-05903-JW-PVT (N.D. Cal. dismissed March 29, 2010).

137. *Borquez v. Ozer*, 923 P.2d 166 (Colo. App. 1995) (disclosure of HIV status by employer was a wrongful publication of private fact), *rev'd on other grounds*, 940 P.2d 371 (Colo. 1997).

138. *See, e.g., Cinel v. Connick* 15 F.3d 1338, 1345 (5th Cir. 1994) (information contained in public record is not "private").

139. *See, e.g., Crumrine v. Harte-Hanks Television, Inc.*, 37 S.W.3d 124, 127 (Tex. App. 2001) (television station story regarding a custody proceeding in which one parent raised concerns for a child's safety is of legitimate public interest and protected by the First Amendment, and facts about sexual orientation and HIV status revealed in court are no longer private and may be published with impunity by media).

140. *Cason v. Baskin*, 20 So. 2d 243 (Fla. 1944). *Cason v. Baskin* was the Florida courts' first opportunity to embrace or to reject the right to privacy, and it embraced it. *Id.* at 244 ("The first and the main question presented here is whether an action may be maintained in this State for an invasion of the right of privacy."). The papers concerning the trial and its defendant are archived at the University of Florida, George A. Smathers Libraries, *A Guide to the Cross Creek Trial (Cason v. Baskin) Papers,* http://web.uflib.ufl.edu/spec/manuscript/guides/CasonvBaskin.htm.

141. *See generally* Patricia Nassif Acton, *Invasion of Privacy: The Cross Creek Trial of Marjorie Kinnan Rawlings* (1988).

142. Marjorie Kinnan Rawlings, *Cross Creek* (1942).

143. *See generally* Anita L. Allen & Erin Mack, "How Privacy Got Its Gender," 10 N. Ill. U. L. Rev. 441 (1990) (arguing that concerns about the need to protect women's privacy spirited the early development of privacy law); *cf.* Robert E. Mensel, "The Anti-Progressive Origins and Uses of the Right to Privacy in the Federal Courts 1860–1937," 3 Fed. Cts. L. Rev. 109, 112 (2009) (citing nineteenth-century federal court cases in which judges rendered opinions "valuing female privacy more than male" and reflecting "prevailing bourgeois understandings of gender and race").

144. *See generally* Allen & Mack, *supra* note 155.

145. Acton, *supra* note 153, at 24.

146. *Cason*, 20 So. 2d at 244–45.

147. Rawlings, *supra* note 154. See the blog devoted to the Cross Creek trial, which includes discussion of the woman-as-man discourse, http://crosscreektrial. com/2009/12/a-bunch-of-mannish-hussies/.

148. *Cason*, 20 So. 2d at 245.

149. *Id.* at 245–46 (quoting passages from Rawlings, *supra* note 154).

150. *Cason*, 20 So. 2d at 245.

151. *Id.* at 245–46.

152. *Id.* at 247. The memoir was offensive to Cason more because of what it called attention to than because of what it revealed.

153. Acton, *supra* note 153, at 31, 92–94.

154. *Id.* at 30 ("She wore pants at every possible opportunity, taught her niece and nephew to shoot, and enjoyed an occasional boxing match. And she was not above a show of violence if it suited her purposes.").

155. *Cason*, 20 So. 2d at 247.

156. *Id.*

157. *Id.*

158. *Schuyler v. Curtis*, 15 N.Y.S. 787, 788 (N.Y. Sup. Ct. 1891) (family sought to prevent the public display of a bust created in the image of a woman philanthropist who was a "woman of great refinement and cultivation").

159. Prosser, *supra* note 10, at 393.

160. Acton, *supra* note 153, at 144. *But see id.* at 144 ("Though she was never completely happy with her portrayal in Cross Creek, Zelma found it in her heart to forgive Marjorie. . . .").

161. *Id.* at 24, 25.

162. *Id.*

163. *Id.* at 80–81 ("As Zelma knitted, her ball of yarn—through intent or accident—repeatedly fell from her lap and rolled under the table. [The defendant's husband, Norton] Baskin, being the gentleman that he was, stooped down each time to retrieve it.").

164. *Id.* at 24; *see also Id.* at 115 (counsel for plaintiff arguing rhetorically that defendant Baskin might be unaware that in the deep South "'old maid' is a fighting term").

165. 923 P.2d 166 (Colo. App. 1995), *rev'd on other grounds*, 940 P.2d 371 (Colo. 1997).

166. *Id.* at 169.

167. *Id.* at 169–70.

168. *Id.* at 170.

169. *Id.* at 171.

170. *Id.* at 179.

171. *Id.* at 172.

172. *Id.*

173. *Id.* at 173.

174. *See, e.g., Uranga v. Federated Publ'ns, Inc.*, 67 P.3d 29, 33 (Idaho 2003).

175. *Crumrine v. Harte-Hanks Television, Inc.*, 37 S.W.3d 124 (Tex. App. 2001); *see generally* Hilzendeger, *supra* note 12.

176. *Cinel v. Connick*, 15 F.3d 1338, 1345 (5th Cir. 1994).

177. *Id.* at 1340.

178. *Id.* at 1341.

179. *Id.*

180. *Id.* at 1342–43.

181. *Id.*

182. *Id.* at 1343.

183. *Id.* at 1345.

184. *Id.* at 1346.

185. *Id.*

186. *Id.*

187. *Id.*

188. *Id.*

189. *Uranga v. Federated Publ'ns, Inc.*, 67 P.3d 29 (Idaho 2003).

190. *Id.* at 31.

191. *Id.* at 30.

192. *Id.* at 31.

193. *Id.*

194. *Id.* at 30. The high court rejected the intrusion claim because Uranga did not state any kind of intrusion into a place, or any uncomfortable investigation. The newspaper only investigated what was in the public record and did not intrude on Uranga's seclusion. *Id.* at 32. Uranga abandoned the false light claim, perhaps because he believed the court would find a duty of verifying every court document quoted or reproduced to be an unreasonable burden on newspapers.

195. *Id.* at 33.

196. *Id.*

197. *Cox Broad. Corp. v. Cohn*, 420 U.S. 469 (1975) (The First Amendment bars media liability for broadcasting the lawfully obtained identity and photograph of a rape and murder victim despite a Georgia statute prohibiting the publication of the identities of rape victims.).

198. *Uranga*, 67 P.3d at 35.

199. *Id.*

200. *Id.*

201. 443 U.S. 97 (1979).

202. *Uranga*, 67 P.3d at 35.

203. *Id.*

204. *Id.*

205. Uranga's actual sexual orientation is unclear. He denied the sexual involvement he felt was implied by the statement and its republication in the *Idaho Statesman*.

206. *Simpson v. Burrows*, 90 F. Supp. 2d 1108, 1125 (D. Or. 2000).

207. *Id.* at 1112.

208. *Id.* at 1113.

209. *Id.* at 1114.

210. *Id.*

211. *Id.* at 1115.
212. *Id.* at 1114.
213. *Id.*
214. *Id.* at 1121.
215. *Id.*
216. *Id.*
217. *Id.* at 1120.
218. The court rejected Simpson's libel claims because they were barred by the statute of limitations and because defendants were entitled to their offensive opinions about the plaintiff's lesbian sexual orientation. *Id.* at 1124.
219. *Id.*
220. *Id.* at 1125.
221. *Id.*
222. *Id.* at 1131.
223. *See* Lior Jacob Strahilevitz, "A Social Networks Theory of Privacy," 72 U. Chi. L. Rev. 919 (2005).
224. *Melvin v. Reid*, 297 P. 91 (Cal. Ct. App. 1931) (filmmakers violated the privacy of a woman whose past life as a prostitute and accused murderer was resurrected and turned into a motion picture using her real name); *see also Briscoe v. Reader's Digest Ass'n*, 483 P.2d 34 (Cal. 1971). *But see Sidis v. F-R Publishing Corp.*, 113 F 2d 806 (2d Cir. 1940).
225. *Diaz v. Oakland Tribune, Inc.*, 188 Cal. Rptr. 762 (Cal. Ct. App. 1983).
226. *Id.* at 765.
227. *Id.*
228. *Id.*
229. *Id.*
230. *Id.*
231. *Id.*
232. *Id.*
233. *Id.* at 766.
234. *Id.*
235. *Id.*
236. *Id.*
237. *Id.*
238. *Id.*
239. *Id.* at 762.
240. *Id.* at 766.
241. *Id.* at 768.
242. *Id.*
243. *Id.* at 762.
244. *Id.* at 769.
245. *Cox Broad. Corp. v. Cohn*, 420 U.S. 469 (1975).
246. *Id.*; *see also Diaz,* 188 Cal. Rptr. at 771 (discussing the holding in *Cox*).
247. *Cox*, 420 U.S. at 496.
248. *Diaz,* 188 Cal. Rptr. at 771.

249. *Id.*
250. *Id.*
251. *Id.*
252. *Id.*
253. *Id.* It is worth noting that original birth certificates are commonly sealed and not available even to the people they concern; in most U.S. jurisdictions, adults adopted as infants and seeking their "true" identities are for that reason alone not granted access to their original birth certificates.
254. *Id.* at 766.
255. *Id.* at 773.
256. *Id.*
257. *Id.*
258. *Id.*
259. *Id.*
260. *Id.* at 773–74.
261. *Id.* at 774.
262. *Id.*
263. *Id.* at 774.
264. *Id.*
265. *Id.* at 774–75.
266. *Id.* at 774.
267. *Id.*
268. *Id.* at 775.
269. *Schuler v. McGraw-Hill Cos.*, 989 F. Supp. 1377 (D.N.M. 1997).
270. *Id.* at 1382.
271. *Id.* at 1383.
272. *Id.*
273. *Id.* at 1384–85.
274. *Id.* at 1389–90.
275. *Id.* at 1390.
276. *See U.S. Dep't of Justice v. Reporters Comm. for Freedom of the Press*, 489 U.S. 749, 770 (1989) (that "an event is not wholly 'private' does not mean that an individual has no interest in limiting disclosure or dissemination of the information"); *Id.* at 780 ("The privacy interest in maintaining the practical obscurity of rap-sheet information will always be high.").
277. *Schuler,* 989 F. Supp. at 1390.
278. *Id.* Today, calling attention to personal facts about a person is the kind of thing we might regard in ordinary parlance as intrusive. But to plead the intrusion privacy tort, a plaintiff must allege and prove facts that go to the elements of the tort. Even when the facts are alleged and a paradigm instance of intrusion is seemingly proven, as in *Plaxico v. Michael*, 735 So. 2d 1036, 1038 (Miss. 1999), an LGBT plaintiff may lose.
279. *Schuler,* 989 F. Supp. at 1390.
280. *See Id.* at 1384–89.
281. *Id.* at 1386–87. Schuler's reference in her argument to "multiple personality disorder" displayed a regrettable lack of knowledge about this psychiatric condi-

tion—a condition it was unfair to say *Business Week* attributed to her. People with the rare, controversial condition dissociative identity disorder ("multiple personality disorder") typically develop two or more distinct personalities, often in response to a serious emotional trauma. They do not typically surgically alter their external appearances in order to satisfy the gender identities of one of their personalities. *See generally* David H. Gleaves, Mary C. May, & Etzel Cardeña, "An Examination of the Diagnostic Validity of Dissociative Identity Disorder," 21 Clinical Psychol. Rev. 577 (2001).

282. *Schuler,* 989 F. Supp. at 1386–87.

283. *Id.* at 1390.

284. *See Id.* at 1391–92.

285. *Borquez v. Ozer,* 923 P.2d 166 (Colo. App. 1995), *rev'd on other grounds,* 940 P.2d 371 (Colo. 1997).

286. *Greenwood v. Taft, Stettinius, & Hollister,* 663 N.E.2d 1030, 1034 (Ohio Ct. App. 1995).

287. *Borquez,* 923 P.2d at 173. The Supreme Court of Colorado reversed the case, stating that the trial court erred by instructing the jury that the plaintiff's claim could be based on "publicity" of private fact rather than "publication." 940 P.2d 371 (Colo. 1997).

288. *Greenwood,* 663 N.E.2d at 1034.

289. *Id.* at 1031.

290. *Id.* at 1032.

291. *Id.* at 1036.

292. *Id.* at 1034.

293. *Id.* at 1035.

294. *Id.* at 1035–36.

295. *Id.* at 1036.

296. *Sipple v. Chronicle Publ'g Co.,* 201 Cal. Rptr. 665 (Cal. Ct. App. 1984).

297. *Id.* at 666.

298. *Id.*

299. *Id.*

300. *Id.*

301. *Id.* at 667.

302. *Id.*

303. *Id.*

304. *Id.*

305. *Id.* at 668.

306. *Id.* at 669.

307. *Id.*

308. *Id.*

309. *Id.* at 669–70.

310. The plaintiffs availed themselves of the only privacy right New York embraces, the right codified in Sections 50 and 51 of the New York Civil Rights Law. N.Y. Civ. Rights Law § 50, 51 (*McKinney's consolidated laws of New York annotated,* 1994. St. Paul, Minn.: West Group) (liability for nonconsensual use of a person's name or likeness for business or trade purposes).

311. *Merriwether v. Shorr*, No. 116582/94, 1995 WL 461265 (N.Y. Sup. Ct. Feb 6, 1995).

312. *Id.* at 1.

313. *Id.*

314. *Id.*

315. *Id.*

316. *Id.*

317. *Id.*

318. *Id.*

319. *Id.* at 2.

320. *Id.*

321. *Id.* at 3.

322. *Id.*

323. *Id.*

324. *Id.*

325. *See, e.g., Sipple v. Chronicle Publ'g Co.*, 201 Cal. Rptr. 665 (Cal. Ct. App. 1984) (holding that Sipple's sexual orientation was not a private fact because he was a known gay figure in San Francisco) *cf. Merriwether v. Shorr*, No. 116582/94, 1995 WL 461265, at 2 (N.Y. Sup. Ct. Feb. 6, 1995) ("plaintiffs do not deny being lesbians, but contend that they have 'always been extremely private and discreet about their long-standing relationship. . . .' [T]hey never told any of their co-workers of the nature of their relationship . . ."); *Prince v. Out Publ'g*, No. B140475, 2002 WL 7999 (Cal. Ct. App. Jan. 3, 2002) (rejecting plaintiff's claim that the article disclosed to a large number of people that he was gay, information that he had shared previously with only certain family members and close friends, because the article was newsworthy).

326. Prosser, *supra* note 10, at 398. The Restatement (Second) of Torts provides: § 652E. Publicity Placing Person in False Light
One who gives publicity to a matter concerning another that places the other before the public in a false light is subject to liability to the other for invasion of his privacy, if the false light in which the other was placed would be highly offensive to a reasonable person, and the actor had knowledge of or acted in reckless disregard as to the falsity of the publicized matter and the false light in which the other would be placed. Restatement (Second) of Torts § 652E (1977).

327. Prosser, *supra* note 10, at 398.

328. *Id.*

329. *See Id.* at 399 nn.140 & 143; *Martin v. Johnson Publ'g Co.*, 157 N.Y.S.2d 409 (N.Y. Sup. Ct. 1956) ("Man Hungry" woman); *Semler v. Ultem Publ'ns*, 9 N.Y.S.2d 319 (N.Y. City Ct. 1938).

330. Prosser, *supra* note 10, at 400.

331. *D.C. v. Harvard-Westlake Sch.*, 98 Cal. Rptr. 3d 300 (Cal. Ct. App. 2009) (defendant school's motion to compel arbitration reversed).

332. *Langford v. Sessions*, No. 03-255 (CKK) (D.D.C. July 29, 2005), https://ecf. dcd.uscourts.gov/cgi-bin/show_public_doc?2003cv0255-17.

333. *Douglass v. Hustler Magazine, Inc.*, 769 F.2d 1128, 1135 (7th Cir. 1985) (reversing a large judgment in favor of a plaintiff, reasoning that "*Hustler* is a magazine

for men. Few men are interested in lesbians. The purpose of showing two women in an apparent sexual embrace is to display the charms of two women."); *cf. Schomer v. Smidt*, 170 Cal. Rptr. 662 (Cal. Ct. App. 1980) (holding that a false attribution of homosexuality is "slander per se" in a case where a flight attendant sued a fellow employee for slander, invasion of privacy, battery, and intentional infliction of emotional distress after she falsely represented to others that the plaintiff was a lesbian).

334. *Geisler v. Petrocelli*, 616 F.2d 636, 639 (2d Cir. 1980).

335. Complaint for Thompson, *supra* note 53, at 3–4.

336. *Id.* at 4.

337. *Cf. Jews for Jesus, Inc., v. Rapp*, 997 So.2d 1098, 1114 (Fla. 2008) (declining to recognize a claim for false light invasion of privacy separate from defamation).

338. *Nazeri v. Missouri Valley Coll.*, 860 S.W.2d 303, 312 (Mo. 1993).

339. *Albright v. Morton*, 321 F. Supp. 2d 130 (D. Mass. 2004).

340. *Id.* at 132–33.

341. *Id.* at 140.

342. *See Id.* at 136. The court also rejected the false light claim because the tort was not recognized in Massachusetts. *Id.* at 140. Albright asked the court to recognize the false light claim, and the court held that it was not essential to recognize the tort for this case. *Id.* In Massachusetts there was a cause of action for invasion of privacy, but in this case all the information in the book was delivered with the permission of Albright, so there was no invasion of privacy. *Id.* The court rejected all the other claims. *See Id.* at 133.

343. *Id.*

344. *Id.*

345. *Id.*

346. *Id.* at 133–34.

347. *Id.* at 133.

348. *Id.* at 134.

349. *Id.* at 136.

350. *Id.* at 136.

351. *Id.* at 138.

352. *Dworkin v. Hustler Magazine, Inc.*, 867 F.2d 1188 (9th Cir. 1989).

353. *Willliams v. Sun Microsystems, Inc.*, No. H029828, 2007 WL 2254301 (Cal. Ct. App. Aug 7, 2007) (false light claim time dismissed as barred by statute of limitations).

354. *Schuler v. McGraw-Hill Cos.*, 989 F. Supp. 1377 (D.N.M. 1997).

355. *Id.* at 1384–85.

356. *Id.* at 1385.

357. *Id.* at 1390.

358. *Id.*

359. *Whitaker v. A&E Television Networks*, No. G040880, 2009 WL 1383617, at 1 (Cal. Ct. App. May 18, 2009).

360. *Id.* at 1.

361. *Id.*

362. *Id.*

363. *Id.*

364. *Id.*

365. *Id.* at 3.

366. *Id.* at 4.

367. *Id.*

368. In the *Uranga* case, the plaintiff had to abandon his false light claim because the publication that placed him in false light relied on a court record, and the court held that it would be an unreasonable burden on newspapers to verify every court document. *Uranga v. Federated Publ'ns, Inc.*, 67 P.3d 29 (Idaho 2003). In *Prince*, the court rejected a gay model's claim that he was falsely portrayed as attending a type of party popular with a segment of the gay community because the party was a public event. *Prince v. Out Publ'g*, No. B140475, 2002 WL 7999 (Cal. Ct. App. January 3, 2002). Furthermore, in *Raymen v. United Senior Ass'n, Inc.*, a picture of same-sex spouses kissing was published without their permission as part of an advertising campaign to which they objected. 409 F. Supp. 2d 15, 18–19 (D.D.C. 2006). The newspaper photographer had photographed the couple while they waited their turn to marry. *Id.* at 18. The men unsuccessfully argued that the publication falsely portrayed them as "unpatriotic American citizens who do not support the United States Military." *Id.* at 22. Neither their false light nor their appropriation claims were sustained. *Id.* at 18.

369. *Dominick v. Index Journal Co.*, No. 99-CP-24-370, 2001 WL 1763977 (S.C. Ct. Com. Pl. Mar. 15, 2001).

370. *Id.* at 1.

371. *Id.* at 3.

372. *See Gignilliat v. Gignilliat, Savitz, & Bettis, L.L.P.*, 684 S.E.2d 756, 759 (S.C. 2009) ("In South Carolina, there are three separate and distinct causes of action for invasion of privacy: 1) wrongful appropriation of personality; 2) wrongful publicizing of private affairs; and 3) wrongful intrusion into private affairs.") (citing *Swinton Creek Nursery v. Edisto Farm Credit*, 514 S.E.2d 126 [1999]).

373. *Dominick*, 2001 WL 1763977, at 1.

374. *Id.* at 2–3.

375. *Id.* at 4.

376. *Id.*

377. *Id.* at 5.

378. *Id.*

379. *Id.* at 4.

380. *Id.*

381. *Albright v. Morton*, 321 F. Supp. 2d 130, 136 (D. Mass. 2004) ("I could not find that such a statement is capable of a defamatory meaning. . . . [I]n this day and age, I cannot conclude that identifying someone as a homosexual discredits him, that the statement fits within the category of defamation per se."). The *Albright* court argued that in the wake of *Lawrence v. Texas* accusations of homosexuality no longer imply criminality and that describing someone as a homosexual is no longer properly viewed as defamatory per se. *Id.* at 137.

382. *Weaver v. Nebo Sch. Dist.*, 29 F. Supp.2d 1[279], 1284 (D. Utah 1998) (citing *Rowland v. Mad River Local Sch. Dist.*, 470 U.S. 1009, 1012 [1985] [Brennan, J.,

dissenting from denial of certiorari]). The court went on to conclude: "Thus, it could be said that a voluntary 'coming out' or an involuntary 'outing' of a gay, lesbian or bisexual teacher would always be a matter of public concern." *Id.*

383. *Prince v. Out Publ'g*, No. B140475, 2002 WL 7999, at 9. (Cal. Ct. App. January 3, 2002).

384. *Id.* at 7–8.

385. I refer to Sipple, Uranga, Prince, Cinel and other individuals extensively discussed herein.

386. *Pavesich v. New England Life Ins. Co.*, 50 S.E. 68, 68 (Ga. 1905).

387. *See* Restatement (Second) of Torts § 652C (1977) ("One who appropriates to his own use or benefit the name or likeness of another is subject to liability to the other for invasion of his privacy.").

388. *See* Prosser, *supra* note 10, at 401.

389. *See, e.g., Pavesich*, 50 S.E. at 74 (citing Warren and Brandeis).

390. *See Langford v. Sessions*, No. 03-255 (CKK) (D.D.C. July 29, 2005), https:// ecf.dcd.uscourts.gov/cgi-bin/show_public_doc?2003cv0255-17. *But see Douglass v. Hustler Magazine, Inc.*, 769 F.2d 1128, 1135 (7th Cir. 1985); *Raymen v. United Senior Ass'n*, Inc., 409 F. Supp. 2d 15 (D.D.C. 2006).

391. *Langford*, No. 03-255 (CKK), at 1.

392. *Id.* at 1.

393. *Id.* at 4–6.

394. *Id.* at 5.

395. *Id.* at 4.

396. *Id.* at 1.

397. *Id.* at 15.

398. *Id.* at 10.

399. Prosser, *supra* note 10, at 403.

400. *Langford*, No. 03-255 (CKK), at 10.

401. *Id.* at 11–12.

402. *Id.* at 10–11.

403. *Id.* at 11 (citing *Kitt v. Capital Concerts, Inc.*, 742 A.2d 856, 862 [D.C. 1999]).

404. *Id.* at 14.

405. *Id.* at 13.

406. *Id.* at 13 n.6 (citing *Albright v. Morton*, 321 F. Supp. 2d 130, 139 [D. Mass. 2004]).

407. *Albright*, 321 F. Supp. 2d 130 at 139 (D. Mass. 2004).

408. *Id.* at 139–40.

409. *Id.*

410. 409 F. Supp. 2d 15, 18–19 (D.D.C. 2006). In Albright the alleged appropriation was in a detergent publication glitch, whereas in *Raymen* the use of the plaintiffs' photographs was intentional and for political gain unrelated to the beliefs and values of the plaintiffs. *Id.* at 18.

411. *Id.*

412. *Id.*

413. *Id.* at 19.

414. *Id.*

415. *Id.*

416. *Id.*

417. *Id.* at 19–20.

418. *Id.* at 20.

419. *Id.*

420. *Id.* at 23.

421. *Id.* at 25.

422. The court dismissed all claims, holding that the plaintiffs failed to establish libel because the advertisement was not defamatory and a reasonable person could not interpret the advertisement as stating that the plaintiffs were unpatriotic. *Id.* at 21–22. The court similarly dismissed the couple's false light claim on the ground that there was no reasonable link between the advertisement and the pictured men's belief system. *Id.* at 25. The kissers' intentional infliction of emotional distress claim was denied because the defendant's conduct was not so outrageous in character as to go beyond all possible bounds of decency. *Id.* at 29–30.

423. *Prince v. Out Publ'g*, No. B140475, 2002 WL 7999, at 10. (Cal. Ct. App. January 3, 2002).

424. Prosser, *supra* note 10, at 422.

425. *Id.*

426. *Cf. Stewart v. Rolling Stone LLC*, 105 Cal. Rptr. 3d 98, 111 (Cal. Ct. App. 2010) ("California has long recognized a common law right of privacy for protection of a person's name and likeness against appropriation by others for their advantage.").

427. *See generally* Neil M. Richards & Daniel J. Solove, *Privacy's Other Path: Recovering the Law of Confidentiality*, 96 Geo. L.J. 123 (2007).

428. *Simpson v. Burrows*, 90 F. Supp. 2d 1108, 1131 (D. Or. 2000).

429. *Id.* at 1124.

430. *Id.* at 1125.

431. *Id.* at 1123–24.

432. Courts ruling this way include *Raymen v. United Senior Ass'n, Inc.*, 409 F. Supp. 2d 15 (D.D.C. 2006); *Langford v. Sessions*, No. 03-255 (CKK) (D.D.C. July 29, 2005), https://ecf.dcd.uscourts.gov/cgi-bin/show_public_doc?2003cv0255-17; *Albright v. Morton*, 321 F. Supp. 2d 130 (D. Mass. 2004); *Doe v. Templeton*, No. 03 C 5076, 2004 WL 1882436 (N.D. Ill. August 6, 2004); *Uranga v. Federated Publications, Inc.*, 67 P.3d 29, 31 (Idaho 2003); *Madsen v. Erwin*, 481 N.E.2d 1160 (Mass. 1985); *Merriwether v. Shorr*, No. 116582/94, 1995 WL 461265 (N.Y. Sup. Ct. Feb 6, 1995); and *Dominick v. Index Journal Co.*, No. 99-CP-24-370, 2001 WL 1763977 (S.C. Ct. Com. Pl. Mar. 15, 2001).

433. *Templeton*, 2004 WL 1882436.

434. *Id.* at 1.

435. *Id.*

436. *Id.*

437. *Id.*

438. *Id.*

439. *Id.*

440. *Id.* at 3.

441. *Id.*

442. *Id.* at 5.

443. *Id.*

444. *Id.*

445. *Id.*

446. *See* Luke 12:3 (King James) ("Therefore whatsoever ye have spoken in darkness shall be heard in the light; and that which ye have spoken in the ear in closets shall be proclaimed upon the housetops."); *cf.* Matthew 10:27 (King James) ("What I tell you in darkness, that speak ye in light: and what ye hear in the ear, that preach ye upon the housetops.").

447. Some critics have suggested that Prosser failed to include a fifth privacy tort, "breach of confidentiality." *See, e.g.*, Richards & Solove, *supra* note 439, at 125.

448. Edward J. Bloustein, "Privacy as an Aspect of Human Dignity: An Answer to Dean Prosser," 39 N.Y.U. L. Rev. 962, 971 (1964).

449. *Pavesich v. New England Life Ins. Co.*, 50 S.E. 68, 80 (Ga. 1905) ("[H]e is in reality a slave without hope of freedom, held to service by a merciless master. . . .").

450. *See, e.g., Schuler v. McGraw-Hill Cos.*, 989 F. Supp. 1377 (D.N.M. 1997) (a transgender woman alleged that publication of a magazine article critical of her constituted defamation, intentional infliction of emotional distress, false light, publication of private facts, and intrusion); *Prince v. Out Publ'g*, No. B140475, 2002 WL 7999 (Cal. Ct. App. January 3, 2002) (gay man alleged that publication of his photographs without consent constituted both libel and invasion of all four privacy torts); *Sipple v. Chronicle Publ'g Co.*, 201 Cal. Rptr. 665 (Cal. Ct. App. 1984) (gay ex-marine whose sexual orientation was publicized in the press after he thwarted the assassination of President Ford alleged intrusion, publication of private facts, false light, and intentional infliction of emotional distress); *Madsen v. Erwin*, 481 N.E.2d 1160 (Mass. 1985) (lesbian fired from her job at the *Christian Science Monitor* alleged defamation, intrusion, publication of private facts, and intentional infliction of emotional distress).

451. *See generally* Bloustein, *supra* note 460.

452. Sadly, the intimate lives of LGBT Americans are still subject to unwarranted invasion. On September 22, 2010, Rutgers University freshman Tyler Clementi committed suicide after his roommate and another student used hidden webcams to stream over the Internet live images of Clementi having sex with a male partner in a supposedly private dorm room.

3

Toward Identity Rights beyond Privacy

Andrew Clement
University of Toronto

There is growing recognition that conventional privacy rights and protective measures are inadequate for dealing effectively with the civil liberties challenges posed by the ongoing explosion in personal information trafficking. To address some of the major shortcomings of current privacy frameworks, this chapter explores the prospects for an allied but distinct identity rights framework for dealing with personal information handling by large organizations. In particular, we introduce the notion of "identity impairment," not subsumed by "privacy violation." We further propose a view of citizen-centric identity rights relevant to interactions between individuals and organizations that make categorical judgments about individuals based on information, regardless of whether this information should enjoy privacy protection. Drawing from the Canadian Charter of Rights and Freedoms and borrowing heavily from fair information practices more generally, we articulate a set of fundamental identity integrity rights and associated "fair identity practice" principles. Such a citizen-centric-identity-based approach to personal information handling, by focusing on the decisions that directly affect individuals in transactional situations, promises to be more easily understood and actively supported by members of the public than privacy-based arguments.

"ID, please." In one form or another, whether in person or online, individuals increasingly hear this request when initiating a service transaction with an organization. Typically the expected response of handing over a document with a name, number, and picture, or entering an account name

This chapter is an extensively revised and expanded version of chapter 8, Identity Policy Principles, in *CAN ID? Visions for Canada's Identity Policy: Understanding Identity Policy and Policy Alternatives* (Boa et al. 2007, 96–105).

and password, produces the desired result, and the individual can proceed with the transaction smoothly. Occasionally however, providing identification has the opposite result, and the transaction is denied. Sometimes the person is then treated with suspicion, especially if she questions the decision, and may even be apprehended. Too often the reasons for this denial of service or access are not clear, and no adequate justification is provided. When someone is not permitted to enter a building, pick up a parcel, buy liquor, or the like, the person may be inconvenienced or embarrassed. In the case of making an important application, such as for a loan, welfare benefit, housing, job, or student admission, a refusal can diminish one's life chances. Often no clues are given about the grounds on which the "data subject" has been sorted into a disadvantaged category or even that this categorizing has occurred. At borders or when boarding an airplane, the consequences can be more serious yet. The recurring, well-publicized trouble that Ted Kennedy faced in U.S. airports because a variant of his name appeared on a no-fly watch list offers insight into the difficulties facing thousands of other innocent travellers similarly listed, few of whom have the resources that the late senator could muster in repairing his situation.[1] An extreme example of such challenges involves Canadian engineer Maher Arar, who was detained by U.S. officials while in transit at JFK airport and underwent "extraordinary rendition," including torture and solitary confinement in his native Syria. After he was released an extensive public inquiry cleared his name, and the Canadian government awarded him $10.5 million in compensation. However, the United States still does not allow him to cross its borders.[2]

While there are important differences across all the various cases of unwarranted access or service denial sketched above, which we may refer to as "identity impairments," there are also some key similarities promising of a unified corrective approach. Whether it is a mail recipient trying to collect a package with a former address still on her driver's license, an innocent victim of extraordinary rendition intercepted because his records appear to fit some terrorist profile, or someone in the myriad of other life situations where one's legitimate business is thwarted after trying to comply with an ID request, each case is characterized by an adverse organizational judgment based on information previously recorded about the individual. The conventional approach to dealing with harms related to the misuse of personal information, i.e., about an identifiable individual, is to treat it as a form of privacy violation. Privacy protection usually involves withholding one's information in anticipation of potential violation or once collected ensuring it is neither used nor disclosed in ways inconsistent with the original purpose. However, in the ID cases mentioned here, this approach is not likely to be effective. Another way of thinking about promoting the rights of information subjects that address these identity impairments needs to be explored.

This chapter takes up the challenge of articulating a new information right that is applicable to ID-demanding situations, one that addresses the limitations of privacy as the overarching framework. It proposes a distinctive "identity right," allied with the right to privacy but going beyond it in terms of the problematic situations that it can help resolve. We begin the exploration of identity rights by examining some of the shortcomings of privacy and how a focus on identity can shift the focus of attention from the point of personal information collection onto the categorical judgments organizations make about individuals. This leads into looking at constitutional sources, notably the Canadian Charter of Rights and Freedoms, for the legal foundations for a right to identity integrity. Extending the widely adopted principles of fair information practice and incorporating the seven laws of identity, we then articulate eighteen fair identity/information practice principles. The chapter closes by discussing some of the expected challenges in establishing identity integrity as a well-recognized and supported information right.

LIMITATIONS OF A PRIVACY FRAMEWORK

Privacy is the broad term commonly used in referring to incidents when information about a person is used by others in ways considered harmful, risky, or socially inappropriate. Public opinion surveys have long indicated that privacy violations are a widespread concern. Privacy advocates, however, lament that, in spite of high public awareness of privacy conflicts, conventional measures are inadequate for dealing with the problems associated with the burgeoning collection and use of personal information. Furthermore, privacy concerns do not translate readily into practical action by individuals, who often relinquish control of their information for immediate, but relatively modest, benefits.

Semantically Complex

Various reasons are given for the current privacy crisis (note other chapters in this volume). Drawing on conceptual and situational perspectives, we examine three limitations that are especially relevant to this discussion of problematic ID-based transactions. Many authors have pointed out confusion and lack of clarity about what is meant by "privacy" in informational contexts. It appears to mean very different things to different people in different situations. Part of the confusion arises from the origins of the modern treatment of privacy rights in the classic Warren and Brandeis (1890) formulation as "the right to be let alone," which is not directly appropriate to transactional settings when, far from wanting seclusion, people seek to be active in the public realm, by traveling, conducting business, and the like. The more recent informational self-determination interpretation[3] partly overcomes this difficulty but brings others related to the still-growing variety and subtlety of situations in which individuals act with their personal information. While there are some important advantages to having a broad umbrella term such as *privacy* widely used for referring to a variety of forms of personal information abuse, it brings serious shortcomings when probing problematic situations more deeply. Solove (2002) provides a survey of the various conceptualizations of privacy, which while helpful in better appreciating the complexity of the term, does little to clarify things from an individual person's perspective. If scholars have trouble articulating a coherent common ground for understanding privacy, it is not surprising that the lay public adopts varied and inconsistent meanings.[4]

Situationally Impractical

A second major area of difficulty that the prevailing privacy framework presents is the burden of vigilance and restraint it places on anyone trying to exercise effective control over her personal information. In situations where one is explicitly requested to provide information, such as filling in an application form during an enrollment process, there is a strong bias against the data subject taking the steps necessary to make good judgments about whether the risk of loss of control over personal information is worth the payoff. The benefit for providing the requested information is usually immediate and tangible—the application is accepted, the desired service is provided, the transaction proceeds smoothly. Even the attempt to assess the privacy risks and tradeoffs involved in providing or withholding information brings an immediate cost in terms of delay. Simply reading and understanding the privacy policy related to an online transaction is beyond the patience and expertise of even the most dedicated privacy advocate (Akalu 2005). Assessing the likely risks of providing information requires additional experience and anticipation of future events that are inherently impossible to evaluate confidently. The situation is exacerbated by the realization that, if one's information was handled improperly, it would be extremely difficult to determine whether such mishandling had happened and then would be expensive and time-consuming to correct. Acting on privacy concerns during in-person transactions further involves an awkward and time-consuming exchange with the service agent, who is typically not used to answering detailed questions about what is done with the information collected and may hold up other clients waiting in line. Any possible benefits from this kind of privacy diligence are typically remote in time and place. And these are the data collection situations that are best covered by privacy protection measures. The challenge is exacerbated in situations where the personal data capture is implicit, embedded within the transaction as is normal when using ID in the form of a credit/debit, library, membership, or other type of digitally enabled card linked with an organizational database. The organization in effect "holds all the cards" in the implicit negotiating process, with the cognitive burden placed squarely on the shoulders of largely isolated individuals. From this situational perspective, who can be surprised then that even those most concerned about their privacy will generally comply, without delay or voicing misgivings, with the data collection regimes they encounter in everyday life?

Focus on Data Collection

A third limitation of privacy is its strong emphasis on the early data collection stage of the information life cycle within organizational information systems while having relatively little to say about the organizational actions based on the collected information. This limitation relates directly to the previous point about the difficulty that an individual data subject faces in anticipating how his information may be used. Much more important to an individual than whether the collecting organization strictly follows fair information practices is whether the outcome will be detrimental to the individual's interest. If an individual is adversely affected, it matters little to her that her data were collected and processed lawfully. Conversely, if information handling was sloppy but the results benign, the individual is not likely to be as concerned, even though this sloppy handling might constitute a technical violation of privacy principles and perhaps even the law. This point was driven home during fieldwork on a study of attitudes and everyday practices of domestic Internet use. We were struck by the contrast between the widespread awareness of privacy issues among our informants and the almost complete ignorance or indifference to the fair information practice principles that provide the foundation for privacy protection. While everyone in the relatively small sample was aware of privacy risks, they had little expectation that once they released personal information that it would be handled accountably. They appeared to make an assessment of the trustworthiness of the site and likelihood that any harm would come to them, and based on this assessment decided whether to provide personal information (Viseu, Clement, and Aspinall 2004). Once a data subject has consented to data collection, the only opportunity provided by fair information practices for dealing with the substantive outcomes of personal information process is through the Access/Participation principle, which provides individuals with the ability to view the data collected and to verify and contest its accuracy. It gives no right to contest the validity of the results that are based on the collected data, such as whether a benefit is denied. By focusing only on the procedural aspects of information handling and providing the data subject with decisional authority only at the point of data collection rather than when the organization acts on the information, a privacy approach offers very little in the way of remedial tools for addressing problematic personal information situations.

Informational Scope

The fourth and final major limitation of a privacy framework for addressing ID-based transactions is that privacy regulations are confined to handling only what is considered personal information and hence do not include information about an individual that is publicly available. Information about an individual that has been obtained from a published source, such as the home address and phone number that appear in a telephone directory or date and city of birth posted to a social networking site, does not enjoy privacy protection, yet it is commonly used as the basis for distinguishing individuals and making decisions about them.

Table 3.1 summarizes the various limitations of the conventional privacy framework related to failure in organizational systems to properly use per-

Table 3.1. Summary of Privacy Framework Limitations

	Privacy Framework Limitations
Semantic Complexity	Broad, Ambiguous Privacy, in organizational transactional situations, has a wide range of sometimes conflicting meanings (e.g., withholding information versus expecting organizational accountability for information provided).
Semantic Complexity	Difficult Requires an anticipatory assessment of the risks at a time when the data subject is at a negotiating disadvantage. Benefits of complying with organizational requirements are immediate and tangible. Benefits of personal data protection are distant and uncertain.
Focus of Attention	Collection Procedure Focuses mainly on the procedural aspects of data collection, before the data subject is aware of how she will be treated based on the information provided.
Informational Scope	Limited to "Personal" Information Excludes attention to data from public sources or that which is generated by the organization.

sonal information in making service or other transactional decisions. These limitations help account in part for why it is hard for individuals to act in pursuit of their own immediate privacy concerns. This failure further undermines any willingness to join others similarly positioned in building a social movement around privacy rights that could develop sustained pressure for reform of prevailing personal-information-handling practices (Clement and Hurrell 2008). These limitations also provide a strong incentive for exploring other more promising frameworks for addressing such situations. In particular, the key shortcomings of the privacy framework that an alternative needs to overcome are the adverse judgments made about individuals and the heavy onus it places on them to make prudent decisions about the release of information about themselves. It is the central claim of this chapter that an identity rights framework offers such a promising alternative approach. It is to articulating such an identity framework that we now turn.

AN IDENTITY FRAMEWORK ALTERNATIVE TO PRIVACY

A first step in developing an alternative identity rights framework for addressing unwarranted denial of a service or access request is to recognize that identity is a common and central feature. We introduced earlier the term *identity impairment* to characterize such situations because it draws attention to the fact that a person's standing or reputation, his "identity" in short, at least in the eyes of the organization, is compromised and/or unjustified. Identity here refers not to a singular, all-encompassing ideal of the entire person, but more simply to who the person *is* in relation to a particular organization, and possibly even to a specific time, place, and transactional context.

Earlier we observed that a shortcoming of a privacy framework was the imprecision of the term *privacy* because it is subject to multiple and even contradictory readings. *Identity* potentially faces a similar, or even more severe, limitation, given its very wide use and disparate interpretations across a broad range of disciplines and settings. Often identity refers to a form of collective affiliation, such as through gender, race, nationality, ethnicity, or linguistic competence, that unite a potentially large number of people with a common, shared "identity." These factors, and many others, are no doubt important from the point of view of an individual in her own sense of who she is and perhaps also for the organizations she encounters. This chapter, however, takes a much narrower interpretation of "identity" in the context of interacting with organizations and their information systems. In this setting, identity is typically about individuating persons from one another to address a person according to the specificities of her situation, as reflected in the organizational database records associated with that particular person. This individuation is often a precondition for assigning individuals to predefined categories for subsequent treatment in a process Gandy (1993) has termed more generally the panoptic sort.

These situations of social sorting are increasingly common as governments and private sector enterprises respond to growing pressures to provide service in online environments and as authenticating individual identities is viewed as one of the principal security tools at a time of heightened insecurity associated with the "war on terror." Establishing the identity of individuals in transactional settings, or simply identification, is thus becoming a major preoccupation of service-providing organizations. From their point of view, the essential first step in a transaction is to determine whether the person presenting herself is already in their database and then to look up her records to assess eligibility and otherwise determine how to respond to the particular request. A good indication of this organization-centered view of identity comes from the authoritative definition used by the Government of Canada. The Senior Director, Identity Management and Security, Chief Information Office Branch, Treasury Board Secretariat,[5] gave this standard interpretation of identity at an annual joint meeting of U.S. and Canadian government officials: *Identity: a reference or designation used to distinguish a unique and particular individual* (Boucher 2007, slide 8).

Typically the "reference or designation" is in the form of a unique identifier, such as a driver's license number, social security or insurance number,[6] passport number, student number or bank account number, that directly links the person to the records about that individual in the organization's database. Often this number, together with the person's name, facial image, and other information about the data subject stored in the organizational database is printed on an ID card issued to the individual for presentation on the occasions of subsequent service or access requests (Lyon 2009). The main function of the ID card in this case is to expedite the location of correct database records to use in determining the authoritative organizational handling of the transaction.

A Citizen-Centered Definition of Identity

The interpretation and practices around the concept of identity discussed so far clearly and quite understandably reflect an organization-centered identity perspective, consistent with a central objective of "making sure we are dealing with the right person" (Boucher 2007, slide 7). However, from the point of view of individuals encountering a service transaction, who overwhelmingly are legitimate and law-abiding, this form of unique individuation is not their primary concern. They already know they are the persons they claim to be, so the key identity question for them is whether they will be recognized by the organization as entitled subjects or more generally enabled to proceed with the requested transactions (Clement et al. 2008).

In shifting away from an exclusively organization/system-centered view of identity to incorporate what also matters to the identity subject—being recognized as a legitimate and entitled person in relation to the specific organization and transaction—we can refine the definition of a person's "identity" given previously to the following: *Identity: a reference or designation associated with an individual, consisting of information about that person enduringly linked with categorical judgments assigned by an organization to confirm a status or conduct a transaction.*

There are three key points to note here about this more "citizen-centric" interpretation of identity.[7] First, that the essence of identity for citizens or clients is not just their personal information (e.g., name, date of birth, etc.) but also their standing vis-à-vis the organization with which they are dealing. In short, it is mainly about the person's "reputation" with respect to the organization in question.

Secondly, and flowing from this first point, is that identity records are more than the "personal information" normally considered in privacy discourse and specifically include the categorical assignments made by (identity assigning and data holding) organizations. This wider view shifts attention from the data collection, storage, and management practices that are central to privacy protection and helps focus on the key judgments organizations make about individuals based on the information so collected. Arguably, from the point of view of the individual "identity-subject," the organizational actions taken that affect the outcome of everyday transactions as well as cumulatively a person's life chances are more consequential than those related to privacy concerns.

Thirdly, this definition of identity does not presuppose a singular, essential identity that is applicable across all transactions and which opens the door to all appropriate service and access entitlements. Rather, analogous to the multiple cards carried in one's wallet, a person will possess multiple, partial identities that are each specific to purpose, organization, and other contextual features. Indeed, according to this view identity is not simply a static "fact" about a person but is closely akin to the possible roles that a person can present or perform in the various facets of her life.[8]

This refined, more citizen-centric, contextually sensitive understanding of identity also helps show better how much is at stake for individuals as well as organizations in the decision-making process, and hence why identity is a sensitive concern and so politically charged for many people.

Comparing Identity and Privacy Interests

With this understanding of identity in mind, we are now in a position to begin comparing identity and privacy frameworks in dealing with identity impairments. In particular we will review how an identity integrity perspective addresses the limitations of privacy frameworks discussed earlier.

The service transactions discussed so far present several aspects of interest from a privacy and fair information practice point of view. Briefly, the focus is mainly on the points of data collection and whether the information is "minimal" for the stated purposes and is obtained with appropriate authority and/or consent. And once collected from the data subject, as long as the organization maintains the security, confidentiality, and accuracy of the personal information, uses it only in keeping with the stated purpose, and ensures that any third parties who have access to the personal data comply with the same terms, the privacy interest is satisfied. Nor is there a privacy interest in any information about the person that is not considered "personal" such as that obtained from public sources. This situation is represented schematically in figure 3.1.

The organization has no *privacy* responsibility to account for the decisions it makes based on the data, regardless of how unfair the decision making may be nor how detrimental the consequences. There may be other forms of accountability and responsibility that the organization may be subject to, but these will be specific to the particular context of the decision.

An identity perspective on personal information attempts, as a privacy one does as well, to apply to a wide range of situations where information about

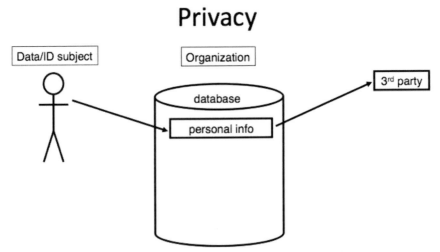

Figure 3.1. Privacy interests in an organizational database of personal information.

a person is directly involved. When we adopt such an identity perspective, the interest shifts to the points where the organization makes judgments about the status or entitlements of the individual. It is helpful here to distinguish between two different processes—initial enrollment in the organization's information system (represented schematically in figure 3.2), and subsequent authentication and authorization for transactions (represented schematically in figure 3.3).[9] In particular, in the enrollment process, the identity interest centers on decision making about whether the subject is eligible to be enrolled (the "OK?" decision diamond in figure 3.2), issuing an ID token or card, and assigning the subject a particular status or category of "member." These are all matters beyond the scope of privacy interest because this is how an organization produces new data about the person, *not* how it collects it from the person. This point is made clearer in the case where the organization collects data from public sources. The organization is exempt from any privacy claim from the individual, regardless of what it does with the data about that person. However, an identity interest can be invoked once the organization makes a judgment about that person.

An identity interest is principally invoked in the authentication/authorization stage because this is when any decisions the organization makes become

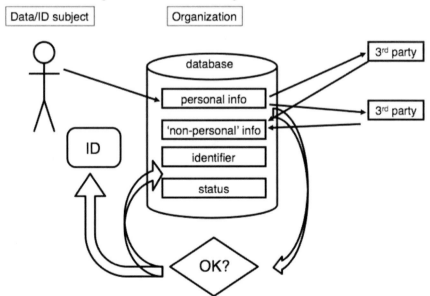

Figure 3.2.   Identity interests in enrolling a person in an organizational ID scheme.

directly consequential for the individual. If either the person is not recognized as a "member" of the organization, or if is so recognized but deemed ineligible, the transaction request will be denied. This point is represented by the "OK?" decision diamond in figure 3.3; this time, however, it refers to denying or granting the requested service, rather than whether to enroll an applicant. This authentication/authorization situation is devoid of any new privacy interest, while an identity interest can focus on whether the denial is justified. This is the point at which an identity subject experiences the consequences of an organizational decision and is likely well motivated to complain, request explanations, enroll allies, and generally attempt to hold the organization to account. Such holding to account will likely not be easy, particularly because the aggrieved person has to start from the position of an isolated individual. But he will be in a much stronger bargaining position than if he has to rely on privacy arguments, which would involve reconstructing the data trails and then challenging consent procedures at the earlier point of collection.

We can now return to consider in turn each of the four limitations a privacy framework faces in dealing with identity impairments. These are summarized in table 3.2. We can see from this analysis that by focusing mainly on organizational judgments about individuals, an identity ap-

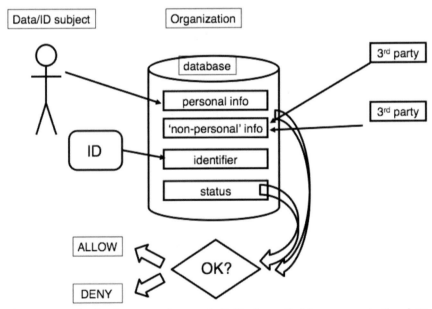

Figure 3.3. Identity interests when an individual enrolled in an organizational ID scheme requests service or access.

Table 3.2. Summary Comparison of Privacy and Identity Frameworks

	Privacy Framework Limitations	*Identity Framework Relative Advantages*
Semantic Complexity	*Broad, ambiguous* Privacy, in organizational transactional situations, has a wide range of sometimes conflicting meanings (e.g., withholding information versus expecting organizational accountability for information provided).	*Tight* Identity, in organizational transactional situations, refers exclusively to the categorical judgments made by an organization about an individual.
Situational Practicality	*Difficult* Requires an anticipatory assessment of the risks at a time when the data subject is at a negotiating disadvantage. Benefits of complying with organizational requirements are immediate and tangible. Benefits of personal data protection are distant and uncertain.	*Less Difficult* The aggrieved data/identity subject can challenge the organizational judgment at the point she becomes aware of it, when the matter is still fresh and she has less to lose.
Focus of Attention	*Collection Procedure* Focuses mainly on the procedural aspects of data collection, before the data subject is aware of how she will be treated based on the information provided.	*Decision Stage* Focuses mainly on the decisions and their outcomes, the points at which an organization makes a judgment that affects a person.
Informational Scope	*Limited to "Personal" Information* Excludes attention to data from public sources or that which is generated by the organization.	*Unrestricted* Focuses on categorical judgments, regardless of the source or type of information these judgments are based on.

proach enjoys a relative conceptual tightness that has so far been hard to achieve with an exclusively privacy focus. While it may be difficult for an individual to challenge an adverse decision, she will nevertheless be in a much better position motivationally to assert rights and seek redress. An identity framework places the attention on the proximate phenomenon (the adverse decision), whereas tracing back the personal data trails to

determine whether there was any improper handling, as a privacy orientation would call for, would be very much more difficult and discouraging.
This difference is due in large part because the privacy interest is mainly
invoked during data collection, which may have been scattered across time
and space. And finally, the identity approach would not be diverted by having to consider whether the information upon which a particular decision
was based was "personal" in legal terms. Regardless of the source of its
information, an organization should still be accountable for its judgment
about the individuals it deals with.

TOWARD IDENTITY RIGHTS

A clear conception of identity is only one ingredient of an identity framework. It is common for organizations when developing identity rules and
procedures, as with other complex policy areas, also to formulate concise sets
of overarching principles. These are intended to focus discussion on central
identity questions and guide subsequent action. The Government of Canada's
efforts in this regard provide useful insight into how a large organization
approaches the complex challenges of creating a consistent and workable
identity management regime. The Treasury Board Secretariat, the central
coordinating body for the Canadian Government, articulated a set of eleven
Identity Principles "intended to apply throughout the entire government in
contexts where identity is an issue or consideration."[10]

These government principles provide a useful basis for developing organizational identity management policies and practices. They address some of
the central concerns of identity management, such as the need for lawfulness,
transparency, and public trust. Each principle is distinctively valuable, and all
are necessary. However, this list, as well as the conceptual framework and the
assumptions that underlie them, are limited in several important respects and
so are not a sufficient foundation for proper identity management. In addition
to the reconceptualization of basic identity definitions as discussed above,
such limitations call for additional principles derived more broadly. Reflecting a drafting process conducted exclusively within the Government of
Canada, this formulation understandably adopts a organization-centered view
of identity. Appropriately, the various principles repeatedly begin with the
phrase, "The Government of Canada will . . . " However, several important
dimensions of identity policy are missing—most notably a client-centered
focus incorporating the perspectives of individual "identity subjects" as well
as a grounding in constitutional human/civil rights rather than just organiza-
tional/bureaucratic mandates.

Guiding Identity Precept

One of the greatest risks run by a government or other organization in establishing rules and procedures related to identity is political (Boa et al. 2007). That is, identity rules and procedures, like any others involving personal data collection and processing (especially ones that decisively define status in society or in relation to powerful organizations as identity schemes of broad scope do), hinge on public trust. If the identity authority does not earn public trust in its identity scheme, it risks rejection of the scheme and its own legitimacy. The recent UK elections provide a vivid example of the political consequences that can befall a government that attempts to impose an identity scheme without garnering popular support. The *first* legislative act of the Conservative–Liberal Democrat coalition was the introduction of the Identity Documents Bill 2010, which repeals the previous Labour Government's Identity Cards Act 2006, cancels the National ID card program, and requires the destruction of the information held on the National Identity Register.[11] Posed positively, this change suggests the following broad precept for guiding identity policy development:

> For any jurisdictional or organizational identity system to be legitimate and effective in achieving its intended purposes, it must earn wide acceptance and trust among the relevant public or client group based on transparency and accountability.

To give this precept practical value, more specific principles are needed. There are various ways for developing such principles, depending on the perspective one adopts. Rather than combining these principles into a single integrated list from the start, we will here explore several approaches to identity, each from a different perspective, bringing along their associated conceptual presumptions and interests. At this point we are aiming for a relatively comprehensive treatment, which will mean some overlap and duplication, which provides the basis for a subsequent consolidation into a tighter framework with less redundancy.

Some Fundamental Rights in Relation to Identity

Identity documentation is the *sine qua non* of "citizenship," in any of its forms, such as for voting, traveling abroad, claiming a entitlement, or receiving a benefit. Hence it needs ultimately to rest on, as well as reinforce, the fundamental rights of formal citizenship. In Canada, these citizenship rights are most definitively spelled out in the Canadian Charter of Rights and Freedoms.[12] This Charter, passed in 1982 as part of the Constitution Act, is relatively young in comparison with constitutions internationally, and it draws extensively on them for core principles. There have so far been few cases in the personal information area on which the Canadian Supreme Court has rendered authoritative rulings, giving more precise interpretation of the Charter's sweeping ideals. Nevertheless, the Charter represents a clear and succinct statement of societal norms, specifying the rights that everyone, including those charged with serious crimes, can enjoy. It therefore offers a good starting point for thinking about the rights individuals should enjoy in their dealings with any organization in society. Sections 7, 8, 9, 10, 11, 15, and 27 of the Charter are the most pertinent to identity rights:[13]

Sec. 7. Everyone has the right to life, liberty and security of the person and the right not to be deprived thereof except in accordance with the principles of fundamental justice.

Sec. 8. Everyone has the right to be secure against unreasonable search or seizure.

Sec. 9. Everyone has the right not to be arbitrarily detained or imprisoned.

Sec. 10. Everyone has the right on arrest or detention

a) to be informed promptly of the reasons therefore;

b) to retain and instruct counsel without delay and to be informed of that right; and

c) to have the validity of the detention determined by way of habeas corpus and to be released if the detention is not lawful.

Sec. 11. Any person charged with an offence has the right . . .

d) to be presumed innocent until proven guilty according to law in a fair and public hearing by an independent and impartial tribunal;

Sec. 15. (1) Every individual is equal before and under the law and has the right to the equal protection and equal benefit of the law without discrimination and, in particular, without discrimination based on race, national or ethnic origin, colour, religion, sex, age or mental or physical disability. (2) Subsection (1) does not preclude any law, program or activity that has as its object the amelioration of conditions of disadvantaged individuals or groups including those that are disadvantaged because of race, national or ethnic origin, colour, religion, sex, age or mental or physical disability.

Sec. 27. This Charter shall be interpreted in a manner consistent with the preservation and enhancement of the multicultural heritage of Canadians.

Based on a lay reading of these particular sections, here are four proposed rights pertaining to identity:

1. *Integrity of (Personal) Identity. Everyone has the right to the integrity of her personal identity.* This is the most fundamental of the distinctive iden-

tity rights. Like the closely related right to privacy, it can be based directly on the constitutional right of "security of the person" (sec. 7) and "to be secure against unreasonable search and seizure" (sec. 8). In keeping with the definition of identity mentioned above, this right includes the right to reliable identity documentation and goes beyond personal information protection to include the judgments about the person made by an authority based on these data, such as profiling, categorical treatment, and the like.

2. *Presumption of Anonymous Entitlement. When an individual asserts a claim for entitlement or to conduct a transaction, the initial presumption is that he is so entitled by virtue of his existence. Where there is a requirement to deviate from this presumption, the responsibility is on the authority to justify the need to go beyond anonymity and establish some form of pseudonymity or collective or individual identity.* This right is founded on sec. 11d: presumption of innocence. The presumption of innocence is designed to protect the relatively weak individual in the face of a more powerful organization by placing the burden of proof of "suspicion" or "guilt" on that organization. Similarly, it should be possible for individuals to conduct many of their everyday affairs anonymously, without having to reveal who they are. There are, of course, also many instances where it is necessary for an organization to know some specific details about the person it is transacting business with, such as when making a delivery to a particular address or determining whether an age requirement is met. Strict anonymity is therefore not an absolute right. In such cases, starting with an initial presumption of anonymity, an organization that needs more personal information should demonstrably justify the specific additional information it needs.

3. *Judgmental Transparency and Accountability. Where an agency has made an (enduring categorical) adverse judgment about an individual, this judgment shall not be made arbitrarily. That person has the right a) to be informed promptly of the reasons therefore; b) to retain and instruct expert advice without delay and to be informed of that right; and c) to have the validity of the judgment determined by way of habeas corpus and to be reversed if the judgment is not justifiable.* This right is based in sec. 9 and 10: Arrest or detention. Being denied access or service that one is normally entitled to is a form of arrest, albeit typically much milder than arrest and detention by law enforcement authorities. Similarly, requiring personal information of an individual is akin to search and seizure, again milder than when performed by police backed by arms. Nevertheless, no organization should deny access or demand personal information in an arbitrary, opaque, or unaccountable fashion. Everyone whose identity is impaired in some way by an organization should be informed of the reasons and given the opportunity to challenge the judgment in a timely fashion, assisted as needed by competent experts.

4. *Equality, Diversity, and Cultural Inclusion. Every individual will be treated equally in terms of identity documentation and practices, recognizing our multicultural heritage.* This right is based in sec. 15: Equality, and sec. 27: Multicultural heritage. Many of the principal elements for determining identities, such as names, their number, ordering, spelling, and length; and facial images have differing meanings and sensitivities across various cultures. Dominant Anglo-American norms about names and facial images do not translate easily to other linguistic, cultural, and religious traditions. ID schemes need to be sufficiently flexible to adapt to the preferences of significant minority communities.

Fair Identity/Information Practice Principles?

It is evident that the policy issues around identity management are closely related to those around privacy protection. Indeed, in some cases they are indistinguishable. However, with the making of enduring categorical judgments about individuals by organizations recorded as part of the person's "identity package," there are some important distinctive and novel elements about identity that warrant reformulating the familiar privacy principles of fair information practice to take account of these organizational judgments about individuals. The U.S. Department of Health, Education, and Welfare provided the first comprehensive articulation of fair information practice principles (FIP) in 1973. The other jurisdictions that have developed privacy or data protection legislation have drawn on and extended these principles.[14] The most widely applied Canadian version of fair information practices is articulated in the Canadian Standards Association (CSA) Model Code,[15] subsequently incorporated into the Personal Information Protection and Electronic Documents Act (PIPEDA),[16] which largely governs private sector personal information in Canada. In light of our identity concerns, we have modified each of the ten CSA FIP principles to highlight the corresponding identity issue. This Code and the principles it enumerates reflect the perspective and responsibilities of an organization that is a custodian of personal information and that makes and records judgments about individuals on the basis of this information. In what follows, the phrase *identity judgments* refers to the categorical assignments made by the organization about the individual that become part of the stored records about that individual. Changes to the original privacy/data protection text are shown *italicized*.

   1. Accountability. An organization is responsible for personal information *and identity judgments* under its control and shall designate an individual or individuals who are accountable for the organization's compliance with the following principles.

2. Identifying Purposes. The purposes for which personal information is collected *and identity judgments made* shall be identified by the organization at or before the time the information is collected.

3. Consent. The knowledge and consent of the individual are required for the collection, use, or disclosure of personal information, *as well as in making identity judgments*, except where inappropriate.

4. Limiting Collection. The collection of personal information *and making of identity judgments* shall be limited to that which is necessary for the purposes identified by the organization. Information shall be collected *and identity judgments made* by fair and lawful means.

5. Limiting Use, Disclosure, and Retention. Personal information, *including identity judgments,* shall not be used or disclosed for purposes other than those for which it was collected *or made*, except with the consent of the individual or as required by law. Personal information, *including identity judgments*, shall be retained only as long as necessary for the fulfillment of those purposes.

6. Accuracy. Personal information, *including identity judgments*, shall be as accurate, complete, and up-to-date as is necessary for the purposes for which it is to be used.

7. Safeguards. Personal information, *including identity judgments*, shall be protected by security safeguards appropriate to the sensitivity of the information.

8. Openness. An organization shall make readily available to individuals specific information about its policies and practices relating to the management of personal information *and the making of identity judgments*.

9. Individual Access. Upon request, an individual shall be informed of the existence, use, and disclosure of his or her personal information, *as well as the making of identity judgments*, and shall be given access to that information *and identity judgment-making process*. An individual shall be able to challenge the accuracy and completeness of the information *as well as the identity judgment-making process* and have *them* amended as appropriate.

10. Challenging Compliance. An individual shall be able to address a challenge concerning compliance with the above principles to the designated individual or individuals accountable for the organization's compliance.

These ten principles can be supplemented by eight more, which can also serve usefully to regulate organizational practices around identity.[17]

11. Identity minimization. An organization shall minimize the degree of identification required of an individual, preferably conducting transactions anonymously or pseudonymously.

12. Identity Repair and Mitigation. Where a person's identity has been impaired unjustifiably, the organization shall repair and mitigate the harm done, compensate the individual appropriately, and take reasonable steps to avoid recurrence.

13. Identity Breach Publicity. When an organization breaches its identity management responsibilities, it shall publicize appropriately any such breach, proportionate to its severity and taking due account of the privacy rights of any individuals affected.

14. Universal Accessibility. An organization shall ensure that its identity documentation and practices are accessible for all, regardless of age, disability, language preference, education, and income. In particular, communications must be clear and understandable via interfaces that are humanally comprehensible and controllable.

15. Proportionality. An organization shall ensure that the means, criteria, and costs of assuring identity are proportionate to the intended purposes, benefits expected, risks incurred, and control that can be exercised by each party.

16. Reciprocity. An organization shall ensure that to the greatest extent feasible, identity transactions will be based on reciprocal rights and responsibilities by minimizing the effect of power differentials between it and its clients.

17. Pluralism of Operators and Technologies. The interoperability of different identity technologies and their providers must be enabled by the identity scheme ("universal identity metasystem"). Both the interoperability *and* segregations of identity technologies may offer users more choices and control over the means of identification across different contexts.

18. Consistent Experience across Contexts: Enhanced User Empowerment and Control. The identity scheme ("unifying identity metasystem") must guarantee its users a simple consistent experience while enabling the separation of contexts through multiple operators and technologies.

Identity System Desiderata

Flowing from and assuming compliance with these foundational identity rights and fair practice principles, the following are intended to serve as criteria for assessing jurisdictional identity systems from the perspective of various outsiders, e.g., identity subjects, citizens, consumers, clients, civil society organizations, legislators, and technical experts. In some cases these desiderata repeat themes mentioned above as part of the Fair Identity Practice principles, but here the emphasis shifts from individual usage to the scheme as a whole identity package of organization, technical system, practices, regulation, and governance.

These desiderata range from those deemed important in any large-scale, organizationwide infrastructure to those that are specifically relevant to identity systems:

Transparency of objectives, standards, processes, and redress mechanisms to facilitate individual empowerment and collective accountability.

Acountability of the ID operation and its identity activities to democratic norms and institutions, achieved through independent oversight by competent technical, legal, and political authorities.

Necessity. The need for the identity system is clearly demonstrated.

Clear purpose specification. The identity system has a clear, publicly stated, and broadly accepted purpose.

Effectiveness. The identity system demonstrably achieves the stated purpose.

Cost effectiveness. The identity system demonstrably achieves the stated purpose in an efficient manner.

Client-Centeredness. The identity system is organized around the needs and rights of individuals rather than predominantly administrative priorities.

Proportionality of means to justifiable risks and desired ends.

Minimization of civil liberty risks and effective mitigation of risks where unavoidable.

Multiple, purpose-specific ID token/systems, rather than a single, all-purpose ID token/system.

Open technical standards to avoid reliance on "security though obscurity" and facilitate testing by independent experts.

Technical neutrality, to avoid vendor dependence.

Eligibility authentication rather than identity authentication where feasible (e.g., by using "electronic signature cards" rather than "ID cards").

Two-way device and authority authentication so that individuals conducting identity transactions can as quickly and easily check the authority for the collection of personal information and subsequent judgments as the agency checks the individual for identity assurance.

Back-up ID documents readily available in case of loss or theft.

No central storage of biometrics, as this storage presents unacceptable risks of being compromised.

Identity System Development Desiderata

The principles or desiderata sketched so far pertain to properties of an identity management regime once established. The processes for developing the regime in the first place and keeping it "on track" need to be consistent with the desired outcome. There are many well-recognized principles for developing and maintaining complex institutional information systems. Here we list a few that are especially relevant given the particular challenges that developing a jurisdictional identity system faces:

Participatory Design. Since a jurisdictional or organizational identity system so vitally affects individual clients as well as society more broadly, it is vital that all the stakeholders have an effective influence over its development. This influence requires the active, facilitated, informed, effective, and resourced civil society participation throughout the development process.

Social Impact Assessment-Driven. The development should involve from the beginning social impact assessment (SIA) and design approaches facilitated by competent experts and publicly accountable bodies that take appropriate account of the privacy, civil liberties, equity, and other relevant social/cultural issues. Such SIA's should play a formative role in the early stages where they can help avoid problems before they emerge and become difficult to remedy.

Identity Practice Foundations. The design process needs to be grounded in a clear appreciation of the identity practices of individuals in everyday lived situations. It is conventional in the design of complex informational/institutional systems to take a top-down, deductive approach. But to achieve the good operational fit on which effective performance and public trust rely, the design of identity tokens, systems, and rules need also to be grounded in the particular ways people acquire and handle their identity documents and engage with relevant organizations.

Privacy Enhancing/Preserving Techniques. The full range of up-to-date privacy enhancing (and preserving) technologies (PETs) and methods (e.g., encryption, digital credentials, and others mentioned earlier) should be considered for appropriate incorporation into the identity system.

Ongoing Assessment and Redesign. To ensure that an identity system continues to meet its objectives even as these may shift, there needs to be ongoing mechanisms for feedback about scheme strengths and weaknesses as well as regular systematic assessments of performance, both of which are linked to revising the scheme in light of emerging difficulties, needs, and opportunities.

Prospects for an Identity Rights Framework for Personal Information

The identity framework and specific sets of principles presented above build on and contribute new ingredients to the prior work that has been done in the areas of privacy and identity. However, we are still at an early stage in formulating workable guidelines. Their very number and diversity so far illustrate the complexity of the issues involved but at the same time point to significant limitations in the usefulness of these principles and the need for further refinement.

First, these principles should be subject to usual tests of necessity, completeness, clarity, parsimony, and relevance. It is this last characteristic that is probably the biggest challenge since so little is known about the ways that people engage in identification practices in their daily lives. This lack of knowledge calls for significant empirical research to elicit the understandings people have about identity as well as what their needs and desires are around identity. In the absence of such grounded research, any formulation of general principles is suspect.

A further step is to turn each of these principles into clear tests that can be applied in practice to identity systems, both proposed and in operation. Strong tests, such as those outlined in the final section of *CAN ID? Visions for Canada's Identity Policy* (Boa et al. 2007), will be valuable in assessing clearly whether the corresponding principles have been observed properly or not. Without such operationalization, even the most refined set of principles will be useless, or even dangerous, if they are used to promote identity systems that then cannot be held to account by citizens or independent oversight bodies.

One of the most compelling forms of operationalization of information rights principles is the working implementation of a technology that exemplifies and reinforces the principles. Recent cryptographically based research and development has demonstrated the feasibility of identity schemes that are not based on the conventional full identification approach but rather are based on user-centric principles similar to those mentioned above. Of particular note in this regard is the U-Prove suite of minimal disclosure techniques developed by Stefan Brands (2000) and colleagues at Credentica and released publicly in March 2010 by Microsoft under open licenses (Cameron 2010). U-Prove, in a significant departure from conventional identification methods, relies on cryptographically verifiable certificates of specific identity assertions, such as year of birth, age greater than a given threshold, membership in a particular group, and so on, while withholding all other aspects of a subject's identity that are not needed for the transaction. So far this minimal disclosure approach has mainly been tested experimentally in online transaction settings and has yet to be widely adopted by government or commercial enterprises.[18]

But refined principles, strong tests, and working prototypes taken together will not by themselves reform identification and related personal information handling practices. This transformation will likely require sustained social, economic, and political pressure on the part of the public. And it is here that an identity rights approach to personal information holds the promise of succeeding beyond where privacy measures have taken us. We are shifting the focus of attention from informed consent at the moment of data collection to the categorical judgments made by organizations at the point and moment of service, as well as shifting the burden of proof from the individual toward the organization. By doing so, individuals may be more able to grasp the significance of the mishandling of their personal information and be willing to act on that mishandling. Of course, if individuals suffering egregious identity impairments remain uninformed and isolated from each other, then sustained pressure for reform will remain weak. But a public discourse around identity rights that allows many people to see more clearly the alignment of their personal and collective interests can help overcome these obstacles of fragmentation and inertia. A focus on organizational misjudgments leading to identity impairment could help individuals view their own experiences and potential identity injuries as part of a wider phenomenon in which they have a vital stake. More people coming to regard such routine institutional sorting processes as directly linked to who they are and can be can become a powerful impetus for reform. A robust identity framework (Clement and Hurrell 2008), in combination with privacy protections and as a prominent part of a wider information rights social movement, could help bring the democratically accountable and responsive information environment that we need and deserve.

NOTES

1. For more on no-fly watch lists, such as Secure Flight (U.S.) and Passenger Protect (Canada) and the problems these can lead to for otherwise innocent citizens, see: http://en.wikipedia.org/wiki/No-fly_list and the websites developed by the American Civil Liberties Union (ACLU) http://www.aclu.org/national-security/aclu-challenges-government-no-fly-list and the Canadian-based International Civil Liberties Monitoring Group (ICLMG) http://travelwatchlist.ca/.

2. For a good starting point for the extensive materials on Maher Arar's case, see http://en.wikipedia.org/wiki/Maher_Arar. For the "Commission of Inquiry into the Actions of Canadian Officials in Relation to Maher Arar (Arar Commission)," see http://www.fedpubs.com/subject/govern/arar.htm.

3. See Westin (1970), "The right of the individual to decide what information about himself should be communicated to others and under what circumstances" and the German Federal Constitutional Court decision of 1983, "the capacity of the individual to determine in principle the disclosure and use of his/her personal data." http://en.wikipedia.org/wiki/Informational_self-determination

4. It could be argued that other vital political ideals, such as liberty or free expression, similarly lack precision without jeopardizing their value. But privacy appears to be especially fraught with internal inconsistency and competing concepts, such as "right to be left alone" versus "informational self-determination" mentioned earlier.

5. Treasury Board is the cabinet-level committee in charge of much of the operation of the Canadian government. It is equivalent to the U.S. Office of Management and Budget.

6. Social Security Number (SSN) in the U.S. or Social Insurance Number (SIN) in Canada.

7. Various terms similar to *citizen-centric* can be found in the discussion of identity management frameworks—including *user-*, *consumer-*, *customer-*, and *client-centric* identity. We use *citizen-* here in the informal sense, since the argument applies to rights that individuals should enjoy not only in their relations with governmental agencies, but more broadly in relation to other organizations to which they "belong" in some way and thereby enjoy rights with respect to.

8. This view of identity is consistent with Roger Clarke's interpretation of identities, as distinct from entities (2010).

9. Sometimes, of course, these two processes appear to the data subject to happen simultaneously.

10. Treasury Board Secretariat Identity Principles:

Principle 1. Justify the Use of Identity: The Government of Canada will identify individuals and businesses only when it is authorized by legislation, policy, or program mandates.

Principle 2. Identify with Specific Reason: The Government of Canada will identify individuals and businesses only when there is a specific reason to do so.

Principle 3. Use Appropriate Methods: The Government of Canada will use acceptable and appropriate means to identify individuals and businesses.

Principle 4. Use a Risk-Based Approach: The Government of Canada will use a comprehensive, risk-based approach to identity management that balances all relevant considerations, including privacy and security.

Principle 5. Enhance Public Trust: The Government of Canada will use transparent identity management processes to enhance public trust in government.

Principle 6. Uphold the Rights and Values of Canadians: The Government of Canada will use identity to uphold the rights and values of Canadians.

Principle 7. Ensure Equity: The Government of Canada, in identifying individuals and businesses, will ensure equity.

Principle 8. Enable Consistency, Availability, and Interoperability: Through a governmentwide approach to identity, the Government of Canada will enable consistency, availability, and interoperability of government programs and services.

Principle 9. Maintain Accuracy and Integrity: The Government of Canada will maintain the accuracy and integrity of identity information.

Principle 10. Be Collectively Responsible: The Government of Canada recognizes that identity is the collective responsibility of all governments and the individuals they serve.

Principle 11. Preserve Proportionality: The Government of Canada will ensure that identity management activities remain within their intended scope and jurisdiction and are proportional to the stated goals (Bouma 2006, slide 18).

11. See: http://services.parliament.uk/bills/2010-11/identitydocuments.html.

12. See: http://laws.justice.gc.ca/en/Charter/index.html.

13. Within the U.S. Constitution, these sections correspond most closely to the Fourth Amendment. See: http://www.usconstitution.net/constquick.html.

14. See: http://www.ftc.gov/reports/privacy3/endnotes.shtm#N_27_.

15. Derived from the Canadian Standards Association (CSA) Privacy Principles in Summary. http://www.csa.ca/standards/privacy/code/Default.asp?articleID=5286 &language=english.

16. See: http://laws.justice.gc.ca/en/P-8.6/.

17. The last two principles are inspired by Microsoft's "7 Laws of Identity," notably "laws" 5 and 7 (Pluralism of Operators and Technologies and Consistent Experience across Contexts) that go beyond single organizations and require at least governmentwide or industrywide coordination. The wording here is drawn directly from the Ontario Information and Privacy Commissioner's reinterpretation of these laws (Ann Cavoukian, Information and Privacy Commissioner, Ontario, Canada, 2006. *7 laws of identity: The case for privacy-embedded laws of identity in the digital age.* http://www.ipc.on.ca/English/Resources/Discussion-Papers/Discussion-Papers-Summary/?id=470). As the OPC notes, all seven laws are highly consistent with well-established privacy principles. The other "laws" that are oriented to individual identity handling organizations, notably 1–4 and 6, can be found in the first fifteen principles listed here.

18. One experimental implementation of the U-Prove technology using physical ID cards for use during in-person as well as online transactions is being conducted by the Fraunhofer FOKUS Institute in Germany. It aims to demonstrate interoperability with the German eID card system. The current author (Clement 2010) is also taking a similar approach in the "Proportionate ID Digital Wallet" project, which is using smartphones for prototyping user-centric, minimal disclosure ID tokens (see http://iprp.ischool.utoronto.ca/Prop-ID).

REFERENCES

Akalu, Rajen, et al. 2005. Implementing PIPEDA: A review of Internet privacy statements and on-line practices. A report to the Office of the Privacy Commissioner of Canada.

Boa, Krista, Andrew Clement, Simon Davies, and Gus Hosein. 2007. *CAN ID? Visions for Canada's identity policy: Understanding identity policy and policy alternatives.* Report to the Office of the Privacy Commissioner of Canada. http://archive.iprp.ischool.utoronto.ca/publications/PDFs/CAN-ID/CAN-IDreportv2ga-Jul3.pdf

Boucher, Pierre. 2007. Identity management in the Government of Canada. Presentation at North America Day. http://www.usaservices.gov/intergovt/documents/CanadaPierreBoucherIDmanagement.ppt

Bouma, Tim. 2006. Identity: Setting the larger context, achieving the right outcomes. Presentation at CACR Privacy and Security Conference. Slides and a video of the presentation at http://www.cacr.math.uwaterloo.ca/conferences/2006/psw/agenda.html

Brands, Stefan. 2000. *Rethinking public key infrastructures and digital certificates: Building in privacy.* Cambridge, MA: MIT Press.

Cameron, Kim. 2010, March 2. U-Prove minimal disclosure availability. Identity Weblog, http://www.identityblog.com/?p=1094

Clarke, Roger. 2010. A sufficiently rich model of (id)entity, authentication and authorisation. Review Version of 15 February 2010. http://www.rogerclarke.com/ID/IdModel-1002.html

Clement, Andrew. 2010. A privacy protective 'proportionate ID digital wallet' for Canadians: Open prototyping and public policy alternatives. Research proposal funded by the Office of the Privacy Commissioner of Canada. http://www.ipsi.utoronto.ca/research.html

Clement, A., Krista Boa, Simon Davies, and Gus Hosein. 2008. Toward a national ID card for Canada? External drivers and internal complexities. In *Playing the identity card: Surveillance, security and identification in global perspective*, ed. Colin Bennett and David Lyon, 233–50. London: Routledge.

Clement, Andrew, and Christie Hurrell. 2008. Information/communications rights as a new environmentalism? Core environmental concepts for linking rights-oriented computerization movements. In *Computerization movements and technology diffusion: From mainframes to ubiquitous computing*, ed. Ken Kraemer and Margaret Elliott, 337–58. Medford, NJ: Information Today.

Gandy, Oscar H. Jr. 1993. *The panoptic sort: A political economy of personal information.* Boulder, CO: Westview Press.

Lyon, David. 2009. *Identifying citizens: ID cards as surveillance.* Malden, MA: Polity.

Solove, Daniel J. 2002. Conceptualizing privacy. *California Law Review* 90, no. 4: 1087–1155.

Viseu, Ana, Andrew Clement, and Jane Aspinall. 2004. Situating privacy online: Complex perceptions and everyday practices. *Information, Communication & Society* 7, no. 1: 92–114.

Warren, Samuel, and Louis Brandeis. 1890. The right to privacy. *Harvard Law Review* IV, no. 5: 193–220.

Westin, Alan. 1970. *Privacy and freedom.* New York: Atheneum.

4

Privacy-Invasive Technologies and Their Origins

James Harper
CATO Institute

Many proponents of privacy do their work unaware of the structural bias against privacy in the protocols and technologies around them. The struggle to protect privacy is harder because of social and technical systems that have either as their purpose, or as a principal side effect, the undoing of privacy. Few recognize the role of governments in producing privacy-invasive technologies—the role of the U.S. government in particular. Yet time and again, government initiatives and funding have produced the privacy-invasive technologies that surround us today.

Historically, for example, governments pressed uniform naming systems on the populations within their borders. Hundreds of years ago, governments replaced vernacular names with standardized naming systems, pulling people out of obscurity and making them more amenable to taxation and conscription (Scott 1998, 64–71). With the failure of traditional naming to suit modern purposes and circumstances, more abstract identifiers have arisen. A dominant governmental and commercial "naming" protocol in the United States now is the Social Security number (SSN) (Harper 2006, 30–31). In short order after its creation, the federal government promoted the SSN for uses well beyond administering the Social Security Act. The SSN is a highly useful protocol, widely used for tracking Americans and, of course, for providing them services.

Identity cards follow a similar trajectory in more recent history. Governments originated them and are now pressing them into service for more and more purposes throughout society. Governments currently fund research on facial recognition technologies (and the protocols within those technologies) that will join or supplant SSNs and ID cards in the identification arsenals of governments and corporations. Real-time or near-real-time DNA identification may soon follow.

Understanding why society is slanted against privacy may reveal correctible institutional biases or behaviors in governments or the business sector. The search might reveal steps privacy advocates could take to fundamentally reconfigure privacy conflicts. Knowing how antiprivacy tools, technologies, and architectures originate and propagate may help privacy advocates get the upper hand, perceiving emerging threats before they are integral to society.

The idea of assigning responsibility for privacy-invasive protocols and technologies involves some poorly defined terms and challenging premises. The starting point must be to whittle down the problem and give contour to the many concepts at play, including "privacy" itself and what a "privacy-invasive technology" is.

Privacy in its strongest sense is having control of personal information and using that control well. The ability to control information in a given technological environment is a capacity that people build up over time through experience. Privacy expectations and privacy-protective behaviors in the "natural" world have grown up over millennia. As a literal matter, technologies are always privacy neutral—their effects on privacy depend on their application. What we call here "privacy-invasive technologies" are those that have arrived at a pace that outstrips individuals' capacities for maintaining information control.

It does not follow from calling some technologies "privacy invasive" that we should reject them. Privacy is a price paid for many benefits of modern living. And it would take more than a book chapter to analyze all the inputs that produce new technologies, implying credit or blame for their benefits and burdens. But a strong theme in the history of information technology does exist: government projects and spending have speeded technology development, at a cost to privacy.

Perhaps technologies adopted at a "natural" pace, unaided by government promotion, may have posed less threat to privacy as they emerged. Consumers may have chosen them more carefully, and adopted them more slowly, adjusting their behaviors to protect important values like privacy as they went. Perhaps society can be more circumspect in the future or look at today's government-sponsored research and purchasing with an eye on future results. The starting point for exploring all these ideas, of course, is to define more carefully what we mean when we use the word *privacy*.

WHAT IS PRIVACY?

As the chapters in this volume demonstrate, there may be as many senses of the word *privacy* as there are commentators. Privacy is highly valued—on that nearly all agree—but there is hardly uniform usage of the term.

Privacy sometimes refers to the interest violated when a person's sense of seclusion or repose is upended. Telephone calls during the dinner hour, for example, spam emails, and—historically—the quartering of troops in private homes undermine privacy and the vaunted "right to be let alone" (Brandeis 1928, 478). For some, it is marketing that offends privacy, or at least targeted marketing based on demographic or specific information about consumers. Many people feel something intrinsic to individual personality is under attack when people are categorized, labeled, filed, and objectified for commerce based on data about them. This shade of privacy offense is worst when the data and logic get it wrong. A couple that recently lost their baby receives a promotion for diapers or children's toys, for example. Informally, communities sometimes attack individuals because of the inaccurate picture gossip paints using the powerful medium of the Internet (Solove 2007, 50–75). The "privacy" damage is tangible when credit bureaus and other reputation providers create an incomplete or inaccurate picture. Employers and credit issuers harm individual consumers when they deny people work or credit based on bad data or bad decision rules.

Other kinds of privacy violations occur when criminals acquire personal information and use it for their malign purposes. The scourge of identity theft is a well-known "privacy" problem. Drivers' privacy protection statutes passed in many states and at the federal level after a stalker murdered actress Rebecca Schaeffer, having acquired her residence information from the California Department of Motor Vehicles.

Privacy is also under fire when information demands stand between people and their freedom to do as they please. Why on earth should a person share a phone number with a technology retailer when she buys batteries? The U.S. federal government has worked assiduously to condition air travel on the provision of accurate identity information to the government, raising the privacy costs of movement. Laws banning or limiting medical procedures dealing with reproduction offend many people's sense of a right to privacy. There are a lot of privacy problems out there.

The version of privacy we examine here, though, is its "control" sense—privacy as control over personal information. In his germinal 1967 book *Privacy and Freedom*, Alan Westin characterized privacy as "the claim of individuals, groups, or institutions to determine for themselves when, how, and to what extent information about them is communicated to others" (7). A more precise, legalistic definition of privacy in the control sense is "the subjective condition people experience when they have power to control information about themselves and when they exercise that power consistent with their interests and values" (Harper 2004, 2). The "control" dimension of privacy alone has many nuances.

A Personal, Subjective Condition

Importantly, privacy is a subjective condition. It is a situation with respect to one's information circumstances that one alone can define as satisfactory or unsatisfactory. One person cannot decide for another what his sense of privacy is or should be. To illustrate this situation, one has only to make a few comparisons: some people are very reluctant to share their political beliefs, refusing to divulge any of their leanings or the votes they have cast. They keep their politics private. Their neighbors may post yard signs, wear brightly colored pins, or go door-to-door to show affiliation with a political party or candidate. The latter have a sense of privacy that does not require withholding information about their politics.

Health information is often deemed intensely private. Many people closely guard it, sharing it only with doctors, close relatives, and loved ones. Others consent to have their conditions, surgeries, and treatments broadcast on national television and the Internet, hoping to enjoy catharsis through sharing or to help others in the same situation. More commonly, people relish the attention, flowers, and cards they receive when an illness or injury is publicized. Privacy varies in thousands of ways from individual to individual and from circumstance to circumstance.

The Role of Law

The legal environment determines whether people have the power to control information about them. Law has dual, conflicting effects on privacy: much law protects the privacy-enhancing decisions people make. Contract law, for example, allows consumers to enter into enforceable agreements that restrict the sharing of information involved in, or derived from, transactions. Thanks to contract, one person may buy foot powder from another and elicit as part of the deal an enforceable promise never to tell another soul about the purchase. Real property law and the law of trespass mean that people have legal backing when they retreat into their homes, close their doors, and pull their curtains to prevent others from seeing what goes on within. The law of battery means that people may put on clothes and have all the assurance law can give that others will not remove their clothing and reveal the appearance of their bodies without permission.

Whereas most laws protect privacy indirectly, a body of U.S. state law protects privacy directly. The privacy torts provide foundational protection for privacy by giving a cause of action to anyone whose privacy is invaded in any of four ways (Privacilla.org 2002). The four privacy causes of action, available in nearly every state, are:

- Intrusion upon seclusion or solitude, or into private affairs;
- Public disclosure of embarrassing private facts;
- Publicity that places a person in a false light in the public eye; and
- Appropriation of one's name or likeness.

While those torts do not mesh cleanly with privacy in the control sense—they range across control, fairness, and (of all things) trademark—they are established, fundamental, privacy-protecting law.

Law is essential for protecting privacy, but much legislation plays a significant role in undermining privacy. Privacy-protecting confidentiality has long been an implied term in many contracts for professional and fiduciary services, like law, medicine, and financial services, but legislation and regulation of recent vintage have undermined those protections. Regulatory, tax, and entitlement programs routinely deprive citizens of the ability to shield information from others—to control government's and fellow citizens' access to personal information. Such access is not always a wrong result, but it is real. The helping hand of government often strips away privacy before that hand goes to work.

Consumer Knowledge and Choice

Perhaps the most important, but elusive, part of privacy protection is people's exercise of power over information about themselves consistent with their interests and values. This exercise requires awareness of the effects behavior will have on exposure of information.

Asking people to understand how information moves in society is asking a lot, but it may not ask as much as some might assume. Consider privacy protection in the physical world. For millennia, humans have accommodated themselves to the fact that personal information travels through space and air. Without understanding how photons work, people know that hiding the appearance of their bodies requires them to put on clothes. Without understanding sound waves, people know that keeping what they say from others requires them to lower their voices.

From birth, humans train to protect privacy against physical depredations. Over millions of years, humans, animals, and even plants have developed elaborate rules and rituals of information sharing and hiding based on the media of light and sound. In these media, privacy protection is easy, habitual, and (perhaps) natural. Unfortunately, this protection is not easily available with modern technology and communications media. People do not yet have well-developed privacy habits around digital technology.

"PRIVACY-INVASIVE TECHNOLOGIES"

As we augment our lives and society with new information technologies, controlling personal information seems to be getting harder. Average people—and many experts—do not know what effects their behavior will have on information about themselves. The worlds of communication and commerce are rapidly changing, and personal information is both ubiquitous and mercurial. The result? We are surrounded by "privacy-invasive technologies."

But think again of the privacy-invasive quality of photons. In their near-infinite numbers, they bounce off everything all the time, revealing the activity of anyone to any nearby sensor. Why does the Internet threaten privacy so much, while light bulbs do not get rapped as a "privacy-invasive technology"?

It turns out that "privacy invasiveness" does not turn on the characteristics of a technology. It turns on the ability of humans to understand its effects and amend their behavior to control information. Privacy invasiveness is a function of how little time humans have had to adapt to their high-tech information inventions.

It may be easier to call a protocol or technology "privacy invasive" when the benefits it produces are unclear. And calling a technology "privacy invasive" may seem to imply that society would be better off without it. But it would be a mistake to leap to that conclusion, omitting the many economic and social benefits of protocols and technologies simply because they also have privacy costs. Many privacy-invasive technologies are entirely valuable. The computer and the Internet are huge privacy threats that have made the society much better off in other ways—and probably better off on balance.

A privacy-invasive technology is not bad because it has that quality. And a privacy-invasive technology does not become "privacy neutral" just because it adds value to other dimensions of life. "Privacy invasive" is just a description indicating that a protocol or technology has outrun society's capacity to digest its consequences for information control.

The questions are: How are privacy-invasive technologies created, and how are they propagated? How is it that we have so much technology that has propagated too quickly? Who is to blame for all these threats to privacy? And also . . .

WHAT IS WRONG WITH TEXAS?

In October of 1978, the Attorney General for the state of Texas, John L. Hill, issued an opinion to Commissioner W. K. Harvey Jr., of the Texas Rehabilitation Commission about a new system for maintaining the state's financial accounts. Commissioner Harvey had asked whether the state could refuse to pay an otherwise valid request for payment if the request lacked a "Comptroller's Sales Tax Permit Number" or "Comptroller's Vendor Number." The Attorney General found that the Texas Comptroller could refuse payments on that basis. And it was all right to use the Social Security number as a vendor number.

The Attorney General's conclusion flies in the face of the Privacy Act of 1974, which says, "It shall be unlawful for any Federal, State or local government agency to deny to any individual any right, benefit, or privilege provided by law because of such individual's refusal to disclose his social security account number" (Privacy Act of 1974, §7(a)(1), P.L. 93-579, codified at 5 U.S.C. §552a note). This law probably inspired Commissioner Harvey's question, and it would seem to foreclose Texas from requiring Social Security numbers as a condition for receiving payments from the state. But the Texas Attorney General found some more law on point. The federal Tax Reform Act of 1976 says:

It is the policy of the United States that any State (or political subdivision thereof) may, in the administration of any tax, general public assistance, driver's license, or motor vehicle law within its jurisdiction, utilize the social security account numbers issued by the Secretary for the purpose of establishing the identification of individuals affected by such law, and may require any individual who is or appears to be so affected to furnish to such State (or political subdivision thereof) or any agency thereof having administrative responsibility for the law involved, the social security account number (or numbers, if he has more than one such number) issued to him by the Secretary. (Tax Reform Act of 1976, codified at 42 U.S.C. § 405(c)(2)(C)(i))

"[T]o the extent that any provision of Federal law heretofore enacted is inconsistent with the policy set forth [above]," the federal law continues, "such provision shall . . . be null, void, and of no effect" (Tax Reform Act of 1976, codified at 42 U.S.C. § 405(c)(2)(C)(ii)). Given how the Tax Reform Act shaded back on the Privacy Act, the Texas Attorney General concluded, "Since the vendor identification number system is largely designed as a program of collection of delinquent taxes we believe it is covered by the exemption" (Texas Attorney General, Opinion No. H-1255 [October 11, 1978]).

To summarize, although Congress had barred states from collecting Social Security numbers in 1974, it turned around two years later and allowed SSN collection for administering taxes, public assistance programs, and driver licensing. In another short two years, the Texas Attorney General found that anyone receiving payments from the state—something quite different—could be required to submit a Social Security number. So today, an outsider who has never owed a tax to Texas, never accepted public benefits in Texas, and never been licensed to drive by Texas, must submit a Social Security number to the state if he will be reimbursed for flying to a conference at a Texas public university.

How did we arrive at such a state of affairs? Why would privacy protections in federal law evaporate so quickly? How could Attorney General Hill be so cavalier about privacy? What is wrong with Texas?

There is nothing wrong with Texas. And there was nothing wrong with Attorney General Hill. The state's policies followed the same course as other states, federal entities, and private businesses. The demands of institutions for Social Security numbers were drawn forth by the existence of the SSN, a data collection tool so efficient that it quickly bowled over statutory protections against its use. Texas's 1978 privacy problem began in Washington, DC, forty-three years earlier.

THE SOCIAL SECURITY NUMBER

When President Franklin D. Roosevelt signed the Social Security Act on August 14, 1935, the Social Security Board (predecessor of the Social Security Administration) was tasked with registering over two million employers and twenty-six million workers in short order. The law did not require a numerical scheme or card, but the Board selected a number to be issued on a card with the worker's name. In 1936, Treasury Department regulations established that workers covered by Social Security had to apply for a Social Security number—a unique number to be used in lieu of names for tracking receipts and payments by Social Security participants.

Because of the short time frame for commencing the Social Security program, the Social Security Board opted to accept without verification a person's assertions about personal identifying information (such as name, date and place of birth, sex, parents' names, address, etc.). This was a rational choice: employers were to collect and remit the tax, giving workers no incentive to lie. Indeed, by lying or omitting information, workers stood only to deny themselves benefits.

The choice set an important trajectory, too, because the Social Security card has never become an identification document. It only asserts that the name on the card has been associated with the Social Security number printed on it. It is a national identifier, but not a national identification system. Making it into a national ID would be difficult and expensive.

Shortly after the Social Security program began operations, though, use of the Social Security number was extended beyond the purposes of the program—by the Social Security Board itself. The Board decided that the Social Security number should be used for all workers insured under state unemployment insurance programs, rather than having each state agency develop its own identification system. Many workers not covered by the Social Security program received Social Security numbers for this purpose, and broadened use of the Social Security number was underway. The federal government's promotion of the Social Security number as an identifier has never relented (Social Security Administration).

In 1943, for example, Executive Order 9397 required federal agencies to use the Social Security number in any new system of records to identify persons. Few did. The expense of changing record systems was prohibitive relative to the benefit from doing so. According to the Social Security Administration, use of the Social Security number did not take off until the computer "revolution" of the 1960s when the efficiency gains of giving each person a unique number became clear.

In 1961, the Civil Service Commission adopted the Social Security number as the official identifier for federal employees. A year later, based on Internal Revenue Code amendments requiring each taxpayer to furnish an identifying number, the IRS began using the Social Security number as its official taxpayer identification number. In April 1964, the Commissioner of Social Security approved the issuance of Social Security numbers to pupils in the ninth grade and above. Also in 1964, the Treasury Department, via internal policy, began to require buyers of series H savings bonds to provide their Social Security numbers.

With the enactment of Medicare in 1965, it became necessary for most people sixty-five and older to have a Social Security number. In 1966, the Veterans Administration began to use the Social Security number for admissions and patient record keeping. In 1967, the Department of Defense adopted the Social Security number in lieu of the military service number for identifying Armed Forces personnel. Expanded use of the Social Security number was in full swing.

In the early 1970s, Congress was concerned about welfare fraud and illegal working. It amended the Social Security Act, authorizing the Social Security Administration to assign Social Security numbers to all legally admitted noncitizens at entry and to anyone receiving or applying for a federal benefit. Subsequently, Congress required a Social Security number as a condition of eligibility for federal programs, such as Aid to Families with Dependent Children (now Temporary Assistance for Needy Families), Medicaid, food stamps, school lunch programs, and any federal loan program. The Tax Reform Act, discussed above, authorized states like Texas to use the Social Security number for a wide array of its purposes.

During this period, private institutions such as banks, credit bureaus, hospitals, and educational institutions also began to identify citizens and consumers using the Social Security number. There was no general prohibition on private use of the Social Security number. Nor, of course, was there any general obligation to use it. But there were a series of requirements nestled into federal law that promoted Social Security number use in the private sector.

The Currency and Foreign Transactions Reporting Act (Bank Secrecy Act), passed in 1970, required all banks, savings and loan associations, credit unions, and broker/dealers in securities to obtain the Social Security numbers of their customers. The law required financial institutions to file a report with the IRS, including the Social Security number of the customer for each deposit, withdrawal, exchange of currency, or other payment or transfer of more than $10,000. This requirement, combined with tax reporting requirements keyed to the Social Security number, ensured that private financial institutions collected and used Social Security numbers.

During this period, the credit reporting industry was consolidating and making greater use of computerization and database technology. Credit reporting had begun in the late 1800s as a service to local merchants who needed to keep track of which customers failed to pay credit accounts (Hendricks 2004, 157). In the 1970s, there were 2,250 credit bureaus, but the inefficiency of operating separately in an increasingly mobile society was becoming clear. By affiliating and nesting their data systems, credit bureaus could develop economies of scale. Undoubtedly, use of the Social Security number helped them do so.

The private sector adopted Social Security numbers for a variety of reasons, such as efficiency, but government-mandated issuance of Social Security numbers to all workers laid the groundwork for this private adoption to occur. Mandates on some sectors of the private economy to use Social Security numbers advanced their use further still. In other words, using Social Security numbers for identification was the path of least resistance—down which the private sector was pushed.

Today, the Social Security number is called for in a wide variety of interactions with public and private entities. And Congress continues to press for identification and regimentation of citizens, including by reaching into the province of the family. The Family Support Act of 1988 required states to require parents to give their Social Security numbers in order to get a birth certificate issued for a newborn (PL 100-485, § 125). The Small Business Job Protection Act of 1996 required taxpayers to report the tax identification number of dependents (for all intents and purposes, the Social Security number) when claiming them as a deduction (PL 104-188, § 1615).

The Social Security number is a protocol for distinguishing uniquely among Americans. In so many uses—and misuses when it is treated as a password—consumers and citizens do not know how to control information in the face of the SSN's existence. They give it out regularly, tying records about themselves together in government and private databases. They contribute personal data to the information economy, often not even knowing such an economy exists.

The historical record on the SSN's establishment and propagation is fairly clear. It was created and mandated for use by a government agency, then mandated for additional uses by that agency. Other government agencies adopted it for yet more uses, and it ultimately made its way into the private sector, where it has continued to gain ground. Given the SSN's utility, laws against its use have been ignored or rapidly reversed.

There is no denying, of course, that the SSN is a wonderful administrative tool. For government agencies, it is an essential part of record keeping that allows programs to be carried out at national scale. Private businesses benefit from using the SSN, and consumers do, too. Such things as the robust U.S. credit reporting system, riding on the SSN, allow consumers to buy houses and cars at interest rates that match their histories of financial acumen.

But the fact remains that Americans have less privacy with the SSN than they would have without it, and they are poorly equipped to deal with the information-control challenges the SSN presents. The SSN is a privacy-invasive technology whose invention decades ago set in motion the wheels that drive the state of Texas toward overcollection of data, along with thousands of other organizations in millions of similar cases.

A protocol like the SSN is an information technology that allows for systematic identification of people in the records of organizations. But the technologies more threatening to privacy today are electronic technologies like computers and the Internet. Government technology promotion has had similar effects on privacy in this area, too.

PRIVACY-INVASIVE TECHNOLOGIES AND THE INTERNET STACK

The Internet is one big privacy threat, although this assertion says nothing about whether we want to get rid of it. It is important to remember its many benefits. One way to describe the Internet is to treat is it as a series of layers, a "stack" of different systems that combine to produce all the communications we know and love. One prominent description, for example, refers to the Internet bottom-up, from the physical layer, to the data link layer, the network layer, the transport layer, the session layer, the presentation layer, and the application layer.

To simplify, think of the physical things at the bottom—cables, wires, and computers. Above that is the logic that lets machines send signals to one another. On top of them is the logic that routes information among many different computers. Above that is more logic: the rules by which analog information like a word or picture is rendered into digital form and restored again at the other end of a communication. Another layer is comprised of the rules for displaying information in organized ways—web pages, for example. Yet another layer is made up of the computer programs we are familiar with: email software, web browsers, instant messaging, and the like. Some versions of the Internet stack might place a "content" layer on top of that—the images, sounds, and messages that Internet users experience.

The topmost layer is sometimes jokingly referred to as the CTKI, or "chair-to-keyboard interface"—that is, humans. Humans are the hapless, error-prone agent between the well-functioning chair and the efficient computer. Calling people "CTKI" allows acronym-happy technologists to put them in their place atop the Internet stack. Humans are the Internet's least competent and most unpredictable layer. But like the bride and groom on the top of a wedding cake, they are what it is all about.

There is good reason to worry about how protocols like the SSN affect the CTKI, but, again, today equal or greater concerns with privacy come from computers and the Internet. Here, also, we can ask what forces produced and propagated the technologies that outstrip society's capacity to understand them. Where did the powerful, privacy-invasive technologies and protocols that form the Internet come from? Below, we look at a few especially ripe layers of the Internet to see where they came from and perhaps to learn what agency produced them. We begin with the computer.

The Computer

The computer has so many glorious uses and does so many wonderful things that it is hard to believe where it largely originated: war. In their excellent documentation of the computer's origins, *Computer: A History of the Information Machine*, Martin Campbell-Kelly and William Aspray draw no conclusions about the social agent responsible for producing the computer. But their book shows that the computer was essentially a project of governments from its earliest beginnings, coming into its own as a tool of warfare.

Before today's electronic calculators and computers, mathematical tables were the order of the day, for surveying, astronomy, navigation, and so on. But rote table making had problems: human errors in calculation, transcription, and printing would throw off table users, sometimes with disastrous results. Mechanical computing was invented to reduce the error rates in human-produced tables. The table-making project that inspired Charles Babbage to invent one of the earliest mechanical computers was Napoleon's plan in France to reform the system of property taxation, which required up-to-date maps of the country. "It was by far the largest table-making project the world had ever known," write Campbell-Kelly and Aspray (5).

Charles Babbage applied modern methods to problems like this, inventing a Difference Engine to do the calculations and set the type for mathematical tables. His campaign to promote it included a letter urging government funding of the device, and in 1823 he obtained £1,500 in UK government funds to build his machine. During the 1820s and 1830s, the government advanced Babbage a huge sum for the time, £17,000. Babbage claimed to have spent an equal amount of his own funds, but government subsidy of computing was there from the beginning.

In the United States, it was not property taxation but the 1890 census that brought government funding to computing. The United States had grown to where completing the census by hand was an overwhelming chore—the 1880 census had taken seven years to complete—so an automated system was needed. Herman Hollerith's (1859–1929) development of a punch-card system for tallying census data won a competition sponsored by the Bureau of the Census, and the foundation was laid for IBM.

The creation of the Social Security system in the United States a few decades later was another boon to computing and IBM. Employment records for the entire working population of the country had to be maintained by the government, and private employers had to comply with the stepped-up information demands of the Social Security Act, welfare programs, National Recovery Act codes, and so on. Government subsidies, information demands, and similar mandates produced early machine computing.

Some examples illustrate how computing also failed to advance when government support was absent. While his Difference Engine was built with government support, Charles Babbage's Analytical Engine, a superior effort by Babbage's reckoning, did not enjoy a government subsidy and was "largely a paper exercise" (Campbell-Kelly and Aspray 2004, 47). It may have been a brilliant idea, but it was not a computer.

Likewise, the ideas of Englishman Lewis Fry Richardson, a pioneer of numerical meteorology in the early 1920s, did not come to fruition when he denied them government support. As a Quaker, he was unwilling to work in the military's Air Ministry, which had taken over weather forecasting from the civilian British Meteorological Office. Numerical weather forecasting took another half-decade to show success.

The story of Konrad Zuse is similar. Born in Berlin in 1910, Zuse invented and originally self-financed a machine like Babbage's Analytical Engine to perform calculations relating to airframe designs. When Germany's national aeronautical research laboratory allocated money to it, Zuse was able to produce a fully engineered programmable calculator, but when Hitler cut off funding for it in favor of weapons like the V-2 rocket, the project halted. "Such were the contingencies of war" writes Jon Agar in *Turing and the Universal Machine*, "at one moment fostering fast development, at another halting development altogether" (2001, 41–52).

The relationship of the computer to war is a close one. Computing innovator Leslie John Comrie founded his company, Scientific Computing Service Limited, in 1937. He reportedly liked to boast that within three hours of Britain's declaration of war on Germany he had secured a contract with its War Office to produce gunnery tables (Campbell-Kelly and Aspray 2004, 59).

The Second World War made computing what it is today. "During World War II, virtually all computer research (like most scientific research) was funded directly by the War Department as part of the war effort," writes University of Michigan School of Information professor Paul N. Edwards in his book, *The Closed World: Computers and the Politics of Discourse in Cold War America* (1996, 44). Agar puts it this way: "Without the six-year conflict at the heart of the century, the Second World War (1939–1945), the history of many technologies would look radically different" (2001, 39). Campbell-Kelly and Aspray elaborate:

> World War II was a scientific war: Its outcome was determined largely by the effective deployment of scientific research and technical developments. The best-known wartime scientific program was the Manhattan Project at Los Alamos to develop the atomic bomb. Another major program of the same scale and importance as atomic energy was radar, in which the Radiation Laboratory at MIT played a major role. It has been said that although the bomb ended the war, radar won it. (69)

The Moore School of Electrical Engineering at the University of Pennsylvania, for example, produced the first successful electronic computer to provide ballistics computations for the Aberdeen Proving Ground in Maryland, where artillery and munitions were test-fired and calibrated. Real-time computing—going beyond number crunching to rudimentary interactivity—was developed for training fighter pilots.

At war's end in 1945, "the digital computation techniques that had been developed in secret during the war rapidly began to diffuse into the civilian scientific arena" (Campbell-Kelly and Aspray, 144). The computer produced by World War II was firmly a part of U.S. technological infrastructure.

International conflict did not wait long to hasten the further development of computing. The threat of Soviet nuclear attack emerged in August 1949 with the detonation of a nuclear bomb by the Russians. The United States' awareness that the USSR possessed bomber aircraft capable of delivering such a weapon got the SAGE project—Semi-Automatic Ground Environment—underway, and over the next decade it became a system of air surveillance and weapons deployment with massive computing power at its center. Along with its predecessor, the Whirlwind project, SAGE was the "single most important computing project of the post war decade" (Edwards 1996, 75). And the Cold War made IBM the "king of the computer business," according to company head Tom Watson Jr. (Campbell-Kelly and Aspray, 151).

At one point in the early 1950s, nuclear weapons researcher Herman Kahn had calculations for nuclear bomb designs running on all twelve of the high-speed computers in the United States (Brock 2003, 63). Paul Edwards argues, "The historical trajectory of computer development cannot be separated from the elaboration of American grand strategy in the Cold War" (2).

Government sponsorship of computing research and development from its beginnings, and the close historical relationship between computing and war, say nothing about whether computing is good or bad. Indeed, it is easy to conclude that the economic and social benefits of computing leave us better off despite privacy lost.

The history simply suggests that the wealth governments commanded and directed toward computing caused it to develop more quickly than it otherwise would have. This support helped create the circumstances of today, in which computing challenges people's ability to protect privacy. Thanks to computers and all their good uses, people have a hard time controlling personal information about themselves.

The history of computing gets decidedly more complex, of course, after World War II. Computing technology produced by government sponsorship was picked up in the private sector and put to many new uses. Governments may have dominated the invention of computing, but they had a relatively smaller role in propagating computers to where they are today.

American Research and Development was the prototype venture capital firm founded by Harvard Business School professor George F. Doriot, a retired military general. Its purpose was to finance the commercial exploitation of technologies created during the war. Doriot today is known as the "father of venture capital" (Campbell-Kelly and Aspray, 200).

Financial innovations like his met up with technical ones such as the integrated circuit (first produced for the military) to produce a number of new computing products. The minicomputer made computing power available to smaller businesses. Calculators and digital watches came available to individual consumers. Rudimentary video games like Pong made their way on to store shelves (Campbell-Kelly and Aspray, 204). And by the mid-1970s, a commercial market for personal computers came into existence.

Electronics hobbyist Ed Roberts produced one of the first personal computers, the Altair 8800, through his small Albuquerque, New Mexico, electronics kit supplier, Micro Instrumentation Telemetry Systems. The launch of the Altair 8800 ended up transforming life for a young Bill Gates and his business partner Paul Allen, who together wrote a BASIC programming language system for the machine. Their company, Microsoft, would grow to epic size based on its authorship of an operating system for IBM-compatible computers. A similarly well-fated pair, Stephen Wozniak and Steve Jobs, began work around this time on what would become the Apple II, a consumer-friendly, all-purpose computer. Today most people have multiple computers on or about them, in their homes, and in their cars (Campbell-Kelly and Aspray 2004, 205, 206, 217–19).

The historical record is utterly clear: computing itself was a government project. But propagation of computing power throughout society was a project of variegated private-sector efforts. This complexity complicates any suggestion that privacy-invasive technologies are entirely governments' "fault." A subtler thesis might be that governments produce technologies that the private sector eventually propagates, as we saw also in the example of the Social Security number.

Of course, computers have limited capacity to threaten privacy if they are not strung together. Other important layers of the Internet provide this function. The modem and the technology of packet switching are Internet layers that reveal something more about where "privacy invasiveness" comes from.

The Modem

A modem (or modulator-demodulator) is a device or program that enables a computer to transmit data over such things as telephone or cable lines. It modulates data at one end of a communication and demodulates the data at the other, restoring the data to the form that the computer can work with. Without the modem, computers would sit quietly alone. There would be no accessing the Internet.

The development of the modem shows less of the government involvement we saw in the computer. Use of the voice band electronic infrastructure (that is, phone lines) for sending nonvoice information began with the Teletypewriter Exchange system created by AT&T in 1931. This system used the existing phone system to route and transfer Teletype information (Hochfelder 2002, 705–32). Modem technology undoubtedly got a boost from the U.S. government's Cold-War-era SAGE program, though, which some authors credit with spurring the device's invention (Abbate 2002, 122; Brock 2003, 78). In 1963, the AT&T system was upgraded from offering only 45 baud service (45 signaling pulses per second) to 110 baud service using the newly introduced ASCII standard (Jennings n.d.). This was the direct precursor system to the Bell 103A, the first widely used standard for data transmission over the standard phone lines, developed in 1962 (History of Computers and Computing).

Although AT&T originally retained a monopoly over devices that connected electronically to the telephone lines, a 1956 court decision allowed users of the telephone system to attach third-party products to their phones (*Hush-a-Phone v. United States*). This decision lead to the development of acoustically coupled modems. The *Carterfone* decision in 1968 finally allowed consumers to connect devices directly to phone lines, so long as they did not interfere with telephone service or the telephone system itself (*Carterfone v. AT&T*).

Once connecting the modem directly to the phone system became legal, third-party modem manufacturers could enter the market, and private-sector modem innovation took off. Speeds over the next decade improved from 300 bits/sec to 1,200 bits/sec because technologists improved both the rate at which the modem could issue signals and the number of bits each signal conveyed. The next huge innovation in modem design would come in 1981, with the release of the Smartmodem by Hayes Microcomputer Products (Shannon n.d.). The Smartmodem could dial and terminate calls itself, a significant improvement over prior modem technology.

With the Smartmodem came the rise of Bulletin Board Systems (BBS), a precursor to the Internet message board. And with the popularity of BBSes came a rising level of competition in the modem market, especially between the three major U.S. manufacturers: Hayes, U.S. Robotics, and Telebit.

Between 1981 and 1990, speeds further increased as various technological barriers were overcome, primarily by research teams associated with major telecommunications or computer companies. The International Telecommunication Union's Telecommunication Standardization Sector, based in Geneva, Switzerland, coordinates standards for telecommunications on behalf of the International Telecommunication Union (ITU). Though the ITU is a United Nations agency, sponsored by governments around the world, there is little to suggest that its role in standardization was a prime mover in the development or propagation of the modem. The development of the voice band modem culminated with the V.34 standard in 1994, the basis for the 28.8 Kbit/sec modem that dominated the market for home Internet connections until the broadband revolution (Forney et al. 1996).

Where computers show a history of development almost exclusively through government funding, modems follow no similar path. This piece of the privacy-invading Internet was mostly a product of private invention and commercial forces. "Blame" for its role in privacy invasion can be placed on the private sector.

The ability to send data across telephone lines did not make the Internet what it is, though. BBS systems communicating via modem were still just one-to-one conversations, like telephone calls. Packet switching was the invention that took computer communication to new heights. The language that computers use to network together has different origins and more roots in government policy.

Packet Switching

According to a history written by several "founders" of the Internet, the first recorded description of what the Internet would become was a series of memos J. C. R. Licklider of MIT wrote in August 1962 about a "Galactic Network" (Leiner et al. n.d.). The earliest iteration of the idea may have been the H. G. Wells "World Brain" concept, which he sought to promote in 1937. His appeal to President Franklin Delano Roosevelt did not garner interest, and the project went nowhere. Licklider envisioned a globally interconnected set of computers through which everyone could quickly access data and programs from any site. Leonard Kleinrock at MIT published the first paper on packet switching theory in July 1961 (Kleinrock 1961).

Licklider was the first head of the computer research program at ARPA, the U.S. Defense Department's Advanced Research Projects Agency, starting in October 1962. While at DARPA he convinced his successors of the importance of this networking concept. In late 1966, one of them, Lawrence G. Roberts, went to ARPA to develop the computer network concept, quickly putting together his plan for the ARPANET. At a conference where he presented a paper on it, there was also a paper on a packet network concept from UK researchers who told him about parallel work at RAND, a U.S.-government-supported think tank, where a group had written a paper on packet-switched networks for secure voice communications in the military in 1964.

Although ARPANET is the most famous of the early packet-switched networks, the early 1970s saw the development of several other independent packet-switching systems. Of these other systems, many were closely linked to ARPANET such as Telenet, established in 1974 by the former head of AR-PANET to commercialize the packet-switching technology (CyberTelecom n.d.). At Tymshare, a computer time-sharing company based in Palo Alto, a former Lawrence Livermore National Labs employee used the same basic research to create Tymnet (Cap-lore.com n.d.).

ARPANET's TCP/IP protocol (Transmission Control Protocol/Internet Protocol) was not the only specification for general network communications using packet switching. The ITU-T created a standard called X.25, mainly based upon the internal network architecture of Telenet. Indeed, X.25 became the standard for many international networks, and even networks with proprietary internal architectures began to present X.25 gateways to other networks. While at MCI in 1983, "father of the Internet" Vint Cerf was unable to convince IBM, Digital Equipment Corporation, and Hewlett-Packard to support TCP/IP (Hafner and Lyon, 248).

However, many saw X.25 as an inferior protocol to TCP/IP (Padlipsky 1982; Bush and Meyer 2002). In the end, their view prevailed within ARPANET, which transitioned to TCP/IP on January 1, 1983. Importantly, the U.S. Department of Defense established TCP/IP as the standard for military networks the same year. Over time, the simplicity of TCP/IP combined with the market advantage of U.S. government sponsorship to produce its universal adoption. The U.S. government's packet-switching protocol became the world's packet-switching protocol.

There was no one piece of legislation that created the Internet, and no politician "took the initiative in creating the Internet" (McCullagh 1999), but the government produced the Internet. Technology historian Janet Abbate has written of the factors that contributed to its successful founding: "Liberal funding from the government got the project started at a time when the technologies were not attractive to corporations" (2002, 127).

Part of the reason that advanced communications technologies were not interesting to the corporate sector may have been that AT&T, the government-monopoly telephone provider, was not experiencing the spur of market competition and had no need to improve its systems. As communications historian Gerald Brock notes:

> If AT&T failed to implement new technologies, its core market position was protected through regulation and network interconnection effects. If it undertook risky projects, it would receive criticism from regulatory authorities for failures . . . but could not receive financial rewards for success. AT&T established a conservative engineering approach to managing telephone service. (2003, 114)

Ironically, government regulation of the communications marketplace may have suppressed incremental advances in technology until government subsidized packet-switching technology burst onto a society unprepared to digest its consequences. Many in the public have yet to grasp how the Internet affects their ability to control personal information and what to do about it. The packet-switching technology at the heart of the Internet, which government produced and promulgated, is a privacy-invasive technology.

CONCLUSION: NOT TO BLAME BUT TO BE AWARE

The short, uneven histories in this chapter are not up to the task of determining exactly which economic and social engines brought about and popularized the technologies that challenge privacy as they do. Accordingly, there is no absolute conclusion to draw about responsibility for privacy-invasive technology. But in many instances, government spending and programs have been big drivers of the technologies that threaten privacy most—computing itself and the protocols at the heart of the Internet, for example. The history of the electronic computer shows its deep roots in war, which political radical and writer Randolph Bourne called "the health of the state." The business sector seems to have played an important but arguably subsidiary role, propagating technology and filling in interstices.

There is contrary evidence. Governments did not produce all privacy-invasive technology. Hypertext, in particular, was the idea of 1960s countercultural figure Ted Nelson. His manifesto, Computer Lib (short for Computer Liberation), imagined easy-to-use computers and a worldwide database of information—privacy menaces we face today. Tim Berners-Lee's work on hypertext at CERN, the European laboratory for particle physics, and Marc Andreessen's at the University of Illinois at Urbana-Champaign (and later Netscape) do not have the hallmarks of government projects.

And the relationship between government funding and privacy-invasive technology may not be a basis on which to draw conclusions about the future. It may be a simple historical contingency that governments were the only bodies with the capital needed to produce big new technologies in the past. Today's highly professionalized lobbying practices may be fusing the government and corporate sectors together in a way that diminishes the relevance of distinguishing the two.

But government power and money has been the necessary condition for production of many privacy-invasive technologies. In the forward to their volume, *From 0 to 1: An Authoritative History of Modern Computing,* editors Atsushi Akera and Frederik Nebeker write, "Computers did not emerge through the isolated efforts of electronic engineers, but through a multiplicity of developments in physics, mathematics, communications, accounting, and an assortment of other fields." They also cite "a productive tension between diverse military, commercial, and academic interests" (2002, 4–5). They underplay the role of government money in the development of computing. As Robert Seidel writes in the closing chapter of their book, "It cannot be said that computing would not have emerged without the intervention of the federal government. The emerging computer industry, however, could not have developed without government patronage, which supplied the market and the means for its development" (2002, 200–01).

Governments today are instituting policies and funding technology research that may continue to cut deeply into individual privacy. The U.S. national ID law, proposals for additional national ID systems, and policies built on the premise of a national ID all could result in another dramatic setback for privacy. Success in governmental efforts to procure facial recognition and real-time or near-real-time DNA identification technology could devastate the privacy people still enjoy today. These are technologies that are inevitable given a long enough time horizon, but their rapid emergence would not give society time to digest their consequences and respond in privacy-protective ways.

It would be wrong to conclude that technologies are bad solely because they have their roots in war. Indeed, the capacity of the computer to produce wealth, to educate populations, and to procure a more peaceful world than ever could make reparation many times over, transcending the computer's founding in government-sponsored bloodshed.

It would also be wrong to conclude that technologies are bad because they are "privacy invasive." They may have benefits that outweigh privacy losses along other dimensions. It is important to recognize, simply, that some technologies have developed at a pace outstripping society's capacity to understand and control their information consequences. As we acculturate to the technologies that make up the Internet—as both privacy expectations and our skills with information hiding and sharing advance—these technologies will grow less privacy invasive.

The important thing is to be aware of trade-offs, to be aware that some technologies have been developed and deployed at something faster than their "natural" pace. Often this development has been thanks to government investments oriented toward security and war. If the Internet had taken thirty years more to develop, or if it was one of several competing communications networks, our privacy problems would be fewer, although our economic wealth might be lower as well. Privacy advocates would do well to watch out for government projects that could again outrun society's capacity to protect privacy.

In his 1967 book *Privacy and Freedom*, Alan Westin mused about the possibility that citizens, consumers, and the press might one day have the computing power that governments and corporations had then (326). Early computer visionary J. C. R. Licklider had talked about it years earlier:

Lick saw a future in which, thanks in large part to the reach of computers, most citizens would be "informed about, and interested in, and involved in, the process of government." . . . "The political process," he wrote, "would essentially be a giant teleconference, and a campaign would be a months-long series of communications among candidates, propagandists, commentators, political action groups, and voters." (Hafner and Lyon, 34)

Today, indeed, the public has computing power that might rival that of governments and corporations, because of the personal computer, a product of the market, and because of the Internet, produced by the U.S. government and built by private industry.

But the protocols and technologies that reveal individuals to government and business are further along in development than those that reveal governments and business to the people. Privacy advocates should be aware of that, and they should work on building the data infrastructure that makes governments and corporations equally transparent to consumers and citizens. Projects like my own WashingtonWatch.com and many others work for the realization of J. C. R. Licklider's dream that mass computing would empower civil society more than it threatens it. If privacy is to be undone, official secrecy must be undone, too. Such is the vision of David Brin's prescient book, *The Transparent Society*. With outcomes uncertain, government transparency is an essential counterpart to the fight for privacy.

REFERENCES

Abbate, Janet. 2002. Computer networks. In *From 0 to 1: An authoritative history of modern computing*, ed. Atsushi Akera and Frederik Nebeker, 122–32. Oxford, UK: Oxford University Press.

Agar, Jon. 2001. *Turing and the universal machine*. Reading, UK: Icon Books.

Akera, Atsushi, and Frederik Nebeker, ed. 2002. *From 0 to 1: An authoritative history of modern computing*. Oxford, UK: Oxford University Press.

Brandeis, Louis. 1928. Dissenting, *Olmstead v. United States*, 277 U.S. 438.

Brin, David. 1998. *The transparent society*. New York: Basic Books.

Brock, Gerald W. 2003. *The second information revolution*. Cambridge, MA: Harvard University Press.

Bush, R., and D. Meyer. 2002. Some Internet architectural guidelines and philosophy. RFC 3439 http://www.rfc-editor.org/rfc/rfc3439.txt.

Campbell-Kelly, Martin, and William Aspray. 2004. *Computer: History of the information machine*, 2nd ed. Boulder, CO: Westview Press.

Cap-lore.com. n.d. The origins of Tymnet. http://www.cap-lore.com/Tymnet/ETH.html

CyberTelecom. n.d. Industry, GTE->Genuity. http://www.cybertelecom.org/industry/genuity.htm

Edwards, Paul N. 1996. *The closed world: Computers and the politics of discourse in cold war America*. London: MIT Press.

Executive Order 9397. (1943, November 30). Number system for federal accounts relating to individual persons. *Federal Register* 8, no. 237: xx–xx.

Forney, G. David Jr., Les Brown, M. Vedat Eyuboglu, and John L. Moran III. 1996, December. The V.34 high speed modem standard. *IEEE Communication Magazine*. http://research.microsoft.com/en-us/um/people/costa/cn_slides/v34.pdf

Hafner, Katie, and Matthew Lyon. 1996. *Where wizards stay up late: The origins of the Internet.* New York: Simon and Schuster.

Harper, Jim. 2004. Understanding privacy—and the real threats to it. Cato Policy Analysis No. 520.

———. 2006. *Identity crisis: How identification is overused and misunderstood.* Washington, DC: Cato Institute.

Hendricks, Evan. 2004. *Credit scores and credit reports: How the system really works, what you can do.* Cabin John, MD: Privacy Times.

History of Computers and Computing. n.d. The *Modem* of Dennis Hayes and Dale Heatherington. http://www.history-computer.com/ModernComputer/Basis/modem.html

Hochfelder, David. 2002. Constructing an industrial divide: Western Union, AT&T, and the federal government, 1876–1971. *Business History Review* 76, no. 4: 705–32.

Hush-A-Phone Corp. v. United States, 238 F. 2nd 266 (D.C. Circuit 1956).

Jennings, Tom. n.d. An annotated history of some character codes or ASCII: American Standard Code for Information Interchange. World Power Systems. http://www.wps.com/projects/codes/index.html

Kleinrock, Leonard. 1961, May 31. *Information flow in large communication nets: Proposal for a Ph.D. thesis.* http://www.cs.ucla.edu/~lk/LK/Bib/REPORT/PhD/

Leiner, Barry M., Vinton G. Cerf, David D. Clark, Robert E. Kahn, Leonard Kleinrock, Daniel C. Lynch, Jon Postel, Larry G. Roberts, and Stephen Wolff. n.d. A brief history of the Internet. http://www.isoc.org/internet/history/brief.shtml

McCullagh, Declan. 1999. No credit where it's due. *Wired News.* http://www.wired.com/politics/law/news/1999/03/18390

Padlipsky, M. A. 1982. A critique of X.25. RFC 874. http://www.rfc-editor.org/rfc/rfc874.txt

Privacilla.org. 2002. The privacy torts: How U.S. state law quietly leads the way in privacy protection.

Scott, James C. 1998. *Seeing like a state: How certain schemes to improve the human condition have failed.* New Haven, CT: Yale University Press.

Seidel, Robert W. 2002. Government and the emerging computer industry. In *From 0 to 1: An Authoritative History of Modern Computing,* ed. Atsushi Akera and Frederik Nebeker, 189–201. Oxford, UK: Oxford University Press.

Shannon, Victoria. n.d. The rise and fall of the modem king. *International Herald Tribune* http://www.textfiles.com/news/vs010799.txt.

Social Security Administration. n.d. Social Security Numbers: Social Security Number chronology. http://www.ssa.gov/history/ssn/ssnchron.html

Solove, Daniel J. 2007. *The future of reputation: Gossip, rumor, and privacy on the Internet.* New Haven, CT: Yale University Press.

Use of the Carterfone device in message toll telephone services. (1968). 13 F.C.C. 2nd, 420.

Westin, Alan F. 1967. *Privacy and freedom.* New York: Atheneum.

2

INFORMATION TECHNOLOGY

5

Doing the DPI Dance

Assessing the Privacy Impact of Deep Packet Inspection

Alissa Cooper
Center for Democracy and Technology
and Oxford Internet Institute

Massive growth in data processing power has spurred the development of deep packet inspection (DPI) equipment that potentially allows providers of Internet service and other intermediaries to collect and analyze the Internet communications of millions of users simultaneously. DPI has come to permeate numerous Internet policy discussions, including those related to net neutrality, behavioral advertising, content filtering, and many others. Although the policy concerns that DPI raises differ in each case, one theme that recurs is the potential for DPI to eliminate online privacy as it exists today, absent the pervasive use of encrypted communications. As a technology that can provide Internet service providers (ISPs) and their partners with broad and deep insight into all that their subscribers do online, its potential to facilitate privacy invasion has been described in the most dire of terms: as "wiretapping" the Internet (Barras 2009, 1), "unprecedented and invasive ISP surveillance" (Ohm 2009, 1417), and even "the end of the Internet as we know it" (Riley and Scott 2009, 1).

Residential ISPs' use of DPI has drawn scathing privacy criticism—and attention from policy makers in both the United States and the EU—despite the fact that numerous other entities are capable of conducting content inspection. Content delivery networks and caching services could have similar capabilities, as can individual Internet users employing firewalls, home gateways, or packet sniffers. Likewise, web- and software-based service providers have been providing many of the services that DPI can facilitate for ISPs—security protections, behavioral advertising, and content filtering, for example—for years.

There are several characteristics inherent to residential ISPs and their use of DPI that significantly increase the privacy stakes as compared to these other entities, however. ISPs are uniquely situated in three respects: they serve as gateways to all Internet content, changing ISPs can be difficult for Internet users, and the use of a tool as powerful and versatile as DPI makes it prone to invisible mission creep. All of these characteristics are difficult or impossible to mitigate, and together they form the fundamental basis for the heightened privacy alarm that has characterized DPI discussions. To some, these characteristics are enough to reject DPI altogether and call for its prohibition (NoDPI 2008).

Few legal prohibitions of such technologies exist today, however. The application of existing communications privacy laws to new uses of DPI is unclear at best and inadequate at worst, providing space for ISPs to experiment with many different uses of DPI. In the United States, for example, the Wiretap Act as amended by the Electronic Communications Privacy Act (PL 99-508, 1986) prohibits the interception and transfer of electronic communications. But both of these prohibitions have exceptions for business-related uses that are not well defined, and the application of the law depends on the arrangement of flows of intercepted data between network operators and other parties. Furthermore, the case law that exists to interpret the prohibitions comes largely from outside the Internet context, leaving uncertainty about the meaning of the law in the DPI context.

ISPs, meanwhile, see promising opportunities of many kinds in the growth of DPI. The technology can provide them with a powerful tool to address constantly evolving challenges in managing network congestion and security threats. It can provide insight into how their networks are being used, allowing them to make more informed decisions about network upgrades and architecture. And perhaps most importantly, DPI is among a set of tools that can provide ISPs with new revenue streams, whether by funneling data about users to advertisers, selling expedited delivery to content providers, or levying extra fees on heavy network users. As the services that telephone and cable companies have traditionally relied on for the bulk of their revenue—multichannel video and voice—are increasingly forced to compete with similar web- and IP-based offerings from unaffiliated applications providers, developing and monetizing intelligence in the network's core is becoming increasingly tempting.

ISPs around the world are taking up DPI for all of these different reasons (Finnie 2009); one DPI vendor claims that its ISP clients serve 20 percent of the world's fixed broadband subscribers (Verhoeve 2009). Given the attractiveness of deep packet inspection for ISPs and the nebulous legal landscape, ISPs are likely to continue to deploy and experiment with DPI on their networks for the foreseeable future. Under these circumstances, the potential that DPI creates for privacy invasion should be examined, the tools available to mitigate its associated privacy risks should be explored, and both of these concerns should be assessed against deep packet inspection's benefits as perceived by Internet users. This chapter takes on those tasks. The first section articulates a clear, comprehensive definition of the term *deep packet inspection* for use in conducting privacy analysis. Using that definition, the following section explores the inherent privacy risks of ISPs' use of DPI. The second half of the chapter delineates DPI's most prevalent uses and discusses how a set of techniques to mitigate privacy invasion could be applied in each case. The chapter concludes with a summary of the entire analysis.

UNDERSTANDING DEEP PACKET INSPECTION

Taken together, the meanings of "deep," "packet," and "inspection" describe both a technology and a practice that warrants analysis from a privacy perspective. This section explores the meaning that each component contributes to the term as a whole by discussing the different parts of a packet, defining "deep" in terms of which of these parts might be examined and taking an expansive view of the types of analyses that might be performed of packet data.

"Packet"

All Internet communications are comprised of packets: small pieces of data that get transmitted from one end of a communication medium to the other. Internet packets follow a layered structure, with each successive layer of information inside a packet corresponding to a particular function that is necessary to have the packet successfully delivered to and used by the recipient. One generic network model that is often cited as a basis for this layered structure is the Open Systems Interconnection (OSI) Reference Model (International Organization for Standardization 1996). The OSI model consists of seven layers: (1) physical, (2) data link, (3) network, (4) transport, (5) session, (6) presentation, and (7) application. These layers form a complete representation of the network, from its physical capabilities (electrical signals sent on a cable or telephone wire, for example) at layer 1 to applications and services (email or web browsing, for example) at the highest layers.

For the purpose of defining DPI and understanding its privacy impact, a mapping between the structure of Internet packets and the OSI layers is useful (see figure 5.1). Internet packets are addressed according to the Internet Protocol (IP) (Postel 1981b). Every Internet packet contains an IP header—a

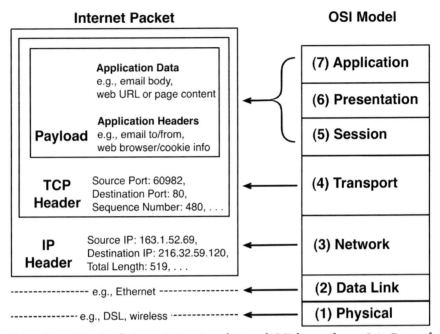

Figure 5.1. Mapping between Internet packets and OSI layers (layers 3 to 7 are of interest for defining DPI).

set of metadata fields that describe characteristics of the packet that allow it to successfully reach its destination. IP header fields include the source and destination addresses for the packet, the length of the packet in bytes, and several other items. The IP header corresponds to OSI layer 3, the network layer. Historically, ISPs' inspection of packet data has been limited to data in the IP header, with the remainder of the packet treated as the data to be delivered. This distinction between headers and data exists at each successive layer of Internet packets.

Beyond IP headers, Internet packets also contain transport-layer headers. Although several transport-layer protocols are in wide use, the most common one is the Transmission Control Protocol (TCP) (Postel 1981a). TCP serves several layer-4 functions, including identifying a device-level address (known as a port) where packets should be delivered and providing error detection for when packets get dropped. The port and sequence number fields shown in figure 5.1 are used for each of these purposes, respectively. As with IP, a division exists between TCP headers and data—the network nodes that implement TCP can find all the information they need in the headers and treat the remainder of the packet as data to be delivered.

For simplicity, this chapter will use the term *payload* to refer to the data portion of a packet carried by TCP, although in practice a packet's TCP headers and data together can also be considered as a "payload" carried by IP.

The payload, which comprises OSI layers 5, 6, and 7, contains all of the application- and content-related information in the packet. All of the bits that comprise an email message, Voice over IP (VoIP) call, or web surfing session reside in this section of the packet. Although the OSI model separates the payload into three separate layers of functionality, for the purpose of analyzing the privacy impact of DPI, the entire payload can be considered as a single unit.

Just as with IP and TCP, many Internet applications use the header/data model, with the headers facilitating some functionality necessary for the application to function and the data portion containing the data communicated by the application. Web requests, for example, usually contain headers that serve various functions in executing the request, including providing information about the user's browser or cookies. The data portion is the URL being requested (which in many cases also includes search terms) or the content of the web page. Similarly, the "to," "from," and "subject" fields of an email message have in some circumstances been considered to be application headers, whereas the body of an email message has been treated as application data, although in some cases all email fields are considered as application data.

"Deep"

There has been some controversy about just how "deep" the inspection of packets needs to be for it to qualify as DPI and potentially jeopardize users' privacy. The strictest conception of "deep" draws a line between IP addresses and all other headers and data in the packet, claiming that the use of any data other than the destination IP address constitutes DPI (Bowman 2009). A slightly more expansive conception makes a distinction between IP headers and the rest of the packet: inspection of any packet data other than IP header fields is considered deep (Reed 2008). Parsons (2008) provides an even more nuanced definition by classifying three levels of depth: "shallow," which uses OSI layers 1–3; "medium," which uses OSI layers 1–5; and "deep," which uses data at all OSI layers.

Taking these definitions together with an understanding of the layered structure of Internet packets, a conception of how "deep" DPI needs to be before it raises its own privacy implications begins to emerge. It seems quite clear that Internet service providers' use of IP headers, at OSI layer

3, is unobjectionable. IP headers have always been used by ISPs to route packets to their destinations, and thus it would be difficult to argue that their continued use creates some new privacy risk that has not existed since the Internet Protocol was first developed.

TCP headers provide a minimal amount of additional information about an Internet user's online activities, primarily in the form of port numbers. Many applications adhere to specific registered port numbers; for example, HTTP uses port 80, and email frequently uses port 25. Thus, by inspecting TCP headers, ISPs may glean some limited information about their subscribers' activities that goes beyond what IP headers reveal. However, in part because web browsing is a popular form of Internet usage, many nonweb applications have migrated to port 80 in order to take advantage of web optimizations or to avoid restrictions placed on other ports. Some applications also use non-standard ports, or they change the ports they use over time. Thus, while TCP headers provide some application-level information, using them in isolation raises limited privacy concerns.

Determining the user's privacy interest in packet payloads is a thornier task. Payloads often contain application headers, and many of these headers—such as the HTTP version type and content encodings cited earlier—are fairly innocuous from a privacy perspective. However, other kinds of headers can reveal much more sensitive information about a person's Internet activities, such as URLs, email recipient addresses, user names, addresses, and many other kinds of data.

Furthermore, for most application headers, it is next to impossible for an ISP to pluck out the header information without also inspecting at least a small number of other data within a payload. While IP and TCP headers have standardized formats, there is no standard format for all payloads, nor a mechanism for ISPs to know definitively from only IP or TCP header information whether a particular packet will contain an HTTP request, email to/from headers, or any other specific application data. ISPs can make good guesses about what a packet contains by observing the characteristics of the traffic flow—the sequences, sizes, and timing of streams of packets—together with TCP port information (Allot Communications 2007), but ultimately, correctly identifying the application requires inspecting the packet payload itself.

The same analysis holds true for application data, including the content that Internet users access online and generate themselves. Internet users may not have a particularly strong privacy interest in some of these data—the content of an online weather report, for example. But the breadth of activities that Internet users engage in is increasingly large and can incorporate information at all levels of sensitivity. Email, instant messaging, VoIP, file sharing, and the innumerable list of web-based activities—from reading the news to visiting social networks to searching for health information—each carry with them a particular set of privacy expectations. To attempt to ferret out particular bits that an ISP could inspect without sweeping in privacy-sensitive content is not likely to be feasible.

The thread tying all of these pieces together is the inspection of application-level data. When ISPs go beyond their traditional use of IP headers to route packets, they begin to implicate data that their subscribers have an interest in protecting. The privacy interest may be minimal, as with the mere inspection of TCP headers. But beyond OSI layer 4, drawing any firm conclusions about which parts of a packet are or are not privacy sensitive becomes exceedingly difficult. Thus, the data of concern from a privacy perspective are application-level data—any data above OSI layer 3 that relate to an application—with the understanding that the inspection of OSI layer 4 data alone may incur limited privacy risk.

"Inspection"

Although common understandings of "inspection" include merely scrutiny or examination, in the DPI context it has taken on a much broader meaning that may encompass interception, collection, observation, analysis, and storage of application-level data. This expansive conception of "inspection" suits DPI because the technology that comprises a single DPI system—and that DPI vendors sell as a single product—can be put to so many different uses. Some of these uses require only real-time analysis of individual packets crossing the network, while others involve intercepting, storing, and later analyzing users' packet content. This broad meaning of the word is likewise a suitable foundation for privacy analysis because it is not merely the inspection of data that may create privacy risks but also what happens before (collection) and after (analysis and storage) data inspection. Not all DPI systems will necessarily perform every one of these functions, but all of the functions that are performed should be included in the privacy analysis of any DPI system.

Combining this notion of inspection with the discussions of "deep" and "packet" yields the following definition of DPI for use in analyzing its privacy impact: *Deep packet inspection is the collection, observation, analysis, and/or storage of data related to an application that is found in Internet packets above OSI layer 3*. Figure 5.2 shows the subset of packet data and OSI layers that are covered by this definition.

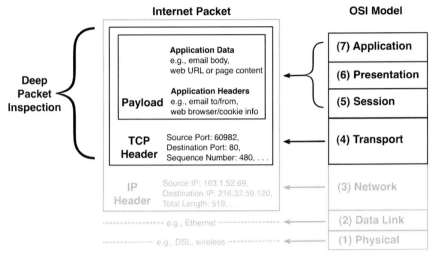

Figure 5.2.   Subset of packet data and OSI layers involved in DPI.

SINGULAR CHALLENGES OF ISP
USE OF DEEP PACKET INSPECTION

The definition of DPI given above is highly generic and not limited to any particular service or functionality that an ISP might want to implement. But even at its most generic, abstract level, an ISP capable of observing, analyzing, and storing application-level data presents unique risks to privacy that do not apply to other kinds of service providers with the same capability. As compared to their web- and software-based kin, ISPs using DPI are uniquely situated in three respects: they serve as the gateways to the Internet, the costs of switching ISPs are high, and their use of DPI is prone to invisible mission creep. Each of these characteristics is both inherent to ISPs' use of DPI and difficult or impossible to mitigate, raising the privacy stakes above and beyond those for other service providers in many cases.

ISPs as Internet Gateways

The Internet is often thought of as a dramatically free medium for speech, where little stands between an Internet user and the expression of her ideas to friends, colleagues, and the world at large. It is also an intensely personal medium used to maintain familial and social ties, to find information related to personal activities and pursuits, and to transact personal business. The Internet provides a single communications platform that supports services traditionally offered by disparate infrastructure providers, including broadcasters, telephone companies, banks, and many others. Millions of Internet users worldwide trust the medium enough to engage in a wide range of personal and commercial communications and transactions online. While "the medium" is composed of many services and applications providers at different levels, the foundation for this trust is the connectivity itself as provided by ISPs. Ohm (2009, 1446) has aptly described this service provider trust as the "sense of repose" that Internet users have as they use the network to conduct their lives.

DPI has the potential to disrupt this sense of repose by inserting a middleman—and potentially a gatekeeper—between Internet users and those with whom they communicate. To the extent that Internet users find themselves at ease conversing and transacting online, ISPs' increased use of DPI presents the potential to chip away at that sense of security by introducing surveillance where it did not exist previously. ISPs are an important element of the trust that Internet users place in the network, and increased use of DPI calls that trust into question.

The effects of this loss of trust could be wide-ranging. As with other technologies of surveillance, increased use of DPI creates the potential for self-censorship and inhibition online (Lyon 2007). It may also serve to deter online commerce if consumers and businesses question the confidentiality of their transactions. These risks are plausible whether specific uses of DPI are known to Internet users or indeed breach confidentiality, because even a general awareness that surveillance may be occurring can prompt people to alter their behavior (Foucault 1977). Introducing DPI on the network thus has the potential to turn what was a trusted conduit into a suspicious eavesdropper, even if Internet users are only vaguely aware that DPI is in use.

Many other trusted service providers exist on the Internet, and many of them would be similarly capable of damaging users' trust should they begin to examine their users' communications in an unexpected way. In fact, there are clearly intermediaries in existence today that are capable of collecting more application-level data about many more Internet users than any single ISP could—Google is the obvious example. But neither Google nor any other service provider is as capable as an ISP of comprehensively monitoring the entirety of each individual subscriber's online activities. Every one of a subscriber's packets, both sent and received, must pass through the ISP's facilities. What separates ISPs from other service providers is the potential for their gaze over their subscribers to be omniscient.

ISPs may be far from realizing that potential, and encryption tools exist to help protect Internet users from the prying eyes of their ISPs. But as long as the majority of Internet users pursue their online activities without encrypting their communications, the mere existence of DPI on the network jeopardizes the bond between them and their ISPs.

High ISP Switching Costs

The potential for ISPs to abuse their gate-keeping power is further exacerbated by the fact that switching to a new ISP is comparatively more difficult than switching between other services like search engines or web browsers. While the latter may involve a simple mouse click or software download, changing ISPs can be a much more elaborate process, involving a time investment to explore new alternatives and bundled services, installing new equipment, setting up new bill payments, and time at home waiting for an engineer to hook up new service (Krafft and Salies 2008). Because of these barriers to switching, subscribers may be unwilling or unable to switch ISPs even if their current ISPs introduce DPI-based practices to which they object. Internet users may perceive their choice of ISP to be much more binding than their choice of other online services, which reduces their ability and inclination to avoid ISPs' privacy-invasive practices. Moreover, users in many U.S. markets may have few competing ISPs to choose from (Horrigan 2009).

Notably, even where consumers have many ISP choices, switching costs may still impede consumers from changing ISPs because of DPI concerns. For example, in the competitive UK market, many ISPs indicate in their website disclosures that they are using DPI of some form to manage congestion, and the majority of Canadian ISPs that responded to a recent regulatory inquiry indicated that they are using DPI for some network management purpose (Parsons 2009). Whereas competition for privacy is appearing in other online sectors with low switching costs—the major search engines, for example, continue to improve upon each others' data retention policies (Center for Democracy & Technology 2007)—higher ISP switching costs may reduce ISPs' incentives to compete on privacy.

While there may be limited steps that ISPs can take to make changing easier—lowering or eliminating contract termination fees, establishing flexible schedules for hooking up new service, and so forth—the burdens of changing to a new ISP are in some ways inherent to the provision of Internet service. Because these burdens are largely unavoidable, relying on competition to discipline ISPs' privacy behavior is not likely to be sufficient.

Invisibility of Mission Creep

Another distinguishing feature of ISPs' use of DPI is the potential for mission creep: having DPI equipment that was installed for one purpose used for multiple new purposes over time (Werbach 2005). The potential uses of DPI are nearly as wide as computing itself. Many of the capabilities of DPI equipment are generic computing capabilities: intercepting packets, pattern-matching their content, and storing the raw data, aggregations of the data, or conclusions drawn from the data. Because the wide variety of DPI uses employs some or all of these generic capabilities, DPI vendors are finding it more efficient and less costly to build their equipment to suit multiple uses. Several vendors tout the fact that a single one of their products can be used for congestion management, usage monitoring, and prioritized or tiered service offerings, for example (Arbor Networks 2010; ipoque 2008). The trend is toward more functionality built into individual DPI products, not less.

When mission creep occurs, it may be invisible to users. Because ISPs' use of DPI occurs in the middle of the network, there need not be any indication to subscribers that inspection takes place. There is also no technical reason why DPI equipment should leave any trace on users' computers; although, for some uses, DPI can work in conjunction with files or software stored on users' computers. This lack of visibility is in contrast to other kinds of technologies that can perform similar functions to those of DPI. For example, while many web-based behavioral advertising networks deposit cookies on users' computers for tracking purposes, an ISP could employ a DPI-based behavioral advertising system without storing anything on users' machines. Furthermore, one of the core design goals of DPI vendors is to build equipment that has the least possible impact on the network's performance and users' experiences (Allot Communications 2007). The combination of these technological elements creates the potential for DPI to be deployed—and subsequently put to new uses—mostly invisibly on the network.

Perhaps because of the fact that DPI technology does not need to reveal itself, several early DPI systems were deployed without any indication to users (European Commission 2009; Federal Communications Commission 2008). Furthermore, despite the limited public scrutiny that ISPs' DPI practices have been subjected to thus far, one large ISP has already admitted that "even though DPI equipment was originally intended to introduce usage data collection functionality . . . it was subsequently determined that DPI should be used for traffic shaping" (Engelhart 2009, 3). This sort of mission creep is precisely what raises concerns about the misuse of the technology and its ability to erode consumers' trust in the network. Features of the technology that are not easy to overcome drive concerns over mission creep: the cost effectiveness of producing general-purpose DPI equipment and its lack of transparency on the network.

PRIVACY ANALYSIS OF DPI USES

Internet service providers' use of DPI thus creates unique challenges to privacy—because ISPs serve as the trusted on-ramp to a medium that is intensely expressive and personal, Internet users may not easily extricate themselves from an ISP whose DPI practices they disagree with, and DPI presents particularly promising territory for invisible mission creep. For many stakeholders, these characteristics together are so serious that the stakeholders insist on its prohibition (NoDPI, 2008). ISPs, however, will continue to experiment with DPI as long as the legal landscape remains unsettled. A comprehensive privacy analysis of any DPI system cannot end with these generic considerations because the specific purposes for which DPI is used can create additional privacy challenges—and opportunities. The following sections discuss DPI's prevalent uses and a set of potential mitigation techniques that create particular challenges and opportunities in the DPI context.

DPI Uses

Various actors have already used DPI for a wide variety of purposes, and new uses will no doubt emerge. The following categories of prevalent DPI uses are discussed below: congestion management, prioritized service offerings, behavioral advertising, proactive security measures, troubleshooting, usage monitoring, and content filtering. While all of these functions can be performed using other means, the discussion below emphasizes how ISPs are using DPI, or are envisioning its use, in each case.

Congestion management—DPI can be used in a number of different ways to help ISPs manage congestion on their networks. Because deep packet inspection captures application-level data, ISPs can use DPI to identify applications with a particular set of network usage characteristics. For example, real-time applications such as VoIP transfer small amounts of data and require minimal network delay (known as latency) to ensure good call quality, whereas bulk transfer applications such as peer-to-peer file sharing may transfer high amounts of data and be more tolerant of higher delays. ISPs can use DPI (usually in combination with other techniques) to determine the application in use by each packet stream. They can then apply a particular bandwidth management rule to particular applications or classes of applications, such as prioritizing low-latency traffic or deprioritizing delay-tolerant traffic during times of congestion (Werbach 2005). ISPs in the United States (Casserly et al. 2008; Wilson et al. 2010) and Canada (Engelhart 2009; Henry and Bibic 2009; MacDonald 2009) have experimented with or deployed this technique on their networks, drawing significant attention from regulators and privacy advocates in the process.

ISPs may also use DPI to as a tool to implement pricing practices aimed at managing traffic (Henry and Bibic 2009). For example, ISPs may charge subscribers based on which applications they use (Anderson 2007). Or an ISP may allocate to each subscriber a particular monthly volume of application-specific traffic—gaming or VoIP, for example—and levy fees on only those users who exceed their monthly thresholds. In either case, ISPs need the ability to determine which applications each subscriber is using, and DPI provides that capability. If ISPs institute bandwidth usage caps such that subscribers who exceed the caps are charged additional fees, they may want to exempt certain content (such as software upgrades) from counting against subscribers' usage allotments. DPI provides the tools necessary to make such distinctions.

Prioritized service offerings—The same kinds of capabilities that DPI provides for congestion management could also be used to provide affirmative prioritization to particular applications and services. For example, an ISP could use DPI to identify its own video content on the network and expedite the delivery of that content, it could charge other video content providers for such expedited delivery, or it could offer expedited delivery of specific video content to subscribers for an additional fee. These kinds of prioritized service offerings have been at the center of net neutrality controversies (Felten 2006), but the fact that DPI could facilitate prioritized services has been somewhat overlooked.

Behavioral advertising—Internet users' online activities present a wealth of information to advertisers seeking to better target their online advertisements. Web-based advertising companies have for many years used web-based technologies (such as cookies) to track the sites that users visit, allowing the companies to compile profiles of users' behavior for advertising purposes. DPI creates that same possibility for ISPs by allowing them to identify the websites that their subscribers are visiting, the content of those sites, and the other kinds of applications and data that subscribers are using. ISPs or their advertising partners can extract this information from individual packets and compile it into profiles that can later be used to show targeted ads to subscribers as they surf the web. ISPs in the United States (Johnson 2008; Martin 2008; Post 2008) and the UK (Bohm 2008; Clayton 2008) have experimented with the use of such systems.

Proactive security measures—ISPs provide many kinds of proactive security protections to their networks: filtering spam, blocking malware and viruses, and monitoring for intrusions and attacks. DPI, in combination with other tactics, can be useful for all of these purposes because it allows ISPs to screen the traffic crossing their networks and identify potentially malicious content within packet payloads. DPI vendors claim that ISPs have been using DPI for security purposes for many years (Bowman 2009; Mochalski and Schulze 2009), and many ISPs reserve the right to do so (or to do something vaguely DPI-like) in their terms of service.

Troubleshooting—DPI can also help ISPs address network problems, including security issues, as they arise. An ISP may receive signals from below OSI layer 4 that indicate the presence of a problem, such as a denial-of-service attack or a failing router; the ISP can switch on a DPI system to investigate further. ISPs may also switch on their DPI tools in response to customers' service calls (MacDonald 2009). While some kinds of customers' problems, such as network outages, may not require application-level data to be resolved, others may be caused or exacerbated by specific applications or content, in which case DPI can provide better or more relevant information than information from lower layers.

Usage monitoring—Information about network usage can be helpful to ISPs as they seek to understand how usage differs across subscribers in different regions or with different service plans and where network upgrades may be necessary. While ISPs have long collected information about the volume and frequency of transmissions on their networks in the aggregate, DPI provides an extra level of insight into which applications and services are generating more or less traffic. Application-level insight in turn allows ISPs to manage their networks according to the performance demands of different applications (as discussed in the congestion management section) by adding bandwidth, changing congestion management policies, or rerouting traffic depending on its application or application type. ISPs all over the world are using DPI in this manner (Cho et al. 2006; MacDonald 2009).

Metrics describing web usage—namely, which websites are most popular among an ISP's subscriber base—may be of particular interest, both internally for the ISP and externally for website owners and advertising companies. Website owners have a keen desire to understand the volume of traffic to their sites, as do advertisers and advertising companies seeking to draw the largest or most targeted audiences possible to their ads. DPI can facilitate the process of compiling data about the volume of traffic to individual websites that can then be shared or sold to website owners and marketers. Some ISPs have partnerships with data vendors that purchase these data from ISPs and sell them to website owners and marketers (Hindman 2008).

Content filtering—DPI can serve as the basis for content filtering schemes of many flavors, including those aimed at child pornography, unlicensed uses of copyrighted works, or content that an ISP deems to be objectionable. Although government-mandated filtering—which in many cases makes use of

DPI—has garnered significant attention throughout the world, there have also been many instances of ISPs using DPI or contemplating its use for content filtering in the absence of any regulatory mandate (Hunter 2004; Mateus and Peha 2008). DPI is also a tool for ISPs to use in offering content filtering services, such as parental controls, that individual subscribers may elect to apply to their Internet connections, as opposed to ISPs applying a blanket filtering mechanism to all subscribers' traffic.

Lawful intercept—ISPs and DPI vendors frequently cite the interception of communications at the behest of law enforcement or government intelligence officials (Bowman 2009; Henry and Bibic 2009; Werbach 2005). This function is often known as lawful intercept, although as Bendrath (2009) notes, DPI may be used whether a particular government request is lawful or not. Because this use case arises purely as a result of government requirement or coercion, it introduces a host of privacy concerns that the other uses, which result largely from ISPs' own initiative, do not share. Thus, government-requested interception will not be considered in the privacy analysis below.

Although the list above represents the most prevalent use cases, the list is by no means exhaustive. As Reed (2008) has pointed out, DPI constitutes a general-purpose capability whose evolution is directly tied to the evolution of processing power and functionality built into Internet routing and switching devices. As such, its potential uses are as diverse as computing itself, and new uses are likely to continue to be invented at a rapid pace.

The extent to which Internet users perceive the benefits of DPI will vary from use to use and will also depend on whether users already have software or use web-based services that serve the same functions. Proactive security measures and troubleshooting capabilities are likely to be the most easily appreciated uses, especially if Internet users experience reduced levels of spam, malware, or loss of connectivity on the network as a result. For congestion management, prioritized service offerings, and content filtering, users' judgments will likely depend on how their own online activities are affected by the services. If their user experiences are dramatically improved once DPI technology is deployed, they may be more likely to accept such offerings. Conversely, if their experiences worsen as a result of DPI—because their content is targeted for throttling or filtering—they may be less likely to accept them. Congestion management, content filtering, and prioritization are three uses that are likely to be better appreciated as they are deployed as user empowerment tools that users can turn on and off as they wish. Since usage monitoring is primarily conducted for the benefit of ISPs, users may have difficulty perceiving its value. Finally, because many Internet users appear hesitant to embrace behavioral advertising (Turow et al. 2009), that use case may prove to be the least compelling from the user perspective.

Mitigations of Privacy Risk

Although the uses of DPI vary widely, many of the steps that ISPs can take to mitigate the privacy risks of their DPI systems are common to multiple uses of the technology. Among the many privacy protections that data collectors of all sorts have at their disposal, several create particular challenges and opportunities for ISPs using DPI: limiting the depth of inspection, limiting the breadth of inspection, limiting data retention, disclosing the presence of DPI, and offering users choices. This selection by no means exhausts the scope of protections that ISPs could apply, but each tactic provides a useful illustration of how ISPs can reduce some privacy concerns and how mitigating privacy risk may be similar across multiple DPI uses.

Limiting the depth of inspection—As the discussion of the term *deep* alluded to, the depth of DPI—the extent to which DPI tools delve into individual packets—can vary greatly, from the mere inspection of port numbers to the capture and analysis of entire packet payloads. At its core, DPI concerns pattern matching: inspecting packets to determine if the bits they carry matches some predetermined sequence of bits that is of interest to the ISP. The depth of DPI measures how much of each packet is subjected to this pattern matching. ISPs seeking to mitigate privacy risk can limit their inspection to only the depth necessary for the purpose at hand.

Only some DPI uses provide the ISP with a choice of how deep inspection can be. For example, some peer-to-peer protocols declare their names in their application headers, so that when a peer-to-peer file transfer is first initiated, the name of the protocol in use is always visible at the same location inside the packet. When DPI is used to identify these protocols as part of congestion management or a prioritized service offering, the ISP could seek to inspect only the portion of the packet payload where it is possible for peer-to-peer protocol names to appear as opposed to inspecting entire payloads. Likewise, an ISP looking to generate approximate usage data about the amount of email traffic on its network could inspect only port numbers to identify traffic using common email ports, or alternatively it could inspect entire payloads to look for well-known email protocol signatures or "to," "from," and "subject" fields. The ISP's choice will likely depend on a number of factors, including the perceived accuracy of each alternative. If shallower inspection is sufficient for the ISP's purpose and it chooses to do deeper inspection, however, it would be introducing additional privacy risk unnecessarily.

Other uses, such as blocking viruses (a proactive security measure), filtering objectionable content, and behavioral advertising likely necessitate the capture and inspection of entire payloads in order to determine if the traffic on the network matches a virus signature or a content fingerprint that is known to the ISP or contains information that indicates a particular user's interest. Troubleshooting, because of its investigatory nature, is also likely to be designed to capture entire payloads.

Limiting the breadth of inspection—Breadth measures the volume of packets that are subject to DPI. The possible levels of breadth of DPI are wide-ranging, from just a sample of packets from a small number of an ISP's subscribers to every packet of millions of subscribers. As with depth, ISPs can limit the breadth of inspection to what is necessary for the DPI system's purpose. Cost and performance likely also factor in to decisions about breadth. Although today's DPI equipment is capable of processing vast amounts of data at high speeds, deploying it on a large scale may be costly or may introduce performance losses that ISPs must also take into account.

One way that breadth can be calibrated is by changing the number of an individual user's packets that pass through DPI equipment. When an application running on a user's computer initiates a communication with another computer on the Internet, the sequence of packets exchanged between the two computers is known as a "flow." Each individual user and many applications can sustain multiple flows simultaneously. For many DPI uses, conducting a pattern match on only the first few packets in a flow may provide sufficient information for the ISP to take whatever action is appropriate (Mochalski and Schulze 2009). In the peer-to-peer protocol-matching example from above, the ISP may know that the protocol name appears only in the first packet of a flow between two computers. If the first packet of a flow contains the peer-to-peer protocol name, the ISP can apply its congestion management or prioritization rules to the entire flow without further inspecting its packets. Otherwise, it can ignore the flow altogether. The same logic applies to filtering content of particular types, e.g., images.

Similarly, some networks experience congestion much more frequently in one direction (upstream or downstream), and some content slated for prioritization may travel in only one direction. ISPs can limit their DPI use to the relevant direction only, thereby limiting the number of packets that get inspected. Behavioral advertising presents a similar choice. The behavioral advertising firm Phorm inspects traffic flowing in both directions between a user and a website, collecting data about both the user's website request (the URL and, for searches, the search terms) and the website content sent to the user (Clayton 2008). In contrast, the system used in a trial by NebuAd, another DPI-based firm, captures only URLs and search terms, not the content of web pages (McCullagh 2008), thus requiring inspection in only one direction. Both companies have limited their inspection to web traffic, and, upon identifying a flow destined for certain sensitive sites (web-based email sites, for example), they have exempted the remainder of the flow from inspection (Clayton 2008; Dykes 2008). Thus, the breadth of packets involved in Phorm's system is far greater than that of the NebuAd system, but both companies have sought to limit breadth in particular ways.

Another breadth-related design decision concerns the total number of subscribers whose packets pass through a DPI engine. ISPs can deploy DPI throughout the network such that all subscribers' traffic is subjected to inspection, or they may selectively deploy it on certain groups of subscribers or at certain network nodes. For usage monitoring and troubleshooting, it may be sufficient to inspect traffic at only a sample of network nodes that give an indication of how subscribers are using the network or to diagnose a specific network problem, rather than monitoring every single subscriber. For other uses, such as behavioral advertising or content filtering, the efficacy of the DPI solution likely increases with each subscriber whose traffic is subjected to it, giving ISPs an incentive to include as many subscribers as possible.

Finally, DPI's breadth depends on whether a DPI system proactively monitors traffic or only in response to other network events or signals. The difference between the proactive security and troubleshooting use cases highlights this distinction. For proactive spam management, for example, an ISP may scan every email message to determine whether each message matches any predefined spam signatures. Conversely, ISPs employing the troubleshooting approach might wait for subscribers or other ISPs to report spam problems, and only then would they use DPI to investigate. For some use cases, such as behavioral advertising and prioritized service offerings, the only reasonable choice is to deploy DPI proactively because the continual monitoring of the network is what allows the ISP to offer the DPI-based service.

Limiting data retention—Only a handful of DPI use cases demand that some individualized (per-user) data be retained beyond a short time, and even in those cases the data need not be raw packet payloads. For behavioral advertising to work, behavioral profiles need to be retained, but DPI systems, as Phorm and NebuAd have done, can draw their conclusions about users' behavior immediately and retain those conclusions without keeping the packet payloads. Proactive security measures may require retaining information about specific traffic patterns coming to or going from certain IP addresses, but again these logs need not necessarily contain all collected packet data.

ISPs may have reasons to retain more detailed individualized records of what their DPI systems are doing, however. These records can help ISPs evaluate the effectiveness of their congestion management, prioritized service offerings, troubleshooting arrangements, or content filters. ISPs need to balance the benefit of storing additional records in individualized form against the privacy risks associated with storing data, which include accidental or malicious disclosure, compelled disclosure to litigants and governments, and internal misuse (Brown and Laurie 2000; Cooper 2008a).

There are also performance trade-offs involved between doing analysis in real time with little data storage and storing packet data for later analysis. Behavioral advertising and usage monitoring, for example, do not necessarily require real-time analysis because behavioral profiles and usage data can be calculated based on stored data. Performing sophisticated analysis in real time on large quantities of traffic can affect the network's performance (Messier 2009). On the other hand, given the vast streams of data that may potentially pass through a single DPI unit, the storage costs associated with retaining the data for any significant length of time may be prohibitive for some ISPs. Both of these factors come into play in cases where ISPs have a choice about when to analyze packet data.

Disclosing the presence of DPI—Disclosing the presence of DPI is one of the most basic steps that ISPs can take to mitigate the privacy impact of DPI. For most uses, the level of detail included in the disclosure can be quite specific, providing details of the circumstances under which packets are inspected, the purpose for conducting the inspection, the data retention policy, the choices that users have with respect to the DPI system, and the mechanism they can use to access the data collected about them. With regard to proactive security, however, ISPs may have cause to refrain from disclosing much so as to prevent attackers from circumventing the system.

ISPs' lack of proximity to their subscribers complicates the task of disclosure (Ohm 2009). While interaction with online service such as search engines or social networks is usually obvious, it is not immediately obvious to Internet users when they are interacting with their ISPs' service infrastructures. Frequent visits to search engines or social networks can create for Internet users a strong sense of their personal relationship or association with those sites. Conversely, their ISPs contact them only infrequently, usually only to send a bill. Despite the fact that an ISP transmits all of a subscriber's online communications, the subscriber is unlikely to feel as though he is directly communicating with the ISP on a frequent basis, whereas it may be much more obvious to Internet users that they directly communicate with the websites they visit.

ISPs have several conventional mechanisms available to them to try to bridge this gap, including their own websites (Bell Canada n.d. provides one example) and written rules and procedures, their printed communications sent to subscribers or potential subscribers, and media campaigns and press reports. ISPs and vendors can also seek innovative ways to raise awareness about DPI more generally. German DPI vendor ipoque, for example, has released an open source version of its DPI engine for bandwidth management (Anderson 2009), showing exactly how the pattern matching works for a wide variety of protocols. Third parties have developed tools that allow

Internet users to detect some of the potential effects of DPI, such as packet modification (Dischinger et al. 2008; Electronic Frontier Foundation 2008). ISPs could incorporate and expand such tools to show their users how DPI is functioning on the network.

Offering users choice about DPI—For some uses of DPI, offering users a choice about whether to have their packet data inspected contravenes the purpose of deploying DPI in the first place. For congestion management or the filtering of unlawful content, for example, offering subscribers a choice about their participation may defeat the purpose of conducting DPI; those who create substantial congestion or transmit illegal content could simply choose not to have their communications subject to inspection. For the offering of prioritized services, ISPs may build terms into their contracts with content providers that require them to prioritize content delivered to all subscribers, thus eliminating their ability to offer users a choice.

For the other DPI uses, however, the idea of offering subscribers a choice is reasonable, and the challenge for ISPs is to facilitate that choice. Conventional mechanisms available to ISPs for offering choice each have their own drawbacks and benefits. ISPs may reach all their subscribers by sending printed materials or including the choice option in the initial contract for Internet service, but it may be difficult to draw subscribers' attention to printed disclosures. Sending a notice and obtaining subscribers' consent via email may also be possible, but many ISPs do not collect their subscribers' primary email addresses. Phone calls may be a good way to engage subscribers directly, but calling millions of subscribers may be prohibitively expensive.

ISPs also can show subscribers an online pop-up or overlay notice to inform them about DPI and what their choices are. There are at least two ways such a notice could work: as a captive screen or walled garden that forces subscribers to make a decision before they can use their Internet connections for other purposes (similar to how some hotels and WiFi hotspots operate), or as a recurring notice that shows up from time to time if subscribers click away from it without making a decision. Opperman (2009) discusses this type of pop-up for a purpose unrelated to notification of DPI. In either case, ISPs will need to account for the fact that the novelty of receiving a pop-up from the ISP may take many subscribers by surprise. Furthermore, the task of deciding when to insert the notice in the midst of subscribers' online activities may itself require some form of DPI. If the ISP wants to display a web-based pop-up, for example, it will need to intercept a user's web request in order to deliver the notice as part of the web response. For web-based notices, at least, it is not immediately obvious how to bypass the conundrum of using DPI to inform subscribers about the use of DPI.

ISPs face additional challenges because many Internet connections are shared by multiple members of a household. To give individuals control over whether their communications will be monitored, ISPs would need to find ways to offer choice separately to different household members and to treat different individuals' traffic differently depending on their individual preferences. For most residential Internet connections, ISPs do not seek to differentiate between users within a household, and doing so may not be technically feasible or could create privacy risks of its own by revealing more to the ISP about which person is associated with each online activity. Thus, for any particular use of DPI, ISPs face the need to weigh the ability of a single individual to choose on behalf of the entire household against the potential that individuals within the household may have differing preferences.

For the choice about a DPI-based service to be meaningful, ISPs would need to differentiate between users who do and do not choose to participate, and the traffic of those who decline should not be subject to inspection above OSI layer 3. Early DPI-based behavioral advertising technologies were configured such that opting out merely discontinued the creation of an advertising profile for the user but did not discontinue the use of DPI on that user's traffic (Clayton 2008; Cooper 2008b). Moreover, given high ISP switching costs, offering a meaningful choice would also require ISPs to provide mechanisms for users to change their preferences over time so they are not locked in to their initial decisions.

Summary of Analysis

There is obviously a great deal of variability in determining exactly which privacy protections can be applied to each kind of DPI deployment, but the analysis above provides some insight into the kinds of steps available to ISPs for each particular use case. The chart in figure 5.3 summarizes this analysis, using a plus sign to indicate a protection that is feasible to apply, a minus sign to indicate a protection that is not likely feasible, and a bullet to indicate a protection whose application is unclear or highly specific to each individual DPI deployment. The three overarching ISP challenges discussed earlier are overlaid across all uses and mitigations.

The summary aptly depicts why individual uses of DPI deserve their own purpose-specific privacy analyses. Proactive security, for example, likely one of the most acceptable uses of DPI to users given its potential to help safeguard their network connections, is also the least amenable to the privacy risk mitigations, with little opportunity to limit retention, disclose the presence of DPI, or offer users choice about its use for security. Behavioral advertising, meanwhile, might raise greater privacy concern for users, but it

		Privacy Risk Mitigation				
		Limiting Depth	Limiting Breadth	Limiting Retention	Disclosing DPI	Offering Choice
Use Case	Usage Monitoring	+	+	+	+	+
	Congestion Management	+	+	+	+	−
	Prioritized Services	+	•	+	+	-
	Troubleshooting	−	+	•	+	+
	Behavioral Advertising	−	•	•	+	+
	Content Filtering	-	•	•	+	-
	Proactive Security	−	-	•	•	•

Figure 5.3. A summary of the application of privacy mitigations to the DPI use cases and the overarching challenges for ISPs using DPI.

also better accommodates mitigations, with clear means available to offer disclosure and choice and some possibility for limiting breadth and retention. The differences among all of the DPI uses demonstrate that a one-size-fits-all assessment of DPI is inadequate to the task of understanding DPI's practical privacy impact.

CONCLUSION

Given the above analysis, the cause for concern over DPI is warranted. As a technology with the capacity to provide targeted insight into Internet communications on a mass scale, it has the potential to dramatically alter the way that people approach the Internet and the trust that they place in the network. Because of ISPs' unique position as network on-ramps, their use of DPI creates singular privacy challenges that may be difficult or impossible to overcome.

The proliferation of DPI is likely to continue, however, as long as the legal landscape remains somewhat flexible, evolving network usage profiles continue to create new challenges for congestion and security, and ISPs continue to feel the pressure to monetize the content crossing their networks. The ability to address the privacy concerns has not yet been fully explored or exploited. As DPI-based systems are designed and developed, ISPs have many tools at their disposal to help mitigate privacy risks. A comprehensive privacy analysis of DPI must explore the details of individual uses and deployments because the applicability of each mitigation tactic and the benefits of DPI systems that Internet users perceive are highly dependent on the specific use(s) to which DPI is put. The extent to which public attention will be devoted to DPI-related privacy issues will likely continue to depend on the specific policy issue under discussion. For example, while privacy has been (and will likely continue to be) a core focus for policy makers in analyzing behavioral advertising, the same has not been true for net neutrality, and thus the focus on DPI-related privacy has been stronger in the former context than in the latter. But as long as ISPs continue to use DPI-based solutions, the privacy of Internet users will hang in the balance among ISPs' unique power as Internet gateways, the steps that ISPs take to mitigate privacy risk, and the benefits that users perceive of DPI-based systems.

REFERENCES

Allot Communications. 2007. Digging deeper into deep packet inspection. http://www.allot.com/Common/FilesBinaryWrite.aspx?id=3053.

Anderson, Nate. 2007. Deep packet inspection meets 'Net neutrality, CALEA. ars technica. July 26. http://arstechnica.com/hardware/news/2007/07/Deep-packet-inspection-meets-net-neutrality.ars.

———. 2009. Deep packet inspection engine goes open source. ars technica. September 9. http://arstechnica.com/open-source/news/2009/09/deep-packet-inspection-engine-goes-open-source.ars.

Arbor Networks. 2010. Arbor e100 datasheet. http://www.arbornetworks.com/de/docman/arbor-e100-data-sheet-english/download.html.

Barras, Colin. 2009. Tim Berners-Lee: Internet at risk from "wiretapping." *Computer Weekly*, March 16. http://www.computerweekly.com/Articles/2009/03/16/235279/Tim-Berners-Lee-Internet-at-risk-from-39wiretapping39.htm.

Bell Canada. n.d. Bell: Network management. http://service.sympatico.ca/index.cfm?language=en&method=content.view&content_id=12119.

Bendrath, Ralf. 2009. Global technology trends and national regulation: Explaining variation in the governance of deep packet inspection. International Studies Annual Convention, February 15–18, New York City. http://userpage.fu-berlin.de/~bendrath/Paper_Ralf-Bendrath_DPI_v1-5.pdf.

Bohm, Nicholas. 2008. The Phorm "Webwise" system—A legal analysis. Foundation for Information Policy Research, April 23. http://www.fipr.org/080423phormlegal.pdf.

Bowman, Don. 2009. Sandvine presentation to the Canadian Radio-television and Telecommunications Commission. CRTC Public Notice 2008-19, July 6. http://www.crtc.gc.ca/public/partvii/2008/8646/c12_200815400/1241688.DOC.

Brown, Ian, and Ben Laurie. 2000. Security against compelled disclosure. In *Proceedings of the 16th Annual Computer Security Applications Conference*. New Orleans, LA, USA. http://www.apache-ssl.org/disclosure.pdf.

Casserly, James L., Ryan G. Wallach, Daniel K. Alvarez, Joseph W. Waz, Kathryn A. Zachem, Mary McManus, Thomas R. Nathan, and Gerard J. Lewis. 2008. Comments of Comcast Corporation in the matter of broadband industry practices, WC Docket No. 07-52. February 12. http://fjallfoss.fcc.gov/ecfs/document/view?id=6519840991.

Center for Democracy & Technology. 2007, August. *Search privacy practices: A work in progress.* http://www.cdt.org/privacy/20070808searchprivacy.pdf.

Cho, Kenjiro, Kensuke Fukuda, Hiroshi Esaki, and Akira Kato. 2006. The impact and implications of the growth in residential user-to-user traffic. In *Proceedings of the 2006 conference on applications, technologies, architectures, and protocols for computer communications*, 207–18. Pisa, Italy: ACM. doi:10.1145/1159913.1159938. http://portal.acm.org/citation.cfm?id=1159938&dl =GUIDE&coll=GUIDE&CFID=69766487&CFTOKEN=47276760#.

Clayton, Richard. 2008. The Phorm "Webwise" system. May 18. http://www.cl.cam. ac.uk/~rnc1/080518-phorm.pdf.

Cooper, Alissa. 2008a. A survey of query log privacy-enhancing techniques from a policy perspective. *ACM Transactions on the Web* 2, no. 4: 1–27. doi:10.1145/1409220.1409222. http://portal.acm.org/citation.cfm?id=1409220.1409222.

———. 2008b, July 17. Statement of Alissa Cooper before the House Committee on Energy and Commerce, Subcommittee on Telecommunications and the Internet: What your broadband provider knows about your web use: Deep packet inspection and communications laws and policies. http://energycommerce.house.gov/ images/stories/Documents/Hearings/PDF/Testimony/TI/110-ti-hrg.071708 .Cooper-testimony.pdf.

Dischinger, Marcel, Alan Mislove, Andreas Haeberlen, and Krishna P. Gummadi. 2008. Detecting bittorrent blocking. In *Proceedings of the 8th ACM SIG-COMM conference on Internet measurement*, 3–8. Vouliagmeni, Greece: ACM. doi:10.1145/1452520.1452523. http://portal.acm.org/citation.cfm?id=1452520.14 52523&coll=Portal&dl=GUIDE&CFID=75047289&CFTOKEN=91399611.

Dykes, Bob. 2008, July 17. Summary of testimony of Bob Dykes, CEO NebuAd, Inc. before the House Subcommittee on Telecommunications and the Internet, What your broadband provider knows about your web use: Deep packet inspection and communications laws and policies. http://archives.energycommerce.house.gov/ cmte_mtgs/110-ti-hrg.071708.Dykes-testimony.pdf.

Electronic Communications Privacy Act. 1986, October 21. PL 99-508.

Electronic Frontier Foundation. 2008, August 1. EFF releases "Switzerland" ISP testing tool. http://www.eff.org/press/archives/2008/07/31.

Engelhart, Kenneth G. 2009. Response to Interrogatory: Rogers(CRTC)4Dec08-1. CRTC Public Notice 2008-19, January 13. elecom Public Notice CRTC 2008-19. http://www.crtc.gc.ca/public/partvii/2008/8646/c12_200815400/1005723.zip.

European Commission. 2009. Commission launches case against UK over privacy and personal data protection. IP/09/570, April 14. http://europa.eu/rapid/press ReleasesAction.do?reference=IP/09/570&format=HTML&aged=0&language=EN &guiLanguage=en.

Federal Communications Commission. 2008. *Memorandum opinion and order in the matters of Free Press and Public Knowledge against Comcast Corporation for secretly degrading peer-to-peer applications; Broadband industry practices; Petition of Free Press et al. for declaratory ruling that degrading an Internet application violates the FCC's Internet policy statement and does not meet an exception for "reasonable network management."*

Felten, Edward W. 2006, August. Nuts and bolts of network neutrality. *AEI-Brookings Joint Center for Regulatory Studies*, no. 6. http://www.reg-markets.org/admin/authorpdfs/redirect-safely.php?fname=../pdffiles/php9e.pdf.

Finnie, Graham. 2009, January. *ISP traffic management technologies: The state of the art.* Heavy Reading. http://www.crtc.gc.ca/PartVII/eng/2008/8646/isp-fsi.htm#_toc219621630.

Foucault, Michel. 1977. *Discipline and punish: The birth of the prison*, trans. Alan Sheridan. New York: Pantheon Books.

Henry, Denis E., and Mirko Bibic. 2009. Response to Interrogatory: The Companies(CRTC)4Dec08-1 PN 2008-19 Abridged. CRTC Public Notice 2008-19, January 13. Telecom Public Notice CRTC 2008-19. http://www.crtc.gc.ca/public/partvii/2008/8646/c12_200815400/1006810.zip.

Hindman, Matthew. 2008. *The myth of digital democracy.* Princeton, NJ: Princeton University Press.

Horrigan, John. 2009, June 17. *Home broadband adoption 2009.* Pew Internet & American Life Project. http://pewinternet.org/Reports/2009/10-Home-Broadband-Adoption-2009.aspx.

Hunter, Philip. 2004, September. BT's bold pioneering child porn block wins plaudits amid Internet censorship concerns. *Computer Fraud & Security* 2004, no. 9: 4–5. doi:10.1016/S1361-3723(04)00109-5. http://www.sciencedirect.com/science/article/B6VNT-4DCVHTP-7/2/b091ae807e76df39019a04ddeadcfaa8.

International Organization for Standardization. 1996. Information technology—Open Systems Interconnection—Basic reference model: The basic model. ISO/IEC, June 15. http://webstore.iec.ch/preview/info_isoiec10731%7Bed1.0%7Den.pdf.

ipoque. 2008. Datasheet PRX-10G. http://www.ipoque.com/userfiles/file/datasheet prx10g.pdf.

Johnson, Roger L. 2008, August 8. Knology Letter RE: Internet advertising inquiry. http://markey.house.gov/docs/telecomm/knology.pdf.

Krafft, Jackie, and Evens Salies. 2008, May. The diffusion of ADSL and costs of switching Internet providers in the broadband industry: Evidence from the French case. *Research Policy* 37, no. 4: 706–19. doi:10.1016/j.respol.2008.01.007. http://www.sciencedirect.com/science/article/B6V77-4S2VFTM-1/2/114350a2884bda8 e3a889cb706498606.

Lyon, David. 2007. *Surveillance studies: An overview.* Oxford, UK: Polity.

MacDonald, Natalie. 2009. Response to Interrogatory: Bragg (CRTC) 4 December 08-1 PN 2008-19. CRTC Public Notice 2008-19, January 13. Telecom Public Notice CRTC 2008-19. http://www.crtc.gc.ca/public/partvii/2008/8646/c12_200815400/1005749.zip.

Martin, D. Craig. 2008, August 13. WOW! Letter to Hon. John D. Dingell, Hon. Joe Barton, Hon. Edward J. Markey, and Hon. Cliff Stearns. http://markey.house.gov/docs/telecomm/20080808_wow_to_ejm.pdf.

Mateus, Alexandre M., and Jon M. Peha. 2008. Dimensions of P2P and digital piracy in a university campus. In *Proceedings of 2008 Telecommunications Policy Research Conference (TPRC)*. Alexandria, VA. http://digitalcitizen.illinoisstate.edu/press_presentations/documents/mateus-peha-TPRC-paper.pdf.

McCullagh, Declan. 2008. Q&A with Charter VP: Your web activity, logged and loaded. *CNET News*, May 15. http://news.cnet.com/8301-13578_3-9945309-38.html.

Messier, Michel. 2009. CRTC File No: 8646-C12-200815400—Telecom Public Notice CRTC 2008-19, Review of the Internet traffic management practices of Internet service providers—Cogeco reply comments. CRTC Public Notice 2008-19, April 30. http://www.crtc.gc.ca/public/partvii/2008/8646/c12_200815400/1110488.pdf.

Mochalski, Klaus, and Hendrik Schulze. 2009. *Deep packet inspection: Technology, applications & net neutrality*. http://www.ipoque.com/userfiles/file/DPI-Whitepaper.pdf.

NoDPI. 2008. No deep packet inspection FAQ. https://nodpi.org/faq/.

Ohm, Paul. 2009, September. The rise and fall of invasive ISP surveillance. *University of Illinois Law Review* 2009, no. 5: 1417–96. http://lawreview.law.uiuc.edu/publications/2000s/2009/2009_5/Ohm.pdf.

Opperman, Jay. 2009. Security scene: Introducing constant guard. Comcast Voices. October 8. http://blog.comcast.com/2009/10/security-scene-introducing-constant-guard.html.

Parsons, Christopher. 2008, January. Deep packet inspection in perspective: Tracing its lineage and surveillance potentials. *The new transparency: Surveillance and social sorting*. https://qspace.library.queensu.ca/bitstream/1974/1939/1/WP_Deep_Packet_Inspection_Parsons_Jan_2008.pdf.

———. 2009. *Summary of January 13, 2009 CRTC filings by major ISPs in response to Interrogatory PN 2008-19 with February 9, 2009 Updates*. February 13. http://www.christopher-parsons.com/PublicUpload/Summary_of_January_13_2009_ISP_filings_with_February_9_2009_Updates_version_1.0%28for_web%29.pdf.

Post, Glen F. 2008, August 7. CenturyTel letter to Chairman Dingell, ranking member Barton, Chairman Markey, and ranking member Stearns. http://markey.house.gov/docs/telecomm/centurytel_080708.pdf.

Postel, Jon, ed. 1981a. RFC 793, Transmission Control Protocol. Internet Engineering Task Force, September. http://www.rfc-editor.org/rfc/rfc793.txt.

———, ed. 1981b. RFC 791, Internet Protocol. Internet Engineering Task Force, September. http://www.ietf.org/rfc/rfc791.txt.

Reed, David P. 2008. Statement of Dr. David P. Reed to Subcommittee on Telecommunications and the Internet Committee on Energy and Commerce U.S. House of Representatives. July 17. http://energycommerce.house.gov/images/stories/Documents/Hearings/PDF/Testimony/TI/110-ti-hrg.071708.Reed%20-testimony.pdf.

Riley, M. Chris, and Ben Scott. 2009, March. *Deep packet inspection: The end of the Internet as we know it?* Free Press. http://www.freepress.net/files/Deep_Packet_Inspection_The_End_of_the_Internet_As_We_Know_It.pdf.

Turow, Joseph, Jennifer King, Chris Jay Hoofnagle, Amy Bleakley, and Michael Hennessy. 2009. Americans reject tailored advertising and three activities that enable it. *SSRN eLibrary* (September 29). http://papers.ssrn.com/sol3/papers.cfm?abstract_id=1478214.

Verhoeve, Michael. 2009, July 28. Final reply: Telecom Public Notice CRTC 2008-19. http://www.crtc.gc.ca/PartVII/eng/2008/8646/c12_200815400.htm#reldoc.

Werbach, Kevin. 2005. Breaking the ice: Rethinking telecommunications law for the digital age. *Journal on Telecommunications & High Technology Law* 4, no. 1: 59. http://heinonline.org/HOL/Page?handle=hein.journals/jtelhtel4&id=65&div=&collection=journals.

Wilson, Alexandra M., Lauren M. Van Wazer, Grace Koh, John P. Spalding, and Alysia M. Long. 2010, January 14. Comments of Cox Communications, Inc. In the matter of preserving the open Internet; Broadband industry practices. http://fjallfoss.fcc.gov/ecfs/document/view?id=7020378714.

6

Future Biometric Systems and Privacy

Shimon Modi and Eugene H. Spafford
Purdue University

Increasingly, concerns about security—protection from criminal acts, terrorism, and fraud, especially online fraud—are causing government and businesses to demand better-authenticated identity. One of the first formal initiatives by the U.S. "cyber czar's" office is the NSTIC, the National Strategy for Trusted Identities in Cyberspace (NSTIC 2010). In this context, identity is the binding of some instance of a class (e.g., U.S. citizen, police officer) or attribute (e.g., a name, age) to an individual; authentication is some process or mechanism that attests to the validity of the binding of the instance to the individual. Traditional methods of authentication, e.g., presentation of a token such as an ID card or knowledge of a PIN code, have proven to be insufficient because malfeasors with sufficient motivation, resources, and access to information resources can find ways to defeat or circumvent these methods.

Traditionally, authentication has been based on some combination of something a person knows (e.g., a social ID number, mother's maiden name, password) or something the person has (e.g., a passport or a key). Items a person knows may be guessed given sufficient time and resources. If the person being identified has generated the known items, they are often "weak" and can be determined using profile information and data mining. Authenticators held by the person may be stolen, duplicated, or counterfeited. The holder of the legitimate authenticators may *repudiate* their unauthorized use, but this repudiation enables a new abuse: fraudulently repudiating use of authenticators. For example, someone might buy a stock only to experience a significant decline in share price, then claim that the purchase was made by someone else using stolen authenticators.

Once authenticators are compromised, it is extremely difficult to determine if repudiation is real or fraudulent using knowledge- and token-based authentication methods. Considering these weaknesses, a third category of authentication is gaining popularity, based on biometrics. Biometrics is defined as the automated recognition of individuals based on physiological or behavioral traits. Fingerprint recognition, facial recognition, and iris recognition are examples of biometric technologies. Biometric technologies are assumed to prevent duplication or surreptitious stealing of a credential because they tie the physical instantiation of that credential to an individual. They also prevent fraudulent repudiation.

Resolving an individual's identity can be categorized into two different processes, each of which comes with its own set of complexities. The first part of resolving a trusted identity is called identification. Identification is the process of establishing an identity without any a priori claims. This claim on identity can be made based on knowledge, token or biometrics. The second process of resolving an identity is called authentication, or verification. Authentication is the process of confirming a claimed identity is true relative to some trusted authority. The process of identification, in the context of biometrics, is far more challenging than verification of that identity because of the complexity of comparisons of a claimant's input against the entire database of registered users. The process of verification in biometrics is implicitly a multifactor authentication of the claim made by the user.

It is the collection and misuse of biometric information in either identification and/or verification that may lead to privacy concerns. These concerns will be discussed in detail later in the chapter.

For a physiological or behavioral characteristic to qualify as a biometric, it currently must fulfill the following properties (i) Permanence: The trait should stay invariant over time; (2) Universality: The trait should be present in the entire population of interest; (3) Uniqueness: The trait should be relatively unique to the individuals in the population; (4) Collectable: The trait should be easily collectable and measured quantitatively (Jain 2007). There are system-based requirements such as psychological acceptability, performance, and robustness that need to be taken into account to ensure that the biometric technology can be used in a real application. Some researchers believe that the comparison of the trait requires near real-time performance to be considered a true biometric; collection of DNA and subsequent genome matching may take days or months using current technology and thus would not be considered as a biometric by this measure.

BIOMETRIC SYSTEM MODEL

Any biometric system can be represented as a collection of five subsystems: data collection, signal processing, data storage, matching, and decision (see figure 6.1). The architecture of the biometric system will determine if all the subsystems are located in the same physical system or distributed over a networked environment. The figure shows the biometric system model as described by the ISO/IEC SC37 subcommittee on biometric standards (International Standards Organization 2006).

The data collection subsystem is responsible for collecting the sample from a user. This is the only point of interaction between the user and the biometric system. The signal processing subsystem will take the biometric sample from the data collection subsystem and extract the relevant features to be used in matching. The signal processing subsystem involves identifying the region of interest, checking quality of the features, and extracting features from the sample. The output of this subsystem typically is a feature vector without any extraneous details, also called a template, which requires considerably less storage room than the sample. For example, a fingerprint image contains graphical information whereas the template will contain only geometric information about minutiae points used for matching.

The data storage subsystem stores the template that is created during the initial registration process. The registration template could be stored on a centralized server, local machine, or a smart card and will be used during the identification or verification process.

The matching subsystem compares the registration template with the sample provided by the individual during identification and verification and

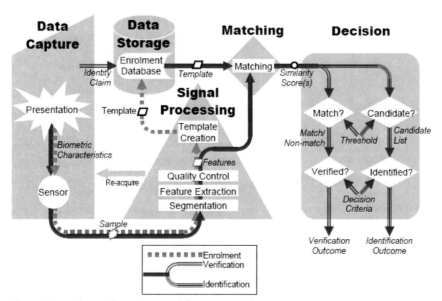

Figure 6.1. Biometric system model.

provides a similarity score. This score indicates a level of confidence by the matcher that the two samples are of the same individual. We will discuss similarity scores in the next section of the chapter.

The decision subsystem compares the similarity score to a predefined threshold and makes a determination of identity. The threshold is a reflection of an acceptable level of risk and the authentication policies of the entity implementing the system. Every biometric system will have a threshold that is adjustable: these thresholds are based on empirical evidence from large-scale testing of the matching system.

Biometric System Processes and Identity Claims

To use a biometric system, a user must *register* with the system through the enrollment process. During enrollment the user's credentials and identity are vetted, her biometric template is created for the first time, and that template is stored for future use. The storage location is determined according to the system architecture. Once a user is enrolled she can use the biometric system for identification or verification.

In the verification process the user first makes a claim to an identity. Next, the enrolled template associated with the claimed identity is matched against the biometric sample provided at the time of claim. In the identification process the user provides only her biometric sample, and the matching subsystem compares the sample against all enrolled templates to make a determination of identity. Depending on the type of application, the decision subsystem provides a result of "closest matching identity" or a list of identities called a "candidate list." A candidate list is used in law enforcement applications where a human expert makes the final determination of identity.

Error Rates

The biometric matching process provides a probability of match output based on the types of input it receives for comparison. A matching system based on passwords or tokens will require input exactly the same as the registration to declare a true match. This type of matching process is binary—the decision is always a yes or a no. Biometric matching and decision making, in contrast, are based on a similarity score and a predetermined threshold value. The reason for this difference deserves some additional explanation.

The capture of two biometric samples from the same individual can never be exactly the same because of the interaction between the user and the biometric sensor. For example, every successive fingerprint capture will be slightly different because of interaction between the finger and sensor. This is true for any type of a biometric system because randomness and variation will always be introduced into the resulting sample. As a result, errors can occur in the decision-making process because biometric systems must use a probabilistic matching process.

Biometric systems can make two forms of decision errors: false rejects (also known as Type I errors) and false accepts (also known as Type II errors). False rejects occur when an enrolled user is incorrectly rejected as not being that user. False accepts occur when a user is incorrectly accepted as another enrolled user. In standard statistical terminology, a Type I error is caused by incorrectly rejecting the (true) null hypothesis, and a Type II error is caused by incorrectly failing to reject the (false) null hypothesis. For a biometric system, the null hypothesis would state that the two samples being compared are from the same individual. A Type I error is equivalent to a false reject error, and a Type II error is equivalent to a false accept error.

The threshold and the distribution of genuine and impostor matches determine the proportion of false accepts and false rejects. Changing the threshold will result in a change in the proportion of false accepts and false rejects—in opposite directions. So if a system administrator wants to reduce the proportions of false accepts, it is likely that the number of false rejects will increase. The type of application will determine the relative importance of these two errors. For example, a physical access control system for a nuclear power plant might be required to minimize the number of false accepts at the cost of increased false rejects. This tradeoff can also be viewed as a conflict of security versus convenience, and the policies surrounding the application will determine the acceptable trade-off cost.

Overview of Biometric Technologies

Fingerprint Recognition. Fingerprint recognition has a long history of use as a means of identification. The surface of the skin on each fingertip contains friction ridges that facilitate different physiological processes and provide a gripping surface. The friction ridges have discontinuities known as minutiae points. The pattern of minutiae points on friction ridges provides uniqueness to an individual fingerprint. The minutiae points can be described using characteristics such as their type (ending or bifurcation), their spatial location using x and y coordinates, and their orientation angle. Fingerprint recognition algorithms also use global features such as the overall shape of the pattern, as well as local features including minutiae points. Tests have shown that fingerprints are unique, even among twins, triplets, and other multiple birth children.

There are several ways of capturing fingerprints, including traditional ink-based techniques and new techniques based on optical, capacitive, thermal, and other technologies (Prabhakar, Maltoni, Maio, and Jain 2003). Finger-print recognition has been used in law enforcement for over a century and has the highest adoption of all biometric technologies commercially as well.

Facial Recognition. Facial recognition is something humans use every day to recognize acquaintances and is one of the least intrusive biometric technologies. Images for face recognition can be captured using single capture devices, surveillance video, and specialized thermal and infrared cameras. Face recognition first identifies the region of interest and then uses facial features for recognition. Face recognition algorithms can generally be categorized into either *appearance-based* or *landmark-based* methods. Appearance models examine a large area of the face as a whole, whereas landmark methods examine the relationship of certain key features, e.g., lips and eyes.

Face recognition applications are gaining popularity with law enforcement and government operators because results can be verified by human operators in real time and can be determined at a distance. Face recognition technology is affected by environmental conditions such as ambient illumination and background, as well as large physiological changes. These challenges place restrictions on face recognition's ability to achieve optimal performance.

Iris Recognition. The iris is the circular, colored part of the eye that surrounds the pupil and controls its contraction and dilation. The iris contains complex texture patterns that may include features such as furrows, ridges, crypts, rings, and the like (Downing and Daugman 2001). Iris recognition technologies use a near-infrared illumination to create an image of the iris. This illumination allows for capture of the most texture information and minimal color information. Iris recognition has been growing in acceptance over the last decade with advancements in capture technology and processing capabilities. Iris recognition has been shown to work well for verification and identification in border control applications.

Hand Recognition. Hand geometry recognition uses the features of the physical composition of a hand. Contrary to popular belief, hand geometry recognition uses an infrared-illuminated image of the back of the hand to extract features rather than the palm. Some of the features used in hand recognition include length of fingers, width of fingers at different points, and distance between features of the hand. Hand recognition technology is resilient to environmental factors, but its form factor and size makes it suitable primarily for physical access control. Hand geometry technology is typically also used in verification applications that require the user to provide an identification number, password, or a smart card to make a claim of identity.

Voice Recognition. Voice recognition uses the acoustic features of speech to recognize individuals. A person's voice reflects both physiological features such as size and shape of vocal cords as well as behavioral features. Voice recognition models are based on text-dependent and text-independent modes. Text-dependent models require users to speak a specific phrase, whereas text-independent models can work with conversational speech. With the increase in mobile telephony over the last decade, voice recognition is becoming popular for identity management in financial applications.

Vein Pattern Recognition. Vein pattern recognition uses the pattern of veins on different parts of the body to recognize individuals. The absorbance of near-infrared waves between blood vessels and surrounding tissues is not uniform across individuals, so recognition can be based on an image of the vein pattern made using near-infrared illumination. Currently, vein pattern recognition technology is based on the back of the hand, the palm, and the fingers. Research has shown that vein patterns of the same part of the hand are different even between twins, and currently this technology is used in several consumer identity management applications in health care and finance.

Limitations of Biometric Identifiers

Currently, all of these biometric methods have deficiencies that limit their use. Because of the range of genetic variability and injury, not everyone has each biometric marker in a useful form. For instance, some people do not have eyes with visible irises, some people are missing fingers, bricklayers may have worn down their fingerprints, and so on. Injury, disease, and aging may also cause a biometric to deviate from its initial registered value: someone may have an injury to her hand, a persistent cough may change one's voice, and diabetes may change vein patterns. Thus, biometrics must be periodically re-registered for accuracy, and false negative errors are common.

Future Developments in Biometrics

In addition to some of the more mature technologies, technologies including DNA recognition, gait recognition, odor recognition, ear recognition, knuckle recognition, knee x-ray recognition, and more are being investigated and developed to assess their capabilities for identifying and verifying individuals. The ability to recognize individuals at a distance of tens to hundreds of meters is also receiving attention from the military and law enforcement communities, and existing iris recognition and face recognition technologies are being modified for such purposes. The ability to use multiple biometric technologies to improve confidence in a person's identity is called multimodal biometric recognition and has been an active area of research in both the commercial and research domains over the last five years.

BIOMETRICS AND PRIVACY

Use of Biometric Technologies

Any type of a system or application that requires management of identities is a prime candidate for biometric authentication. With the increased scrutiny of password and token methods and some highly publicized identity theft events, biometrics technology has gained attention because it can mitigate some of the risks present with other technologies. Biometric devices have provided physical access control at nuclear facilities for over a decade, and commercial firms are adopting similar devices to control physical access to other critical resources. Biometrics has made the largest impact in logical access control as a single-sign-on (SSO) technology that eliminates the need to remember multiple passwords for different accounts. Several commercial applications that provide SSO integration using a biometrics technology of choice are available and in use as of 2010.

The financial and health care industries have been prime candidates for improved authentication because of the legally required safeguards for data in those sectors and the increased conversion of these data to computerized systems. Regulations and recommendations from industry bodies have required financial and health care service providers to consider authentication techniques beyond simple passwords, and biometrics are being adopted to satisfy requirements of stronger authentication. The Federal Financial Institutions Examination Council (FFIEC) released guidance in 2005 on risk management controls necessary to authenticate the identity of customers accessing Internet-based financial services. The guidance reflected the need to protect customers' information as a result of identity thefts and to mitigate risks in an online environment. Although the guidance did not endorse any particular technology, the Council recommended multifactor authentication as the preferred means of authentication.

The health care industry is on a similar trajectory with electronic health care records system adoption, and risk management controls necessary to authenticate the identity of clients will become one of the first major technical challenges. Identity management in health care for patients, nurses, doctors, pharmacists, and other stakeholders will become integral to safeguarding e-health care records and increasing efficiency.

Several governments are exploring biometric programs to improve government-to-citizen (digital government) services such as welfare payments; one example is the Unique ID (UID) project instituted by India. The goal of the UID project is to provide a unique ID to all residents to consolidate more than a dozen different types of identity cards recognized by the government. To ensure that each individual receives only one unique ID number, fingerprint recognition and iris recognition will be used to identify people already enrolled in the program. Further, before the 2008 elections in Bangladesh, eighty million citizens were registered in a fingerprint database as part of the Voter Registration Project. The goal of the project was to use fingerprint recognition to reduce voter fraud.

The International Civil Aviation Organization (ICAO), which is responsible for setting international passport standards, published guidelines for incorporating electronic information in passports with the ability to transmit the information in a wireless fashion. The next generation of e-passports will contain biometric information that can be used to authenticate the holder of the passport against the information stored on the passport. These e-passports are being designed to reduce identity fraud and improve border control. Several governments have implemented additional border control applications for visitors to their respective countries. One such example is the US-VISIT program that currently collects fingerprints from all ten fingers and a facial image to compare against a checklist. Dubai, which is part of the United Arab Emirates, has been using iris recognition to identify individuals who have previously been expelled.

The review of biometric technologies and their applications until now raises a host of policy-related questions about its usability, safety, security, and the privacy of individuals involved. The challenge regarding privacy has four different aspects (Breebaart, Busch, Grave, and Kindt 2008):

1. Unauthorized collection: covert collection of persons' biometric traits without their explicit consent or knowledge. Biometric technologies that can capture features using hidden sensors, and cameras raise the most concern for individuals. An example is face recognition in surveillance mode that can be used to collect facial images from a crowd of people and compare them with a list of suspects.
2. Unnecessary collection: collection of biometric traits that have no relation to current systems and do not improve security or convenience of authentication.
3. Unauthorized use and disclosure: use of biometric traits without the expressed consent of the individual. An example is sharing of biometric information between two nonrelated entities for authentication. In 2008, a company providing services for a registered traveler program attempted to sell the biometric data of individuals who had agreed to enroll in the program. Although the company was eventually not allowed to sell the data of its customers, this incident put focus on the need to control the disclosure of biometric data.
4. Function creep: an expansion of the scope of the biometric system. This concern is raised most often in discussion of a national ID program,

where a biometric identifier could be used to link identities across multiple databases and be used as an information-gathering tool.

In addition to these concerns, biometric systems operate on the probability of a match. A misidentification error that would allow an unauthorized person to gain access to a system under another identity is also a privacy challenge. As we discussed before, simple identification does not require a person to make a claim to a specific identity. Performance of the biometric system also affects privacy—this challenge is unique to identity management using biometrics.

The National Security and Technology Council Subcommittee on Biometrics published a report that outlined several challenges facing biometric systems (National Science and Technology Council Subcommittee on Biometrics 2006). One of the categories of challenges was based on "Communications and Privacy" and stated that the following were high-priority needs that had to be addressed:

- Fundamental understanding of biometric operations, technologies, and privacy principles to enable discussion of usage of biometric systems;
- Embedding privacy functionality at every level of the biometric subsystem;
- Privacy-protecting applications that enhance public confidence and safeguard information.

This report, along with several others, has acknowledged the need to address privacy concerns to increase adoption of biometric technologies and use them effectively.

Potential Unintended Uses of Biometrics

There are some obvious privacy implications involved in the gathering and storage of biometric information and in the use of these data to authenticate identity. Some of those implications are visible with current technology, and some may become possible in the not-too-distant future, with additional technological changes. Many of those concerns are identical to those related to the use of any identifier/authenticator system: failure to protect collected information, undisclosed collection, unauthorized cross-matching of data, and so on.

However, some biometric techniques have the potential to provide subtler disclosures of private information when the data gathering is made more precise and/or data are repeatedly sampled over time. Some biometric collection methods may also be expanded to collect somewhat related but unnecessary details that are then used for other purposes, either at the time of collection or retrospectively when examining historical data. Specifically, small physiologic indicators may be noted that reveal information about personal behavior and conditions that are incidental to authenticating identity but which may be of interest to some parties who are able to examine those data.

One of the most obvious instances of this concern is DNA analysis. Individual DNA is unique: sampling DNA of an individual and matching against enough gene locations can provide definitive authentication, barring some special cases such as identical twins and triplets, some transplant cases, and rare medical oddities such as chimerae. Future technology will likely produce systems that can process DNA for identification and authentication cheaply and quickly enough for it to be commonly used. Current systems may be used to collect cellular material clandestinely for slower and more costly analysis; for instance, a hand scanner might vacuum cells from each person who uses it. The concerns with DNA collection involve how that information is collected, stored, and made available to others.

Analysis of DNA can be used for identification, but it also may reveal the presence or absence of a number of medical syndromes and characteristics that an individual might not choose to reveal as part of the process of identification. Such information might include what the subject does not know and does not wish to know, such as whether the subject is a carrier of ALS (Amyotrophic Lateral Sclerosis, also known as Lou Gehrig's disease) or has any of the BRCA genes that are a strong indicator of susceptibility to breast cancer. Information about these syndromes has been suggested as useful not only to medical practitioners but also to insurance carriers, employers, potential mates, and to governments making immigration decisions. In each case, a decision may be made because of the presence or absence of a genetic marker.

Furthermore, comparing DNA from multiple subjects may expose familial relationships (or nonrelationships) that the subjects do not wish to expose or have known. DNA may show, for instance, that a child is adopted and that her real parents are two other prominent people in the DNA database. This discovery could result in emotional trauma for all involved as well as open the potential for extortion.

Simple hand geometry scanners may also be used to gather data beyond their intended use. For instance, there is some evidence that particular kinds of lines in the palm are indications of underlying medical conditions (medical palmistry). Temperature of the hand may be an indication of thyroid imbalance or Reyes syndrome. The sudden appearance or lack of a ring on a specific finger in a scan can indicate a change in relationship. Subtle fluctuations in the size of the hand may indicate timing of alcohol consumption, menstrual cycles or pregnancy, and overall weight gain or loss. Joint structure may indicate arthritis. Particular patterns (or absence) of calluses may indicate certain forms of tool use. In some circumstances, a bright enough light at the right spectra can also determine pulse rate and blood oxygen levels. There is some evidence that the relationship of length of the index finger to the middle finger may relate to fetal exposure to testosterone, affecting later development. Given these indicators, other information may be obtained, overtly or surreptitiously, to add to these indicators, e.g., note that weight gain is a result of stress or depression.

Facial recognition may also result in additional monitoring, recognizing tanning or pallor, changes in hair color and style, appearance or change in facial hair presence and thickness, weight gain or loss, lack of sleep, and so on. Some changes in facial geometry may indicate medical information, e.g., "moon face" revealing use of steroids. These kinds of information could all be used for purposes different from simple identification or verification when tracked over time. Other concerns may also develop using demographic characteristics coupled with facial scans. For instance, some changes in complexion could indicate the use of birth control pills, and puffiness under the eyes could be matched to determine whether it is seasonal allergies (many others have it) or it is related to some emotional upset, e.g., from crying.

Other biometric collection systems might also be misused for extraneous data gathering. Although we are unable to imagine all of what might be possible with enhanced technology, we are able to conjecture a few more:

- Gait recognition may be used to detect problems related to joint health (e.g., arthritis), weight, and balance. Balance may be affected by various inner ear difficulties (e.g., Menier's disease), stroke, or consumption of alcohol.
- Voice recognition can detect slurring from alcohol, drugs, or stroke.
- Chemical analysis of mouth swabs used for DNA capture may be used to determine levels of certain medications present in the subject, as well as possible indicators of recent meals. In some cases, samples of fluids taken from the mouth may reveal more than one DNA pattern, indicating recent sexual contact with the person(s) indicated in the other patterns.
- Hair samples taken for DNA analysis of the root may be examined for certain chemical exposures to determine recent drug use, whether the subject uses hair coloring, and possibly even some recent travel based on marker element isotope ratios.

It is possible to also augment the biometric capture process with other mechanisms that are privacy invasive. For instance, chemical sensors may be hidden in the microphone used for vocal recognition. These could be used to detect alcohol metabolites as well as telltale traces of ketoacidosis present in diabetes. Alternatively, while present for one biometric sample, a suspect's weight may be taken clandestinely, and the subject scanned for radiation and chemical signatures. These tests might reveal where the subject has recently traveled, concerns about personal hygiene, and some recent medical procedures.

In each of these cases, an argument can be made that discovering these facts is useful to some entity, thus justifying the infringement of privacy. For instance, it could be argued that detection of ketoacidosis could help save the eyesight (or even life) of someone with as-yet-undiagnosed diabetes. It might also be argued that an employer might wish to intervene with counseling in a case where a highly trusted employee is showing signs of emotional trauma and excessive alcohol use. Law enforcement personnel may justify knowledge of recent travel and personal association as useful in their investigations.

However justified, collection performed without consent is usually unethical and an invasion of privacy. Likewise, collection of additional data beyond what is needed for identification without a specific and traceable likelihood that the subject will match on the indicators is equally a privacy violation—similar to how collecting the fingerprints of everyone in a village because one of them might someday commit a crime is considered a violation of privacy today.

What Is Needed?

Policies for Biometric System Usage. Biometric system administrators and vendors must address the various privacy concerns that are being raised by current users and privacy advocacy groups and discuss the advances in biometric technologies. They must also anticipate future concerns, such as those mentioned above. These concerns can be addressed using both technical controls and appropriate policies. Policy makers will have to ensure that the scope of any biometric authentication is clearly defined and enforced. A comprehensive set of policies addressing privacy concerns at every stage of the biometric system process along with usage of the biometric information is required. Such rules and procedures guide collection of information, use and disclosure of biometric information, flow of information between entities, revocation of biometric information, storage, and accountability. Defining ownership of the biometric data is extremely important for reducing any ambiguity about the usage of the data. Auditing of biometric controls is important as well because it leads to examination of risks and countermeasures to using biometrics. The Information System Audit and Control Association created a biometric controls document that outlines detailed procedures for auditors of biometric systems (2007). A clearly defined set of policies is a necessary requirement for preventing intentional and unintentional misuses of biometric information and for maintaining privacy.

Privacy-Enhancing Technologies in Biometrics. Some concerns surrounding the misuse and abuse of biometric technologies have already been acknowledged by the biometrics community. Vendors and researchers alike have been working actively to address some of these concerns by incorporating privacy-enhancing technologies in biometrics. The European Union, under the Seventh Framework Program, initiated a project called Trusted Revocable Biometric Identities (TURBINE). The focus of the TURBINE project (EU 2008) is on fingerprints as a biometric identifier with the goal of providing assurance that:

- The data used for authentication, generated from the fingerprint, cannot be used to restore the original fingerprint sample;
- The individual will be able to create different "pseudo-identities" for different applications with the same fingerprint, while ensuring that these different identities (and hence the related personal data) cannot be linked to each other; and
- The individual is able to revoke an identity for a given application if it should not be used anymore.

The overall goal of this project is to meet usage requirements of biometrics in applications in government-to-citizen and business-to-citizen applications in areas such as health care, finance, and e-commerce. Although the EU TURBINE project is a relatively new initiative, the project participants have generated a body of publications that attempts to address privacy conflicts using numerous different cryptographic techniques.

Another idea that has been investigated concerns cancelable biometrics. It is based on the idea of providing transformation parameters that will change the biometric template so that a matching operation cannot be conducted without the transformation parameter. This technique raises a question about the use of traditional cryptographic techniques for securing biometric information. The variability involved in successive biometric samples from the same individual means that comparison of biometric templates in their encrypted form is not possible. Biometric systems are also inherently susceptible to false positives, which introduces an additional layer of complexity to the problem.

Industry-Specific Groups and Vendors. Biometric standards are an important indicator of technology maturity. These standards enable creation of integrated systems that are interoperable, vendor neutral, and reduce the cost of development. Although the national and international biometric standards committees have focused mainly on data interchange formats, application interfaces, and conformance testing, they have also made efforts to address privacy concerns. The Ad Hoc Group on Biometrics and E-Authentication (AHGBEA) published a report in 2007 with the goal of discussing strengths and weaknesses of use of biometrics for e-authentication over open networks. Along with technical specifications, this report outlined a list of best practices to protect the privacy of users.

Standards have created a consistent sense of understanding of the technical characteristics of different biometric systems, and the same approach needs to be applied to privacy protection of individuals using biometric systems. The EU TURBINE project mentioned earlier is a prime example of an international effort to create standardized privacy-enhancing biometric technologies and a consistent sense of what these should achieve.

In 2001 the Biometrics Institute in Australia published the Biometric Privacy Code report that recommended guidelines for how biometric data should be collected, used, and disclosed to protect the privacy of users. The report outlined three specific goals of the code: (1) to facilitate the protection of personal information provided by, or held by, biometric systems; (2) to facilitate the process of identity authentication in a manner consistent with the Privacy Act and the National Privacy Principles (NPPs); (3) to promote biometrics as privacy-enhancing technologies (PETs).

Biometric vendors are equally important in improving privacy. They are the best suited to build privacy protection into their products. Data communication between components of the biometric system should be encrypted. Liveness detection techniques should be used to ensure appropriate collection of samples. Compliance with standards and certifications enhance trust in the system, and vendors need to be involved in this process. Education of users about what information is being collected by the biometric system is one of the most overlooked aspects of addressing privacy concerns. For example, it is important to explain to users if their fingerprint images or templates being stored will prevent potential misuse of information in case of a data theft. It is similarly important to reassure them that the data collection entity follows best privacy practices. Further, the portrayal of biometrics in television programs and movies is one of the most common sources of information about biometrics for the everyday person, and that portrayal is quite often inaccurate. Another concern is misinformation about the workings of the biometric system because designers are forced to address citizens' and others' perceptions of biometric systems, whether those perceptions are accurate or not. For example, iris recognition systems take an image of the iris using infrared illumination that is not harmful to the eye, but it is a common misconception that lasers are always harmful to the eyes.

CONCLUSION

Biometrics systems are here to stay and are undoubtedly going to be more frequently used in the future. Questions about identity and authentication will become more important as the world population becomes more mobile and more resources are tied to online presence instead of physical world locations. As these changes continue to occur, crime and abuse will also continue to adapt to the changes and present an evolving challenge to authorities.

Privacy itself is a special property embraced by individuals of every culture, although often in a culture-specific manner. One of the truisms is that good security—both as technical protections and as official responses, e.g., law enforcement—must exist to provide assurance of privacy. Someone without protections and without recourse to official aid cannot be certain of privacy. Thus, we must have strong security measures in place to protect the privacy interests of everyone.

One of the challenges in protecting privacy, however, is that any attempt to ensure absolute security is itself likely to result in egregious privacy violations. Collection of too much information is itself a violation of some of the same privacy principles that law enforcement officials may be seeking to protect. As noted by Spafford and Antón (2008), it is critical that users, designers, and policy makers discuss the "big picture" of how far we should go in compromising privacy to deter crime and bad behavior rather than face instances after the fact. The relentless pace of technological change will not stop simply because we have fallen behind in policy formation.

REFERENCES

Breebaart, J., C. Busch, J. Grave, and E. Kindt. 2008. A reference architecture for biometric template protection based on pseudo identities. In *BIOSIG 2008, Special Interest Group on Biometrics and Electronic Signatures*, 25–37. Darmstadt, Germany: Springer LNCS.

Downing, C., and J. Daugman. 2001. Epigenetic randomness, complexity and singularity of human iris patterns. *Proceedings of the Royal Society of London. Series B: Biological Sciences* 268, no. 1477: 1737–40. http://rspb.royalsocietypublishing.org/content/268/1477/1737.abstract.

European Union. 2008. *Trusted revocable biometric identities.*

Information System Audit and Control Association. 2007. *G36 Biometric controls.* Rolling Meadows, IL.

International Standards Organization. 2006. *ISO/IEC 19795-1: Information technology—Biometric performance testing and reporting—Part 1: Principles and framework*, 56. Geneva: ISO/IEC.

Jain, Anil K. 2007. Biometric recognition. *Nature*, 449: 38–40. http://www.nature. com/nature/journal/v449/n7158/pdf/449038a.pdf.

National Science and Technology Council Subcommittee on Biometrics. 2006. The national biometrics challenge. National Science and Technology Council. http:// www.biometrics.gov/Documents/biochallengedoc.pdf.

NSTIC. 2010. Available online from DHS as http://www.dhs.gov/xlibrary/assets/ ns_tic.pdf.

Prabhakar, S., D. Maltoni, D. Maio, and A. Jain. 2003. *Handbook of fingerprint recognition*, 2nd ed. Springer.

Spafford, E. H., and A. I. Antón. 2008. The balance between security and privacy. In *Controversies in science and technology*, vol. II, ed. D. L. Kleinman, K. A. Cloud-Hansen, C. Matta, and J. Handelsman, 152–68. New York: Mary Ann Liebert.

7

Emerging Privacy and Security Concerns for Digital Wallet Deployment

Andrew Harris, Frank S. Park,
Seymour Goodman, and Patrick Traynor
Georgia Institute of Technology, Atlanta

The mobile phone is now a ubiquitous device in virtually every corner of the globe. The widespread adoption of mobile phones has made them a necessity in personal, business, and governmental affairs. Cell phones are used not only for phone calls but also to send email, surf the web, manage daily calendars, store contact information, keep personal photos, play games, and perform a host of other activities. The utility of such a product does not come without a price. Mobile phones and their users are just as susceptible to the ills that plague the Internet such as phishing, malware, and personal data collection. The dangers are greater on a cell phone, however, since the portability of the device makes it easily lost or stolen. Further, mobile devices' limitations on processing power and battery life inhibit the ability to deploy any applications that require frequent monitoring or transmission, such as the conventional antivirus and host-based malware detection systems. This limitation means that much of the information associated with cell phones is more susceptible to theft, snooping, and alteration than that of personal computers.

As societies continue to integrate cell phones into every aspect of life and work, the potential privacy and security problems only grow. Payment by mobile phone is rapidly becoming the next significant use of mobile phones in daily life (Sutter 2009). Successful test runs have been applied worldwide, and the method has become common in Japan and Korea. Although there are multiple methods cell phones use to complete consumers' transactions, the

This material is based upon work supported by the National Science Foundation under Grant No. 0911886. Any opinions, findings, and conclusions or recommendations expressed in this material are those of the author(s) and do not necessarily reflect the views of the National Science Foundation. Research for this study was also made possible through the support of the Science Applications International Corporation (SAIC).

model most likely to be employed uses Near Field Communication (NFC) technology, a form of Radio Frequency Identification (RFID). NFC-enabled phones allow users to purchase goods by waving their phones directly in front of NFC readers that initiate a user authentication. The integration of consumer credit and banking capabilities with mobile phones adds substantial privacy and security concerns to the relatively vulnerable platform. In this chapter, we seek to explore the proposed pay-by-mobile ecosystem, analyzing both the technical and policy gaps that leave users vulnerable. By offering a critical examination of the proposed models before they are fully implemented, we hope to offer substantive solutions to a set of problems in order to ensure a safe and useful platform once fully deployed. Further, we believe these solutions will improve the security of the mobile phone's payment abilities and of a wider range of potential uses.

ENABLING TECHNOLOGY

Near Field Communication

Near Field Communication is a short-range communication technology that enables data exchange between two devices within extremely close proximity. Because NFC is an extension of the ISO 14443 proximity card standards used by RFID, this section will focus primarily on its predecessor. Radio Frequency Identification is a contactless identification that uses radio frequency. Current applications of RFID include supply chain logistics, livestock tracking, and electronic highway toll collection. Unlike NFC, RFID can be used for distances up to and exceeding fifty feet. NFC's distance bounding capability, however, allows security-relevant applications such as building access keys (HID Global n.d.), financial credentials (American Express n.d.; Speedpass n.d.), and event or temporary tickets.

There are two RFID components: a reader and a tag. A reader interrogates available tags, which provide any stored information, usually a unique ID. A tag can be powered either by the reader's emitting electromagnetic energy (passive mode) or through its own power source (active mode). Because active mode has significantly more electric current available, it can communicate from much farther from the reader than can a tag in passive mode. Both modes commonly communicate over 13.56 MHz and use either inductive coupling or backscatter coupling methods to acquire information from the tag (Finkenzeller 2003).

Inductive coupling is used "near-field" when the distance between the reader and the tag does not exceed 0.16 of the wavelength, approximately 3.54 meters at 13.56 MHz. Through inductive coupling, a tag is powered

Magnetic Field

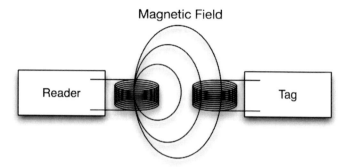

Figure 7.1. Inductive coupling.

using the electromagnetic field that crosses through the coil area. The communication between the devices is done by altering the reader's emitting energy from the magnetic field using a load resistor that switches on or off based on the data it is transmitting. A reader can observe the effects of amplitude modulation of the antenna voltage and receive the transferred data. Backscatter coupling uses the concept of RADAR technology by using the reflection of the electromagnetic waves. Through lessons learned from RADAR technology, we know that an object that is bigger than half of the wavelength is reflected back. Using this theory, a dipole antenna is used by the tag to capture energy for powering on the device. Other power sources can be used (active mode) in lieu of the emitted energy. Similar to the inductive coupling, a tag alters the reflection characteristics by switching on and off the load resistor based on queried data. A received reflection can be observed by the reader to check the deviation from the expected reflection characteristics to gather transmitted data.

Unlike the RFID and the Bluetooth technologies that are already deployed and commonly used today, NFC offers a distance-bounded capability that limits its accessibility to much shorter range of transmission, up to 20 cm. This fea-

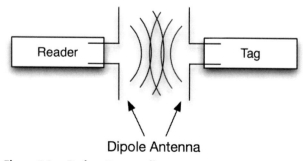

Dipole Antenna

Figure 7.2. Backscatter coupling.

ture ensures that no two devices will establish communication unless explicitly placed next to each other and enables the use of such devices in a crowded area where multiple tags may be present. In addition, the manual configuration of the initial pairing between two Bluetooth devices can be eliminated using NFC, simplifying the initialization of the device communication. NFC also offers both active and passive modes, which not only consume less battery power than that of Bluetooth but also allow the device to communicate with nonpowered devices like smart posters and other contactless smartcards.

RFID technology has created controversies among some users with concerns of such devices' releasing information without the knowledge of the user. A third party could potentially interrogate an RFID tag in order to keep track of a user's movements and infer the user's interests and activities. A well-designed supporting application and proper implementation of the NFC feature on mobile devices will, however, have a switching capability that turns the tag off unless explicitly turned on by the user. An adequately encrypted over-the-air communication along with mutual authentication, when powered on, can secure the physical channel of NFC communication and eliminate unsolicited transmission.

Credit Card Infrastructure

More than $1.75 trillion in purchases were made in 2009 in the United States (Nilson Report 2010), and credit cards are one of the most commonly used forms of payment. The country's high reliance on the credit card infrastructure makes it necessary for this technology to be available at all times and to provide an adequate level of security and privacy for the use of such infrastructure. In response to this expectation, credit card companies have deployed many security features in both the infrastructure and the method of fiscal transactions through various forms of electronic credentials and Personal Identification Numbers (PINs). Despite this effort, both forms of electronic credentials (the magnetic strip and Europay, MasterCard, and VISA [EMV] cards) are vulnerable, as shown through numerous documented attacks (Zetter 2009; Drimer and Murdoch 2007).

In the United States, almost every credit card uses a magnetic strip to store credential information. This strip contains pertinent information to automate the transaction at the retail register. Such information includes the account number, the cardholder's name, and the card's expiration date, and can be read by almost any magnetic reader without any authentication or decryption. This openness to private information allows virtually anyone who has a magnetic reader to capture credential information that can be reused simply by replicating the magnetic strip on another card. In fact, research shows that the primary sources of credit card fraud include card cloning (making physical copies of a card), card skimming (capturing credit card numbers as they are read), and transaction replay (making the same charge multiple times at the expense of the client) (Smart Card Alliance 2009). These vulnerabilities emerge mainly because the magnetic strips are easily read and duplicated with little cost to criminals. To address control of credentials and eliminate reusability, many foreign countries have adopted a technology named after the letters of Europay, MasterCard, and VISA (EMV), also known as Chip-and-PIN (EMVCo n.d.). This method uses a smart card embedded on the traditional credit card that issues a unique digital signature for the authorizing transaction based on the PIN entered at the terminal.

Although the introduction of the Chip-and-PIN has shown improvement in security based on the reports from the Smart Card Alliance, a recent study has shown that, while fraud from lost and stolen cards is down, the overall fraud level has increased (Murdoch et al. 2010). Criminals shifted their efforts to methods of fraud other than fabrication of the stolen card. Some have started targeting the U.S. credit card infrastructure because of the lack of Chip-and-PIN deployment. This rising threat to the United States has further increased the need to replace the existing magnetic-card-based systems with other secure systems. In response, U.S. financial industries have started deploying contactless payment methods, which generate a dynamic signature similar to that of the EMV. However, this implementation has already led to several well-documented attacks (Heydt-Benjamin et al. 2007; Juels 2005), which highlight the need for further evaluation.

Smart Card

A smart card is a small, integrated circuit that is typically embedded on a plastic surface. This device is commonly used in the United States as a subscriber identity module, or SIM card, which is inserted in all GSM-based cell phones; GSM stands for Global System for Mobile Communication and is the most widely used mobile phone standard worldwide. Its tamper resistance and ability to provide confidentiality of stored information make this device ideal for authentication and storing other digital credentials. In addition, a smart card is capable of performing cryptographic functions that can generate a unique signature with nonrepudiation properties. Current applications of smart cards include ATM or credit cards (EMV), high-security access control cards, health care identity cards (Smart Card Applications 2010), and other identification cards that can store an encrypted digital certificate for external use, such as secure disk storage, authentication, and encryption.

A contactless smart card uses both the RFID and smart card technology to offer the security of the smart card while communicating over the air using

RFID or NFC. Such devices are widely deployed around the world for public transportation tolls because of their quick and convenient accessibility (MI-FARE.net n.d.; MARTA n.d.). The security of this technology, however, has been tested and found to be vulnerable to potential cloning and replay attacks (Garcia et al. 2009). Although the chip provides many security features, researchers have found crude attacks aimed at retrieving private information from the chip. In one such attack, researchers were able discover the encryption/decryption algorithms used by the smart card simply by analyzing the electrical current used by the smart card. Also, other attacks include physically destroying parts of the card to gain access to the secure segments of the memory.

For the last several years, smart cards have been used in many security-related applications. Because of this deployment, smart cards have undergone a handful of security tests that have found the device to be quite secure unless physically tampered with. Other attacks are related to trusting the terminal that the smart card is connected to and users' inability to verify the authenticity of the terminal they are using to enter the PIN.

Digital Wallet—Convergence of Technologies

The digital wallet application combines all the technologies mentioned above to offer consumers a single device that can integrate many of the items that one typically carries (such as a phone, wallet, and payment media). NFC-equipped mobile devices will provide physical communication channels between a reader and the device. This physical layer establishes communication and provides adequate power for nonpowered devices when used in reader mode. In the application layer, a smart card (in GSM phones) is used to store and provide proper credentials based on the context in which the authentication is required (credit card or building access). Service providers, such as credit card issuing banks, can then authorize or reject the transaction based on the cryptographic data presented by the smart card. A cell phone's interface may also be used in lieu of the point-of-sale terminal to reduce threats associated with malicious terminals that can log PINs and credit card numbers for future use. There are several other entities involved to support the digital wallet infrastructure, such as the trusted service manager, which is discussed below.

Digital Wallet Uses—An NFC-enabled mobile phone has a small and relatively inexpensive NFC chip embedded within allowing the phone to communicate with point-of-sale (POS) terminals, subway turnstiles, and even "smart" posters advertising specific products or events. A mobile phone's display and input buttons will allow the consumer to perform transactions, interact with bank accounts, and access transportation information immediately, thus providing even greater levels of convenience. For instance, after purchasing a subway ticket using the phone's over-the-air (OTA) capabilities, the customer can pass through the turnstile by waving her phone past an NFC reader and also access trains' arrival and departure times and interact with a system map. The same goes for financial transactions. A consumer who has arranged for his debit card to be accessible through his mobile phone can make purchases, both large and small, by simply waving his phone past an NFC-reading POS terminal and inputting an authenticating PIN. The history of this transaction, along with all of his other account information, can now be viewed and even managed on the same phone that initiated the purchase. Of further note, just as customers can interact with banks via their NFC-enabled phone, they can also interact with retailers. For instance, a retailer might post a product advertisement with an embedded NFC chip. When the customer taps the poster, product information and discounts would then be accessible through the phone. A retail center with numerous smart posters or kiosks can provide opportunities for the consumer as well as allowing retailers to directly interact with customers through the digital wallet (NFC Forum 2008).

The NFC Ecosystem—An NFC-enabled mobile phone system comprises multiple players. On the side of the physical device, mobile network operators, handset manufacturers, and the producers of the various necessary chips—near-field communication, the universal integrated circuit chip (SIM card for GSM phones only), and integrated circuit—will each play a vital role in creating a usable NFC phone. Card Issuing Banks (CIBs), merchants, acquirers, payment solution companies, and POS terminal manufactures comprise the payment side. Completing the ecosystem is, of course, the customer (GSM Association 2007). Other actors likely to engage in the system are marketers and adversaries such as identity thieves.

Among the entities of this ecosystem that are of greatest concern for this study are the mobile network operators and CIBs. These are the respective central actors on the device and financial sides of the ecosystem. By their nature, mobile network operators and CIBs also possess the most sensitive user data and would serve as the primary distributors of these data for the provision of services and marketing. Since proposed NFC models call for payments to be processed using the current infrastructure, this chapter assumes that little will change from the point where a purchase is initiated with a merchant through the end of the processing of the payment. Whatever flaws might occur in this process, it is assumed that they are present regardless of the method of payment and are outside the scope of this chapter. Therefore, on the financial side of the ecosystem, this chapter will focus primarily on the CIB that enables the consumer to initiate an NFC payment. Similarly, while device and chip manufactures are vital in the creation of the NFC ecosystem, none of the entities will deal directly with the customer and her personal information. Therefore, on the device side of the system we will focus on the mobile network operators and their relationship with the customer.

In order to complete an NFC ecosystem, it will be necessary to create a new entity to facilitate the merger of the physical device and banking institutions. This new entity, the Trusted Service Manager (TSM), will perform a host of duties. The TSM will primarily manage the NFC-payment application and ensure the security of financial transactions. Further, the TSM will serve as an intermediary between the CIB and the mobile network operator (GSM Association 2007c). Because no one NFC model has yet been agreed upon, there is no consensus as to who will play the role of the TSM. A third party could perform these tasks, as could the mobile network operator or CIB (GSM Association 2007a). Since the TSM will not be responsible for the actual transaction, it is not necessary for a financial institution to perform this role. The TSM will, however, be a repository for sensitive personal information.

Within such an ecosystem, trust among all parties is crucial. The CIB's ability to issue new credentials and an application to the mobile SIM card requires the mobile network operator's trust that the application will behave as expected without affecting the underlying cellular infrastructure. Reciprocally, the CIB must be able to trust that the mobile network operator will ensure a level of security on all data exchanged over the air. Offloading sensitive data to be stored in the TSM may assist in increasing the trust between the two parties. The ultimate control of the TSM stored device, however, depends on the entity that manages the role of the TSM. Regardless of the TSM's managing party, the essential elements of the NFC ecosystem are represented in figure 7.3.

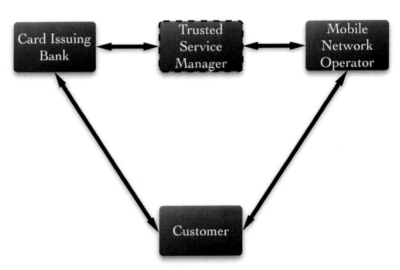

Figure 7.3.   NFC ecosystem.

PUBLIC POLICY CONCERNS

Data Flow

The digital wallet uses described above provide convenience to consumers as well as extensive marketing opportunities to retailers and service providers. Industry papers proposing an NFC-enabled mobile phone system have not been shy about this point. One describes the possibility as "a marketer's dream come true, opening up a world of new possibilities for 'high touch' value-added services" (Gemalto 2008, 5). Another proclaims that, "Consumers can also receive instant and specialized offers based on their shopping patterns and enjoy benefits provided by retailers and financial institutions based on their profiles and lifestyle choices" (Smart Card Alliance 2007, 15). None of these marketing opportunities would be possible without extensive data collection and sharing among phone companies, financial institutions, and marketers. The "profiles and lifestyle choices" refers to a consumer database that compiles a consumer's behavior—such as types, times, and place of purchases—allowing marketers to send advertising believed relevant. As can be seen, two significant problems arise in the NFC-enabled mobile phone system. First, a consumer's financial records and other personal information would be integrated with a device possessing known vulnerabilities. Second, the opportunity for targeted advertising portends the extensive collection and sharing of personal information.

As mentioned earlier, the NFC-enabled mobile phone is a "marketer's dream." Such a device provides marketers the opportunity to develop user-specific advertising delivered to a most personal interface—the mobile phone. A marketer fully integrated into the ecosystem described above would seek to obtain a consumer's purchasing record from the CIB, relevant phone and NFC records from the mobile network operator, and personal preferences supplied directly by the consumer via the smart posters with which he interacts (see figure 7.4).

Compiling such information would then allow marketers to develop accurate personal profiles that would inform the most effective advertisements for that consumer. While this situation may represent a marketer's dream, it presents thorny issues of privacy for the consumer, especially since the consumer is likely to be unaware that such personal information is being collected and shared.

The collection and use of such personal information is problematic on multiple levels. Primarily, it represents an invasion of privacy that many would find disconcerting. Further, collection of personal and sensitive information can expose an individual to fraud or misrepresentation. The sharing of personal information bred by an NFC-enabled mobile phone system means that information about a device owner would become more widely collected and

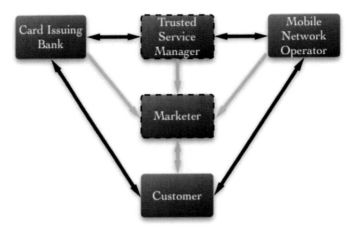

Figure 7.4.   NFC ecosystem with integrated marketers.

held, potentially increasing incidents of data theft and profiling leading to identity theft. This concern is demonstrated in figure 7.5, in which the lighter arrows represent possible origins for data breaches, malicious or inadvertent.

Any NFC-enabled mobile phone system poses questions regarding the security and privacy of the device owner's personal information. By their nature, banks and phone companies obtain significant levels of sensitive data about their customers. These data are potentially valuable to marketers—es-

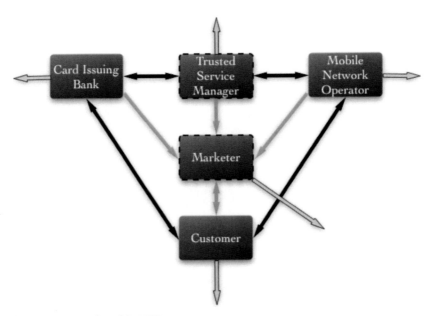

Figure 7.5.   A vulnerable NFC ecosystem.

pecially when the financial and communication services are merged—and parties with fraudulent intent. It is therefore vital that a proper regulatory system be in place to protect individuals against theft and abuse of such personal information.

The American regulatory system presents numerous problems and in its present state is a matter of concern should the public widely adopt an NFC-enabled phone system. While most developed nations provide citizens with protection of personal information through one comprehensive law, the United States offers a sectoral approach in which various industries are regulated through different laws, each with its own standards of security and privacy. Further, with regard to how personal information is marketed to third parties, the American system places the burden on the consumers who typically have to opt out of any data-sharing schemes. Privacy advocates prefer an opt-in system in which "an individual's personal information cannot be used, say, for marketing unless that person gives affirmative consent" (Givens 2009).

The Financial Sector

The Gramm-Leach-Bliley Act (GLBA) or The Financial Services Modernization Act of 1999 (Public Law 106-102) provides financial institutions with guidelines regarding the security and privacy of personal information. Specifically, Title V of the act places three requirements upon institutions in the handling of their customer's personal information (United States 1999). First, institutions must securely store and actively protect confidential information. Second, these institutions are required to inform customers regarding the sharing of personal information with third parties. Finally, banks must offer customers the opportunity to opt out of third-party sharing of certain personal information (EPIC n.d., b). The law's allowance for data sharing poses the greatest threat for the NFC-enabled mobile phone system.

For the purpose of GLBA, nonpublic personal information is any information provided directly to the institution by the customer, any transaction information, or any other information the financial institution obtains (Stevens 2009). Financial institutions may share this nonpublic personal information with any affiliated company without the consent of the customer, while customers must be given the opportunity to opt out of sharing with any nonaffiliated third party. There are exceptions to this opt-out requirement, however. If the financial institution is engaged in a joint marketing venture with a third party or if the third party is providing services on behalf of the institution, then financial institutions may share personal information without providing the customer an opportunity to opt out. Third parties are restricted from further sharing of personal information.

In the NFC mobile phone system, both mobile network operators and marketing firms would classify as nonaffiliated third parties, leading to an opt-out requirement for any information sharing. The exceptions noted above, however, would likely allow card-issuing banks to consider mobile network operators and marketers as joint venture partners or service providers. The mobile network operator is engaged in a joint venture with the CIB while marketers perform the service of providing product and services information to the consumer. It is therefore likely that GLBA will allow the card-issuing bank to share personal information with the mobile network operator and marketers without allowing the customer to opt out of the sharing scheme. This circumstance means that transaction histories and demographic information could be freely shared among the members of the NFC mobile phone system.

GLBA does provide more adequate direction regarding the physical security of the consumer data that financial institutions compile and maintain. As mentioned earlier, security is one of the primary requirements listed in Title V of GLBA. Various agencies overseeing the financial institutions have written and implemented security guidelines for entities under their supervision. These guidelines require financial institutions to sufficiently and periodically assess risks and implement appropriate security measures, including staff training (Stevens 2009). Further safeguarding data about consumers' is the Payment Card Industry Data Security Standard (PCI DSS). This industry association requires that all bank cards adhere to particular security guidelines, including how data should be stored (PCI Security Standards Council n.d.). Although this system of government and industry regulation is not without flaws, it provides a reasonable level of security that would apply to an NFC framework. The greater regulatory concern lies with the sharing of personal information discussed earlier.

The regulatory system offered by GLBA provides consumers with inadequate protection of personal information. By allowing financial institutions to share data with affiliates and exempted third parties without allowing consumers to opt out, the law ensures a steady flow of personal information from banks to marketers. Even when institutions must provide the consumer a chance to limit data sharing, it is only through opting out, which places the burden on the consumer. Further, the opaque language of most privacy policies tends to confuse the average consumer and discourage opting out. This flow of personal information is likely only to increase as the use of NFC-based systems becomes more common. While some states, most notably California, have pushed back against the lack of consumer protection by requiring banks to receive consent *before* sharing personal data, the lack of a single comprehensive law protecting personal information leaves an environment ready for abuse should an NFC-enabled mobile phone system be implemented (EPIC n.d., b).

The Telecommunications Sector

U.S. policies regarding the manner in which telephone companies may share information about customers provide a greater level of protection than those related to the financial industry. The Telecommunications Act of 1996 (PL 104-104, 110 Stat. 56) amended the Communications Act of 1934 to include protections for customers' privacy. Section 222 sets out to explicitly define personal telephonic records and establish rules for the sharing of that information. The provision defines Customer Proprietary Network Information (CPNI) as:

> Information that relates to the quantity, technical configuration, type, destination, location, and amount of use of a telecommunications service subscribed to by any customer of a telecommunications carrier, and that is made available to the carrier by the customer solely by virtue of the carrier-customer relationship.

The Act also stipulates that any information contained in a customer's bill is also considered CPNI (section 222, h.1). Section 222 further describes how this information can be used and how it must be protected.

Generally, section 222 allows telephone companies to share CPNI in only three instances: when required by law, with a customer's approval, and in the provision of services (Ruane 2008). These general regulations were first clarified in 1998 when the Federal Communications Commission issued its CPNI Order. In this order, the FCC required that telephone companies obtain express consent from customers before sharing any CPNI for marketing purposes—an opt-in requirement. The ruling was opposed by the phone companies and eventually overturned by the 10th Circuit Court of Appeals in *U.S. West v. FCC*. Forced to reissue CPNI directives, the FCC altered regulations to require phone companies to receive opt-in consent from customers before sharing CPNI with any noncommunication affiliates and all third parties while allowing for opt-out consent when sharing information with "affiliated parties, joint venture partners, and independent contractors" (Ruane 2008, 7).

The FCC's weakening of privacy standards prompted privacy advocates such as EPIC to lobby the Commission to reconsider the rules regarding CPNI. In 2007, CPNI standards were altered again, this time tightening the regulations on phone companies. Whereas the FCC's previous regulations allowed the sharing of information with joint venture partners and independent contractors, the 2007 directive required phone companies to receive prior consent from customers before sharing with these entities. Only sharing with communication-related affiliates was permitted on an opt-out basis. While the ruling itself stands alone as an acknowledgment that the FCC was seeking to guard consumers' privacy, the ruling also explicitly stated this belief:

While many customers accept and understand that carriers will share their information with affiliates and agents—as provided in our existing opt-out rules—there is less customer willingness for their information to be shared without their express authorization with others outside the carrier-customer relationship. (FCC 2007)

The 2007 ruling also provided significant regulations regarding phone companies' duties regarding the secure protection of CPNI. The order placed responsibility squarely in the hands of the telephone company, ruling that safeguards such as passwords and PINs must be used when customers access CPNI. Further, stored data must be actively and adequately protected. While the order acknowledges that data encryption is one such protection method, the FCC did not require that encryption be used. Therefore, the particular method of security is not dictated, only requiring that companies employ some adequate method.

The FCC's latest ruling on CPNI was challenged again by the phone companies, but a Federal Appeals Court in Washington, DC, ruled in early 2009 that the FCC's opt-in requirements met the spirit of section 222 and could remain in place (EPIC n.d., a). Therefore, the current regulations clearly define personal information, require phone companies to obtain consent before sharing personal information with any nonaffiliated entity, and force phone companies to properly secure personal information. While the current standards certainly provide consumers with a greater level of protection than those regulating the financial industry, the prospect of a pay-by-mobile system offers potential problems nonetheless.

The first issue one must consider concerns the definition of personal information. As mentioned above, section 222 clearly defines the information collected by phone companies and labels it CPNI. However, the definition states that CPNI is data collected in the provision of telecommunications services. So while call data clearly fall under this category, it is not clear that the pay-by-mobile service would be properly classified as a telecommunications service simply because it is provided by a telecommunications company. This particular wording might allow phone companies to view pay-by-mobile data as information collected in the provision of nontelecommunications services and thus not restricted as CPNI.

A second concern regards the opt-in requirement for data sharing. While privacy advocates prefer opt in, the FCC rulings do not adequately describe the manner in which consent must be obtained. This lack of specificity allows phone companies to obtain consent with murky language that is buried in a broader, equally confusing service agreement. Thus, phone companies have the opportunity to obtain consent for data sharing without the customers knowing he has given such consent.

Regarding the security of personal data, since the FCC does not require stored data to be encrypted or protected by any other particular technology, current regulations leave data vulnerable once a pay-by-mobile system is adopted. The additional sensitive information that will be available to phone companies in this system makes any collected yet inadequately protected information especially vulnerable.

Finally, even though the rules for phone companies provide some protection for consumers, this protection is obviated by the weak link of financial institution regulations discussed earlier. The most sensitive and valuable data are collected by the banks and any other entity engaging the NFC consumer (merchants and marketers using smart posters). Since these entities can share data with few restrictions, the flow of information is ensured regardless of the restrictions placed on the mobile network operator.

Data Brokers

Personal data created through digital wallet transactions can legally be shared among stakeholders without much awareness or control by consumers. Facing even less regulation than the telecommunication companies and financial institutions are the data brokers that currently engage in collecting and selling the data (e.g., shopping habits, web-browsing habits, and the like) of nearly all consumers. Many of these data brokers have been responsible for the loss and theft of significant amounts of personal data. Notoriously, ChoicePoint inadvertently sold personal information of nearly 150,000 individuals to data thieves in 2005 (Solove and Hoofnagle 2006). As mentioned earlier, the mobile wallet creates excellent opportunities for marketers to deliver targeted advertisements directly to the personal device that consumers will use to make purchases. The high incentives to do so make the work of data brokers particularly valuable. However, the American sectoral approach to privacy rights leaves data brokers an unregulated entity. According to Sarah Ludington of Duke Law School, this lack of regulation allows brokers "to sell personal information without the consent of the subject, to deny individuals information about the quantity or categories of lists that contain their information, and to deny any requests to remove personal information from these lists" (2007, 143). In place of federal regulation, data brokers employ a regime of self-regulation, the Individual Reference Services Group Principles. These principles, however, offer little protection to consumers and allow brokers to sell private information "without restriction" (Solove and Hoofnagle, 365).

While data brokers are already engaged in building data dossiers about individuals, the employment of the digital wallet would provide these brokers with even more data. Under current regulations, data brokers could purchase personal information collected by card-issuing banks (CIBs) and mobile network operators only if the consumer had granted prior approval. Because the generated information would allow data brokers to build even more accurate dossiers, the incentives will be high to seek to purchase such data from banks and phone companies. The banks and phone companies will in turn be motivated to secure the permission of customers to share their data. While permission must be explicitly granted, the ability to use long and confusing privacy statements makes such approval a relatively simple task for the CIBs and mobile network operators. Once permission is obtained, data brokers will be able to purchase personal information and use it without regulatory oversight or control by consumers. The ability then of data brokers to further erode the privacy of digital wallet users is significant and must be considered prior to employment of digital wallets.

Addressing Public Policy Concerns

The pay-by-mobile system, which seems poised to shortly spread across the United States, will offer great convenience to consumers while significantly decreasing the security and privacy related to much of their sensitive information. A highly integrated pay-by-mobile system will offer sufficient incentives for marketers to obtain personal information from the various information-collecting entities in the ecosystem. This data sharing is facilitated by American regulations that allow corporations to engage in such activity, often with customers having little knowledge. The spreading of personal information across numerous corporations increases the likelihood that that information will be abused, stolen, or lost.

A pay-by-mobile system in the United States will be much safer for consumers if it is accompanied by a comprehensive national privacy policy that requires all entities to obtain consent—in a clear, unambiguous manner—before sharing personal information. Both Japan and Europe offer examples of comprehensive privacy policy instruments that protect personal information while still allowing for the responsible use of private information in the marketplace (Act on the Protection of Personal Information 2003; Directive 95/46/EC of the European Parliament 1995). A comprehensive privacy regime would ensure that consumers could use their digital wallet to purchase goods, ride public transportation, and interact with advertisements with confidence that the data generated through those transactions would not be bought, sold, or traded.

While there is no substitute for the strength of a national comprehensive privacy law for fulfilling the spirit of fair information practices, the passage of such a law is politically difficult. Should privacy advocates deem that entrenched corporate interests would prevent the passage of such a law, a strengthening of the current sectoral approach could greatly improve the protections afforded to consumers. By strengthening the relevant laws pertaining to CIBs and mobile network operators, Congress and federal regulators could help provide consumers with greater control over their personal information. As mentioned earlier, section 222 of the Telecommunication Act defines CPNI as data collected in the provision of telecommunications services. Since not all NFC transactions constitute the provision of telecommunications services, however, mobile network operators may have access to nonprotected information. Recognizing that the business of telecommunications companies is expanding, Congress can amend section 222 to define CPNI as any nonpublic information obtained by the carrier. This change would protect all data generated from NFC transactions obtained by mobile network operators. Further, in keeping with the spirit of section 222, the FCC can take two additional steps. First, privacy statements should be standardized according to a simple and digestible format. When mobile network operators ask a customer for permission to share information, the customer should know all the implications of that request. Second, the FCC can demand that mobile network operators encrypt or otherwise protect CPNI technologically. Such a regulation aligns with section 222's assignment of responsibility for personal information in the hands of telecommunications companies.

Congress could also take steps to improve the privacy protections in Title V of the GLBA. A simple amendment that requires financial institutions to obtain opt-in consent prior to sharing any personal information with any affiliate or third party would significantly strengthen consumers' privacy. As described earlier, the current law allows banks to share personal data with affiliates, joint marketing partners, or service providers without any consent from the consumer. In today's world of megabanks, these exceptions encompass a web of entities with legal accessibility to data about consumers. In the absence of a comprehensive national privacy regime, strengthening Title V of the GLBA is a necessity.

With the ability to collect, purchase, and sell data from and to numerous sources without federal regulation, data brokers must also be addressed in order to ensure a safe digital wallet platform. Any attempt to limit data trading must address the fact that individuals have no contractual relationship with brokers. They cannot simply call the customer service line of the numerous brokers collecting and sharing their data—primarily because the brokering is occurring without consumers' knowledge. Daniel Solove and Chris Jay Hoofnagle recently proposed a privacy protection regime to address the complications surrounding the nebulous data trade. A law to protect individuals from data brokers must require any collector of personal information to register with the FTC and notify individuals of their activities. Further, before using this data in any way, brokers must first obtain permission from individuals. A centralized do-not-share list should be created that would allow individuals to stop all personal data sharing with a single call. Finally, this centralized list should provide consumers with access to the collected information (Solove and Hoofnagle 2006). The digital wallet holds the potential for unprecedented data accumulation and sharing; in light of this fact, consumers' privacy relies on the willingness of political leaders to address data brokers.

Finally, digital wallet developers must consider sensible privacy statements designed specifically for mobile phones. Companies including Google are currently investing significantly in the development of phone-specific advertisements. These ads will be read on mobile phones and targeted to the consumers' locations and interests. Similar care should be put into developing privacy statements for mobile phones, particularly with the advent of the digital wallet. Nancy King of Oregon State University points out that current privacy statements are incomprehensible when viewed on a mobile phone. Long and legalistic, the documents make no sense when seen on a small screen. But with consumers using these devices to purchase goods and interact with marketers, it is essential that potential data collectors provide privacy statements directly on the mobile device. King (2008) therefore proposes a code for mobile phone privacy statements that recognizes the particular aspects of the device. Specifically, the statements should be multilayered, comprehensible, legally compliant, consistently formatted, and brief. It is doubtful that mobile advertisers will take such steps without federal requirements. Therefore, Congress, the Federal Trade Commission, and the Federal Communications Commission should act to ensure consumers are fairly informed about data collection and sharing resulting from the use of their mobile phones.

TECHNOLOGICAL SECURITY VULNERABILITIES OF CELL PHONES

Many of today's smart phones have architectures similar to those of personal computers. They are supported by known operating systems such as Linux and MacOS and use familiar platforms such as Java. Although most smart phones are fundamentally identical to the personal computer, cell phones face completely different threats for many reasons. Cell phones are rarely ever turned off and follow the user at all times. In addition to its near-constant proximity to its user, the device is always connected to a critical infrastructure, often employing various local networks using different communication channels such as WiFi and Bluetooth. Each cell phone typically has only one user, and most of the stored information is considered private (phonebooks, pictures, and email messages). Because of these differences, security tactics for cell phones require a dramatically different approach than that demanded by personal computers. This section of the chapter discusses various security concerns of mobile technology and introduces new and existing threats to digital wallet implementation as suggested by the industry.

Network/Communications Security

Many cell phones are now equipped with an array of communication channels, which include Cellular (GSM/CDMA), WiFi, Bluetooth, and GPS. Because of the various possible points of entry, mobile phones are targeted to aid propagation of malware to personal computers and other cell phones. Mobile phones are commonly connected to an enterprise network while at work, making them a perfect vehicle through which to bypass the traditional firewall set up at the border of the network.

There are a number of antivirus applications for mobile phones distributed by several vendors. Yet, these are simple extensions to existing desktop applications, which are mostly signature-based detection mechanisms. Unlike the situation with desktops and laptops, a simple task of scanning files for known signatures significantly drains the battery life of the cell phone, making this security strategy impractical. In order to offload such processing, researchers have suggested methods to send information about any particular activity on the cell phone to a known server for analysis (Cheng et al. 2007; Bose et al. 2008). A SIM card application that uses external resources, however, may go undetected using these detection methods.

A cellular network is built with a set of assumptions different than that of the Internet. Thus, the propagation characteristics of cellular malware differ from threats on the Internet and can burden the workload of the cellular infrastructure. In addition to malware propagation and denial of service attacks, there are potential attacks that can impose financial burdens on victims by initiating outbound calls to premium numbers and by sending unintended short message service (SMS) and medium message service (MMS). Such attacks can be used by spammers for voice, email, and SMS spamming.

Enhanced SIM Card

In order to enable existing phones to support NFC capability, the cell phone industry has proposed adding required hardware on the SIM card, for GSM network, or on the media card, for CDMA network (GSM Association 2007b). Such enhanced devices are equipped with their own processors and the memory storage to independently support wireless transmission and pertinent applications. In addition to storing nonvolatile data such as the application, memory storage will be used to store all the credentials needed to enable the application. The types of credentials stored on the device include financial, building access, and temporary access credentials. Because an NFC-enabled phone would contain a user's most sensitive personal information that can potentially jeopardize physical security, secure storage of this information is vital. Each NFC-enabled phone would contain a Secure Element (SE) that "hosts the firewall applications and user credentials, and controls security and cryptography using an onboard microprocessor and software" (Gemalto 2008, 5). The SE may be included within the SIM card (on GSM phones) or on a separate embedded chip.

The SIM card is currently used in GSM networks to securely store a unique International Mobile Subscriber Identity (IMSI) and an authentication key (K_i) that is used to identify the subscriber on the mobile device. The SIM card is designed not to allow the release of sensitive information such as K_i but rather to provide an indirect cryptographic response to the challenges that the authenticator requests. This property enables the mobile device using the SIM card to answer any challenges received by the mobile network operator without ever knowing the key stored in the SIM card. Despite a handful of security features provided by the SIM card, researchers have been able to compromise the SIM card to recover the authentication key, enabling attackers to duplicate the credential for attacks (Hack Watch 1999; Smartcard Developers Association 1998). Using these methods to store credentials to support NFC on a SIM card may create vulnerabilities similar to those that can compromise the authentication key, making the security of SIM card storage questionable.

In addition to the vulnerability that exists in storage, the enhanced version of SIM will be equipped with sufficient processing power to execute more complex applications than previously possible. This increase in processing power would allow potential attackers to install malware in the SIM card, executed using an external processor and memory, bypassing any security detection that may be installed on the mobile device. The installed SIM application will have access to many functions native to the mobile device, such as the ability to control radio transmissions, send SMS, and initiate voice calls. Attackers can use these functions to leak personal information (such as credentials, phonebooks, and call logs) stored in the SIM card or on the device.

Public Awareness

Although there are many technical vulnerabilities that may compromise mobile devices, many attacks can be mitigated by educating users. Almost every application installation requires human interaction and explicit consent before installing. Despite warnings, studies have shown that a majority of the users blindly approve the installation of malware when given legitimate-looking messages. For this reason, many mobile devices now require code signing before applications are authorized for installation on a device. Although this mechanism reduces unauthorized downloads, other methods of propagation exist that do not require application installation. A user with the ability to detect malicious or unexpected behavior can significantly reduce the effectiveness of malware; therefore, educating users must complement technical mitigation of security threats.

Securing the Digital Wallet

Research in personal computers strives for faster performance and smaller size. The same computing power that once required equipment that filled an entire room now fits in the palm of a user's hand, while processing power has followed Moore's law. This exponential growth has always surpassed the advancement of security that protects the device and the user. As the reliance on technologies such as mobile phones increases, the level of damage caused by a security breach affects not only the privacy of users but also the physical security of the assets that are digitally protected.

Reaching 100 percent security is impossible. But available security features should provide a large number of possible combinations to increase the workload of any attackers. Many users increase their vulnerability to attack through their lack of technological understanding as well as a high level of trust when interacting with other parties. Therefore, public education campaigns are vital to deterring criminal activity online. In addition to public education to identify illegitimate devices, there should be a mechanism to mutually authenticate the legitimacy of communicating devices and an alerting system to notify the user before the user discloses her private information.

Currently, the proposed implementation of digital wallets introduces additional hardware to mobile devices: the NFC transmitter, the enabling platform for the applications, and secure storage. Although SIM cards provide an adequate level of secure storage, the interacting devices may not provide the equivalent level of security. Regardless, the user expects security when indirectly interacting with the SIM card. This vulnerability has not yet been a threat mainly because most users do not interact with the secure storage of the SIM card daily. Digital wallets will significantly increase the level of users' interaction with the card, requiring authentication and the establishment of a secure channel. Such mechanisms are required to provide protection from unauthorized applications.

CONCLUSION

The dangers of the digital wallet, or pay-by-mobile system, illustrate only one example of the privacy and security concerns associated with mobile phones. As these devices become repositories of more and more personal information and increasingly integrated in numerous aspects of everyday life, we as a society open the door to significant harm. The devices on which we have come to rely so greatly are quickly becoming vulnerable targets for those who choose to exploit these weaknesses. Whether targeted for identity theft, personal tracking, targeted advertising, snooping, or spying, cell phones provide an open and accessible window into our lives. What is more, the high commercial incentives associated with mobile technology add to an environment of continuously degraded personal privacy. Many individuals will gladly accept this loss of privacy in exchange for new services and conveniences. But without a robust reconsideration of federal privacy laws, those individuals who wish to protect their privacy will be left with fewer means to do so. The pay-by-mobile system provides an excellent opportunity to imagine the potential of mobile technology while demonstrating that we are inadequately prepared to fully enjoy those possibilities. It is therefore essential that we understand both the opportunities and the dangers presented by these devices. The safe and responsible deployment of emerging mobile technologies requires not only additional understanding but also the willingness of government, corporations, and civil society to confront these challenges expeditiously.

REFERENCES

Act on the Protection of Personal Information. 2003, May 30. Government of Japan. *Law Number 57.* Tokyo.

American Express. n.d. *American Express.* Retrieved March 19, 2010, from https://www124.americanexpress.com/cards/loyalty.do?page=expresspay

Bose, Abhijit, Xin Hu, Kang G. Shin, and Taejoon Park. 2008. Behavioral detection of malware on mobile handsets. *Proceeding of the 6th international conference on mobile systems, applications, and services,* 225–38. New York: ACM.

Cheng, Jerry, Starsky H. Y. Wong, Hao Yang, and Songwu Lu. 2007. SmartSiren: Virus detection and alert for smartphones. *Proceedings of the 5th international conference on mobile systems, applications, and services (MobiSys),* 258–71. New York: ACM.

Communications Act of 1934 as amended by the Telecommunications Act of 1996. 1996, March. Public Law 104-104, 110 Stat. 56.

Directive 95/46/EC of the European Parliament and of the Council of 24 October 1995 on the protection of individuals with regard to the processing of personal data and on the free movement of such data. 1995, November 23. *Official Journal of the European Communities.*

Drimer, Saar, and Steven J. Murdoch. 2007. Keep your enemies close: Distance bounding against smartcard relay attacks. *Proceedings of 16th USENIX security symposium on usenix security.* Boston: USENIX Association.

EMVCo. n.d.. Retrieved January 10, 2010, from EMVCo: http://www.emvco.com

EPIC. n.d. *CPNI (Customer Proprietary Network Information).* Retrieved July 19, 2009, from EPIC: http://epic.org/privacy/cpni/#overview

EPIC. n.d. *The Gramm-Leach-Bliley Act.* Retrieved August 31, 2009, from EPIC: http://epic.org/privacy/glba

Federal Communicationss Commission. 2007, April 2. *Customer proprietary network information and other customer information; IP-enabled services.* Federal Communications Commission: http://hraunfoss.fcc.gov/edocs_public/attachmatch/FCC-07-22A1.pdf

Finkenzeller, Klaus. 2003. *RFID handbook.* West Sussex, UK: John Wiley & Sons, Ltd.

Fraud in the U.S. payments industry: Chip card technology impact on fraud. 2009, December. Smart Card Alliance: http://www.smartcardalliance.org/pages/news letter-200912-feature?issue=200912

Garcia, Flavio D., Peter van Rossum, Roel Verdult, and Ronny Wichers Schreur. 2009. Wirelessly pickpocketing a Mifare classic card. *Proceedings of the 30th IEEE symposium on security and privacy,* 3–15. Washington, DC: IEEE Computer Society.

Gemalto. 2008, Winter. *The Review.* Retrieved August 23, 2009, from Gemalto: http://www.gemalto.com/brochures/download/2008_02_review.pdf

Givens, Beth. 2009, April. *Privacy today: A review of current issues.* Privacy Rights Clearinghouse: http://www.privacyrights.org/ar/Privacy-IssuesList.htm#s

Gramm-Leach-Bliley Act. 1999, November 12. Public Law 106-102.

GSM Association. 2007a, February. *Mobile NFC services.* GSM World: http://www.gsmworld.com/documents/nfc_services_0207.pdf

GSM Association. 2007b, November. *Mobile NFC technical guidelines.* GSM Association: http://www.gsmworld.com/documents/gsma_nfc2_wp.pdf

GSM Association. 2007c, November. *Pay-buy-mobile: Business opportunity analysis.* GSM World: http://www.gsmworld.com/documents/gsma_nfc_tech_guide_vs1.pdf

Hack Watch. 1999, December 7. *GSM phone hack recovers key in one second.* http://www.hackwatch.com/gsmpaper.html

Heydt-Benjamin, Thomas S., Daniel V. Bailey, Kevin Fu, Ari Juels, and Tom O'Hare. 2007. Vulnerabilities in first-generation RFID-enabled credit cards. In *Financial cryptography and data security,* ed. Sven Dietrich and Rachna Dhamija, 2–14. Berlin/Heidelberg: Springer.

HID Global. n.d. http://www.hidglobal.com/

Juels, Ari. 2005, February 28. *Attack on a cryptographic RFID device.* RFID Journal: http://www.rfidjournal.com/article/print/1415

King, Nancy J. 2008. Direct marketing, mobile phones, and consumer privacy: Ensuring adequate disclosure and consent mechanisms for emerging mobile advertising practices. *Federal Communicationss Law Journal* 60, 2: 229–324.

Ludington, Sarah. 2007. Reining in the data traders: A tort for the misuse of personal information. *Duke Law School Legal Studies Research Paper Series* 66, 140–93.

MARTA. n.d. http://itsmarta.com/

MIFARE. n.d. http://www.mifare.net/

Murdoch, Steven J., Saar Drimer, Ross Anderson, and Mike Bond. 2010. Chip and PIN is broken. *Proceedings of 2010 IEEE Symposium on Security and Privacy.* Oakland, CA.

NFC Forum. 2008, October. *Essentials for successful NFC mobile ecosystems.* http://www.nfc-forum.org/resources/white_papers/NFC_Forum_Mobile_NFC_Ecosystem_White_Paper.pdf

Nilson Report. 2010, February. no. 943: 8–9. http://www.nilsonreport.com/issues/2010/943.htm.

PCI Security Standards Council. n.d. *About the PCI data security standard (PCI DSS).* https://www.pcisecuritystandards.org/security_standards/pci_dss.shtml

Ruane, Kathleen Ann. 2008, March 10. *Selected laws governing the disclosure of customer phone records by telecommunications carriers.* Federation of American Scientists: http://www.fas.org/sgp/crs/misc/RL34409.pdf

Smart Card Alliance. 2007, September. *Proximity mobile payments: Leveraging NFC and the contactless financial payments infrastructure.* http://www.smartcardalliance.org/resources/lib/Proximity_Mobile_Payments_200709.pdf

Smart Card Applications. 2010. http://www.smartcardalliance.org/pages/smart-cards-applications

Smartcard Developers Association. 1998, April 13. *Smartcard Developer Association clones digital GSM cellphones.* http://www.scard.org/press/19980413-01/

Solove, Daniel J., and Chris Jay Hoofnagle. 2006. A model regime of privacy protection. *University of Illinois Law Review* 2006, no. 2: 357–404.

Speedpass. n.d. http://www.speedpass.com

Stevens, Gina. 2009, January 29. *Federal information security and data breach notification laws.* Open CRS: http://assets.opencrs.com/rpts/RL34120_20090129.pdf

Sutter, John D. 2009, August 13. *Wallet of the future? Your mobile phone.* CNN: http://www.cnn.com/2009/TECH/08/13/cell.phone.wallet/index.html

Traynor, P., Michael Lin, Machigar Ongtang, Vikhyath Rao, Trent Jaeger, Patrick McDaniel, and Thomas La Porta. 2009. On cellular botnets: Measuring the impact of malicious devices on a cellular network core. *Proceedings of the 16th ACM conference on computer and communications security (CCS),* 223–34. New York: ACM.

U.S. West v. FCC, 182 F.3d 1224 (10th Cir. 1999).

Zetter, Kim. 2009, August 17. *Threat level. Wired:* http://www.wired.com/threatlevel

3

OTHER PERSPECTIVES: INFORMATION STUDIES, HISTORY, AND SOCIOLOGY

8

Privacy, Reading, and Trying Out Identity

The Digital Millennium Copyright Act and Technological Determinism

Philip Doty
University of Texas at Austin

> Science and technology embody values, and have the potential to embody
> different values.
>
> —Judy Wajcman, *TechnoFeminism* (2004, 126)

This chapter examines how U.S. maximalist copyright law, especially the 1998 Digital Millennium Copyright Act (DMCA, PL 105-304), poses threats to the privacy of readers through the embrace of technological determinism. The DMCA does so by granting copyright holders new rights to surveil and limit readers' actions. The technological determinism of the DMCA undermines the autonomy of individuals and the agency of the American polity more generally, thus undermining privacy. This perspective on privacy of reading and maximalist copyright is new; while there is a growing literature about privacy and copyright, no author has explored the relationship between copyright and the technological determinism that characterizes much of contemporary American culture and much of the policy discussion of copyright and digital materials.

Before beginning, it is useful to consider three important terms: *reading*, *privacy*, and *identity*. First, reading in this chapter means "reading, listening, and viewing," and I will use the simple locution of "reading" and the longer locution of "reading, listening, and viewing" throughout. Second, Agre (1997, 7) gives a useful working definition of *privacy* for our purposes: "the freedom from unreasonable constraints on the construction of one's own identity." This conception of privacy leads to the third "definitional" concept: *identity*. By this term, I mean a sense of self, or more accurately, the many senses of many selves that human beings experience phenomenologically by virtue of being in the world. This chapter does not view identity as unitary, static or immutable, abstract, or "in" the body. Instead, identity is multiple, always changing through time and circumstance, embodied especially in material practices, and as part of an integrated, embodied self. Jodi O'Brien (1999) and David Shoemaker (2009), despite their many differences, are useful sources in this regard.

Agre's link between identity and privacy is common in the philosophical literatures about privacy but is unusual in policy and legal studies. Those literatures tend to focus only on expressive freedom and other formal elements of First Amendment jurisprudence when discussing privacy, generally ignoring reading or conflating it with writing. Similarly, in computer science and other information systems contexts, identity is usually limited to concerns about identification (Waldo et al. 2007, 82–83), e.g., with authorization of a particular person to perform particular functions on particular systems, established by name, institutions, documents, and the like. The traditional troika of authentication of identity involves: (1) what one is, usually biometric identifiers like fingerprints, retina patterns, facial recognition, and the like; (2) what one knows, e.g., a password or digital signature; and/or (3) what one has, e.g., a key, cardkey, or other material token.

Drawing usefully on the theories of the performative and dynamic self of Erving Goffman, Agre argues that those theories of self and privacy are important to the consideration of digital technologies in particular because "a technology shapes individuals' abilities to negotiate their identities" (8). Using the wide literature about privacy, this chapter also uses the concept of autonomy or agency to explore the privacy threats posed by the DMCA. More specifically, the chapter sees agency from two perspectives, the microscopic and macroscopic. The microscopic perspective emphasizes the individual autonomy of users of online materials to choose what to read, when to read it, how to read it, and how to quote, integrate, cut, paste, and otherwise actively "read" all kinds of texts, images, and sounds. The primary means by which threats to the privacy of reading are realized are the digital rights management (DRM) technological protections given by copyright holders to their online material which, among other things, track users' opening, use, and closing of digital files. Limitations on copying digital files are enforced in part by limitations on access to those files, especially through cryptography and by surveillance of the use of those files. As argued below, such limitations and surveillance are, on their face, violations of the privacy protections given to reading materials and one's papers and effects in the U.S. Constitution and those provided by more than two hundred years of American jurisprudence. It is through the privacy of reading that individuals try out and express identity and exercise the personal autonomy widely recognized as important to privacy interests.

The macroscopic perspective on autonomy and the DMCA involves the American polity more generally. From this perspective the Digital Millennium Copyright Act was the result of national and international initiatives by policy actors in the United States to force the Congress to adopt the strong copyright protections of the DMCA. This effort was purportedly to implement and to achieve "harmonization" with two World Intellectual Property Organization (WIPO) treaties of 1996: the Copyright Treaty and the Performances and Phonograms Treaty. The WIPO Treaties, however, had many of the maximalist provisions they possess because the U.S. representatives to the talks that produced the treaties pressed for them, particularly because the U.S. Congress had largely already rejected those provisions. This story is told more fully below.

PRIVACY AND AUTONOMY

A well-known typology of privacy identifies *informational* privacy, *decisional* privacy, and *accessibility* privacy (see, e.g., Baruh 2007; Grodzinsky and Tavani 2005; Shoemaker 2009). The first element of the typology concerns control of information about one's self, the second the ability to make decisions autonomously and largely free of unjustified constraints, and the third the protection from physical and attentional intrusion. A widely cited concept of privacy, particularly "why privacy is important," is that developed by James Rachels (1975). Rachels's paper is widely anthologized with reason. Rachels argues that part of what makes privacy distinctive is its direct support of the moral and ethical nature of human beings as self-directed, autonomous beings, especially in choosing to establish and maintain relations to other particular human beings or choosing not to. It is here that Rachels's argument intersects with the tripartite typology of privacy mentioned above. Autonomy, the ability to choose freely, is key to all three of the ways of considering privacy above, and, thus, important to readers in allowing them to choose how and what to read but also how what they read helps them make themselves.

READING AND IDENTITY

Reading is one important way in which people reflect about who they are and try out identity in a number of ways (Long 2003) and is linked to the protection of intellectual privacy (Cohen 1996 and 2003). There is a growing body of empirical and other research about the relationship between reading and identity. Some important themes in this research include how learning to read is a defining part of childhood and familial relationships; how reading particular books or other materials is tied to important personal relationships; how particular works are key to personal growth and change, especially in trying circumstances such as the loss of a loved one, the formation and evolution of sexual identity, and decisions related to education and career choice; and how our political, aesthetic, and other identities are forged in reading, writing about our reading, and talking to others about our reading (Bilal 2007; Boyarin 1993; Long 1993 and 2003; McKechnie et al. 2007; and Nahl 2007). This last theme, the way that reading, listening, and viewing are essential to how we tell our narratives of self and thereby form and maintain identity, is one that this chapter discusses only briefly.[1]

Erving Goffman's work on *The Presentation of Self in Everyday Life* (1959) emphasizes the performative and dramaturgical elements of identity in ways of particular interest to discussions of reading, identity, and privacy. His discussion of "secret consumption" is particularly useful, citing the then-recent Kinsey reports about American's sexual behavior (42). Goffman's primary example of secret consumption is the display of a "high-culture" magazine like *The Saturday Evening Post* for others to see and form a good impression of the household and its members, while the household explains away a copy of the "low-brow" *True Romance* as "'something the cleaning woman must have left around.'" While the evocation of a cleaning woman and the examples of reading material are telling about social relations and the state of mid-twentieth-century bourgeois American culture, that is not the most important reason to cite them here. Instead, we should consider Goffman's theme of managing others' impressions of us; in this case, trying to determine what they think of us by determining what they think we read and do not read. Maintaining the privacy of reading is central to the formation of others' impressions of us. We simply do not want other persons, even our intimates and, in some cases, especially our intimates, to know everything that we read and everything that we have not read. Thus, we arrange an impression of our reading as an important part of our sense of self, as a means of trying out different identities, and as an embodiment of the more general concept of privacy. Further, Goffman reminds us that an important element of our appearing competent in our social roles to others is *not* familiarity with a social or behavioral script but rather "commands of an idiom, a command that is exercised from moment to moment with little calculation or forethought" (74). Surely, practice, both in private and in public, when alone and when observed by others, is what enables us to develop familiarity with the appropriate idioms of a particular social role and to develop a comfortable enactment of the idioms. Here again is a place where privacy, especially of the reading that underlies much of the imagination and enactment of a social identity, is important to the self.

Unfortunately, those of us in disciplines such as information studies and cognate fields fall prey to the cognitivism and information fetishism common in contemporary culture, and we too often forget that reading is more than informative. To read is to make ourselves and, thereby, make ourselves subject to important cultural discriminations and judgments. Again, it is this making through reading that demands privacy.

Some of the literatures about identity and gender, in particular, give us insight into the interdependence of identity and narrative. Of course, reading (and listening and viewing) materials are constituted by narratives of many kinds, but, just as importantly, one of the important ways of our narrating ourselves, of using stories to make ourselves, is the telling of what and how we read, listen, and view. In discussing masculinity and technologies, Brandth and Haugen argue that people "use storylines to speak and write themselves into existence" and that we use narratives to "constitute our social identities" to make ourselves (2005, 151). The ethnographic work of Elizabeth Long on book clubs gives countless examples of how such groups allow their members "different ways to 'narrate the self,' that is, to understand their lives or vicariously to live through other choices, other ways of being in the world" (2003, 60). Such behaviors, of course, thereby evoke concerns about privacy if they are surveilled, whether by government or by copyright holders.

Document Use, Communities of Practice, and Learning to Be

The links between identity and reading (and listening and viewing), seen from another perspective, rest on a deeper foundation: the documents we read and create are expressions of the communities to which we belong and/ or aspire to belong. As is clear from the scholarship of many disciplines, e.g., psychology, sociology, information studies, philosophy, anthropology, and others, the self and communities are mutually constitutive. The literature about communities of practice is a particularly rich source for understanding how documents are important to the formation and maintenance of communities. This literature also shows how learning to use particular documents in particular ways is essential to learning to be a member of communities, to forming one's identity as a member of a community of practice. In these contexts the status of reading and the privacy to try out identities without interference are particularly important.

In the Western tradition, reading has been closely identified with autonomy and identity formation of many kinds. Research in information studies and related fields has clearly shown that documents, among other ends, establish and maintain communities. Further, community membership (thus document use) involves learning to be, not only changing "what one knows" but changing how one imagines oneself in the world and changing how one realizes identity through practice (Lave and Wenger 1992; Wenger 1998). Even more particularly, in community, we learn what to read, how to read it, and how to be informed by what we read.[2]

Similarly, Martin Heidegger gives us some insight into the value of practice in this context, recognizing that reading, viewing, and listening are not just cognitive, atomistic individual behaviors (not just the acts of Cartesian individuals). In I.1§ 12 of *Being and Time*, Heidegger, citing earlier work by Blattner, asserts that self-understanding is a "form of competence or ability, a practical phenomenon, rather than a cognitive one. Our self-understanding is embodied in the way we live, rather than in how we think or talk about our lives." While we might argue with the dismissal of the importance of narrative in making the self, we can just as easily embrace the importance of doing, of embodying our selves through our behavior. Listening, viewing, and reading are essential parts of that doing and embodying, and documents of all kinds are essential means of that doing and embodying (Litman 2007).

This presumed connection among identity, autonomy, and reading (or document use) is especially strong in the classical liberal tradition closely tied to the Enlightenment ideology that privacy, private property, and political autonomy are mutually reinforcing.[3] According to the ideological tradition these and other scholars describe, religious, political, and economic autonomy and freedom of action are tied to the ability to decide what to read and to keep others, most especially the government, from saying what one should read or from knowing what one reads.

Open Texts, de Certeau, and the Autonomy of the Reader as Poacher

While writing has long been a matter of attention for scholars of many kinds, reading has been less so. In society more generally, metaphors of reading resemble those of receipt—the writer writes and the reader receives. For the past several decades, however, literary theorists and others have developed much richer and more complex understandings of reading, some of which are based on richer understandings of the social matrix from which creative works' writing and reading emerge. For example, Roland Barthes in *S/Z* describes "writerly texts . . . [that] require a reader who is 'no longer a consumer, but a producer of the text'" (1974, 4, quoted in Roe 1994, 24). This idea is part of a larger conversation about reader-response theory,[4] the active reader, and open texts. For example, Julia Kristeva's work on intertextuality tells us how creative works are produced from other works, echoing Northrup

Frye's statement that all poems are made from other poems. Both of these ideas, of course, have important implications for the creativity thought to be at the basis of the ability to copyright original works (for example, see Boyle 1996 and 2008) and are useful here in prompting us to examine the presumably well-understood and simple processes of writing and reading, viewing, and listening.

The work of French theorist and historian Michel de Certeau is widely cited in reading studies and is particularly useful here. Various chapters of his collection *The Practice of Everyday Life* (1984) are of value in this context, beginning with the collection's General Introduction. There de Certeau lays out a critique of our contemporary, easy distinction between producers of cultural commodities and those who are presumed to be nonproducers. While this distinction has important implications for copyright doctrine, I will use it here instead to investigate the agency, the activity of readers, viewers, and listeners. These presumed nonproducers are thought to be simply passive receivers or voyeurs of culture, and their receipt is marginal to cultural activity as it is commonly imagined. In contrast to this supposed passivity, de Certeau posits a very active reader, viewer, or listener:

> In reality, the activity of reading has on the contrary all the characteristics of a silent production: the drift across the page, the metamorphosis of the text effected by the wandering eyes of the reader, the improvisation and expectations of meanings inferred from a few words, leaps over written spaces in an ephemeral dance. . . . [The reader] insinuates into another person's text the rules of pleasure and appropriation: he poaches on it, is transported into it, pluralizes himself [*sic*] in it like the internal rumblings of one's body. (xxi)

Thus the theorist embraces open texts, intertextuality, and reader response theory instead of a solid, unchanging text that imposes its meaning on its audience.

The chapter "Reading as Poaching" in this collection is de Certeau's single, best-known work. Here de Certeau more fully specifies the activity of the reader, viewer, and listener, insisting that the audience makes the cultural expression, further, longer, and more deeply than the original creator. He insists that we should see "cultural creativity where it has been denied that any exists" by challenging "consumption" as conceived and instantiated by privileging "authorship" and "scriptural imperialism" (167 and 169). As noted above this assertion poses a fundamental threat to the presumption of originality that copyright rests upon, but it is the agency of the reader that matters most here. De Certeau, like many other contemporary scholars, stresses the "plurality of meanings" that cultural expressions like books and television shows give rise to, meanings that are key to identity and emerge only through the agency of readers themselves (169). He further asserts that reading "eludes the law of information," the supposed conveyance of information from writer through the text to the reader that overdetermines what the reader makes of the text (173). As elsewhere, de Certeau contrasts this reductive conduit metaphor with the plurality of activities, multitudes of meanings, and heterogeneity of behaviors that readers, viewers, and listeners exhibit.[5]

As argued below, maximalist copyright doctrine and maximalist copyright policy instruments like the Digital Millennium Copyright Act rest on a number of mutually reinforcing but faulty assumptions—two of the most important of those assumptions are the assumed passivity of the reader and the presumed passivity of the polity in the face of technological determinism.

TECHNOLOGICAL DETERMINISM

The concept of technological determinism is rife in American thought and has been for quite some time (see Smith and Marx 1994 for a review). Such determinism is one element of the secular American *mythos* of technology as liberatory, self-driven, and part of the American Edenic ideal. As leading technology studies scholar Merritt Roe Smith puts it, "Technology and science not only became the great panacea for everyday problems, they also stood for values at the core of American life" (1994, 23). It is this symbolic value of technology and thus technological determinism that provides these ideas with their power, including their power in making public policy narratives. Space does not allow the investigation of any of these ideas in depth.[6] One important element of research in American technology studies of special interest here, however, is the link between technological determinism and the rhetoric of the "taming of the American west" (e.g., Smith and Marx 1994). For example, Michael L. Smith argues that, after the close of the American frontier, "Americans would have to find a substitute for westward migration to signify the nation's progress" and "placed new emphasis on an alternate iconographic terrain: the technological frontier" (1994, 43). Much of the rhetoric leading to the adoption of maximalist copyright statutes recalled the "wild West," "taming the lawless frontier of the Internet," and the like. This powerful cultural trope is very difficult to resist and has proven persuasive for policy makers and others when presented with outraged copyright holders' arguments for longer, wider, and more comprehensive protection of copyrighted materials online. And, recalling the determinist arguments of the "taming of the U.S. frontier" by technologies like the steam engine, the rifle, barbed wire, telegraphy, and the steel plow, the DMCA became and remains technologically determinist.

Several scholars can give us insight into technological determinism. Leo Marx and Merritt Roe Smith, two of the most important and generative thinkers about technology in American culture for decades, generally describe technological determinism: "agency (the power to effect change) is imputed to technology itself, or to some of its intrinsic attributes; thus the advance of technology leads to a situation of inescapable necessity" (1994, xii). Their mention of agency and its meaning as "the power to effect change" is especially important to the argument of this chapter and is explored further below. In the same collection, Michael L. Smith notes that technological determinism is "the belief that social progress is driven by technological innovation, which in turn follows an 'inevitable' course" (1994, 38). Judy Wajcman, a widely known and influential theorist in science and technology studies and in gender studies, defines technological determinism as the "view of technology as an external, autonomous force exerting an influence on society" (2004, 33). While gendered analysis of technologies, of determinism, and of the use of digital technologies in particular are of interest to considerations of privacy of reading, space limitations do not allow their examination. See Lerman et al. (2003), particularly their introduction and bibliographic essay, and Wajcman (1991 and 2004) for some foundational sources.

The origins of technological determinism in the Western tradition, especially in the United States and related to digital information and communication technologies, are many. These include (see, e.g., Smith and Marx 1994; Williams 1994):

- The Enlightenment ideology of technology as politically liberatory
- A general Whiggish view of history, wherein history is seen as an "ever upward" process, usually heading to some utopian goal or *telos*
- The American *mythos* of "conquering" the Western frontier and the technological frontier
- The "emerging iconographic role of technology in American culture" (Michael L. Smith 1994, 47)
- Technological utopianism and dystopianism which, oxymoronically, share a faith in the power of technologies to be irresistible, universal, and monolithic
- The symbolic role of information and communication technologies (ICT's), for example, as emblematic of the modern state and (competitive) organization[7]; as Nye says, "as with electricity in 1910, so much was attributed to the Internet in the 1990s that it became a universal icon of the age" (2006, 64)

- The triumphal rhetoric of traditional liberalism at the fall of the Soviet Union in the early 1990s that saw the presumed "end of history" as a function, in part, of the West's supposed technological superiority
- "[T]he thingness or tangibility of mechanical devices . . . [which] helps to create a sense of causal efficiency made visible" (Marx and Smith 1994, x–xi)

This list is far from comprehensive, but it gives us some understanding of the nexus of cultural and political values that undergirds technological determinism. Similarly, these values clearly demonstrate that technological determinism is not defensible as a robust theory of social change or of history.

Raymond Williams offers a very useful working definition of technological determinism in the second edition of his well-known book on *Television*. Such determinism is:

> an immensely powerful and now largely orthodox view of the nature of social change. New technologies are discovered, by an internal process of research and development, which then sets the conditions for social change and progress. Progress, in particular, is the history of these inventions which "created the modern world." The effects of these technologies, whether direct or indirect, foreseen or unforeseen, are as it were the rest of history. The steam engine, the automobile, television, the atomic bomb, have *made* modern man [*sic*] and the modern condition. (2003, 5, emphasis in original)

Technological determinism is commonly assumed as a fact in much of American culture, as in other societies where laissez-faire economics and the cult of individualism is strong (Nye 2006, 18). Analysts of science and technology, however, have largely abandoned technological determinism as an explanatory tool. In parallel moves, such researchers have also avoided the locution of the "individual inventor (or 'genius') as the central explanatory concept . . . and . . . making distinctions among technical, social, economic, and political aspects of technological development" (Bijker, Hughes, and Pinch 1987, 3).

Other useful critiques of technological determinism include those of Reinhard Rürup that focus on the fact that contemporary technologies and the benefits and costs that we experience because of those technologies seem "the *necessary outcome* of previous innovations and techniques" (emphasis in original, 1974, 174). John Staudenmaier (1994, 263) and others particularly critique the fundamentally ahistorical character of such determinism, and it is to historicity that we now turn.

The Historicity of Technologies as Sociotechnical Ensembles

Four concepts in science and technology studies (STS) help us (1) understand how the technologically determinist character of the DMCA, especially its anticircumvention provisions, undermines individuals' autonomy by undermining their agency and the privacy of their reading and (2) see how the DMCA's technological determinism undermines the American polity's agency by the canonical narrative of the DMCA's passage. According to this narrative, technical systems presumably "required" the law, as did the supposedly irresistible drive to "harmonize" U.S. law with international copyright treaties.

To begin with, STS has largely embraced a view of technologies of all kinds, most especially digital technologies, as *sociotechnical* (a concept originally developed by Thomas Hughes). At its simplest, this concept means that technologies must be understood as both technical and social, that analysis of technologies privileges neither the social nor the technical in discussing the genesis of technologies, discussing their implementation and deployment, or discussing their use. Digital technologies have been the focus of fruitful analysis using the concept of the sociotechnical, including, for example, digital libraries and the documents they include (Levy 2003). David Nye offers some useful insights into the specific character of the *sociotechnical* in *Technology Matters* (2006). According to Nye, historians of technology contend that technologies emerge not just from economic or so-called internal technical imperatives (see the long quotation from Raymond Williams above), but rather they are "shaped by social conditions, prices, traditions, popular attitudes, interest groups, class differences, and government policy" (19).

Given that technologies are generated and used in sociotechnical circumstances, technologies are necessarily *ensembles*. Technologies are ensembles not only in the sense of being combinations of various artifacts, ideas, and practices but also in the sense that the technical is not reducible to the social, nor is the social reducible to the technical. Technologies are the nonresolvable combination of the social and technical, thus are *ensembles*. Gender-sensitive analyses of technologies, both empirical and theoretical, also usefully underscore the sociotechnical character of technologies (e.g., Lerman et al. 2003, *passim*; Wajcman 1991 and 2004). For example, Judy Wajcman reminds us that "political choices are embedded in the very design and selection of technology" and continues:

Technologies result from a series of specific decisions made by particular groups of people in particular places at particular times for their own purposes. As such, technologies bear the imprint of the people and social context in which they developed. (1991, 22)

Besides the sociotechnical character of technologies that these quotations illustrate, they also emphasize the concept of choice, of *agency* important to the sociotechnical understanding of technologies.

Agency in science and technology studies has a number of faces. Anthropologist Lucy Suchman, especially in her 2007 book *Human-Machine Reconfigurations: Plans and Situated Actions*, gives us some powerful insights into the use of the concept of agency in STS. As with other STS scholars, Suchman takes great pains to ensure that agency is seen as a generative outcome of the interface, the intersection of the human and "the machine," *not* a presumed inherent characteristic of an artifact or technology itself. Agency is the result of the combination of the person(s) and the technology, which is another, evocative way of identifying technologies as ensembles, as combinations of the human and the machine.

The fourth and last of the useful STS concepts to discuss here is the *historicity* of technologies. Technological determinism, more than a bit ironically, speaks of technologies as being able to determine history, yet at the same time technology is seen as an exogenous force, *outside* of history. David Nye (2006) is a good example of the many counterarguments to the ahistoricity of technological determinism, offering examples such as the Japanese early adoption of gunpowder, then the resurgence of bows and arrows for cultural and nationalistic reasons despite the supposed superiority of gunpowder as a weapon. He also cites the failure of the presumably technologically superior electric car to this point because of political, economic, and cultural reasons, not the technical abilities of the electric designs. This contingency and complexity go even further in the usual constructivist reading of technology. Bijker (1995, 281), for example, asserts, "the core of technology, *that which constitutes its working*, is socially constructed" (emphasis in the original). Similarly, Misa (1988) identifies major interpretive problems with technological determinism as a system of thought. The most important here is that technological determinism "can level historical processes that were full of conflicting values," thereby ignoring an essential part of the contingency of technological development and an essential indicator of the choices made by particular persons in particular circumstances. What happened then seems foreordained, inevitable, despite being contingent (321).

Given this nexus of ideas about technological determinism and its critique in science and technology studies as well as other disciplines, how is the Digital Millennium Copyright Act technologically determinist? And how does that determinism threaten privacy and thereby undermine identity? The remainder of this chapter addresses those questions and begins with a short review of how the DMCA came to be.

A BRIEF HISTORY OF THE GENESIS OF
THE DIGITAL MILLENNIUM COPYRIGHT ACT

It is useful here to provide some insight into the origins of the Digital Millennium Copyright Act (DMCA) of 1998, particularly of its anticircumvention provisions. Copyright scholar Jessica Litman gives perhaps the most useful recounting of the origins of the DMCA for our purposes in *Digital Copyright* (2001, particularly 122–50), but also see James Boyle (2008, 83–121), Paul Goldstein (2003, 163–85), and Tarleton Gillespie (2007, 105–34 and 174–77).

The DMCA is an expression of what Litman (2000 and 2001) identifies as a fundamental evolution in the metaphors we use to explain copyright. Along with others, Litman traces the dominating metaphors, stories, and models of copyright through four phases that increasingly threaten the many unauthorized uses of copyrighted materials that were legal (2000, 1) and, in fact, strongly encouraged, e.g., fair use. Instead, we are now, under the law and economics paradigm that has long dominated law school training, at the point where we think of copyright as "a tool for copyright owners to use to extract all potential commercial value from works of authorship, even if that means that uses that have long been deemed legal are now brought within the copyright owner's control" (2). The four metaphors were these:

1. The reigning metaphor for copyright in the first decade of the twentieth century was quid pro quo, whereby the polity, through the Congress and the federal courts, granted some limited exclusive rights to creators in exchange for the public distribution of the work and its "eventual dedication . . . in its entirety to the public domain" (4).
2. As the formal requirements for ensuring copyright protection diminished, quid pro quo evolved into the concept of a bargain whereby the public interest in the creation and distribution of creative works was exchanged for limited exclusive rights. Thus creators could reap sufficient financial rewards from the works they created and shared while the polity maintained a balance between what was protected and what was not.
3. Under the law and economics analysis popular in legal training in the past four decades, copyright law was seen as primarily an incentive to creation and distribution of creative works. Such a model, of course, is not based on an empirical analysis of creators. In fact, it may be more reasonable to assert that many, if not most, creative persons create as an expression of who they are, not with a rational, calculating eye toward reward. Similarly, we must recall that the entire edifice of copyright is only a relatively recent product, intimately tied to the concept of the

modern nation state and early modernity, i.e., the first modern copyright law was the English Statute of Anne in 1709/1710.

4. During the past fifteen years or so, according to Litman's and others' analysis (e.g., Boyle 2008; Gillespie 2007; and Lessig 2001, 2004, and 2006), we have seen the growth of a new and hegemonic story about copyright: "[c]opyright is less about incentives today than it is about control" (5).

This evolution in metaphors for copyright establishes a theoretical, economic, and political context for the Digital Millennium Copyright Act.

Despite the contributions of researchers worldwide, it is fair to say that the U.S. federal investment in networked computing was the primary impetus to the rise of the Internet, beginning with the establishment of the Defense Advanced Research Projects Agency initiatives in the late 1960s. Such investment spurred the Internet's communication TCP/IP protocols, production-level packet switching, and major applications of networked computing, e.g., email and file transfer. In the early 1990s, especially after the introduction of the graphical web browser Mosaic in 1993–1994, the first Clinton administration began to rely more explicitly and fully on the private sector to provide Internet services and to guide the development of U.S. telecommunications policy to leverage the decades-long U.S. investment in aggregating an Internet audience. Such increased reliance on the private sector was and remains a cornerstone of U.S. federal telecommunications and information policy, and the Clinton administration demonstrated such reliance by the formation of the Information Infrastructure Task Force (IITF) in the early 1990s and by giving its leadership to Ron Brown, then Secretary of Commerce.

There were several working groups in the Task Force, and, among the most important outcomes of the Task Force's Working Group on Intellectual Property [sic] were its Green Paper in 1994 and the subsequent White Paper in 1995. The vision of copyright and digital communication that these papers expressed was the focus of considerable controversy. The so-called copyright industries embraced the papers' assertion of control—the papers asserted that copyrighted works, and other forms of "intellectual property" online, were just like real property. Thus, the goal of copyright protection was the maximization of copyright owners' return on investment and exclusion of others from benefiting from that property without the express permission (and often rent seeking) of those owners. Opposed to that perspective were parties emphasizing the exceptions to the exclusive rights of rightsholders that have long been built into copyright statutes and jurisprudence in U.S. law, e.g., fair use, the right to dispose of a legally obtained copy largely as one sees fit (the doctrine of first sale), and the use of copyrighted works to create more cultural expression. Strong negative reactions to the Green Paper had little effect on the subsequent publication of the White Paper. The White Paper, in turn, became the foundation for an aggressive legislative agenda in the 104th Congress (H.R. 2441 and S. 1284, 1995). The effort to pass these bills, led by Bruce Lehman, then U.S. Patent Commissioner who had been chair of the IITF Taskforce on Intellectual Property [*sic*], aimed to instantiate the White Paper's vision of control in Congressional law. That effort met with some considerable resistance, especially when members of Congress saw the negative reactions to the IITF agenda from IT companies, Internet service providers and other telecommunication companies, secondary "content providers," and the like (Litman 2001 is especially good here).

So the United States, led by Lehman, pressed for a meeting of the World Intellectual Property Organization, of which the United States is a leading member, to develop a treaty that would instantiate the White Paper's recommendations about digital communication and copyrighted works that would, in turn, demand Congressional adoption of similar provisions. While the resultant treaties did not incorporate all of the White Paper's recommendations and did not adopt the strongest of them, Congress had to respond to WIPO's treaties and did in the Digital Millennium Copyright Act of 1998. Somewhat ironically, the DMCA emphasized control, particularly the strong penalties for circumvention of technological protections of copyrighted works, and supported what were then generally termed "copyright management systems" and are now generally referred to under the rubric of "digital rights management" (DRM). What is particularly important to underscore here is the rationale for passage of the DMCA. Since treaties in the United States are not self-executing, supporters of the IITF's White Paper's provisions of increased control of copyrighted works in digital environments in Congress, encouraged by Lehman and large media companies in publishing, music distribution, and movie making and distribution, used the WIPO treaties to adopt parts of the earlier bills that emerged from the White Paper in 1995/1996. The argument made for the most stringent of the anticircumvention provisions of the DMCA was that the United States had no choice but to adopt those measures, even though the WIPO treaties were considerably less stringent. Otherwise, so the argument went, the United States would not be in compliance with the treaties. More importantly, however, the considerable U.S. trade surplus in copyrighted and other protected goods would necessarily decline. It was the argument for U.S. global economic competitiveness that would otherwise be hopelessly compromised by (so-called) piracy and the presumed refusal of major U.S. copyright holders to mount their protected works online that won the day. Ignored were fundamental questions important to public policy other than copyright owners' interests, especially those questions related to privacy and personal autonomy.

SURVEILLANCE AND THE DMCA

Current digital rights management (DRM) technologies are increasingly powerful, able to make subtle and often invisible distinctions and discriminations among users, devices, and uses. DRM can place the following serious and unprecedented limitations on copyrighted digital information (Boyle 2008; Cohen 1996 and 2003; Gillespie 2007; Katyal 2004; Lessig 2006; Litman 2000; Waldo et al. 2007):

* Identifying readers of digital information
* Tracking how often copyrighted information is read
* Limiting how often copyrighted information can be viewed
* Determining how, if at all, copyrighted information can be read
* Determining how, if at all, such information can be copied
* Tracking if that information is imported to another device owned by the lawful purchaser of the information
* Prevention of that importing to a particular device or class of devices
* Specifying what parts of the information the user can see and what parts the user cannot
* Tracking how long a particular reader has read copyrighted information
* Limiting the length of time a particular reader and/or particular device can read copyrighted information
* Specifying the time(s) that particular functionalities, e.g., searching, browsing, cutting, and copying, will be available to particular readers and on particular devices

Going even further in identifying the moral panic that copyright maximalists react to and further inflame, Patry (2009), Gillespie (2007), and others specify how the DMCA grants rightsholders new rights that emerge from fear, the exaggerated claims about property articulated by rightsholders, and a desire by those rightsholders for increased control of their copyrighted materials online. The DMCA, unilaterally and without being subject to fair use and other exemptions commonly applied to copyright, determines what kinds of players for digital material will be manufactured in, distributed in, and imported into the United States and what kinds of technological means owners can place between users and how they can read, view, or listen to copyrighted works online. What makes these new rights even more threatening to privacy and autonomy online is the union of this narrative of control with the American belief in technological determinism.

This brief list shows the unprecedented powers of surveillance and control that digital rights management technologies give to copyright holders. Loss of anonymity of reading, and loss of the privacy of reading more generally, becomes only collateral damage in the drive to give rightsholders increasingly impregnable means of controlling the use of copyrighted works. This result seems unchallengeable and foreordained, particularly because of the DMCA generally and its anticircumvention provisions particularly. Further, the asymmetry of power between rightsholders and users, unchecked by judicial review and, in fact, reinforced by the judicial privileging of contract, gives readers, viewers, and listeners few ways to protect their privacy interests or their tightly constrained autonomy. The next section considers how the DMCA embodies technological determinism.

THE DMCA AS TECHNOLOGICALLY DETERMINIST

The anticircumvention provisions of the Digital Millennium Copyright Act are in section 1201, which forbids circumvention of any "technological means that effectively controls access to a [protected] work without *explicit* knowledge and permission of the owner of the copyright of the work" (emphasis added). First, this provision plainly controls access to a work, not just copying. Thus the Act clearly overreaches in granting rightsholders new rights. Second, as noted below, this provision makes it illegal to develop and/ or distribute any means to circumvent any copyright-protecting technology even if that circumvention is for a legally recognized privilege, e.g., fair use (see *Universal City Studios v. Reimerdes*, 2000). This, too, is a new right given to rightsholders, and one that many regard as unconstitutional (e.g., Boyle 2008 and Lessig 2006). Further, the right to prevent circumvention of technologies controlling uses of digital copyrighted works lasts in perpetuity, unlike copyright's limited terms. Such constraints without end also give rise to fears about editorial control, i.e., the use of copyright control instantiated in the DMCA to forbid reviewers, parodists, critics, and commentators of all kinds from getting access to a work. Again, the Act seriously undermines the free expression and the wide sharing of a wide variety of views that the First Amendment encourages and which copyright is meant to help support.

As discussed earlier, there are two "layers" of technological determinism in the Digital Millennium Copyright Act. The microscopic "layer" directly threatens privacy through the surveillance of individual readers' behavior. The macroscopic "layer" asserts the supposed inevitability of maximalist copyright because of the state of digital technologies and the presumed ir-resistible force of harmonization of national law with international copyright treaties. These two "layers" of technological determinism in the DMCA result from a number of conceptual bases that link cultural belief to extrem-ist policy actions like passage of the DMCA and support of its controlling provisions in the federal courts.

One such basis includes the technologically dystopian claims of copyright maximalists (there is uncontrolled "piracy" and lawlessness online) and tech-nological utopian claims of many of those same persons and actors ("the an-swer to the machine is in the machine"; see Clark 1996). Jamie Boyle neatly summarizes the effects of these utopian and dystopian claims as enacted by statute: Congress "generally overstated the threat posed by the digital world and underestimated the benefits" (2008, 103). The microscopic layer of technological determinism in the Digital Millennium Copyright Act is the assertion that individuals have no choice but to accommodate themselves to the particular technological arrangements that DRM and other technologies provide. Rightsholders act as if these technologies are demanded by the so-called realities of online communication, as if these technologies themselves had no social origins and no economic rationales or justifications. Thus, users are left with an all or nothing choice that leads us all to believe that such a so-cial arrangement is inevitable given the technologies that exist (Bijker 1995, 284). The agency that Suchman describes as springing from the interface of users and machines, key to STS understandings of technology, is clearly a casualty of this way of thinking and this kind of political relationship between readers and copyright holders.

Even further, however, the technological determinism hidden in utopian and dystopian beliefs about technologies claims that the clash of political, social, economic, and other values that cultural expression involves can be neatly resolved with the wave of a technological hand. It presumes that in-creasingly powerful and integrated technologies like encryption, barriers to copying, finely discriminated fared uses, and the like will end the ever-vexing questions about the status of cultural expression in a free society. Plainly they cannot. Like engineers in Kleif and Faulkner (2003, 319), American policy makers and others regard the technological as a means to eliminate "the un-certainty and ambiguity" in the social and as a "solution" to difficult social and political problems.

This point leads to the more macroscopic way that the DMCA is techno-logically determinist. This argument has two main parts. The first is the story of the passage of the DMCA told above: the failure in the U.S. Congress of the 1995 White Paper's maximalist claims, use of the World Intellectual Property Organization's treaty negotiation process to include copyright

maximalist provisions of those failed Congressional bills, and using the presumed necessity of "international harmonization" to convince the Congress
to pass the DMCA, especially its most extreme forbidding of circumventions
of technologies encapsulating copyrighted works. Gillespie (2007), among
others, describes the second part of the macroscopic character of the DMCA.
For maximalist copyright claims to be understood and legitimated in politics, there must be a dominant narrative of irresistible technological change
that demands political accommodation (the clearest form of technological
determinism). For this narrative to produce the kinds of control desired by
maximalist copyright, however, then there must be a seamless integration
of strongly controlling technologies with business and economic arrangements of control, and with strong, controlling policy instruments passed by
the Congress and enforced by the courts (what Gillespie identifies as locks,
licenses, and laws, 167ff.). Digital rights management, especially as enforced
by the DMCA, makes this tripartite seamless arrangement largely through an
unquestioned narrative of technological determinism.

The DMCA constructs readers as passive individuals, passive "consumers" or receivers of meaning that creators of copyrighted works put into
their works. Distributors of copyrighted works, including those who use
digital rights management technologies to create the trusted systems described by Stefik (1999) and others, then pass along that meaning to users.
These so-called consumers must either accept the political arrangements
supposedly made inevitable by digital technologies or not use copyrighted
works online at all. This form of microscopic technological determinism
is plainly mistaken, roundly contradicted by the work described earlier in
this chapter showing how readers are active, meaning-making poachers,
making themselves as they use documents to learn to be. Such determinism also ignores the four STS concepts discussed in the previous section of
this chapter. Further, the DMCA is based on a clearly misguided analysis
of the supposed imperative of "harmonizing" U.S. copyright law with the
World Intellectual Property Organization treaties of 1996. This form of
macroscopic technological determinism ignores how U.S. representatives
to the talks that preceded the WIPO treaties used those talks, in essence, to
back the Congress into a corner. These representatives far exceeded their
expectations when Congress made the Digital Millennium Copyright Act
even more draconian that the treaties appeared to demand. Thus, the polity leaves unexamined and, worse, reinforces, the supposedly compelling
union of technological, economic, and political arrangements that make
copyright maximalism such a threat to cultural expression. Rosalind Williams reminds us that "[a]uthoritarian technics is designed to be determina-
tive, to place power in the technological system itself" (1994, 228). This

is the virtually unfettered reign of the trusted system, in which people lose agency because of technology's supposedly irresistible power.

PROTECTING PRIVACY: READING AND POLITICAL AUTONOMY

The connection among reading, identity, and autonomy has been widely recognized under the law and in social mores. Further, this connection is explicitly linked to what we now consider privacy interests.[8] Among these are constitutional protections of papers and possessions, e.g., the Fourth and Fifth Amendment protections against illegal search and seizure and protections against self-incrimination; First Amendment and jurisprudential protections of expression and intellectual inquiry, e.g., *Griswold v. Connecticut* (1965) and *Stanley v. Georgia* (1969); state law protection of library circulation records; and federal statutes protecting video rental, cable television subscriptions, and some financial transactions. The First Amendment to the U.S. Constitution maintains that:

> Congress shall make no law respecting an establishment of religion, or prohibiting the free exercise thereof; or abridging the freedom of speech, or of the press; or the right of the people peaceably to assemble, and to petition the Government for a redress of grievances.

It may seem surprising that copyright is not a larger source of litigation related to the First Amendment, especially the freedom of speech, but, on further examination, this fact is not surprising (see Netanel 2001 and 2008 and Lange and Powell 2009 on this paradox of copyright).

The traditional response in American law to questions about copyright as a restraint on free speech are the so-called safety valves protecting copyright from such concerns. Prominent among these safety valves are the limited terms of copyright protection, the fair use exception, the doctrine of first sale (including the protection of users' anonymity), the idea/expression dichotomy (protecting the way that ideas are expressed rather than the ideas themselves), cultural repositories' exemptions from certain kinds of accusations about misappropriation, compulsory licenses for music and broadcast television shows, and the inability of copyright to be extended to "facts." Some of these safety valves, e.g., fair use, first sale, and certain exceptions for libraries and the like, are explicitly incorporated into Title 17 of the *U.S. Code* along with the exclusive rights enumerated for rightsholders. In truth, however, the rather facile assumption that these safety valves are unproblematic and obtain across all kinds of uses of copyrighted works is increasingly under fire.[9] With that said, however, federal judges, practicing attorneys,

Congress, and copyright holders generally rely on the presumption that these safety valves are adequate protections of the right to communicate under the First Amendment.

Further, the legal attention to copyright regarding the First Amendment has largely been limited to the freedom of expression rather than what we might call the freedom to read. Baruh states bluntly that although "the first amendment only incidentally recognizes the rights of the readers, legal precedents establish a concrete understanding of the connection between the right to read, watch and listen and the right to speech," citing a number of Supreme Court and other federal cases recognizing the importance of the right to read (2007, 193). While there has been a steady stream of court cases and law journal commentaries about freedom of speech, there has been relatively little about the freedom to read. A most telling exception, however, is Julie Cohen's influential 1996 paper "A Right to Read Anonymously: A Closer Look at 'Copyright Management' in Cyberspace," which, as the title makes clear, joins together examinations of copyright enforcement with the right to read anonymously.[10] The concept of anonymity online has been the focus of a growing body of literature in the law,[11] but even this literature does not deeply explore the relationship between reading and privacy in the context of copyright.

What makes that lack of special interest, as Cohen (1996) and others make clear, is that the increasingly maximalist copyright doctrine makes it more difficult to read digital material without copyright owners' knowledge and explicit permission. Further, readers of online materials must meet whatever financial and other conditions on reading and subsequent use those owners impose. The focus of Cohen's wide-ranging discussion of copyright management is the First Amendment case to be made to protect readers' anonymity in the face of digital rights management (DRM) systems then developing and what became the anticircumvention provisions of the Digital Millennium Copyright Act. She argues that "reading is so intimately connected with speech and freedom of thought that the First Amendment should be understood to guarantee such a right" (982) and that reading is "so expressive in its own right" that it deserves First Amendment protection (1039).

She bases her argument for the First Amendment interests at stake in reading generally and in reading anonymously online on the kinds of systems that offered copyrighted material in 1996. These systems, now commonly called digital rights management (DRM) systems, have had a mixed record of success, with CD's with strict and intrusive DRM systems laughed out of the marketplace (see, e.g., Gillespie 2007 on SDMI, the secure digital music initiative), but with similar systems accepted and avidly protected by the courts for other media, e.g., books, websites, and journal articles. The DRM

systems protected by the Digital Millennium Copyright Act enable unparalleled aggregation and scrutiny of individuals' reading habits online. These
systems then pose what Cohen and others identify as fundamental threats
to the privacy of reading and the First Amendment interests in individual
expression that the privacy of reading provides. As she cogently argues, the
collection, aggregation, and subsequent use of information about individuals'
reading online need not happen. For example, copyright control could exist
quite easily with anonymizing and automatically self-purging systems that
control interaction with online customers. Instead, we have the current situation where, with few exceptions, we "enable copyright owners who desire it
to maintain comprehensive databases of who is reading what" (989).

Cohen provides a useful list of specific kinds of monitoring that DRM
systems now routinely provide rightsholders and others (983–84). Using the
example of a purchase of a collection of online essays, rightsholders insert
code into the collection that will track (1) each time any one of the essays is
opened, (2) which essay is opened, and (3) which functions are used, from
simple browsing to cutting and pasting, printing, and the like. More importantly from the perspective of identity and autonomy, (4) the rightsholder can
prevent looking at the essay, as well as printing or cutting a section of the
essay, except in the circumstances, in the technological environments, and on
the devices the rightsholder approves.[12] Then, (5) the rightsholder, business
partners, and third-party aggregators like Google Books and similar initiatives can generate profiles of users with important and commercially valuable information such as full name, mailing address, credit card information,
email address, Internet Service Provider (ISP), and the like. Such profiles
related directly to particular reading materials are clearly new violations of
the usual expectations that readers have long had about their reading; it was
largely private absent any compelling reason to make it otherwise. As Cohen
and many other scholars interested in the privacy of users of online materials
assert, "[n]one of these intrusions need occur" (987). The very existence of
copyright owners' "comprehensive databases of who is reading what" has a
chilling effect on what readers want to read.

Later, she has a section in her 1996 paper exploring "A Right to Read
Anonymously" (1003–19). Although it is commonly recognized that anonymous as opposed to pseudonymous use of online materials may not be possible or desirable (see, e.g., Lessig 2006), Cohen's argument in this section
provides a very useful explanation of the status of reading under the First
Amendment and the importance of reading to the free inquiry the First
Amendment seeks to protect. She begins by noting that American jurisprudence has focused on freedom of expression, identifying readers' interests
"only incidentally" (1003). As Cohen discusses, one of the primary causes

of First Amendment jurisprudence's ignoring of reading *per se* is our shared cultural belief that reading is largely passive while speaking is not (see, for example, Michel de Certeau's and other theorists' stringent critique of this faulty assumption discussed above). Reader response theory and the active reading of hypertext are among the examples that she gives to demonstrate that distinguishing "'active' expression and 'passive' receipt is less clear than one might suppose" (1005). It is the term *receipt* of information that characterizes the Supreme Court cases that she cites as the most important to the consideration of the privacy of reading.

Prominent in her argument are *Lamont v. Postmaster General* (1965) and *Stanley v. Georgia* (1969), both expressive of the jurisprudence and doctrinal reasoning that emerged from the McCarthy era in U.S. politics. *Lamont* protected reading of political materials that were presumably communist propaganda, and Cohen cites Justice Clark's opinion warning about "'the chilling effect that disclosure of individual[s'] reading preferences would produce,'" most especially on what people chose to read (1007). In a case related to purportedly obscene materials, Justice Marshall underscored the First Amendment protection in *Stanley* of "'the right to satisfy [one's] intellectual and emotional needs in the privacy of [one's] own home'" and to be "'free from state inquiry into the contents of [one's] library.'" As Cohen notes, "[t]his is privacy language, and has been recognized as such" (1009), and that, in subsequent decisions (see her note 118 inter alia), the Supreme Court clearly asserted that the First Amendment affirms a right to largely unfettered intellectual inquiry and freedom of thought, "a right that necessarily includes the freedom to read unobserved" (1011). Unfortunately, the *Stanley* court and others (e.g., *Griswold v. Connecticut*, 1965) have used language like the "receipt of information and ideas" to describe reading/listening/viewing, plainly reiterating the mistaken view of reading as passive. Cohen later draws the clear link between reading and each person's right to build one's identity unobserved, and it is this point that leads us directly to considering how the unparalleled surveillance of reading made possible by the Digital Millennium Copyright Act and the Act's technological determinism undermine privacy.

WHY COPYRIGHT SURVEILLANCE AND TECHNOLOGICAL DETERMINISM MATTER

As discussed throughout this chapter, there are a number of ill effects from the culture of copyright maximalism and copyright surveillance that led to the Digital Millennium Copyright Act and facilitate the Act's increased surveillance of reading. The first kind of negative outcomes involve *conceptual errors* that twist policy deliberations and decisions. Some of these errors have been discussed earlier in this chapter, but they merit summation here:

1. As discussed by many commentators, e.g., Boyle (2008), Congressional deliberations and hearings, federal statutes, executive branch task forces, and the like have generally overstated the threats of digital technologies for copyrighted works and have systematically underestimated the benefits of these technologies for creators and commercial rightsholders generally.

2. There is a general attitude in American culture about technology and about the politics of technology that we are helpless in the face of current technological arrangements that seem both historically inevitable and irresistible. They are neither (Bijker 1995 and Suchman 2007).

3. There is a concomitant belief that any policy conflicts about privacy, copyright, and technologies can be "solved" by technical means. Certainly, technical means cannot resolve value conflicts, and it is value conflicts that lie at the heart of political conflicts.

4. The larger political and economic context in which the DMCA and its privacy threats exist supports a largely unquestioned ideology of control of copyright that goes hand in glove with controlling technologies and economic arrangements that emphasize control, taking advantage of the asymmetry of relations between large corporate and governmental interests and individuals or groups of individuals (see, e.g., Gillespie 2007 and Lessig 2001 and 2006).

As discussed throughout this chapter, however, the negative implications of copyright surveillance and the DMCA are not just conceptual. Instead, they clearly threaten the privacy of reading.

The DMCA's technological determinism directly undermines the privacy of reading; this is a more microscopic perspective of special interest to public policy, focusing on the ill effects of the Act on individuals and their behaviors. The first of these ill effects is *the chilling effect of knowing one's reading is monitored*.[13] This chilling effect is not merely an abstract problem; it is especially pernicious with regard to material related to what we commonly regard as especially "private" behavior, e.g., sexual identity, group membership, unpopular political opinions, and antigovernmental activity. This surveillance has several results:

1. Copyright surveillance *reduces reading* in a number of direct and indirect ways. Rightsholders can charge for every reading and other use, e.g., porting a digital file from a handheld communication device to an

MP3 player. While rightsholders welcome such revenue streams and the ability to make increasingly fine price discriminations among users, this right is a power rightsholders never had before.

2. Further, *curiosity and leisurely browsing* are directly curtailed, as are quoting, citing, combining, and other uses of copyrighted materials that are among the chief rationales for granting copyright protection in the first place.

3. And, finally, reading is reduced because of the *uncertainty* of being observed. More specifically, there is a clear chilling effect on reading, and thus on using reading to try out identity, by the invasiveness of *not* knowing that one's reading is monitored and shared with rightsholders' business partners. One fears that it might be, that it can be, but one is never sure when or how. Thus, the panoptic discipline of self-imposed limitation of reading occurs.

This interrelated series of inhibitions of reading leads to another negative outcome of copyright surveillance on reading: the stifling of communication.

More particularly copyright surveillance enabled by the DMCA and similar policy instruments put *clear limitations of the First Amendment* goal of ensuring the creation and sharing of many and heterogeneous forms of cultural expression to as many persons as possible (especially see Cohen 1996 and 2003, Lange and Powell 2009, and Lessig 2001 and 2006). Even if we question the easy presumption that more information leads to a more informed electorate, better deliberation, and better democracy, we can still recognize the normative imperative for communication to be open. Less reading means narrower communication, especially for those with unpopular and/or anti-governmental views. Reading is key to writing, and thereby reading widely and deeply is key to freedom of expression. We have, unfortunately, tended to minimize the value of reading, in itself and as the foundation of speech, in our long-held tradition of protecting freedom of speech (Baruh 2007; Cohen 1996). Less reading means less speech and less informed speech. Further, as Wiebe Bijker demonstrates, "[d]eterminism inhibits the development of democratic control on technology because it suggests that all interventions are futile" (1995, 281). Surely this outcome is not what we want from copyright statutes or jurisprudence. In fact, copyright is meant to have the opposite effect; that is, the enhancement of the intellectual vibrancy of the polity and an affirmation of the agency of individuals and the political order as a whole to determine their own fates.

The fourth and final outcome to mention here involves what we might term the temporal character of the anticircumvention provisions of the Digital Millennium Copyright Act. Because these technological measures to protect

digital works under the DMCA do not expire the way that a copyright's limited term does, even works that enter the public domain by virtue of reaching the limitation of the copyright term cannot be used through means such
as reverse engineering that circumvent the technological protections. Such
works, in essence, are given the protection of copyright law (the DMCA's
anticircumvention provisions and copyright more generally) then are made
the expressive property of the rights owners in perpetuity. This outcome is
plainly antithetical to the public policy aims of copyright, a paradoxical additional threat to the robust communication that both copyright and the First
Amendment were established to engender.

As this chapter has endeavored to demonstrate, the formation of self, the very
foundation of making an evolving and responsive identity, needs privacy, especially privacy of reading, to flourish. The intrusion into the privacy of reading
enabled by the Digital Millennium Copyright Act, especially its enactment of
the mistaken belief that the machine is the answer to the machine, ignores the
active reader and the reader making a dynamic, evolving self in concert with
others. The DMCA constitutes citizens only as passive consumers of cultural
goods, not active, self-defining readers, listeners, and viewers. Technological
determinism is an essential tool of this construction that leads to stifling copyright surveillance as much as copyright maximalism does.

CONCLUSION

A major insight of the study of culture over the last several decades has
been that we are never and never could be innocent of the past. Science and
Technology Studies has informed some of the legal and policy literature for
more than a decade (e.g., Boyle 1996 and 2008; Cohen 1996 and 2003), and
an essential insight of STS is that material circumstances and the effects of
history cannot be ignored. Thus, while we made the DMCA and can remake
it, subsequent policy change is *not* entirely open. As a polity, we are substan-
tially constrained by what has happened before and by the particular social
and legal arrangements we have already made. Yet we are *not* powerless in
the face of what we have made. A more realistic view is one that Scranton
(1994, 143) describes: "We recognize that our choices are limited but not
totally determined by the natural and social orders we live in." The embrace
of how things can be different, but not without limit, is key to understanding
how cultural theory and close reading of history can inform policy study.

The argument begins with the recognition that, relying on the Digital
Millennium Copyright Act, especially its technological determinism and
its anticircumvention provisions, rightsholders and others can monitor our

reading and control what we do with what we read, view, and listen to, as never before. As discussed earlier, the DMCA's technological determinism emerges from a number of naïve presumptions.

The first naïve presumption arises from an ahistorical view that the DMCA "had to" be what it is in order to harmonize U.S. copyright law with the World Intellectual Property Organization treaties that preceded the Act. This presumed rationale is mistaken on two counts. First, the DMCA far exceeds the WIPO treaties' demands for surveilling and limiting users of online files, echoing instead the failed legislative agenda that emerged from the IITF White Paper in 1995. Second, what the DMCA implements is the White Paper's mistaken identification of copyright with protections granted to owners of real property.

The second naïve presumption of the DMCA's technological determinism is a simplistic view that information policy supposedly always trails information technology development. This presumption, too, is flawed along at least two dimensions. First, policy often deliberately leads IT development by funding some IT research initiatives and teams (e.g., the National Science Foundation's support of digital library research), aggregating markets for particular technologies (e.g., the Internet), funding particular conferences and travel arrangements, and buying particular software and hardware configurations in the multibillion-dollar-per-year process of government IT procurement. Second, *if there is* a presumed gap between IT and policy development, that gap is often deliberate. That is, such a gap allows important policy issues and actors to emerge, often over decades; it allows competing technologies to demonstrate their strengths and weaknesses in the marketplace (an important ideological element of the so-called marketplace of ideas); and it inhibits the formation of any integrated U.S. industrial policy. This last is another important ideological imperative in the United States which, in contrast to every other "developed" nation, has no formal industrial policy and insists that the development of such a policy would interfere with market forces.

The third naïve presumption underlying the technological determinism of the DMCA is that the online world is primarily chaotic, largely empty if not for major copyright holders' material, and populated by pirates. This presumption ignores the thriving Internet populated by donated, open sources, and other freely given material, which existed for decades before the explosive growth of Internet use facilitated by the release of the first graphical web browser in 1993. This wealth of material persists. Even worse, however, is that this presumption forgets that copyright is a product of only the past five centuries. Put bluntly, saying that people create only because of the incentive of copyright ignores the thousands of generations of cultural creation of things such as language, music, poetry, drama, axes, bows, knots, graphical arts, and on and on that preceded copyright. While this point cannot be further developed here, the question of copyright-as-incentive is one about which lawyers and others make large claims but about which none of us knows much. What is clear is that creative people create because they must and they can. What else is clear is that copyright strongly protects the interests of for-profit distributors, especially large, vertically integrated media companies, not those of creators. These middlemen play vital social and economic roles such as quality control, cultivation of talent, aggregation of audiences, and wide distribution. At the same time, however, these middlemen are rarely creators. The DMCA and its ideological roots ignore these undeniable facts.

What deeper reflection leads us to is a clear need to reassert human agency and autonomy, which are key to privacy and identity formation, in the face of naively unquestioned imperatives of history, technology, and policy. And science and technology studies (STS) can help us do so conceptually and politically.

There is a commonplace in STS that it is important to remember that technologies might always have been otherwise.[14] Lohan and Faulkner (2004, 322) revisit Thomas Hughes's work, the source of the currently widely used concept of the sociotechnical discussed above.[15] This concept is key to the insights of science and technology studies and is of particular use here in that it recognizes that "[t]he possibility always exists that a technology and its outcomes could be otherwise." This sense of contingency and, thereby, human choice and agency, is a direct contradiction to the simplistic and presumed inevitability of technological and historical determinism that undergird the copyright maximalism of the DMCA and similar policy instruments. In his discussion of narrative policy analysis, Emery Roe (1994, 31) offers a very useful reminder, not just to policy analysts but also to historians, political commentators, and scholars more generally: "Contrary to the view of historical determinists, it is precisely history, or at least history as the repository of alternatives, that gives the present its sense of contingency." This theme of alternatives, difference, and contingency must animate our understanding of the policy process, including copyright policy instruments such as the DMCA.

Some legal scholars have long recognized this antideterministic argument, e.g., Cohen (1996). The Congress, the courts, rightsholders, technologists, and others have made the DMCA what it is. We made the DMCA and can remake it. Judy Wajcman provides some useful guidance here. She reminds us that technological determinism, especially its naïveté, "narrows the possibilities for democratic engagement with technology, by presenting a limited set of options: uncritical embracing of technological change, defensive adaptation to it, or simple rejection of it" (2004, 33). This concern echoes the theme of autonomy and agency that animates much of the privacy and STS literatures. While technology is obdurate in many ways, whether artifactual, intellectual, or social technologies, it is not irresistible, and recognizing that fact is key to doing politics. Wiebe E. Bijker provides a valuable perspective on this complex of ideas:

> Arguing for the malleability of technology does not imply that we can forget about the solidity and momentum of sociotechnical ensembles. Overly optimistic expectations based on a false sense of infinite malleability can easily cause disillusionment. A politics and a theory of socio-technology have to meet similar requirements in this regard: a balance between actor and structure perspectives in theory. (1997, 281)

For Bijker, Wajcman, and others, including STS and legal scholars, determinism is paradoxical in many ways—particularly in that it is optimistic about the liberatory possibilities of technology (an essential part of the Enlightenment ideology) but pessimistic about individuals' and polities' ability to resist technologies' supposed inherent characteristics and effects. Not examining this paradox, as these scholars and others remind us, threatens the autonomy that privacy depends upon, particularly the use of cultural expression for identity formation.

We cannot afford "merely gaping" (Heidegger 1997, 314) at either the supposed chaos of the Internet and the presumed resultant uncontrolled "piracy" of copyrighted material or the presumed inevitable, unassailable technological fixes that guarantee a presumed fair return to copyright holders. If we do gape, we are paralyzed politically, especially since we then recognize only the agency of copyright owners to protect their "property," not the agency of the polity to negotiate the copyright bargain to serve the polity's needs, not just those of owners. Further, we must recognize the complex character of reading and the value of protecting the privacy of reading so that we can use reading to make and remake our senses of self. Leaving aside any question about the particular copyright theory on which it rests, the DMCA does *not* demand the surveillance, database construction, and invasions of privacy that it allows. Copyright interests can be protected under the Act without using the Act to invade and compromise the privacy of readers, listeners, and viewers. It could have been and can be otherwise.

NOTES

1. How narratives of reading are essential to the formation of selves through time is a topic that deserves much more sustained attention in the policy and legal literatures.

2. The literature about communities and document use is quite large and growing rapidly in information studies and in many other disciplines. See, e.g., Bishop and Star (1996), Brown and Duguid (1991 and 2002), Levy (2001 and 2003), and Star et al. (2003).

3. The foundational work of Jürgen Habermas (1991) on early modernity, especially on the reading public, newspapers, journals, and books, is quite useful here, as is the work of commentators on his work, e.g., Baker (1992) and Fraser (1992), and that of social historians of the book, reading, and the library, e.g., Augst (2007), Goodman (1994), Johns (1998), and Sher (2006).

4. See Harkin (2005) for a useful history of the adoption of reader response theory.

5. Michael Reddy (1993) provides a well-known and influential critique of the conduit metaphor.

6. The interested reader is encouraged to see, for example, additional work in American technology studies by Merritt Roe Smith, Leo Marx, David Noble, Judith McGaw, Carroll Purcell, and David Nye. The research of Donald MacKenzie is especially valuable in bringing together highly focused technology studies (see, for example, his groundbreaking 1985 work with Judy Wajcman on *The Social Shaping of Technology*), with consideration of information systems, e.g., *Knowing Machines* (1998).

7. Examples of technoenthusiastic studies of the cultural status of ICTs include well-known works such as Castells (1996 and 2001), Negroponte (1995), and Toffler (1980). As is widely recognized, the technophoria of these and similar authors is all too common, with only Castells of the three offering any serious and specific critique of such enthusiasm. Also see Braman (2006) that exhibits a different sort of analytic emphasis.

8. While much of the legal and policy literature tends to ignore the intersection of copyright, privacy, and expression, there are a number of very useful works that merit extended consideration that the author will give them in a subsequent study. This chapter can touch only lightly on these literatures.

9. A good sample of the critiques of the easy assumption that the safety valves protect copyright from First Amendment scrutiny can be found in Boyle (1996 and 2008), Goldstein (2003), Lange and Powell (2009), Lessig (2001 and 2004), Netanel (2001 and 2008), and Vaidhyanathan (2001 and 2004). The books by Netanel (2008) and Lange and Powell (2009) are especially valuable on this point.

10. Also see Baruh (2007), Grodzinsky and Tavani (2005), Katyal (2004), Kerr (2005), and Kerr and Bailey (2004).

11. Useful discussions of anonymity in the law can be found in Kennedy (2006); Lessig (2006); Nicoll, Prins, and van Dellen (2003); and Waldo et al. (2007).

12. See Boyle (2008), Gillespie (2007), Katyal (2004), Netanel (2008), and Patry (2009) about these and other limitations on reading online.

13. Cohen (1996 and 2003), Goffman (1959), Grodzinsky and Tavani (2005), Katyal (2004), and Litman (2007). Of course, any mention of chilling effects of surveillance must mention Foucault's panoptic metaphor despite the critiques of the limiting effects of this metaphor's virtual hegemony in surveillance studies, e.g., Lyon (2006).

14. Bijker (1995), Bijker et al. (1987), and Wajcman (2004) very usefully discuss the contingency of the technological and political orders. Other STS sources cited in this chapter do as well.

15. On the sociotechnical, also see Lerman et al. (2003), Latour and Woolgar (1979), Bijker (1995), and Bijker et al. (1987).

REFERENCES

Agre, Philip E. 1997. Introduction. In *Technology and privacy: The new landscape*, ed. Philip E. Agre and Marc Rotenberg, 1–28. Cambridge, MA: MIT Press.

Augst, Thomas. 2007. Faith in reading: Public libraries, liberalism, and the civil religion. In *Institutions of reading: The social life of libraries in the United States*, ed. Thomas Augst and Kenneth Carpenter, 148–83. Amherst, MA: University of Massachusetts Press.

Baker, Keith Michael. 1992. Defining the public sphere in eighteenth-century France: Variations on a theme by Habermas. In *Habermas and the public sphere*, ed. Craig Calhoun, 181–211. Cambridge, MA: MIT Press.

Barthes, Ronald. 1974. *S/Z*, trans. Richard Miller. New York: Hill and Wang.

Baruh, Lemi. 2007. Read at your own risk: Shrinkage of privacy and interactive media. *New Media and Society* 9, no. 2: 187–211.

Bijker, Wiebe E. 1995. *Of bicycles, Bakelites, and bulbs: Toward a theory of sociotechnical change*. Cambridge, MA: MIT Press.

Bijker, Wiebe E., Thomas Hughes, and Trevor Pinch, eds. 1987. *The social construction of technological systems: New directions in the sociology and history of technology*. Cambridge, MA: MIT Press.

Bilal, Dania. 2007. Grounding children's information behavior and system design in child development theories. In *Information and emotion: The emergent affective paradigm in information behavior research and theory*, ed. Diane Nahl and Dania Bilal, 39–50. Medford, NJ: Information Today.

Bishop, Ann P., and Susan Leigh Star. 1996. Social informatics of digital library use and infrastructure. In *Annual review of information science and technology*, vol. 31, ed. Martha Williams, 301–401. Medford, NJ: Information Today.

Boyarin, Jonathan, ed. 1993. *The ethnography of reading*. Berkeley, CA: University of California Press.

Boyle, James. 1996. *Shamans, software, and spleens: Law and the construction of the information society*. Cambridge, MA: Harvard University Press.

———. 2008. *The public domain: Enclosing the commons of the mind*. New Haven, CT: Yale University Press.

Braman, Sandra. 2006. *Change of state: Information, policy, and power*. Cambridge, MA: MIT Press.

Brandth, Berit, and Marit S. Haugen. 2005. Text, body, and tools: Changing mediations of rural masculinity. *Men and Masculinities* 8, no. 2: 148–63.

Brown, John Seely, and Paul Duguid. 1991. Organizational learning and communities-of-practice: Toward a unified view of working, learning, and innovation. *Organization Science* 2, no. 1: 40–57.

———. 2002. *The social life of information*, 2nd ed. Boston: Harvard Business School Press.

242 *Doty*

Castells, Manuel. 1996. *Rise of the network society*. Oxford, UK: Blackwell.
Castells, Manuel. 2001. *The Internet galaxy: Reflections on the Internet, business, and society*. Oxford, UK: Oxford University Press.
de Certeau, Michel. 1984. *The practice of everyday life*, trans. Steven Rendall. Berkeley, CA: University of California Press.
Clark, Charles. 1996. The answer to the machine is in the machine. In *The future of copyright in a digital environment*, ed. Bernt Hugenholtz, 139–45. The Hague: Kluwer Law International.
Cohen, Julie E. 1996. A right to read anonymously: A closer look at "copyright management" in cyberspace. *Connecticut Law Review* 28: 981–1039.
———. 2003. DRM and privacy. *Berkeley Technology Law Review* 18, no. 2: 575–617.
Foucault, Michel. 1977. *Discipline and punish: The birth of the prison*, trans. Alan Sheridan. New York: Pantheon Books.
Fraser, Nancy. 1992. Rethinking the public sphere: A contribution to the critique of actually existing democracy. In *Habermas and the public sphere*, ed. Craig Calhoun, 109–42. Cambridge, MA: MIT Press.
Gillespie, Tarleton. 2007. *Wired shut: Copyright and the shape of digital culture*. Cambridge, MA: MIT Press.
Goffman, Erving. 1959. *The presentation of self in everyday life*. New York: Anchor Books.
Goldstein, Paul. 2003. *Copyright's highway: From Gutenberg to the celestial jukebox*, rev. ed. Stanford, CA: Stanford University Press.
Goodman, Dena. 1994. *The republic of letters: A cultural history of the French Enlightenment*. Ithaca, NY: Cornell University Press.
Griswold v. Connecticut 381 U.S. 479 (1965).
Grodzinsky, Frances S., and Herman T. Tavani. 2005. P2P networks and the *Virginia v. RIAA* case: Implications for personal privacy and intellectual property. *Ethics and Information Technology* 7, no. 4: 243–50.
Habermas, Jürgen. (1991). *The structural transformation of the public sphere: An inquiry into a category of bourgeois society*, trans. Thomas Burger and Friedrich Lawrence. Cambridge, MA: MIT Press.
Harkin, Patricia. (2005). The reception of reader-response theory. *College Composition and Communication* 56, no. 3: 410–25.
Heidegger, Martin. (1997). The question concerning technology, trans. William Lovitt. In *Basic writings*, ed. David Farrell Krell, 287–317. San Francisco: HarperSanFrancisco.
Johns, Adrian. 1998. *The nature of the book: Print and knowledge in the making*. Chicago: University of Chicago Press.
Katyal, Sonia K. 2004. Privacy vs. piracy. *Yale Journal of Law and Technology* 7: 222–345.
Kennedy, Helen. 2006. Beyond anonymity, or future directions for Internet identity research. 18, no. 6: 859–76.
Kerr, Ian R. 2005. If left to their own devices . . . How DRM and anti-circumvention laws can be used to hack privacy. In , ed. Michael Geist, 167–210. Toronto: Irwin Law.

Kerr, Ian, and Jane Bailey. 2004. The implications of digital rights management for privacy and freedom of expression. *Information, Communication, and Ethics in Society* 2, no. 1: 87–97.

Kleif, Tine, and Wendy Faulkner. 2003. "I'm no athlete [but] I can make this thing dance!"—Men's pleasures in technology. *Science, Technology, and Human Values* 28, no. 2: 296–325.

Lamont v. Postmaster General, 381 U.S. 301 (1965).

Lange, David, and H. Jefferson Powell. 2009. *No law: Intellectual property in the image of an absolute First Amendment*. Stanford, CA: Stanford Law Books.

Latour, Bruno, and Steve Woolgar. 1979. *Laboratory life: The construction of scientific facts*. Princeton, NJ: Princeton University Press.

Lave, Jean, and Étienne Wenger. 1992. *Situated learning: Legitimate peripheral participation*. Cambridge, UK: Cambridge University Press.

Lerman, Nina E., Ruth Oldenziel, and Arwen Mohun, eds. 2003. *Gender and technology: A reader*. Baltimore: Johns Hopkins Press.

Lessig, Lawrence. 2001. *Future of ideas: The fate of the commons in a connected world*. New York: Random House.

———. 2004. *Free culture: How big media uses* [sic] *technology and the law to lock down culture and control creativity*. New York: Penguin.

———. 2006. . New York: Basic Books.

Levy, David. 2001. *Scrolling forward: Making sense of documents in the digital age* [sic]. New York: Arcade.

———. 2003. Documents and libraries: A sociotechnical perspective. In *Digital library use: Social practice in design and evaluation*, ed. Ann Peterson Bishop, Nancy Van House, and Barbara Buttenfield, 25–42. Cambridge, MA: MIT Press.

Litman, Jessica. 2000. The demonization of piracy. Computers, Freedom, and Privacy 2000: Challenging the Assumptions, Toronto, Canada.

———. 2001. *Digital copyright*. Amherst, NY: Prometheus Books.

———. 2007. Creative reading. *Law and Contemporary Problems* 70, no. 2: 175–83.

Lohan, Maria, and Wendy Faulkner. 2004. Masculinities and technologies: Some introductory remarks. *Men and Masculinities* 6, no. 4: 319–29.

Long, Elizabeth. 1993. Textual interpretation as collective action. In *The ethnography of reading*, ed. Jonathan Boyarin, 180–211. Berkeley, CA: University of California Press.

———. 2003. *Book clubs: Women and the uses of reading in everyday life*. Chicago: University of Chicago Press.

Lyon, David, ed. 2006. *Theorizing surveillance: The panopticon and beyond*. Portland, OR: Willan.

MacKenzie, Donald, and Judy Wajcman, eds. 1985. *The social shaping of technology: How the refrigerator got its hum*. Philadelphia: Open University Press.

MacKenzie, Donald. 1998. *Knowing machines: Essays on technical change*. Cambridge, MA: MIT Press.

Marx, Leo, and Merritt Roe Smith. 1994. Introduction. In *Does technology drive history? The dilemma of technological determinism*, ed. Merritt Roe Smith and Leo Marx, ix–xv. Cambridge, MA: MIT Press.

McKechnie, Lynne (E. F.), Catherine Sheldrick Ross, and Paulette Rothbauer. 2007. Affective dimensions of information seeking in the context of reading. In *Information and emotion: The emergent affective paradigm in information behavior research and theory*, ed. Diane Nahl and Dania Bilal, 187–95. Medford, NJ: Information Today.

Misa, Thomas J. 1988. How machines make history, and how historians (and others) help them to do so. *Science, Technology, and Human Values* 13, nos. 3/4: 308–31.

Nahl, Diane. 2007. The centrality of the affective in information behavior. In *Information and emotion: The emergent affective paradigm in information behavior research and theory*, ed. Diane Nahl and Dania Bilal, 3–37. Medford, NJ: Information Today.

Negroponte, Nicholas. 1995. *Being digital*. New York: Vintage.

Netanel, Neil Weinstock. 2001. Locating copyright within the First Amendment skein. *Stanford Law Review* 54, no. 1: 1–86.

———. 2008. *Copyright's paradox*. Oxford, UK: Oxford University Press.

Nicoll, C., J. E. J. Prins, and M. J. M. van Dellen, eds. 2003. *Digital anonymity and the law: Tensions and dimensions*. The Hague: TMC Asser Press.

Nye, David E. 2006. *Technology matters: Questions to live with*. Cambridge, MA: MIT Press.

O'Brien, Jodi. 1999. Writing in the body: Gender (re)production in online interaction. In *Communities in cyberspace*, ed. Marc A. Smith and Peter Kollock, 76–104. London: Routledge.

Patry, William. 2009, November. Blog on his book *Moral panics and the copyright wars*.

Rachels, James. 1975. Why privacy is important. *Philosophy and Public Affairs* 4, no. 4: 323–33.

Reddy, Michael J. 1993. The conduit metaphor: A case of frame conflict in our language about language. In *Metaphor and thought*, 2nd ed., ed. Andrew Ortony, 164–201. Cambridge, UK: Cambridge University Press.

Roe, Emery. 1994. *Narrative policy analysis: Theory and practice*. Durham, NC: Duke University Press.

Rürup, Reinhard. 1974. Historians and modern technology: Reflections on the development and current problems of the history of technology. *Technology and Culture* 15, no. 2: 161–93.

Scranton, Philip. 1994. Determinism and indeterminacy in the history of technology. In *Does technology drive history? The dilemma of technological determinism*, ed. Merritt Roe Smith and Leo Marx, 144–68. Cambridge, MA: MIT Press.

Sher, Richard B. 2006. *The Enlightenment and the book: Scottish authors and their publishers in eighteenth-century Britain, Ireland, and America*. Chicago: University of Chicago Press.

Shoemaker, David W. 2009. Self-exposure and exposure of the self: Informational privacy and the presentation of identity. *Ethics and Information Technology* 12, no. 1, 3–15.

Smith, Merritt Roe. 1994. Technological determinism in American culture. In *Does technology drive history? The dilemma of technological determinism*, ed. Merritt Roe Smith and Leo Marx, 1–35. Cambridge, MA: MIT Press.

Smith, Merritt Roe, and Leo Marx, eds. 1994. *Does technology drive history? The dilemma of technological determinism.* Cambridge, MA: MIT Press.

Smith, Michael L. 1994. Recourse of empire: Landscapes of progress in technological America. In *Does technology drive history? The dilemma of technological determinism*, eds. Merritt Roe Smith and Leo Marx, 37–52. Cambridge, MA: MIT Press.

Stanley v. Georgia, 394 U.S. 557 (1969).

Star, Susan Leigh, Geoffrey Bowker, and Laura J. Neumann. 2003. Transparency beyond the individual level of scale: Convergence between information artifacts and communities of practice. In *Digital library use: Social practice in design and evaluation*, ed. Ann Peterson Bishop, Nancy Van House, and Barbara Buttenfield, 241–70. Cambridge, MA: MIT Press.

Staudenmaier, John M. 1994. Rationality versus contingency in the history of technology. In *Does technology drive history? The dilemma of technological determinism*, ed. Merritt Roe Smith and Leo Marx, 260–73. Cambridge, MA: MIT Press.

Stefik, Mark. 1999. *The Internet edge: Social, legal, and technological challenges for a networked world.* Cambridge, MA: MIT Press.

Suchman, Lucy. 2007. *Human-Machine reconfigurations: Plans and situated actions*, 2nd ed. Cambridge, UK: Cambridge University Press.

Toffler, Alvin. 1980. *The third wave.* New York: Bantam.

Universal City Studios v. Reimerdes et al., 111 F. Supp. 2nd 294 (Southern District of New York), 2000.

Vaidhyanathan, Siva. 2001. *Copyrights and copywrongs: The rise of intellectual property and how it threatens creativity.* New York: New York University Press.

———. 2004. *The anarchist in the library: How the clash between freedom and control is hacking the real world and crashing the system.* New York: Basic Books.

Wajcman, Judy. 1991. *Feminism confronts technology.* University Park, PA: Pennsylvania State University Press.

———. 2004. *TechnoFeminism.* Cambridge, UK: Polity Press.

Waldo, James, Herbert S. Liu, and Lynette I. Millett, eds. 2007. *Engaging privacy and information technology in a digital age* [sic]. Committee on Privacy in the Information Age [*sic*]. National Research Council. Washington, DC: National Academy Press.

Wenger, Étienne. 1998. *Communities of practice: Learning, meaning, and identity.* Cambridge, UK: Cambridge University Press.

Williams, Raymond. 2003. *Television: Technology and cultural form*, 2nd ed. London: Routledge.

Williams, Rosalind. 1994. The political and feminist dimensions of technological determinism. In *Does technology drive history? The dilemma of technological determinism*, ed. Merritt Roe Smith and Leo Marx, 218–35. Cambridge, MA: MIT Press.

9

Privacy in Time of American War

Gesse Stark-Smith, Craig Blaha, and William Aspray
University of Texas at Austin

One of the responses to the 9-11 terrorist attacks and the subsequent "War on Terror" was a pendulum shift in government restrictions on civil liberties and privacy. This shift toward increased government restrictions on privacy is perhaps best represented by the USA PATRIOT Act of 2001 (PL 107-56), which provided law enforcement with new powers to fight terrorism, such as enhanced access to financial, business, and library records. There was little public discussion of the legitimacy of these new powers in the waning months of 2001. But as the public became more aware of the extent of new powers brought to the government, such as the ability to detain immigrants indefinitely and the ability to search telephone and email records without a court order, there began to be greater concern expressed about these powers and about the proper balance between privacy and national security.

Discussions of the USA PATRIOT Act commonly allude to a pattern of abrogation of privacy in times of heightened U.S. national security, and in particular to the internment of Japanese Americans during the Second World War. However, these discussions seldom include substantial historical information. In an August 18, 2003, speech at the American Enterprise Institute in support of the PATRIOT ACT, for example, then-Attorney General John Ashcroft used Winston Churchill's 1941 plea to the United States to "give us the tools and we will finish the job" to underscore the utility of the PATRIOT Act. "The Patriot Act opened opportunity for information sharing. To abandon this tool would disconnect the dots, risk American lives, sacrifice liberty, and reject September 11's lessons" (Ashcroft 2003).

Contrast this plea to save American lives and protect liberty by increasing surveillance with the January 2003 ACLU report entitled *Bigger Monster, Weaker Chains* that warns "Privacy and liberty in the United States are at risk. A combination of lightning-fast technological innovation and the erosion of privacy protections threatens to transform Big Brother from an oft-cited but remote threat into a very real part of American life. We are at risk of turning into a Surveillance Society" (Stanley and Steinhardt 2003).

This chapter provides a modest survey, using only secondary sources, of privacy issues that have arisen in times of American wars, going back to the Revolutionary War and including the War of 1812, the Mexican-American War, the U.S. Civil War, the Spanish-American War, the First and Second World Wars, the Korean War, and the Vietnam War.[1] (For the dates of and authorizations for these wars, see table 9.1.) We stop with the Vietnam War because it is difficult to give sufficient historical perspective on more recent conflicts.

We acknowledge that this account may be somewhat ahistorical in its approach. The notion of privacy has changed over time in the United States, and we apply a modern conception of privacy when analyzing historical events. Until the mid-nineteenth century, privacy was conceptualized as a property right. In the late nineteenth century, the notion was expanded to include the right to be let alone in one's personal affairs. In the late nineteenth century and throughout the twentieth century, uses made of technological innovations such as the telephone, heat scanners, and the Internet helped to redefine privacy rights. In the post–WWII Cold War era, privacy rights expanded to include concerns about intimate human relationships such as contraception and grandparental visitation rights. Thus, incidents from earlier wars that we

Table 9.1. U.S. Wars and Their Authorizations

War	Date	Authorization
American Revolution	1775–1783	Declaration of Independence
War of 1812	1812–1815	Article One
Mexican-American War	1846–1848	Article One
U.S. Civil War	1861–1865	Presidential Authority retroactively approved by Congress
Spanish-American War	1898	Article One
First World War	1914–1918 (U.S. 1917–1918)	Article One
Second World War	1939–1945 (U.S. 1941–1945)	Article One
Korean War	1950–1953	Support of UN Security Council Resolution
Vietnam War	1959–1979 (U.S. 1965–1973)	Gulf of Tonkin Resolution

identify as privacy violations using our modern conception of what privacy means might not have been articulated as such at the time. We believe, nevertheless, that it is useful for understanding today's situation to consider these examples from the past.

Even restricting oneself to today's America, scholars have had a difficult time in articulating what privacy is. There are many different and sometimes contradictory definitions circulating in the academic discussions of privacy.[2] One influential scholar, Daniel Solove, has abandoned the effort to provide a definition that includes all and only the issues one would regard as privacy issues. Instead, he has employed a bottom-up approach to create a taxonomy of sixteen types of privacy that fall into the four general categories of information collection, information processing, information dissemination, and invasion (Solove, 11).[3] We kept Solove's definitions in mind as we considered the various wars, but the main value this taxonomy had for us here was to provide an expansive notion of privacy. In the end, we found that most privacy violations during American wars involved monitoring or control of individuals and groups, usually by government but sometimes by private organizations in their pursuit of what they believed to be the national good. This account locates privacy issues at the heart of the tension between the interests of the state and those of the individual.

We use the term *monitor* to include what Solove describes as surveillance. Solove differentiates surveillance from simple observation by pointing out that surveillance is continuous and recorded:

> Surveillance is a sweeping form of investigatory power. It extends beyond a search, for it records behavior, social interaction, and potentially everything that a person says and does. Rather than targeting specific information, surveillance can ensnare a significant amount of data beyond any originally sought. (109)

We use the term *monitor* in order to extend Solove's definition of surveillance to include observation of behavior and social interaction without creating a record. Using the term *monitor* allows us to include types of behavioral observation that were encouraged during various wars among private citizens in ways that are not sufficiently described by "surveillance," such as between neighbors, family members, co-workers, or perfect strangers.

Solove uses two terms to describe what we mean by the term *control*: social control and decisional interference. When Solove refers to *decisional interference* he means "governmental interference with people's decisions regarding certain matters in their lives" (166). This government interference includes laws that regulate birth control, grandparental visitation rights, and other "private" matters. Social control is a complex topic. Solove refers to political scientist John Gilliom's definition:

Surveillance of human behavior is in place to control human behavior, whether by limiting access to programs or institutions, monitoring and affecting behavior within those arenas, or otherwise enforcing rules and norms by observing and recording acts of compliance and deviance. (108)

Social control is not necessarily harmful. It is the degree of surveillance or social control that "creates the problem; too much social control can inhibit freedom, self-expression, and identity creation" (108).

Solove associates the inhibition of behavior and enforcement of social control with the awareness by an individual that she is the subject of surveillance. "Not only can direct awareness of surveillance make a person feel extremely uncomfortable, but it can also cause that person to alter her behavior. Surveillance can lead to self-censorship and inhibition. Because of its inhibitory effects, surveillance is a tool of social control" (108). If one is not aware that she is under surveillance, the problem can be even more pronounced. The possibility of surveillance can create a panoptic effect, causing the individual to internalize surveillance and self-enforce the expected behaviors, severely limiting choice and individuality. "A more compelling reason why covert surveillance is problematic is that it can still have a chilling effect on behavior. In fact, there can be a more widespread chilling effect when people are generally aware of the possibility of surveillance but are never sure if they are being watched at any particular moment" (109).

In addition to the work of Solove, this chapter was influenced by the characterization of privacy by the political scientist Patricia Boling. (See her chapter in this volume.) Boling provides us with three broad conceptions of privacy: informational privacy (relating to the exchange and storage of information, or to surveillance), privacy of decisional autonomy (the ability to make decisions for oneself about personal matters, without interference from government or individuals), and privacy of (physical and mental) protected space ("a zone into which others may not intrude without our permission"). Not only do most of the instances of privacy assault in times of American war fit under these three broad categories, but this conceptualization also helps us to understand the relationship between privacy and civil liberty, as we discuss in the next section. To give definitive treatments of what privacy is or how privacy relates to civil liberty is beyond the scope of this paper. Our main goal is to provide sound historical examples that can help to inform these ongoing philosophical discussions.

In the end, we decided not to use Solove's or Boling's or anyone else's categorical privacy characterization as the principal organizational scheme for this chapter. For example, we do not present in a single section all examples of surveillance in American wars. Instead, the paper is organized chronologically, by war, allowing these events to remain open for interpretation using different conceptions of privacy.

CIVIL LIBERTIES AND VARIETIES OF PRIVACY

Before turning to our chronological account, it is useful to consider the interactions between civil liberties and privacy, to understand why certain wartime activities that are clearly violations of civil liberties can also be regarded as privacy violations. We will use Boling's three characterizations of privacy—informational privacy, decisional autonomy, and protected space—as the basis for our discussion of the relations between privacy and civil liberties. Each of these characterizations applies well to what we discovered about privacy issues in times of war, and they help to elucidate the relationship between privacy and civil liberties in these cases.

Civil liberties violations implicate privacy rights, inasmuch as part of the foundation of privacy is the belief that an individual is entitled to a personal space where she can formulate her own beliefs and express them. As legal scholar Fred Cate (1987) explains:

> The Supreme Court recognizes in the First Amendment an absolute prohibition on the state interfering with the thoughts and beliefs of the individual. This guarantees to every person an inner sanctum where the state may not intrude and marks the core of U.S. privacy protection. (54)

By this logic, First Amendment violations can be seen as intruding upon this "inner sanctum" and therefore as attacks on privacy. Thus the civil liberty guaranteed by the First Amendment of no state interference in the thoughts and beliefs of the individual are tied most closely to the privacy of protected space as described by Boling.

When the government monitors communications that are regarded as private, we can clearly agree that what Boling characterizes as informational privacy is being involved. Additionally, we argue that when the government controls the behavior of its citizens, privacy issues may also arise of the sort that Boling characterizes as decisional autonomy. Government control of individual behavior has often been accomplished through civil liberties restrictions of action and expression placed on particular groups of people based on identifiers ranging from their ethnicity to their national origins to their political views. These restrictions might dictate who could go where and when, who could vote, or even what opinions could be expressed. Limiting the ability of an individual to express personal opinions or punish individuals when they do express an opinion is abhorrent to the sanctity of the individual, to the development of one's own identity. As we will see below, restrictions that were sometimes enforced by the government and at other times by civilians (acting on their patriotism and beliefs) inhibited the individual's ability to cultivate her identity. Such infringements on an individual's ability to form her own identity can be seen as an extension of Boling's concept of violating decisional autonomy and as assaults on both civil liberties and privacy.

THE AMERICAN REVOLUTIONARY WAR (1775–1783)

In this war for American independence, perhaps as much as one-fifth of the population remained loyal to the British government, and at least twenty-five thousand so-called Loyalists fought on the side of the British. During the war, many restrictions were placed on the civil and economic rights of those who opposed the revolution:

> They could neither vote nor hold office. They could neither collect debts nor buy and sell land. They were barred from the practice of law and such other professions as teaching. For any act of opposition, they felt the pain of fines, imprisonment, exile, loss of property, and even execution. Those were the officially imposed punishments. (Abrahamson 2001, 18)

One could not keep one's political opinions private, and public knowledge of these opinions carried clear consequences during the Revolutionary War.

The government had monitored individuals and groups since the early eighteenth century. In 1753 Benjamin Franklin, who had been placed in charge of the colonial mail by the British government in 1730, required that his employees swear not to open the mail that passed through their hands (Smith 2004, 49). Nonetheless, the privacy of materials sent through the mail was not yet well established by the time of the Revolutionary War, and mail was read freely during the war. In 1774 the British government dismissed Franklin for his sympathies to the colonies, and William Goddard, a newspaper publisher, established a private Constitutional Post the following year to serve the colonies. Goddard claimed of the Crown's mail service: "Letters are liable to be stopped & opened by ministerial mandates, & their Contents construed into treasonable Conspiracies; and News Papers, those necessary and important vehicles, especially in Times of public Danger, may be rendered of little avail for want of Circulation" (USPS 2006, 3). The Continental Congress established a new federal postal system in 1775, with Franklin as Postmaster General. Toward the end of the war, in 1782, Congress passed a law prohibiting postal clerks from reading or tampering with the mail (Seipp 1981).

THE WAR OF 1812 (1812–1815)

The War of 1812, which pitted Britain and what later became Canada against the Americans, was caused in part by the British attempt to stop American trade with France, with which Britain was then at war. A contributing factor was the British support of Native American tribes, whose support had thwarted the American government's expansionist plans along the frontier. Many of the war's battles were fought on the eastern seaboard of the United States and on the land fronting the St. Lawrence River.

The Baltimore riots of 1812 are an important example of private parties' exercising monitoring and control. Baltimore was a town with many French, Irish, and German immigrants who hated the British. The *Federal Republican* was a well-known Federalist newspaper that opposed the war. The offices of the newspaper were destroyed in the first night of rioting in June 1812 (Gilje 1980). Local government, which supported the war, denounced the violence but did nothing to stop it. Mob gatherings continued, with the mob looking for individuals who had been known in the past to express pro-British sympathies, including several free blacks.[4] When the second editor of the *Federal Republican* reestablished the paper in Baltimore a month later, he surrounded himself with Federalist supporters to deter mob action. Local residents became aware of the newspaper's return, and a mob of one thousand people gathered to protest. During the night of July 27, shots were fired on the crowd as they threw stones at the newspaper offices and began to break in through the front door (553). While this is clearly a story about the First Amendment right of the freedom of the press, it is also a story about privacy in that the mobs, with implicit sanction from the local government, violated people's decisional autonomy to hold a pro-British viewpoint.

Another incident occurred further up the coast. In 1807 and 1808 President Thomas Jefferson had taken isolationist action, mostly involving an embargo on American shipping. New Englanders blamed this action for sending their region into an economic crisis. Jefferson's Secretary of State and successor as president, James Madison, supported this isolationist policy. When war was declared in 1812, the New England states initially opposed it. Massachusetts, Connecticut, and Rhode Island refused to place their state militias under federal control, which the Madison administration requested when Britain blockaded the east coast (Hickey 1977, 590). New England voters unseated many of its Congressmen who had prowar leanings.

President Madison insisted on controlling the movements of the militias in those New England states that opposed the war—a punitive measure since the governors of other states that initially supported the war retained the authority to control military maneuvers within their borders. "The administration made it very clear that it would neither advance money nor reimburse the states for any militia serving under state officers in violation of federal rules" (Hickey, 599). In response, the New England states each sent delegates to Hartford, Connecticut, for a secret convention, lasting three weeks in late 1814 and early 1815, to discuss amendments to the U.S. Constitution that would protect the interests of their states (Banner 1988, 25). No records were kept of the proceedings, but a final report was created that proposed five amendments, mostly focused on limiting the power of the president of the United States. Despite efforts by President Madison to monitor those who had spoken out against the war, the New England representatives were able to meet in secret at the Hartford Convention. These secret meetings are an example of informational privacy, in which the federal government attempted to monitor state representatives who held a position contrary to that of the federal government. In the end, however, these meetings did not result in any action. Massachusetts sent representatives to Washington, DC, in February 1815 to negotiate with the federal government. With a decisive American victory in New Orleans and the signing of a peace treaty, however, there was a rush of patriotic sentiment, and the Federalists lost considerable political ground (Banner, 30).

MEXICAN-AMERICAN WAR (1846–1848)

In 1836 American immigrants in Texas declared independence from Mexico and established diplomatic ties as a sovereign nation with Britain, France, and the United States (Meed 2003, 2). The Mexican government did not recognize this declaration. Through an act of Congress in 1845, the United States annexed Texas as a state. The annexation of Texas led Mexico to break diplomatic relations with the United States and the United States to send troops to defend against invasion from Mexico (Perea 2003, 288). When in 1846 the Mexican army attacked a U.S. Army troop on patrol in contested land in southern Texas (in what came to be known as the Thornton Affair, after the U.S. captain in command of the patrol), the United States declared war on Mexico (Wilcox 1892, 44). The war ended with a resounding American victory in 1848, culminating in the signing of the Treaty of Guadalupe Hidalgo, which ceded Texas and much of what is now the American Southwest to the United States.

We have not found any major privacy incidents during the Mexican-American War. For example, we were unable to find any documented instances of government monitoring of individuals and groups directly related to the war effort. There were continuing efforts by slave owners to monitor and control slaves, but these efforts existed before the war and continued after the war, without any significant change. Henry David Thoreau was an outspoken opponent of the war effort, and he was jailed overnight for not paying his poll tax because he did not want these funds used to support the war. His subsequent essay on "Civil Disobedience" encouraged others to go to jail instead of paying taxes that would support the war (Thoreau 1849).

Government control of individuals and groups during the Mexican-American War was limited to the coerced "volunteering" of working-class citizens for U.S. military operations (Foos 2002, 60). Each state had a quota for the number of fighting units they were required to add to the U.S. military effort against Mexico. While these units were trying to fill out their ranks, there were reports of "a mass roundup of men" (61) involving forced enlistment of Irish and German ditch diggers working at Fort Monroe in Virginia. Although forced recruitment is not directly a privacy issue, it does indicate the inability of these individuals to avoid government control in part due to their social class. If these civilians had been working at some higher-level occupation, chances are they would not have been compelled into military service.

THE AMERICAN CIVIL WAR (1861–1865)

In the American Civil War, between the United States of America and the eleven slave states in the South that formed the Confederate States of America, there were three main privacy violations. First, there was regular opening of letters written by prisoners of war and civilians during the Civil War period, by both the Union and the Confederacy:

> Special agents helped deliver mail to Union troops in the South and reestablished service as southern states returned to federal control. Finding individuals willing and able to serve as postmasters in the South was difficult because, until July 1868, all prospective postmasters had to swear that they had not voluntarily aided the Confederacy or Confederate soldiers. (USPS 2006)

The second privacy violation involved telegraphic messages. Samuel Morse invented the first recording telegraph in the 1830s, and the United States installed its first commercial telegraph line in 1844. By the time of the Civil War, the telegraph network was well established across the United States. The Union army took control of the commercial telegraph lines around Washington, and President Abraham Lincoln used the telegraph to keep in daily touch with his commanders in the field. The Confederates resorted to wiretapping, but they were largely unsuccessful because the Union's Military-Telegraph Service developed strong enciphering techniques that were unbreakable by the Confederates:

The most prolonged and successful wiretapping [by the Confederacy] was that by C. A. Gaston, Lee's confidential operator. Gaston entered [the] Union lines near City Point [Virginia], while Richmond and Petersburg were besieged, with several men to keep watch for him, and for six weeks he remained undisturbed in the woods, reading all messages which passed over Grant's wire. Though unable to read the ciphers, he gained much from the dispatches in plain text. One message reported that 2,586 beeves were to be landed at Coggins' Point on a certain day. This information enabled Wade Hampton to make a timely raid and capture the entire herd.

This same Union military-telegraph office deciphered coded Confederate telegrams:

Brilliant and conspicuous service was rendered by the cipher-operators of the War Department in translating Confederate cipher messages which fell into Union hands. A notable incident in the field was the translation of General Joseph E. Johnston's cipher message to Pemberton, captured by Grant before Vicksburg and forwarded to Washington. More important were the two cipher dispatches from the Secretary of War at Richmond, in December 1863, which led to a cabinet meeting and culminated in the arrest of Confederate conspirators in New York City, and to the capture of contraband shipments of arms and ammunition. Other intercepted and translated ciphers revealed plans of Confederate agents for raiding Northern towns near the border. Most important of all were the cipher messages disclosing the plot for the wholesale incendiarism of leading hotels in New York, which barely failed of success on November 25, 1864. (Greely, 2002)

Third was the use of census data for the war effort. The 1850 decennial census was the first to record data for each individual respondent and to include questions about whether the respondent was born in a state or territory of the United States (census.gov), increasing the government's ability to monitor groups and individuals. The Union army's General William Tecumseh Sherman applied census data that he obtained directly from the Census Bureau in his campaign against the South. His march from Tennessee to Atlanta and on to Savannah was a critical blow to the Confederacy. He "used the data in 1864 to rout the very people in the South who had earlier provided the data to the government in the 1860 head count. Census information led his troops to military sites, mills, cotton supplies, population centers, and a lot more in Georgia and the neighboring states" (Smith 2004, 63). This secondary use of information that had been provided by citizens completely unaware of its potential future implications constitutes a clear privacy violation. Had the citizens of the South been aware of this possible future use, they almost certainly would not have provided the information.

THE SPANISH-AMERICAN WAR (1898)

The Spanish-American War was a four-month war in which the United States attempted to wrest from Spain colonial control of Cuba, Guam, the Philippine Islands, and Puerto Rico. The most important privacy issue of this war was governmental monitoring of the mails, particularly of individuals and groups who were against the war. One such case emerged against the Anti-Imperialist League, formed in 1898 to fight American imperialist expansion. The League mailed pamphlets within the United States and to the Philippines, urging young Americans not to enlist or reenlist for military duty. "Denounced as seditious propaganda, the pamphlets were barred from the Philippines by the Secretary of War. This act, in turn, caused an uproar in the press about freedom of speech" (Caterini 1997, 16). Banning the pamphlets is particularly interesting because of the large number of high-profile individuals who were members of the League, including former U.S. presidents Grover Cleveland and Benjamin Harrison, and numerous influential public figures such as Jane Addams, Ambrose Bierce, Andrew Carnegie, Samuel Clemens, John Dewey, E. L. Godkin, Samuel Gompers, William James, and Moorefield Storey.

FIRST WORLD WAR (1914–1918) AND U.S. INVOLVEMENT (1917–1918)

This major world war involved the United States entering the conflict on the side of Britain, France, and Russia in opposition to Germany, Austria-Hungary, and the Ottoman Empire. During the war, the federal government began to exercise strict control over individuals, sharply curtailing freedom of expression through a succession of policies and laws beginning as early as 1916. As the historian John Brinkley writes, "The American involvement in World War I and its aftermath produced one of the most widespread and virulent assaults on civil liberties in American History" (2008, 27). Going into the 1916 election, President Woodrow Wilson:

> cited the need for legislation to suppress disloyal activities. He implied not only that the behavior of such disloyal elements was indefensible, but also that it was not a subject on which there was room for any public debate, since they had sacrificed their right to civil liberties by their own behavior. His posture cast suspicion on the loyalty of all foreign-born. (Murphy 1923, 53)

This rhetoric was an early indication of the way in which the Wilson administration would deal with dissent and the high level of control it would seek to exert over the citizenry. During the war, the Wilson administration "responded to dissent with an aggressive campaign of intimidation and coercion to silence or marginalize opponents of the war" (Brinkley 2008, 30). With the Espionage Act of 1917 (PL 65-24), the Sedition Act of 1918 (PL 150), and Alien Friends and Enemies Acts of 1918 (Stat. 570 and 577, respectively), citizens could be fined or jailed if their words were found to induce unrest or even if the intention behind their words was to produce this sort of effect (USPS 2006).

As Paul Murphy explains in *World War I and the Origin of Civil Liberties in the United States*:

> All that had to be shown to sustain conviction was that words uttered or written had a tendency to cause unrest among soldiers or to make recruiting more difficult . . . This new standard of guilt allowed conviction for any words which indirectly discouraged recruiting and the war spirit, if only the intention to discourage existed. Intention thus became the crucial test of guilt in any prosecution of opposition to the government's war policies, and this requirement became a mere form, since it could always be inferred from the existence of the indirect injurious effect. (1923, 198)

The legislation was problematic in several ways. The intension provision was particularly troublesome in that intension was often confirmed based on the result of the action. The legislation applied not only to words uttered in public but also to private conversations. In his book, *The American Home Front: Revolutionary War, Civil War, World War I, World War II*, James Abramson brings this point home by relating that "[o]n the 'testimony' of his five-year-old daughter, for example, one German in California received five years in prison for privately criticizing the President" (2001, 122). This testimony clearly implicates Boling's concept of protected space in that this man was not allowed to express his own views even within his home.

The extreme civil liberty violations perpetrated during the First World War may have paved the way for future legislation that would protect these same rights:

> Before World War I, support for civil liberties had been largely theoretical. There was no significant jurisprudence capable of giving real meaning to the Bill of Rights; and though people of wealth and standing took freedoms for granted, most others could have no reasonable expectation that the law would protect their right to free speech and other liberties. (Brinkley 2008, 35)

Although the government's conduct during wartime may have illustrated the importance of civil liberties, changes would not be made for some years. The Second World War would bring a similar set of violations, and it would not be until the 1960s and 1970s that the Bill of Rights would have "an expansive meaning in American life for the first time" (Brinkley, 35).

During the First World War there were also extensive efforts by private citizens to control the behavior of others. These efforts often took the form of social pressure to conform to ideals of being American. As Abrahamson explains:

> Before 1914 the public showed little interest in the Americanization movement. But the ethnic tensions and fears that began to build during the neutrality period soon produced a narrow nationalism suspicious of all "hyphenated" Americans and demanding that they prove, in the words of one 1916 banner, "Absolute and Unqualified Loyalty" to their new country. Total conformity to American ways and American values, as defined by the nativist, became the only way to avoid ethnic persecution. (Abrahamson 2001, 15)

Some citizens went further than banners and neighborly snooping, forming citizen groups to investigate cases of dissent. Perhaps the most active of these groups was the American Protective League, a voluntary organization established in Chicago in 1917, which rapidly established chapters across the country. The League was loosely affiliated with the Federal Bureau of Investigation but had no official authority to conduct investigations or make arrests. This lack of authority did not, however, inhibit the APL's activities. As Murphy describes the situation:

> Having no formal statutory authority to make arrests, operatives of the league engaged in a variety of investigations probing the loyalty of citizens, the actions of the draft exemption board, the actual status of conscientious objectors, and the monitoring, in thousands of cases, of suspicious activities reported by people throughout the country in response to appeals for vigilance in detecting spies and persons guilty of sabotage. (1923, 90)

Such actions on the part of private citizens may have been a result of the government's antidissent policies (specifically those enacted by the Espionage Act of 1917, the Sedition Act of 1918, and the Alien Act of 1918) and may, in turn, have driven these policies. In any case, the social pressure exerted by individuals on other individuals served a similar function as governmental monitoring and control in curtailing the ability of individuals to express their political opinions or practice their cultures in both public and private.

SECOND WORLD WAR (1939–1945) AND U.S. INVOLVEMENT (1941–1945)

The Second World War was a major conflict that the United States entered on the side of the Allies, Britain and Russia (and France until its defeat), in opposition to the Axis powers led by Germany, Japan, and Italy. The government monitored the communication of citizens during the war. Franklin Roosevelt and J. Edgar Hoover agreed in 1940 "that wiretapping of suspected agents or collaborators of the Axis powers was necessary to protect national security" (Yoo 2008, 57). This focus on national security reflected their fears about a "fifth column" of spies within the United States.

Much of the information available about the domestic surveillance programs from the late 1940s through 1975 comes from the Church Committee report. The U.S. Senate established the Special Select Committee to Investigate Intelligence Activities in 1974 after the Watergate scandal brought national attention to the need for improved oversight of intelligence activities. The Senate appointed Frank Church (D-ID) as chairperson and charged the committee with a broad mandate to investigate intelligence activities of the federal government and make recommendations for reform. Two years, fourteen reports, and ninety-six reform suggestions later, the committee had documented a thirty-year string of domestic intelligence gathering efforts and abuses. The reports include extensive original sources and interview transcripts that make fascinating reading for the historian and privacy scholar.

The domestic surveillance programs the government implemented in response to fears of Communist espionage and hostile foreign agents remained in place in one form or another for decades to come. These programs included extensive mail opening, wiretapping, the creation and maintenance of a list of individuals to be rounded up in case of a national emergency, warrantless break-ins, and the recruitment of extensive networks of citizen informants.

The Central Intelligence Agency (CIA) and the Federal Bureau of Investigation (FBI) conducted twelve separate mail-opening programs between 1940 and 1973, in most cases without prior authorization from the president, attorney general, or postmaster general. These programs varied in length from three weeks to twenty-six years (Church 1976 Volume 3, 1). During the Second World War, the FBI began a secret program of opening international mail to and from Communist countries, and a list was created to track individuals suspected of belonging to subversive groups or being susceptible to becoming Communist spies (Church 1976 Volume 2, 38).

Between 1940 and 1973, the FBI developed over five hundred thousand domestic intelligence files. In 1939 the FBI created the Custodial Detention List to keep track of subscribers to newspapers with "notorious Nationalistic sympathies" (Church 1976 Volume 2, 31). In 1943, when Attorney General Biddle became aware of the list, he ordered the FBI to eliminate the practice. He reasoned that the FBI lacked the "statutory authority of present justification" (Church 1976 Volume 2, 35). The FBI responded by simply changing the name of the list to the "Security Index" and ordering agents to keep the existence and name of the list secret, avoiding any mention of the list in any reports (Church 1976 Volume 2, 36)

The Second World War offers a combination of government monitoring and personal monitoring and control in the form of human informants. Some 83 percent of FBI cases relied on a human informant. This reliance on human informants resulted in the FBI employing individuals who would participate in the actions of the groups the FBI was trying to monitor. Informants were reported to have participated in murders and beaten people with "blackjacks, chains and pistols" (Church 1976 Volume 3, 9).

There were also privacy violations involving the secondary use of census data during the war. The Military War Command obtained information from the Census Bureau about the distribution of Japanese Americans prior to their "evacuation" and internment. Although the Census Bureau refused to turn over individual names and addresses, it readily turned over aggregate data, which were sufficient for the War Command to select areas of high concentration as the places to open "processing centers" for evacuation (Larson 1992, 53–54). The release of even aggregated data was in violation of the Census Bureau's charter, which reads, "In no case shall information furnished under the authority of this act be used to detriment of the person or persons to whom such information relates" (Burnham 1983, 23). Vincent Barabba, the director of the Census Bureau at the time, argued after the fact that the Second War Powers Act (56 Stat. 176) allowed the Census Bureau to turn over whatever information it gave to the government. However, the Census Bureau began to release data only ten days after the attack at Pearl Harbor, more than a month before the Second War Powers Act was introduced in Congress on January 22, 1942, and more than three months before it was signed into law by President Roosevelt.

Government control of individuals also took an extreme turn during the Second World War with the internment of Japanese and Japanese Americans, particularly on the West Coast. Executive Order 9066, issued in February 1942, allowed the military to restrict particular people from designated military areas. The order resulted in the internment of more than one hundred thousand Japanese Americans and Japanese citizens living in the United States. This exertion of government control over individuals clearly affected privacy. Not only were these individuals not allowed to have a private sphere to express and formulate their own beliefs but also their privacy was violated in the most literal sense in the internment camps. The packed sleeping quarters, flimsy partitions separating family residences, and frequent roll calls seriously eroded the privacy of the individuals in these camps. (See Gentile 1998, 18–24, for further discussion of the conditions of internment camps.)

The Second World War involved some of the most serious and extensive privacy violations of any American war. There were serious informational privacy violations in the federal government programs to open mail, wiretap, keep personal security files on half a million Americans, and use census data for unintended purposes related to Japanese internment and to recruit citizen informants. There were privacy violations against personal space in the warrantless break-ins to homes. The internment camps violated the privacy of the home zone of individuals and their decisional autonomy, robbing them of the ability to make their own choices about where and how to live their lives.

THE KOREAN WAR (1950–1953)

The United States entered the battle on the side of the Republic of Korea (South Korea), which was supported by the United Nations, against the Democratic People's Republic of Korea (North Korea), which was supported by China and the Soviet Union.

Two programs that began shortly after the Second World War continued as significant components of domestic surveillance through the 1970s: the Federal Employee Loyalty Program and Project Shamrock. These were part of the Cold War era that encompassed both the Korean and Vietnam wars.

Executive Order 9835 created the Federal Employee Loyalty Program on March 21, 1947, by President Truman. The program addressed the concern that federal employees might be susceptible to recruitment by Communist intelligence agencies. The Loyalty program became the legal basis for the FBI's investigation into subversive groups for years to come (Church 1976 Volume 2, 42).

Project Shamrock began in 1947, continued through the 1970s, and involved CIA agents and later National Security Agency agents, copying telegraph correspondence sent from foreign organizations operating within the United States or telegraphs that appeared to be encrypted. An agent made daily trips from Fort Meade to New York, returning with "large reels of magnetic tape" to be processed (Moyers 2007).

In addition to these domestic surveillance programs, there were two major examples of government efforts to control individuals and groups: the Hoover plan to suspend *habeas corpus* and the McCarran Internal Security Act (PL 81-831, 1950) during the Korean War.

During President Truman's second term, J. Edgar Hoover approached him with a plan to "suspend habeas corpus and imprison some 12,000 Americans he suspected of disloyalty" (Weiner 2007, para. 1). Hoover had developed his list of names over the previous twelve months as it became clear that the United States was preparing for war. Although Truman rejected Hoover's plan, it stands as an example of a government plan to control individuals during wartime.

In 1950 Congress overrode Truman's veto of the McCarran Internal Security Act, also known as the Subversive Activities Control Act. This act required "communist organizations" to register with the U.S. Attorney General and blocked U.S. citizenship for individuals who were members of a Communist organization (Sutherland 1951, 386). To manage the provisions of the McCarran Internal Security Act, Congress established the Subversive Activities Control Board (390). It maintained a running list of organizations that had registered, as well as individuals belonging to those organizations. This legislation is an example of both government monitoring and control of groups and organizations.

HTLingual is an important example of the ongoing mail-opening program that began during the Korean War. The CIA originally approached high-level postal officials with the idea of determining how best to communicate with American spies inside Russia, arguing that study of the mail flow between the two countries would enable this assessment. Originally known as the New York mail program, since most postal correspondence between the two countries passed through New York, this program became one of the largest mail surveillance programs, with 215,000 mail items documented. These actions involved a violation of informational privacy in that the mail was routinely opened and read by government agents of individuals who were not specifically identified as being likely spies or terrorists but who were simply sending letters to China or Russia.

THE VIETNAM WAR (1959–1979) AND U.S. COMBAT FORCES PRESENT (1965–1973)

The United States fought to defend South Vietnam from takeover by Communist forces, fighting against the North Vietnamese Army and the Viet Cong guerilla fighters. Many of the domestic surveillance programs established from the Second World War continued through the Vietnam War era: the mail covers program, the Security Index list, Project Shamrock, the Federal Employee Loyalty Program [known as the Employee Security Program (E.O. No. 10,450, 1953)], and the ongoing development of domestic intelligence files. In addition, the FBI began the COINTELPRO program in 1956, which continued actively throughout the Vietnam War era.

Congress authorized the counterintelligence program known as COINTELPRO in 1956, predating the placement of U.S. combat forces in Vietnam by nine years. The program continued through the Vietnam War, and the FBI used it to monitor and control individuals and groups. It was designed to "disrupt groups and neutralize individuals deemed to be threats to domestic security" (Church 1976 Volume 2, 10). These goals were achieved in a number of different ways: attempting to influence employers to fire employees who were under investigations, labeling group leaders and members as informants to reduce trust within a group, and trying to initiate Internal Revenue Service investigations into the finances of groups and individuals (10). One poignant example of monitoring private information with the intent to exert control was the letter sent to a female leader in a group "active in draft resistance, antiwar rallies and New Left activities'" (Church 1976 Volume 3, 52). The FBI had learned that the leader's husband was suspicious of his wife having an affair. The FBI sent a letter to the husband and signed the letter "soul sister." This letter asked the husband to keep his wife from having so many affairs with the men in a black activist group to which his wife belonged (53). The FBI later reported "the matrimonial stress and strain should cause her to function much less effectively" (54). The couple was divorced months after the letter was sent.

The U.S. Army began to maintain intelligence files on Americans whose views did not support the government's position on Vietnam. This surveillance program was active between 1967 and 1970 and initially focused on "dissidents" (Church 1976 Volume 2, 136). A precise definition of "dissident" was not offered, but groups or individuals thought to be participants in, instigators of, or subversive elements related to the civil rights movement and the anti-Vietnam war movements were included. These categories were later expanded to include prominent persons and individuals who were friendly with members of these groups. In all, over one hundred thousand Americans came under surveillance (Church 1976 Volume 3, 6). These files were in addition to the FBI domestic intelligence activities, which opened sixty-five thousand intelligence files in 1972 alone (Church 1976 Volume 2, 6).

CONCLUSIONS

In the course of this chapter we have seen the ways in which violations of privacy expose the struggle between individual rights and national security during wartime in America. (See table 9.2 for a summary of privacy infringements in times of war.) In particular, we have seen how, in the interest of national security, the government and private organizations have assaulted individual protections to informational privacy, decisional autonomy, and protected space. This historical struggle between privacy and national security has a clear resonance with our current political landscape. Our conceptions of privacy have developed over time and are affected by our evolving social mores, changing laws, and technologies.

Table 9.2. Summary of U.S. Privacy Violations in Times of War

War	Private Monitoring and Control	Government Monitoring	Government Control	Privacy Violation Type
American Revolution		Monitoring of the mail	Limits on civil and economic rights	Informational, Decisional
War of 1812	Baltimore Riots	Hartford Convention		Decisional
Mexican-American War			Coerced "volunteering" of workers	Decisional
U.S. Civil War		Monitoring of the mail and secondary use of census data		Informational
Spanish-American War		Monitoring of mail; barring of seditious materials		Informational, Decisional
First World War	American Protective League		• The Espionage Act of 1917 • The Sedition Act of 1918 • The Alien Act of 1918	Informational, Decisional
Second World War	Citizen Informants	Wiretapping, mail-opening programs, Custodial Detention List, warrantless break-ins	Japanese Internment	Informational, Personal Space
Korean War		• The Hoover plan to suspend habeas corpus • The McCarran Internal Security Act • Employee loyalty program • HTLingual • Project Shamrock • Security index		Informational, Decisional
Vietnam War	Informants	• Army intelligence files • FBI domestic intelligence files	COINTELPRO	Informational, Decisional

As these conceptions evolve it is important that we measure our policies against them, that we reflect on what we are willing to sacrifice for national security, and that this reflection include an understanding of the consequences of similar sacrifices in our past. As Bruce Andrews describes the situation in "Privacy and the Protection of National Security":

> The problem is not whether electronic surveillance and other attacks on privacy are legal or constitutional, but whether they are socially intelligible—whether they make sense in view of the society which spawned them. Also, the problem is not whether honorable men can strike a balance between national defense and constitutional restraints, but whether the requirements of a social system like that of the United States—in regard to a foreign policy aimed at advancing its interests, for example—will tend to sweep those restraints aside. (1980, 153)

It is not just lawmakers who define what privacy is, or why it matters, but rather our society at large has a role to play in articulating what is acceptable. As we continue to face the challenges of deciding which privacy rights must be defended to have "socially intelligible" policies, understanding the history of the relationship between privacy and national security can help us understand the consequences of our choices. In this chapter we have sought to establish a basis for this method of consideration, opening our current conversations to an understanding of the tensions between national security and individual rights that have developed historically. We hope that these historical examples will be used in the coming years by scholars who are trying to provide an overarching definition of privacy, who are trying to explain the relationships between privacy and civil liberties, and who are trying to determine future policy on the privacy rights of individual Americans in times of war.

NOTES

1. The concept of war itself is problematic. The War of 1812, Mexican-American War, Spanish-American War, and the First and Second World Wars were formally declared by Congress under Article 1 of the Constitution. The Revolutionary War was authorized by the Declaration of Independence; the U.S. Civil War by Presidential Authority only retroactively approved by Congress; the Korean War by American support of a United Nations Security Council Resolution; and the Vietnam War by the Gulf of Tonkin Resolution. Is it unclear whether it is appropriate to extend this study to other activities labeled as wars but without an opposing army, such as the War on Terror or the War on Drugs.

2. The following overview of competing privacy definitions is paraphrased from Solove (2008, 222): Alan Westin published *Privacy and Freedom* in 1967, defining pri-

vacy using four different elements: intimacy, anonymity, solitude, and reserve (Westin 1967). A number of other frameworks of privacy were proposed in the 1990s. In 1992, Ken Gormley defined privacy in the *Wisconsin Law Review* (Gormley 1992), relying heavily on legal terms: tort privacy, Fourth Amendment privacy, First Amendment privacy, fundamental-decision privacy, and state constitutional privacy. In 1997, in her book *In Pursuit of Privacy: Law, Ethics and the Rise of Technology* (DeCew 1997), Judith DeCew offered three categories of privacy that she argued combine to create an overall definition of privacy: informational privacy, accessibility privacy, and expressive privacy. In the *Stanford Law Review* in 1998, in a paper entitled "Information Privacy in Cyberspace Transactions" (Kang 1997), Jerry Kang discussed three overlapping factors that he used to define privacy: physical space, choice, and flow of information.

3. Solove's sixteen types of activities that implicate privacy are: surveillance, interrogation, aggregation, identification, insecurity, secondary use, exclusion, breach of confidentiality, disclosure, exposure, increased accessibility, blackmail, appropriation, distortion, intrusion, and decisional interference.

4. It is not clear that the focus of mob violence was exclusively related to British sympathies or the U.S. engagement in the war. Some of the mob action may instead have been motivated by racial prejudice (including the destruction of two houses owned by a free black man, James Briscoe) and religious prejudice of Irish Catholics against Irish Protestants.

REFERENCES

Abrahamson, James L. 2001. *The American home front: Revolutionary War, Civil War, World War I, World War II*. Washington, DC: National Defense University Press.
Alien Enemies Act, 1 Stat. 570 (1798).
Alien Friends Act, 1 Stat. 577 (1798).
Andrews, Bruce. 1980. Privacy and the protection of national security. In *Privacy, a vanishing value?* W. C. Bier, ed. New York: Garland.
Ashcroft, John. Speech to the American Enterprise Institute, August 19, 2003. Washington, D.C.
Banner, James M. Jr. 1988, September. A shadow of secession? The Hartford convention, 1814. *History Today* 38, no. 9: 24–30.
Brinkley, Alan. 2008. World War I and the crisis of democracy. In *Security v. liberty*, ed. Daniel Faber, 27–41. New York: The Russell Sage Foundation.
Burnham, David. 1983. *The rise of the computer state*. New York: Random House.
Cate, Fred H. 1997. *Privacy in the information age*. Washington, DC: Brookings Institution Press.
Caterini, Dino J. 1977, December. Repeating ourselves: The Philippines Insurrection and the Vietnam War. *Foreign Service Journal*, 11–17, 31–32.
Census—Historical Census Statistics on the Foreign-Born Population of the United States: 1850 to 1990. (n.d.). Retrieved February 10, 2010, from http://www.census.gov/population/www/documentation/twps0029/twps0029.html.

Church Committee: United States Senate Select Committee to Study Governmental Operations with Respect to Intelligence Activities. 1976. Final report of the Select Committee to Study Governmental Operations with Respect to Intelligence Activities, United States Senate (Vols. 1–6, Vol. 1). Washington, DC: U.S. Government Printing Office.

———. 1976. Final report of the Select Committee to Study Governmental Operations with Respect to Intelligence Activities, United States Senate (Vols. 1–6, Vol. 2). Washington, DC: U.S. Government Printing Office.

DeCew, J. W. 1997. *In pursuit of privacy.* Ithaca, NY: Cornell University Press.

Espionage Act, Pub. L. No. 65-24, 40 Stat. 217 (1917).

Executive Order No. 9066. 1942, February 25. Authorizing the Secretary of War to prescribe military areas. *Federal Register* 7, no. 38: 1407.

Executive Order No. 9835. 1947, March 25. Prescribing procedures for the administration of an employees loyalty program in the executive branch of the government. *Federal Register* 12, no. 59: 1935–39.

Executive Order No. 10450, 1953. Security requirements for government employment. *Federal Register* 18, no. 82: 2489–2500.

Foos, P. W. 2002. *A short, offhand, killing affair: Soldiers and social conflict during the Mexican-American War.* Chapel Hill, NC: University of North Carolina Press.

Gentile, Nancy J. 1988. Survival behind barbed wire: The impact of imprisonment on Japanese-American culture during World War II. *Maryland Historian,* 19, no. 2: 15–32.

Gilje, P. A. 1980. The Baltimore riots of 1812 and the breakdown of the Anglo-American mob tradition. *Journal of Social History* 13, no. 4: 547–64.

Gormley, K. 1992. One hundred years of privacy. *Wisconsin Law Review,* 4, 1335–1441.

Greely, A. W. "The Military-Telegraph Service," http://www.civilwarhome.com/telegraph.htm, last updated February 15, 2002; accessed March 4, 2011.

Hickey, D. R. 1977. New England's defense problem and the genesis of the Hartford convention. *New England Quarterly* 50, no. 4: 587–604.

Kang, J. 1997. Information privacy in cyberspace transactions. *Stanford Law Review* 50, 1193–1294.

Larson, Erik. 1992. *The naked consumer.* New York: Henry Holt and Company.

McCarran Internal Security Act, PL 81-831 (1950).

Meed, Douglas. 2003. *The Mexican War, 1846–1848.* New York: Routledge.

Moyers, Bill. 2007. The Church Committee and FISA. *Bill Moyers Journal.* October 26, 2007. Retrieved August 1, 2008, from: http://www.pbs.org/moyers/journal/10262007/profile2.html.

Murphy, Paul L. 1923. *World War I and the origin of civil liberties in the United States.* New York: W. W. Norton and Company.

Perea, J. F. 2003. A brief history of race and the U.S.-Mexican border: Tracing the trajectories of conquest. *UCLA Law Review* 51, no. 1: 283–312.

Second War Powers Act, 56 Stat. 176 (1942).

Sedition Act, PL 65-150, 40 Stat. 553 (1918).

Seipp, D. J. 1981. *The right to privacy in American history.* Cambridge, MA: Harvard University Press.

Smith, R. E. 2004. *Ben Franklin's web site: Privacy and curiosity from Plymouth Rock to the Internet.* Providence, RI: Privacy Journal.

Solove, Daniel J. 2008. *Understanding privacy.* Cambridge, MA: Harvard University Press.

Stanley, J., and Steinhardt, B. 2003. *Bigger monster, weaker chains: The growth of an American surveillance society.* American Civil Liberties Union. http://www.aclu.org/technology-and-liberty/bigger-monster-weaker-chains-growth-american-surveillance-society.

Sutherland, Arthur E. Jr. 1951. Freedom and internal security. *Harvard Law Review* 64, no. 3: 383–416.

Thoreau, Henry David. 1849. *Civil disobedience.* http://thoreau.eserver.org/civil.html

Uniting and Strengthening America by Providing Appropriate Tools Required to Intercept and Obstruct Terrorism (USA PATRIOT ACT) Act of 2001, PL 107-56. 115 Stat. 272 (2001).

USPS. *The United States Postal Service: An American history 1775–2006.* 2006. Washington, DC: United States Postal Service, Government Relations.

Weiner, T. 2007, December 23. *Hoover planned mass jailing in 1950. New York Times.* Retrieved from http://www.nytimes.com/2007/12/23/washington/23habeas.html.

Westin, A. F. 1967. *Privacy and freedom.* New York: Atheneum.

Wilcox, C. M. 1892. *History of the Mexican War.* Washington, DC: The Church News Publishing Company.

Yoo, John. 2008. FDR, Civil Liberties, and the War on Terrorism. In *Security v. liberty,* ed. Daniel Farber, 42–62. New York: The Russell Sage Foundation.

10

Turtles, Firewalls, Scarlet Letters, and Vacuum Cleaners

Rules about Personal Information

Gary T. Marx
Massachusetts Institute of Technology

"You ought to have some papers to show who you are." The police officer advised me. "I do not need any paper. I know who I am," I said. "Maybe so. Other people are also interested in knowing who you are."

—B. Traven, *The Death Ship*

"You know what happens to nosy fellas? They lose their noses."

—R. Polanski to J. Nicholson in *Chinatown*

Thus the young and pure would be taught to look at her, with the scarlet letter flaming on her breast . . . as the figure, the body, the reality of sin.

—N. Hawthorne, *The Scarlet Letter*

As with the ant and the ram in a popular 1950s song, I began this chapter with "high hopes" of generating a morphology for the rules about personal information.[1] But the monumentality of the task overwhelms. My resulting low hopes are now merely to suggest the range of cases that such a mapping must organize and to suggest some questions and concepts toward this mapping. Identifying the major forms of variation in, and classifying the rules that apply to, personal information is necessary for systematic research.

The following examples give a glimmer of the many varied settings of information control in need of a conceptual home. While all are about personal information, each contains a distinctive analytic element (or elements) to account for. How can variation in expectations about the treatment of personal information be ordered and better understood? What patterns can be identified? This chapter's goal is to bring some conceptual order to the multiple and often conflicting rules and settings involving personal information. A sampling of informational control settings would include:

- Persons refusing to participate in the U.S. census are subject to prosecution (Title 13 of the *United States Code*). (Individual must provide information to the state.)
- Under the Fifth Amendment of the United States individuals can refuse to answer questions that might incriminate them. (The state cannot compel answers.)
- Truth Commissions in East Germany and South Africa permit citizens certain rights to learn about their dossiers under previous governments. (The government must provide information to an individual.)
- Bank Sign: "For Security Purposes Please Remove Hat and Sunglasses." (An individual must provide his or her image to a private organization.)
- The wearing of face-covering, burqa-style veils in public is prohibited in France as of April 2011. (An individual must provide her image in a public place.)
- Under the Privacy Protection Act of 1974 (PL 93-579) and later legislation, credit card holders are entitled to know certain kinds of information that organizations have about them and must be notified if data about them are lost or stolen. (Private organizations must provide information to individuals.)
- Records bureaus in some states are prohibited from releasing birth information to adopted persons absent approval of the birth parents. (The state must not provide information to individuals about themselves.)
- Food inspectors for the Michelin and other restaurant guides are prohibited from revealing their occupation. (Individuals representing a private organization must not report information about himself or herself to another private organization or to other individuals.)
- Under the Intelligence Identities Protection Act of 1982 (PL 97-200, 50 U.S.C. § 421-426) it is a crime to reveal the identity of an agent in certain covert roles with a U.S. intelligence agency. (Individuals must not report information about others.)
- The famous "naked man" was arrested many times in Berkeley for walking down the street nude. (An individual must not offer personal information about himself to other individuals.)
- Emergency rooms must report gunshot wounds, and in many states dentists are required to report suspected child abuse if they see facial bruises. (Private agents must report personal information on others to the state.)
- A prostitute under court order is arrested for failure to inform clients she is HIV positive. (An individual must provide information to another individual.)

- Prenuptial agreements may require full disclosure of all assets. (Reciprocal revelation by private parties is required.)
- A job applicant sues for employment discrimination after being asked questions about racial background and sexual preference. (An organization must not seek information.)
- A daycare center is found civilly and criminally liable as a result of an inadequate background search of an arrested employee. (A private organization is derelict in not seeking information.)
- In the United States it is legal to take a photo of another person in public, and property ownership and tax assessments are public records, but not income tax records, while in France it is illegal to take a photo without permission, and in most Scandinavian countries income tax records are public. (There is variation in what is available to the public across cultures.)

We might say that what we see is Hodgepodge City. Many disciplinary strands are needed for ordering and understanding the varied expectations around the control of information. Philosophy identifies values, law offers specific tools, psychology emphasizes perception and the functions of information for personhood, sociology calls attention to inequality and interaction, economics addresses the costs and benefits of information transactions, design and architecture treat space and the environment. The empirical examples above illustrate a range of rules about information behavior and expectations. Each of the disciplines encounters a different aspect. Rules may determine behavior, or if not, at least create conditions around which actors maneuver.

Questions about the control of personal information have become particularly salient with the spread of new surveillance technologies, e.g., computer monitoring, video cameras, cell phones, ambient sensors, Radio Frequency Identification (RFID) chips, and DNA tests. These new soft forms of surveillance with their lower visibility, lessened cost, and greater intensity and extensity in data gathering, analysis, and communication bring new issues. But they also nestle within a more comprehensive set of questions and phenomena far transcending specific technologies and cutting across disciplines.[2] These forms need to be seen as part of broader information questions that do not involve particular technologies such as informing, contracting, liability, and keeping secrets. The multifaceted topic of privacy is too often treated on an *ad hoc,* descriptive basis as a result of the accidents of academic disciplines and whatever is newsworthy. Privacy is unfortunately frequently treated as if it were the only concern in information control. However, privacy, too, needs to be located within a broader framework of rules covering both the *offering,* as well as the *withholding,* of information. Situating privacy within a larger field can temper intemperate claims about the death of privacy or privacy gone wild.

Rules requiring a subject to withhold or reveal, or an agent to seek or not seek, information can be explored in specific institutions and areas such as education, health, work, commerce, families, and government, and for specific behavior functions that cut across institutions such as identity, eligibility validation, and kinds of treatment. Rules appropriate to one context or time period may not be for another (Marx 2001a and Nissenbaum 2010). But before we examine variation based on context, content, or functions, we must first identify general properties that can be used to classify rules.

The rules and expectations that define various information settings need elaboration and contrast. Information gathering and protection rules can involve various combinations of the individual, group, or organization (whether state or nonstate) as subjects and/or agents and various kinds of information. Rules may refer to types and forms of content (the what); to kinds of actor and action (the who) regarding the roles played; and to specific requirements such as timing (the when), appropriate means, the presence or absence of discretion, and to how collected information is to be treated.

Rules vary in their procedural and substantive rationales: constitutional protections, legislation, judicial interpretations, regulatory rulings, organizational policies—or more informal manners and tradition which we often become aware of only when they are violated.

What are the normative conditions, correlates, and consequences of raising and lowering the curtain around the collection, distribution, and treatment of information about a person? Given the focus on individual privacy at the conference where the papers in this volume were given, I will emphasize information about the personal and formal rules, rather than informal expectations as with manners, agreements, and understandings.

The questions raised by rules are part of a broader field of the sociology of information (Marx and Muschert 2007). Systematically identifying the major forms of variation in information rules and exploring the correlates, causes, and consequences is central to scientific understanding (whether descriptive or explanative) and to public policy. This identification requires a conceptual framework.

This paper is organized around a framework for analyzing the rules about personal information based on answers to eight questions. I discuss each of the questions in turn:

1. What kind of information is present? (personal/private or impersonal/public)
2. To whom does a rule apply? (subject, agent, or both)

3. Who has the information? (subject, agent, both, neither)
4. What kind of behavior does the rule involve? (closure or disclosure of information, reveal or conceal for the subject, seek or do not seek for the agent)
5. What is the nature of the rule's requirement? (prescription, optional, or proscription)
6. Are the goals of the subject and agent shared or in conflict?
7. Do different or identical rules apply to subjects and agents? (asymmetrical or symmetrical)
8. Is information protected or available as a result of a rule or a property of the information and setting?

TYPES OF PERSONAL INFORMATION (QUESTION 1)

What is personal information? The definition is central to our individualistic culture that gives special protection to the personal as vital to human dignity and private property. There is often a lack of agreement about what personal information is, given its several forms and haze in the criteria for deciding where a given instance fits into any organizational scheme. Personal information may partly be understood by contrast to what it is not, that is, nonpersonal information. The weather or the cost of pork bellies informs about things, not persons.

The broad category treated in this paper—information about persons— has several forms and is inclusive of the narrower concepts of personal and impersonal information. It can mean impersonal information that is widely shared and nondifferentiating, such as drivers of SUVs. It may be impersonal because it cannot be directly connected to an identifiable and/or locatable individual. It can be personal in involving a name and location or merely an identifiable person. But in another sense such information need not be "personal" as in intimate, sensitive, or stigmatizing. The latter forms bring special qualities.

Personal information may refer to facts of biography and experience; information an individual has about others or other topics, e.g., who pulled the trigger; secret ingredients in a product; a property or ownership right in some information; and scents and sounds associated with an individual (Marx 2006b).[3] Such distinctions offer a means of exploring different patterns of rules, e.g., those regarding sensitive information and even nonsensitive personal information will likely differ from those in which the individual has varying degrees of anonymity. In many instances, a person's email address is likely to be less accessible to others than a home address. Analyzing such variation is needed, but in this chapter information about persons is used in its broadest sense as information linkable to the individual. An issue for future papers is comparing the rules for various kinds of personal information with those pertaining to other forms, such as population aggregates in which data are not directly linked to a given person. The rules for data involving persons also need to be compared to rules about data that do not involve persons. The latter rules, when not addressing proprietary information, are likely to be less stringent than rules for information about persons.

SUBJECTS AND AGENTS (QUESTION 2)

Does a given rule apply to the subject or to an agent? The subject is the person to whom the information pertains. While the emphasis in this chapter is on an individual subject, the information of interest may apply to others as well, as with shared family DNA, intimacies, or conspiracies.

The agent refers to another party as a potential or actual possessor of information about the individual. The agent as collector (or recipient, a broader term) may be acting only as an individual or for an organization. The agent may be the end user or merely a conduit for yet another entity: a third-party repository.[4]

Individuals and organizations go back and forth between being subjects, agents of discovery, and repositories of information for and about others. Sometimes a person plays all three roles simultaneously. This is the case when investigators or inspectors seeking information about others must first identify themselves, or in sequence, as when an agent becomes a repository as a result of gathering data.[5] Such agents are also subjects of their organizations' internal control efforts. The hybrid category of the informer is an interesting variant. Informers are agents reporting on subjects, but their unique access to hidden information means that they often need to be participants and hence are also self-reporting subjects. The roles may also be joined. Consider self-surveillance, as when an individual serves as both subject and agent, e.g., with some forms of health monitoring. Another variation involves self-initiated invitations from subjects to agents. An example is the "How am I driving?" signs on commercial vehicles that list an 800 number to call.[6]

Control of the subject's information may reside with authorized intermediaries. That is the case when a person's cooperation or permission is needed for access to information about *another*, e.g., a minor, a trustee, exhumation of a relative's grave, or releasing papers of the deceased. Second-party reporting for birth and death records fits here. In neither case is the subject of the information responsible for reporting.[7] From a standpoint of control, the agent has the information or is entrusted to grant permission for it to be discovered, often by another agent.

Rules, sanctions, validity, and accountability may differ for second-party reporters as against direct collection or reporting from the subject. This difference is part of a broader question involving who has responsibility for decisions about discovering, reporting, and protecting information and the quality of the information.

WHO KNOWS AND/OR WANTS TO KNOW OR DISCOVER? (QUESTION 3)

Information about a subject may or may not be known by the individual, the individual's direct permission and literal cooperation may or may not be required, and subjects and agents (whatever the role requires) show variation in whether they desire to follow the rule.

The instance in which the subject alone has information contrasts with situations where someone else (or an organization) also has it, as well as with settings where others have information the subject lacks but desires. As an example of the latter, consider individuals denied access to personal information that pertains to them as with risk scores held by financial institutions or (in some states) access to adoption records. Whether the subject can see a letter of recommendation for a job or academic appointment raises some related issues.

The subject may be unaware that particular information exists. As once said, there are things "we know we don't know" as well as "unknown unknowns." Information repositories may not wish to reveal that they have personal information (dossiers, blacklists) or that individuals fit in a given category, such as living in an area with exposure to unsafe levels of chemicals or having been an unwitting subject of secret experiments.[8]

An organization may acknowledge the existence of a record, but not its basis or content. A rule may require that subjects receive notice, there may be leaks, or action taken may reveal the existence of the data, as with persons who discover they are on no-fly lists only when they are denied the right to board at the airport.

The varieties of fit between what the rules require or make possible and what the subject and agent desire offers a rich area for analysis. The individual may or may not wish to know, as with some carriers of a genetic potential for disease such as Huntington's chorea or learning the sex of an embryo.

Situations where the agent desires to know specific information contrast with those where the agent is indifferent or has a strong interest in not knowing.

There are a variety of reasons why agents may not wish to know when they are expected to.[9] Possessing information may trigger rules that require agents to act in ways they prefer not to. The information may reflect badly on those whom agents wish to protect. There are many fascinating questions here around the sociology of ignorance and the actions taken to avoid toxic information and types of unwanted information. The expression, "you don't want to know" suggests a qualification to the cliché that knowledge is power. As the story of Adam the apple eater suggests, there are times when it might be better for the agent not to know.

KINDS OF BEHAVIOR AND MANDATES (QUESTIONS 4 AND 5)

The next two questions involve the kinds of behavior the rule specifies (reveal or conceal) and the conditions for this specification (always, discretionary, never). Since these are so interwoven, even if analytically distinct, they are treated here as a unit.

For the subject the central kinds of behavior involve either revealing or withholding (or at least not volunteering) data. For the agent central behaviors are seeking to discover or not to discover data. Once data are in possession of the agent, additional rules may involve protecting, sharing, merging, altering, repurposing, preserving, or destroying data.

Most contemporary discussions treat privacy only as a discretionary right of the subject connected to the information and divorce it from other key elements of information control. Privacy rights are like a turtle that can choose to expose its head or keep it within. Such rights can be used or waived.[10] For the latter, consider a prospective employee who chooses to reveal personal details, e.g., about lifestyle or ethnicity, that a job interviewer is prohibited from asking about. The right not to offer any information may be asserted even when there is no incriminating, embarrassing, or strategically disadvantageous information to protect. During the red scare of the 1950s some persons refused to cooperate with investigating committees out of principle rather than because they had an affiliation to hide.[11] The concept of choice inherent to privacy as a normative phenomenon is possible only when the agent is under an obligation to neither compel, nor to prevent, disclosure and the subject has discretion regarding revelation.[12]

But as fundamental as privacy's freedom to choose is to modern notions of the democratic citizen, it formally reflects only one of several elements in the control of personal information. Equally important to a robust understanding of privacy are the subject's and others' obligation to withhold or reveal and the agent's obligation to seek or not to seek.

Rather than discretion, some rules involve a prohibition or restriction on revealing information. Consider contractual restrictions, gag orders, secrecy agreements, and rules about confidentiality, classification, leaks, and who within an organization is authorized to speak to outsiders—the First Amendment notwithstanding. There may be an obligation of secrecy on the part of the subject (or repository) not to tell. This moral firewall may apply to the information itself or to the fact that information exists. This instance shares with an exercised privacy right the limitation of information sharing and its denial to others. But unlike the right to privacy, the obligation to keep the secret cannot be waived.

A related aspect of this rule involves limits on subjects as potential agents of expression who are not to unduly intrude on others. Note expectations regarding modesty in dress, closing bathroom and bedroom doors, prohibitions on breastfeeding in public, limits on obtrusive cell phone use, smoking or wearing perfume in public, or on a neighbor's loud music or wafting cooking smells.[13]

An element of information control opposite from privacy (and its less inclusive kin secrecy) is a subject's *obligation of publicity* or better, *disclosure* (or *revelation*).[14] Thus Hawthorne's novella *The Scarlet Letter* and examples of convicted drunk drivers and sex offenders and those quarantined for health reasons from current times are examples of rules mandating the revelation of personal information. Here the subject must reveal. This broadcasting (whether narrow or broad) shares with an unexercised privacy right the *disclosure* of information, but, in contrast to the unexercised right which can be waived, revelation is mandatory.[15] The appropriate metaphor for the subject here is a propelling porcupine rather than a turtle.

What rules apply to the potential agent of discovery or a data repository? What does a rule imply about the discovery, treatment, and communication *rights* and *obligations* of an agent who does not have the information? Must information be sought, is there a prohibition on seeking it, or is a decision made at the discretion of the agent? What rules appear once a repository is in possession of data?

The rules may exclude the agent from any access or limit the agent from compelling and sometimes even from asking or seeking information. There may be a firewall around the agent as well as the subject or the repository. When the agent can seek information the metaphor for rules and tools is a vacuum cleaner with either a broad or a narrow nozzle. Discovery, like flypaper, can gather whatever is in range or have the precise and restricted focus of a laser.

The subject may have a *right* to withhold or offer information, or the subject may have an *obligation* to withhold or offer information. We can also ask whether the rule requires or prohibits a given behavior and ask about the breadth of the rule. Beyond whether the rule involves disclosing, protecting, seeking, or not seeking information, we can ask if the expectation the rule creates is universal/categorical or applies only under restricted circumstances (situationally specific). When personal information is subject to rules regarding protection or revelation, or an agent is prohibited from or required to seek it, are such things demanded under all or under restricted conditions?

Whatever the kind of behavior that is involved or whether the rule says "must" or "must not," we must attend to the conditions for the behavior and rule enforcement. Some information protection rules, techniques, and environmental conditions that are broad and seamless always apply categorically to the righteous and the unrighteous. They present a nearly impenetrable barrier to data going out or coming in or no barrier at all when the mandate is to always reveal or seek to discover. More commonly, information rules are bounded by limiting, rather than absolute, conditions. They tend to be contextual and contingent, rather than rigidly universal in their prescription or proscription; borders are filtered rather than absolute.[16] Here we see rules about rules themselves rather than about content. Such rules indicate what data collection means can be used and under what conditions.

Consider, for example, criminal justice. Leo and Skolnick (1992) note how the acceptability of the police use of deception to gain information varies depending on where in the processes of being in custody and interrogation the deception takes place. Deception apart, police are generally free to ask (and subjects may ignore) any questions before an arrest has been made. The rules change after arrest and also in the courtroom under the hammer of the oath. During a trial a prosecutor can ask, but the accused cannot be compelled to testify. Witnesses can refuse to testify but risk being held in contempt of court. These constraints, of course, lead to numerous end runs as with undercover police efforts to voluntarily illicit what would otherwise be withheld or not permitted with conventional inquires (Marx 1988, Ross 2008, Joh 2009).

After mapping the rules related to questions 4 and 5, we need to ask, Are they honored? Understanding the correlates of greater and lesser fit between the rules and behavior is central for public policy. What factors condition varying connections between the rules and behavior? In situations where agents are prohibited from discovering personal information, but do so anyway, we see privacy violations. When they fail to inquire and are required to, we may see incompetence. Many U.S. states now recognize a civil action involving "wrongful birth" as a result of a doctor's failure to diagnose or disclose the risk of having a child with severe genetic or congenital abnormality.

The expectations involve both asking (as in assessing or testing) and telling the subject. Subjects violating the rules may also be invading the privacy of others by revealing when they should not and be acting irresponsibly by withholding when they are expected to reveal.[17]

A related issue involves enforcement of sanctions that may be associated with a rule's violations whether by subjects or agents. How do the sanctions for violations of, or rewards for, conformity to rules differ by type and context (contrast the failure to tell or the failure to ask when these are mandated)? Seeking unauthorized information, successfully obtaining it, making a record, informing others, or using the information can constitute distinct violations.[18]

Different legal resources such as civil and criminal penalties can be applied to violations, and law and other policy instruments may also offer positive incentives for conformity. For example, if the subject does reveal information, is there a penalty for not telling the truth, whether by outright lying, prevaricating, or deceptively withholding?

Responses to untruthfulness are likely to vary by whether revealing information is optional or mandatory or involves an oath. The latter two alternatives are likely to be accompanied by more costly sanctions. How do penalties for lying, refusing to answer when that is required, or revealing when that is prohibited compare? How do sanctions for subjects compare to those for agents?

Sanctions for discovered (and acted upon) violations can vary from not receiving something desired, such as a loan or a license, to the loss of a job, fines, and civil and criminal penalties. Just how these are distributed across types of violations for the different roles is an important question. Under what conditions do responses to violations emphasize compensating those harmed by the violation rather than sanctioning those responsible?

A full treatment of rules for privacy of personal information must also analyze illegitimate forms of information control such as blackmail, in which threats are brought to bear on either a subject or an agent to protect information. Unlike the incentives for offering information, the logic is reversed here with rewards for not telling.

The compliance means for rule conformity contrast with the means where the subjects have discretion to withhold or reveal information. Where individuals have a right of privacy (the option of whether to reveal information), means of compliance may involve soft surveillance appeals to values, tangible rewards, convenience, and low visibility automated data collection.[19] Those signing nondisclosure agreements are essentially rewarded with jobs and related benefits for not revealing—in contrast to those trading information for consumer goods as with frequent shopper cards.

SHARED AND OPPOSITIONAL GOALS AND
SYMMETRY AND ASYMMETRY IN RULES (QUESTIONS 6 AND 7)

Information control settings can be viewed as a social system that at a minimum involves an interacting subject and agent.[20] The rights and obligations of information *closure* and *disclosure* need to be seen in their systematic relationship to each other for both subjects and agents. The systematic and interactive qualities of information control can be seen when the variables defined above are combined in various ways to classify information settings.

The logical possibilities here are very large. For example, combining the kind of behavior (reveal, conceal, seek, do not seek) with the direction of the rule (prescribe, optional, proscribe) for subjects and agents yields nine analytically distinct combinations, although some of these will be empirically barren. By far the largest number of instances is in the cell that involves the discretion of subjects and agents. There we often see an exchange/contractual model with genuine choice as subjects willingly cooperate. Or there may be a specious choice as in an offer that cannot be refused because the costs of opting out or in are too great. The gathering of data may also simply reflect the practical difficulties of protection. Soft, low visibility means of data harvesting, often done without the subject's knowledge or consent, take advantage of such situations.

Asking and Telling

Table 10.1 brings together subjects and agents with what the rules require. The table calls attention to four situations based on rules for withholding or offering information by the subject and for asking or not asking (more broadly seeking or not) for information by the agent.

What is the historical trend regarding the relative size of these categories? A growth of organizations and social complexity, doom-saying, and a death of privacy perspective would argue that the number of areas (and the amount of information within them) in which individuals must reveal personal data

Table 10.1.   Four Types Based on Rules for Subject and Agents

		RULE for SUBJECT	
		Disclosure	*Closure*
RULE for AGENT	Do ask	1. do tell, do ask (public health doctor-patient)	2. don't tell, do ask (spies, games)
	Don't ask	3. do tell, don't ask	4. don't tell, don't ask (military)

is increasing relative to the number of areas where information is optional or protected. That pattern would be suggested if cell 1 in table 10.1, in which subjects must disclose and agents can (or must) ask, is increasing in size relative to cell 4, in which subjects have discretion to reveal or withhold and agents are prohibited from asking. If that is the case, is the declining power of the individual matched by the weakening power of the individual to know about organizations? In contrast, a view that emphasizes the gradual growth of civil liberties over the last century would argue that the ratio of cell 1 in table 10.1 to cell 4 goes in the opposite direction—the power of agents declines and citizens' discretion to reveal or withhold information increases.

A related question involves trends in the protection of data that have been gathered, apart from the conditions for data collection. What would measuring the connections over time between rules regarding freedom of information, disclosure, and privacy protection reveal about whether personal information is more or less available to individuals—whether about themselves or others?

But any conclusions about historical trends would also have to consider the development of rules for protecting repository information. Thus, while it is likely that there are ever more occasions in which personal information must be revealed or can be demanded, it is also possible that, as the expansion of privacy laws and protections would suggest, there are ever stronger safeguards for the information that is collected. Rules for collection and subsequent protection are part of a system and may move in tandem.[21] Rules often contain contradictory elements in efforts to mediate value conflicts. Thus, freedom of information laws designed to make information available also are stuffed with exemptions to protect information. Distinct rules also conflict, such as those designed to protect whistle-blowing and freedom of speech versus those designed to protect privacy and confidentiality.

This question could additionally be read to concern the specific "amount" of personal information that must, or must not, be offered or asked for, as opposed to concern with the proportion taken of potentially available information. Thus it is possible that, while ever more information must be given up by individuals, the proportion of the information that could possibly be known has been declining and the proportion protected by rules is increasing. A measure of *surveillance slack*, which considers the extent to which personal information is obtained (both legitimately and illegitimately) in relationship to the amount of information that *could* be obtained given available technology and ways of behaving, is needed for comparing time periods or settings (Marx 2002).

When a subject has a right (and a desire) to withhold and the investigator cannot directly ask but is motivated to find out, information may be independently found apart from the subject, whether in violation of the letter or spirit of the rules or in creatively getting around them. The skilled investigator may be able to manipulate the subject into providing information, as with confessions in criminal justice, whether true or false (Leo 2007).

Table 10.2 (engaging questions 6 and 7) highlights four situations determined by whether the interaction involves cooperation or conflict or is unidirectional or bidirectional. I am particularly interested in the *unidirectional conflict* setting emphasized by Erving Goffman (1963, 1969), in which information the subject does not wish to reveal is of interest to the agent who does not know. For the agent to know there must be revelation by the subject or independent discovery through other means, such as undercover tactics, informers, vital tests, accidents, and inferences.[22] This kind of conflict is common both within hierarchical organizations and between organizations and the individual. Examples of a unidirectional conflict can include an employer interested in the off-duty behavior of employees, an insurance company (the agent) interested in learning about clients' prior health conditions, a subject's interest in withholding such information, a voyeur, and an unwilling or unwitting subject or a parent and a rebellious teenager.[23]

In contrast, in the case of *unidirectional cooperative* settings, subjects and agents share the goal of nondiscovery/not knowing or of revelation/knowing. In the doctor-patient case illustrated by table 10.1, cell 1, major goals are ideally shared.[24] The doctor is expected to ask, and the patient to reveal. Cooperative examples can also be seen when the shared goal involves protecting information. Thus in table 10.1, cell 4, the agent is expected to not ask and the subject not to reveal. Consider the meshing of goals in the military's "don't ask, don't tell" policy regarding homosexuality. Whatever their private beliefs, the parties as military role players have a shared (cooperative) interest in protecting information about sexual behavior.[25]

In the reciprocal *bidirectional* case there is usually greater equality between the parties, the rules they are subject to, and their resources to protect and discover. The parties mirror each other in pursing equivalent goals within a common rule environment. Depending on how the kaleidoscope is turned, an actor will be seen as an agent or a subject. In conflict settings the parties seek to protect their own and to discover their opponent's information. Con-

Table 10.2. Direction and Nature of the Interaction

INTERACTION	Cooperation	Conflict
Bidirectional	1. Prenuptial agreements	2. Spies, games
DIRECTION		
Unidirectional	3. Doctor and patient	4. Law enforcement, some licensing and registration

sider games such as poker, the actions of national intelligence agencies, and competitive businesses. The rules may be formal, as with games and legal contracts, or the rules may be looser, as with unwritten understandings among business competitors or national security agencies.

In cooperative settings the rules require mutual revelation. Prenuptial agreements in which parties disclose their assets and health or commercial disclosure agreements for partners are illustrative (see table 10.2, cell 1).

TYPES OF BORDER (QUESTION 8)

As the discussion above suggests, whether information is known or sought is related to kinds of rules. The rules in turn reflect the kind of information and the environment in which information is found.

How does concealed or revealed information that results from a specific rule (a cultural border or antiborder) differ from that whose status is a consequence of the natural environment involving the presence or absence of a physical border? Barriers such as distance, darkness, time, dense undergrowth, and disaggregated data have traditionally protected information. In their absence information is immediately available to anyone with normal senses and cognition; for example, seeing a person's unmasked face or observing his apparent gender, height, and age.

The relationships between properties of the physical world and the presence of rules are understudied. Some natural conditions mean there is no need for a protective rule (when protection is deemed appropriate), at least until technology manages to pierce these protective borders that appear by default. In other cases this very protection can create a perceived need to have a rule and/or technology that overcomes the border.

Table 10.3 highlights four situations that result from considering the presence or absence of cultural and physical borders with respect to the flows of personal information. An example of where both cultural and physical borders are present is a prison (cell 4). In the absence of either border, only manners and limits on the senses prevent seeing and making inferences about a person encountered on the street or overhearing the conversation of nearby persons (cell 1). Antistalking laws and manners, e.g., "don't stare," illustrate cultural borders in the absence of a physical border (cell 3). Being beyond the range of another's unaided seeing or hearing protects information even in the absence of rules (cell 2).

Of course, physical and cultural barriers are not independent, although in general more academic attention goes into understanding how the latter alters the physical than how the physical conditions the culture. Constructed

Table 10.3. Borders and Information

		PHYSICAL BARRIER to CROSSING	
		No (Soft)	Yes (Hard)
CULTURAL (NORMATIVE) BARRIER to CROSSING	No (Open)	1. Looking at a person speaking to you, city borders	2. Sense limitations (darkness, distance, walls)
	Yes (Closed)	3. Staring, backstage regions, privacy and confidentiality expectations, religious and sacred areas	4. Convents, military bases, vaults

environments may seek to create conditions of openness or blockage found in natural environments.

Much energy and invention go into developing impermeable or permeable borders in an effort to hide what would otherwise be in plain sight or easy to discover, or to reveal what is not. Regarding revelation, consider infrared technology that enables night vision; x-rays that "see" through barriers such as clothes, skin, and luggage; cutting trees and foliage to increase visibility; merging data widely dispersed in time, place, and form; and even having a lip reader with binoculars intercept communication too far away to be overheard—whether for law enforcement or in sports.[26] A bank's prohibition of wearing sunglasses and hats also fits here, as do prohibitions on carrying concealed weapons, requirements for see-through school backpacks, and uniforms without pockets and standards for how technologies are to be made.[27]

In other cases the easy availability of information may create incentives for protecting it and rules that require such protection. High walls, encryption for communication, and masks, plastic surgery, elevator shoes, and false IDs for individuals are examples of protecting what otherwise could be seen. Interesting examples of blocking what would otherwise be available can be seen with witnesses who testify behind a screen and whose voices are altered or some symphony orchestras that audition performers behind a screen, hiding their appearance in order to work against discrimination based on gender or race.

Even when the environment provides information or an opportunity to express it, self-control, manners, concern over reciprocity, and a sense of honor or an oath may mean forgone opportunities to observe or share information in the absence of laws, e.g., averting the eyes not to embarrass others, speaking softly in public, or suppressing a cough during a performance or not gossiping.

The qualities of the data offer another area for inquiry. How does whether data are in visual, auditory, olfactory, numerical, or narrative form condition the kind of rule we develop about such information? Similarly, how do the kinds of tools needed to collect, reproduce, and communicate information af-fect the kind of rule we invoke about that information? It is a truism to note that rules are related to motivations and literal possibilities to behave in ways that the rules seek to control. Yet rules also show some realism in not trying very hard to regulate things that are almost impossible to regulate. Note the hollowness of a judge telling a jury to ignore something it has just seen and heard. In our culture there are few rules about information gained through overt, direct hearing and seeing, although there are rules about recording, sharing, or using such data.

CONCLUSION

This chapter has considered eight questions involving rules about the broadly defined topic of personal information. These questions involve (1) the kind of information, (2) the role played as subject or agent, (3) who has the in-formation, (4) whether the behavior involves closure or disclosure and (5) is prescribed, optional or proscribed, (6) whether the goals of the subject and agent are shared or in conflict, (7) whether the rules are asymmetrical or sym-metrical, and (8) borders involving the properties of the information, rules, and the environment.

William James suggested that to phrase a question well already provides half of the answer. I am not sure about that fraction, but good questions cer-tainly are helpful in raising new questions. I hope the questions raised here and the distinctions above can be further analyzed and can guide research.

The multidimensional nature of personal information and the extensive contextual and situational variation occur within dynamic settings of social conflict. These many dimensions prevent any simple conclusions with respect to explanation and judgment regarding the rules about personal information. Such complexity serves us well when it introduces humility, qualification, and research, but not if it immobilizes. Answers, however temporal and qualified, depend on asking appropriate questions. The signposts provided by specifying concepts are not a detailed map, but they are the building blocks out of which one can emerge.

NOTES

1. I will use the terms *information* and *data* as interchangeable, although for some purposes a distinction between "raw" data and "constructed" and "interpreted" infor-mation is needed.

2. However, contrasting new and traditional information tools with an emphasis on the attributes that differentiate these is a major question. Marx (2002) suggests a number of dimensions for contrasting traditional and the new surveillance.

3. That article notes distinctions based on whether information is private or public with regard to its degree of immediate availability to an agent and is personal or impersonal. Using a series of smaller concentric circles, I further differentiate information that is individual, private, sensitive, and unique and involves a core identity.

4. This area can be further differentiated by adding the sometimes independent categories of the initiator and/or sponsor of the activity. The more distinct the categories, the more challenging the policy and ethical questions.

5. Thus once agents have information about others, those agents may become subjects for other agents and data warehouses who seek "their" data (about someone else) for secondary uses. There are far fewer restrictions in the United States on the ability of third parties to obtain and use such information than is the case in Europe.

6. Such report-based data are data about the person driving, but the reporting and interpretation involved in the data are clearly distinct from information about the driver such as age or location.

7. Birth records offer a nice example of the blurry borders of coproduced personal information. Babies left on doorsteps, the filing of false records, or the failure to file in order to avoid taxation, military service, or parental responsibility raise research questions about the degree of compliance with this rule but do not negate the rule.

8. Examples of such experiments and deceptions include the CIA experiments with LSD (Albarelli 2009) and work at the Tuskegee Institute on syphilis (Reverby 2010).

9. These instances offer interesting contrasts with situations where subjects are mandated to reveal but prefer not to and those where subjects must not reveal but would like to. Consider also the related cases where agents are expected to reveal but do not, as with discovery in the legal system. In the case of a criminal justice trial, discovery requires the prosecution to provide information to the defense. If the defense can show it was denied appropriate information the case will be dismissed. That requirement gives prosecutors an incentive for following disclosure rules. However, such information may undercut the prosecution's case and may be withheld if its existence is unlikely to be otherwise known. Police may fail to report information to prosecutors that would work against conviction, such as that provided by an informant (Natapoff 2010).

10. A different aspect of privacy, often referred to as solitude or being let alone, involves the right to control information or data more broadly defined from crossing into one's personal borders. The discretionary curtain can be adjusted to keep information from coming in, as well as from going out. There are, however, some limits here as well.

Note two-way public address systems in schools that are always on and constructing communication tools so they can receive emergency messages. With regard to the latter, the Federal Emergency Management Administration can send safety warnings that override whatever communications device is in use. Efforts are underway through the Digital Emergency Alert System to allow transmission of emergency alerts to computers, cell phones, and pagers beyond their current availability to radio and television. There are also efforts to create an automatic alarm turn-on capability for devices not in use.

11. Communication rights to freedom of speech and association are of course also interwoven with the expression or withholding of personal information, as with the case of membership lists. Note *NAACP v. Alabama ex rel. Flowers*, 377 U.S. 288 (1964), in which the Supreme Court held that it was illegal for the state to demand a list of NAACP members. In a curious twist the Spanish Data Protection Agency in its public relations efforts justifying Spain's new mandatory national identity card claims that the card goes along with the citizen's right to a national identity (Ouzeil 2010). All countries may require those crossing borders to assert this identity; whether and when pedestrians must also do this shows enormous regional variation that may be declining. The well-known demand for "your papers please" has become internationalized. Author B. Traven (1991) would not have appreciated a 2010 Arizona law requiring local police to verify immigration/citizenship status.

12. Whether the agent can even ask the subject questions is another variable. In the arrest situation the answer is "no" unless the right is waived or an attorney is present, while in criminal justice trials the prosecutor is free to ask but cannot compel disclosure.

13. Then, of course, there is the neighborly expectation of control over sounds associated with lovemaking. Consider the British couple who received a conviction for breaching a noise abatement notice. A neighbor complained that she was frequently late to work because she overslept as a result of "having been awake most of the night because of the offending noise." Equipment installed in the complainant's flat by the local city council recorded noise levels up to 47 decibels. Laws and expectations conflict. The offending couple argued they had done nothing wrong and under the Human Rights Act they were entitled to respect for their private and family life (BBC 2009).

14. Publicity follows easily from privacy. But in a strict sense the oppositional meaning of publicity here is made "public," as in known to another, rather than publicity as in something widely broadcast. How large the public is when the disclosure of information is obligatory and the rules (if any) that apply to the recipient of the information are related facets.

15. Private and public (or better nonrevelation and revelation or closure and disclosure) as used here refer to rules rather than the status of the information. When the rules are not followed, information intended to be private may become known as with leaks, and, when disclosure rules are violated, e.g., not reporting conflicts of interest, what is intended to be public remains private (Marx 2001a).

16. The filters around information can be located by asking if the subject is required to always reveal personal information or only if asked. If the subject has discretion not to disclose, is it necessary to opt out of disclosure by a formal request? Requiring subjects to opt out of data provision is the preferred policy of many organizations. That policy permits honoring the privacy of the subject but tilts against the subject's taking the requisite action to protect privacy. Opt-out can also be seen when callers are offered the opportunity to request that a telephone conversation with a company not be recorded. A related phone control concern involves forms some

doctors' offices give out asking seeing instructions about whether and what kind of messages to leave on patients' answering machines.

17. The behavioral and cultural ways that subjects seek to neutralize information rules are treated in Marx (2003). Nondisclosure and gag requirements, for example, can be overcome by anonymous communication. Note the obvious violations of confidentiality and nondisclosure agreements in the spate of political tell-all books such as *Game Change* (Heilemann and Halperin 2010). According to one account, "discretion is on the wane and disclosures on the rise" as a result of new markets created by Internet communication (*New York Times*, January 17, 2010). The formal rules may be buttressed by and reflective of the culture as well as undermined by it.

18. Whether pertinent actors see a violation in any particular circumstance will partly depend on how behavior is interpreted by authorities. The lines between rule conformity and violation are often hazy given the differences between intangible information and tangible material; you know if your wallet has been stolen, but when is a leak a leak? From one viewpoint, in the Watergate case Mark Felt (Deep Throat) clearly broke the law and departmental regulations in giving information about the ongoing Watergate investigation to *Washington Post* reporters Woodward and Bernstein. But from another perspective, he did not, since he spoke only in general terms and offered no names or specific details about the FBI's investigation. Rather, he offered broad hints and some confirmation of whether the reporters were on the right track. Much of the information the reporters had also came from other sources, which may have protected them from committing crimes. The interpretive borderland is even blurrier here, although, as with conspiracies, intent may matter apart from overt behavior in itself (Woodward 2005).

19. Note two meanings of *optional* here—one refers to tolerance by the rules and the other to the capability of violation. With hard-engineered forms of surveillance, there is an effort to eliminate the possibility of withholding personal information.

Soft forms of surveillance, on the other hand, try to alter incentives so individuals either follow the rule or use their option in a way desired by an agent. Included here is an appeal to ethics and conscience. Consider the "Public Health Questionnaire" given out by a cruise line to passengers regarding recent fever, coughs, and the like in which passengers are asked (in the absence of any legal requirement to provide the information) to sign the document that states, "I certify that the above declaration is true and correct and that any dishonest answers may have serious public health implications."

20. It takes two to tango, but sometimes persons can dance alone. At times the interaction will be only in the imagination of the subject or the agent. Consider a person with a secret taking protective action based on anticipating potential moves of an agent or an agent taking steps to avoid discovery.

21. Persons who wish to give blood, for example, donate, as an advertisement promises, in an "individual booth arranged to preserve confidentiality." They are required to provide health histories, and the blood sample is tested. If tests show that blood is HIV positive, the individual receives confidential notification, and the data are protected. Decades earlier another problem with blood appeared with the development of a test for syphilis. Concerned about a potential syphilis epidemic and protecting the unborn in the 1930s and 1940s, many states adopted laws requiring a blood

test before a marriage license could be granted. Now only a handful of states have that requirement. Few cases appeared, and the testing was not seen as cost-effective. This example offers an interesting question related to causation as the technology enables and then undermines the collection of personal information. Blood testing is routinely done on a voluntary basis in the case of pregnancy.

22. Marx (1984) considers a variety of tactics involving deception, coercion, volition, inference, and uncontrolled contingencies for discovering information individuals and organizations do not wish to reveal.

23. A less common form of information control interaction reverses the direction. Consider a case where the subject wishes to reveal and the rules prevent the agent from knowing or the agent at least wishes to avoid knowing.

24. Elements of conflict (or at least potential conflict) can also be seen. Note the lack of reciprocity in doctors' requiring that patients provide extensive personal information and a photo ID and agree to database searches to see if they have previously sued a doctor. Patients do not usually request equivalent information from doctors, e.g., that doctors submit to a database search regarding malpractice, drug abuse, sexual improprieties, or license revocations, nor are the doctor's credentials verified to protect against falsification and impersonation.

25. While not quite a conspiracy of silence, there are unstated or only minimally acknowledged reasons to look the other way and not know or acknowledge what is known or suspected. In this case the military agent has an interest in following the "don't ask" rules and the military subject in following the "don't tell" rules.

26. Consider the famous (infamous?) case of the 1951 playoff game between the New York Giants and the Brooklyn Dodgers, in which the home-run-hitting batter (Bobby Thomson) apparently learned what pitch to expect based on radioed communication from a coach with binoculars in the bleachers who read the catcher's signal to the pitcher (Prager 2008).

27. The 1994 Digital Telephony Act also known as CALEA (103-414, 108 Stat. 4279, codified at 47 USC 1001-1010) for example, requires that digital communication devices be built to permit eavesdropping. More recently there has been an effort to create new legislation that would require Internet companies that provide communication such as Gmail, Facebook, Blackberry, and Skype to be technically capable of quickly complying with a wiretap order (*New York Times*, October 23, 2010).

REFERENCES

Adams, C. 2006. A classification of privacy techniques. *University of Ottawa Law and Technology Journal* 3, no. 1: 35–52.

Agre, P. 1994. Surveillance and capture: Two models of privacy. *Information Society* 10, no. 3: 101–27.

Albarelli, H. P. 2009. *A terrible mistake*. Walterville, OR: Trine Day.

British Broadcasting Channel News Channel. (2009, November 9). Court hears couple's sex sessions.

Farrall, K. 2010. National suspicious activity reporting initiative and the production of U.S. domestic intelligence. Paper delivered at 5th International Conference on the Ethics of National Security Intelligence. Georgetown University, Washington, DC.

Gandy, O. 1993. *The panoptic sort: Towards a political economy of information.* Boulder, CO: Westview Press.

Goffman, Erving. 1963. *Stigma: Notes on the management of spoiled identity.* Englewood Cliffs, NJ: Prentice Hall.

———. 1969. *Strategic interaction.* Philadelphia: University of Pennsylvania Press.

Hawthorne, N. 1994. *The scarlet letter.* New York: Dover Publications.

Heilemann, J., and Halperin, M. 2010. *Game change.* New York: Harper.

Joh, E. 2009. Breaking the law to enforce it: Undercover police participation in crime. *Stanford Law Review* 62 :156–99.

Leo, R. A. 2007. *Police interrogation and American justice.* Cambridge, MA: Harvard University Press.

Leo, R., and Skolnick, J. 1992. The ethics of deceptive interrogation. *Criminal Justice Ethics* 11, no. 1:3–12.

Marx, G. T. 1984. Notes on the discovery, collection, and assessment of hidden and dirty data. In *Studies in the sociology of social problems*, ed. J. Schneider and J. Kitsuse. Norwood, NJ: Ablex.

———.1988. *Undercover police surveillance in America.* Berkeley, CA: University of California Press.

———. 2001a. Murky conceptual waters: The public and the private. *Ethics and Information Technology* 3, no. 3: 157–69.

———. 2001b. Identity and anonymity: Some conceptual distinctions and issues for research. In *Documenting individual identity*, ed. J. Caplan and J. Torpey, 311–27. Princeton, NJ: Princeton University Press.

———. 2002. What's new about the "new surveillance"?: Classifying for change and continuity. *Surveillance and Society* 1, no. 1: 9–29.

———. 2003. A tack in the shoe: Neutralizing and resisting the new surveillance. *Journal of Social Issues* 59, no. 2: 369–90.

———. 2005. Seeing hazily (but not darkly) through the lens: Some recent empirical studies of surveillance technologies. *Law and Social Inquiry* 30, no. 2: 339–99.

———. 2006a. Varieties of personal information as influences on attitudes toward surveillance. In *The new politics of surveillance and visibility,* ed. K. Haggerty and R. Ericson, 79–110. Toronto: University of Toronto Press.

———. 2006b. Soft surveillance: The growth of mandatory volunteerism in collecting personal information—"Hey buddy can you spare a DNA?" In *Surveillance and security: Technological politics and power in everyday life,* ed. T. Monahan, 37–56. Portland, OR: Wilan.

———. 2007a. The engineering of social control: Policing and technology. *Policing: A Journal of Policy and* Practice 1,1: 46–56.

———. 2007b. Privacy and equality. In *Encyclopedia of privacy*, ed. W. Staples. Westport, CT: Greenwood Press.

Marx, G. T., and Muschert, G. 2007. Personal information, borders, and the new surveillance. *Annual Review of Law and Social Science* 3: 375–95. Palo Alto, CA: Annual Reviews.

Natapoff, A. 2010. *Snitching: Criminal informants and the erosion of American justice.* New York: New York University Press.

Nippert-Eng, C. 2010. *Islands of privacy.* Chicago: University of Chicago Press.

Nissenbaum, H. 2010. *Privacy in context: Technology, policy, and the integrity of social life.* Palo Alto, CA: Stanford University Press.

Ouzeil, P. 2010. *The Spanish identity card: Historical legacies and contemporary surveillance.* Unpublished master's thesis. Victoria, BC: University of British Columbia.

Polanski, R. 1974. *Chinatown.*

Prager, Joshua. 2008. *The echoing green: The untold story of Bobby Thomson, Ralph Branca and the shot heard round the world.* New York: Vintage.

Reverby, S. 2010. *Examining Tuskegee: The infamous syphilis study and its legacy.* Chapel Hill, NC: University of North Carolina Press.

Ross, J. 2008. Undercover policing and the shifting terms of scholarly debate: The United States and Europe in counterpoint. *Annual Review of Law and the Social Sciences,* 4: 17.1–17.35. Palo Alto, CA: Annual Reviews.

Rowinski, D. 2010. Police fight cell phone recordings. New England Center for Investigative Reporting / January 12, http://mobile.boston.com/art/21//news/local/massachusetts/articles/2010/01/12/police_fight_cellphone_recordings/.

Rule, J. 1973. *Private lives, public surveillance.* London: Allen-Lane.

Spire, P. 2009. Peeping. *Berkeley Technology and Law Journal* 24, no. 3: 1168–98.

Staples, W. 2000. *Everyday surveillance: Vigilance and visibility in postmodern life.* Lanham, MD: Rowan & Littlefield.

Traven, B. 1991. *The death ship.* Brooklyn, NY: L. Hills Books.

Woodward, B. 2005. *The secret man: The story of Watergate's Deep Throat.* New York: Simon and Schuster.

Index

Abbate, Janet, 131
abortion court cases, 8–9, 11
Abrahamson, James L., 259
accessibility of identity documentation, 103, 104
Access/Participation principle, 89–90
accountability and identity judgments, 102
accuracy of identity judgments, 103
Ad Hoc Group on Biometrics and E-Authentication (AHGBEA), 181
Advanced Research Projects Agency, 130–31
advertising, 115, 151–57, 159–60, 193–95
Agar, Jon, 126
agents of discovery, 276–78
Agre, Philip E., 211–12
AHGBEA (Ad Hoc Group on Biometrics and E-Authentication), 181
airport security measures, 86
Akera, Atsushi, 132
Albright v. Morton, 53–54, 57, 58–59, 79n342
alternative identity rights framework, 91–98
American Civil War, 248, 255–56, 264

American Protective League, 259
American Research and Development, 127
American Revolution, 248, 252, 264
Analytical Engine, 125
Andreessen, Marc, 132
Andrews, Bruce, 266
Angel Plan, 19–20
Aniston, Jennifer, 67–68n47
anonymity, 33, 101, 103, 231–33
Antón, A. I., 183
appropriation, 31, 57–59, 117
Arar, Maher, 86
ARPANET, 130–31
arrest/detention, 101
Ashcroft, John, 247
asking and telling, 282–84
Aspray, William, 124–25, 126, 247–69
AT&T, 131
authentication, 95–98, 167–68. *See also* biometric systems
autonomy and privacy, 213, 250

Babbage, Charles, 125
Baker v. Burlington Northern, Inc., 71n130
Baker v. Vermont, 9–10, 23n3
Ball, Carlos, 34

Hughes, Thomas, 238
Human-Machine Reconfigurations
(Suchman), 222
Hush-a-Phone v. United States, 129
hypertext, 132

IBM, 127
ICAO (International Civil Aviation
Organization), 175
identity: definitions, 211–12;
documentation/practices, 102;
impairment, 91; privacy interests
compared to, 94–98; theft of, 115;
verification. *See* biometric systems
identity cards, 113
identity judgment, 102–4
identity rights: framework alternative,
91–98; limitations of, 87–91;
overview, 85–87; principles in
Canadian government, 98–108
IITF (Information Infrastructure Task
Force), 224–25
illegitimate forms of information
control, 281
IMSI (International Mobile Subscriber
Identity), 204
Individual Reference Services Group
Principles, 199
informants, 261
informational privacy, 4, 250. *See also*
personal information
Information Infrastructure Task Force
(IITF), 224–25
innocence, presumption of, 101
"inspection" definition, 145
integrity of personal identity, 100–101
International Civil Aviation
Organization (ICAO), 175
International Mobile Subscriber Identity
(IMSI), 204
International Telecommunication Union
(ITU), 129
Internet: ISPs, 140–41, 146–49; layers
of, 123–24; modems, 128–30;
sponsorship by government, 130–31;

web usage metrics, 152. *See also*
deep packet inspection (DPI)
Internet Protocol (IP), 141–45
internment of Japanese/Japanese
Americans, 261
interpretations of identity, 91–93
intrusion, 31, 33–40, 48, 117
iris recognition, 172
ISPs, 140–41, 146–49. *See also* deep
packet inspection (DPI)
ITU (International Telecommunication
Union), 129

James, William, 287
Japan, 18, 19–20
Japanese/Japanese American internment,
261
judgmental transparency/accountability,
101

Kahn, Herman, 127
Kennedy, Ted, 86
*Kerrigan v. Commissioner of Public
Health,* 10–11
King, Nancy, 202
Kleif, Tine, 228
Korean War, 248, 262–63, 264
Kristeva, Julia, 216–17

Lamont v. Postmaster General, 233
Langford v. Sessions, 53, 58
lawful intercept of communications, 153
Lawrence v. Texas, 7–9, 11, 27, 34–35
legislation: Bank Secrecy Act, 122;
court cases compared to, 11;
Digital Telephony Act, 291n27;
DMCA, 211, 213, 223–30, 233–39;
Electronic Communications Privacy
Act, 140; Family Support Act, 122;
Financial Services Modernization
Act, 196; McCarran Internal Security
Act, 263; PIPEDA, 102–4; Privacy
Act, 119; right to privacy recognized
by, 63n1; role of, 116–17; Small
Business Job Protection Act, 122;

Contributors

Anita L. Allen (Anita LaFrance Allen-Castellitto) is deputy dean and Henry R. Silverman Professor of Law at the School of Law, and professor of philosophy at the University of Pennsylvania. She is an expert on privacy law, bioethics, and contemporary values and is recognized for her scholarship about legal philosophy, women's rights, and race relations. In 2010 President Obama appointed her to the Presidential Commission for the Study of Bioethical Issues. Her books include *Everyday Ethics: Opinion-Writing about the Things That Matter Most* (2010); *Unpopular Privacies* (forthcoming, Oxford); *Privacy Law and Society* (Thomson/West, 2007); *The New Ethics: A Guided Tour of the 21st Century Moral Landscape* (Miramax/Hyperion, 2004); *Why Privacy Isn't Everything: Feminist Reflections on Personal Accountability* (Rowan & Littlefield, 2003); and *Uneasy Access: Privacy for Women in a Free Society* (Rowan & Littlefield, 1988). She received her BA from New College, her MA from the University of Michigan, her PhD (in philosophy) from the University of Michigan, and her JD from Harvard University.

William Aspray is the Bill and Lewis Suit Professor of Information Technologies in the School of Information at the University of Texas at Austin. He holds additional appointments in the department of computer science and the LBJ School of Public Affairs. He received his PhD from the University of Wisconsin–Madison. His research involves the historical, political, and social study of information and information technologies. Policy interests include the IT workforce and education, offshoring, Internet use, and privacy. Recent books include *Women and Information Technology* (MIT Press, ed. with Joanne Cohoon), *The Internet and American Business* (MIT Press, ed. with Paul Ceruzzi), and *Health Informatics: A Patient-Centered Approach to*

Diabetes (MIT Press, ed. with Barbara Hayes). Two books are currently in progress: *Information in Everyday American Life* (ed. with Barbara Hayes) and *Interdisciplinary Perspectives on Digital Media* (ed. with Megan Winget).

Craig Blaha is a PhD candidate at the School of Information at the University of Texas at Austin. He is a doctoral preservation fellow with the Institute of Museum and Library Services, and his research interests include privacy, digital preservation, federal information policy, and information security. He has more than ten years of experience in information technology, much of it in higher education security, policy, and web development. In addition to his research, he is the manager of special projects at the University of Texas at Austin School of Information. In this role, he identifies, promotes, and maintains research and strategic partnerships in digitization and preservation policy across campus.

Patricia Boling is an associate professor in the Department of Political Science at Purdue University. She holds a PhD from Berkeley. Her research deals broadly with how problems rooted in private life (e.g., the family, sexuality, reproductive matters, intimate relationships) come to be understood as political issues, particularly with respect to feminist democratic theory. She is currently comparing family policies and democratic responsiveness in France, Germany, Japan, and the United States. Her publications include *Privacy and the Politics of Intimate Life* (Cornell University Press, 1996).

Andrew Clement is professor in the Information faculty at the University of Toronto, where he coordinates the Information Policy Research Program. He also holds a cross-appointment in the Department of Computer Science, from where he received his PhD in 1986. His research, teaching, and consulting interests are in the social implications of information technology and human-centered systems development. Recent research has focused on public information policy, Internet use in everyday life, digital identity constructions, public participation in information/communication infrastructures development, and community networking.

Alissa Cooper is the chief computer scientist at the Center for Democracy and Technology and has completed her bachelor's and master's degrees in computer science at Stanford University. Her current work includes consumers' privacy, network neutrality, and technical standards. She conducts research into the inner workings of common and emerging Internet technologies and seeks to explain complex technical concepts in understandable terms. She has testified before Congress and the Federal Trade Commission and writes regularly on a variety of technology policy topics. She currently co-chairs the Geographic Location/Privacy working group (Geopriv) within the Internet Engineering Task Force (IETF). She is a doctoral student at the Oxford Internet Institute.

Philip Doty is associate dean and a faculty member at the School of Information, associate director of the Telecommunications and Information Policy Institute, and a faculty affiliate of the Center for Women's and Gender Studies, all at the University of Texas at Austin. His research and teaching focus on federal information policy (especially copyright, privacy, and IT), information behavior, cultural and gender aspects of information technologies, history and politics of computer networks, research methods, philosophy and information studies, and digital libraries. He has consulted and done research with organizations such as NASA, the U.S. Office of Management and Budget, the U.S. General Services Administration, the U.S. Office of Technology Assessment, the Museum Computer Network, the GTE/Verizon Foundation, New York State's NYSERNET's New Connections Program, New York's Public Services Training Program, the Texas Office of Court Administration, the Greater Austin Area Telecommunications Network, and the Texas Telecommunications Infrastructure Fund.

Seymour Goodman is professor of international affairs and computing, jointly at the Sam Nunn School of International Affairs and the College of Computing at the Georgia Institute of Technology. He serves as co-director of both the Georgia Tech Information Security Center and the Center for International Strategy, Technology, and Policy. His research interests include international developments in the information technologies, technology diffusion, IT and national security, and related public policy issues. Current work includes research on the global diffusion of the Internet and the protection of large IT-based infrastructures. Immediately before coming to Georgia Tech, he was director of the Consortium for Research on Information Security and Policy (CRISP) at the Center for International Security and Cooperation, with an appointment in the Department of Engineering Economic Systems and Operations Research, both at Stanford University; and Professor of MIS and a member of the Center for Middle Eastern Studies at the University of Arizona.

James Harper is director of information policy studies at the Cato Institute, and his work focuses on the difficulty of adapting law and policy to the unique problems of the information age. Harper is a member of the Department of Homeland Security's Data Privacy and Integrity Advisory Committee. *USA Today*, the Associated Press, and Reuters have cited his work. He has appeared on Fox News Channel, CBS, MSNBC, and other media outlets.

His scholarly articles have appeared in the *Administrative Law Review*, the *Minnesota Law Review*, and the *Hastings Constitutional Law Quarterly*. Recently, Harper wrote the book *Identity Crisis: How Identification Is Overused and Misunderstood*. He is the editor of Privacilla.org, a web-based think tank devoted exclusively to privacy, and he maintains the online federal spending resource WashingtonWatch.com. He holds a JD from the University of California–Hastings College of Law.

Andrew Harris earned an MS degree from Georgia Tech's Sam Nunn School of International Affairs in 2010. While at Georgia Tech, he focused on the use of information and communications technology for political and economic development, particularly in Africa. Specific topics of research included African undersea fiber cables, the diffusion of mobile telephony in Africa, and Liberia's Truth and Reconciliation process. Prior to his graduate work, he served in the U.S. Navy as a Surface Warfare Officer and graduated cum laude from Vanderbilt University in 2001 with a BA in political science. In 2010, he earned an appointment as a (U.S.) presidential management fellow. Through this fellowship, he intends to pursue a career with the U.S. Department of State, working on international policy related to information and communications technology. The views expressed in his chapter do not necessarily represent the views of the State Department or the United States.

Gary Marx is professor emeritus at the Massachusetts Institute of Technology. Widely published in scholarly and popular sources, he was the inaugural Stice Memorial Lecturer in residence at the University of Washington and has been a UC–Irvine Chancellor's Distinguished Fellow, the A.D. Carlson Visiting Distinguished Professor in the Social Sciences at West Virginia University, and the Hixon-Riggs Visiting Professor of Science, Technology, and Society at Harvey Mudd College, Claremont, California. Major works in progress are books on new forms of surveillance and social control across borders. He received his PhD from the University of California at Berkeley. He has been a consultant to, or served on panels for, national commissions, the House Committee on the Judiciary, the House Science Committee, the Senate Labor and Human Resources Committee, the General Accounting Office, the Office of Technology Assessment, the Justice Department, and other federal agencies, state and local governments, the European Community and European Parliament, the Canadian House of Commons, the National Academy of Sciences, SSRC, the American Association for the Advancement of Science, the UK Association of Chief Police Officers, public interest groups, foundations, and think tanks.

Shimon Modi is director of research of the Biometric Standards, Performance, and Assurance Laboratory at Purdue University and currently teaches about the application of biometric technologies. He received his PhD in technology from Purdue University, where his dissertation focused on statistical testing and analysis of fingerprint sensor interoperability on system performance. He has a master's degree in technology with specialization in information security from the Center for Education and Research in Information Assurance and Security (CERIAS), and a bachelor's degree in computer science from Purdue University. His research interests reside in the application of biometrics to authentication, statistical analysis of system performance, enterprise-level information security, and standards development. He is actively involved in biometric standards, both at the national and international level, as a member of the U.S. delegation to the ISO JTC1 SC37 biometrics standards committee, as a technical editor for the BioAPI-Java project, and as Purdue University's voting member on the INCITS M1 biometrics standards committee.

Frank S. Park focuses his research on the effects of physical security through advancement of mobile technology. In addition to his work on security implications of near field communications (NFC) for financial institutions, his prior work includes fraud prevention methods using multilevel authentication via mobile devices and potential methods to monitor keypresses through surface acoustics using the iPhone accelerometer at the Converging Infrastructure Security (CISEC) Lab at Georgia Tech. His earlier research has been in areas of voice over IP (VoIP) and IP multimedia subsystems (IMS) security, focusing on identifying new vulnerabilities on the application and infrastructural levels. He earned a bachelor's degree in computer science and a master's degree in information security, both from the Georgia Institute of Technology.

Eugene Spafford is professor of computer science with courtesy appointments in electrical and computer engineering, communication, and philosophy at Purdue University. He is also the director of the Center for Education and Research in Information Assurance and Security. His current research interests focus on computer and network security, cybercrime and ethics, and the social impact of computing. Among many professional activities, he is chair of ACM's U.S. Public Policy Committee and is the academic editor of the journal *Computers & Security*.

Gesse Stark-Smith is a native of Seattle, Washington. She received her BA in philosophy from Macalester College in 2007 and her MSIS from the University of Texas at Austin in 2010. She has wide-ranging academic interests, and her most recent research has focused on the use of communication technologies by young people. She currently works as a librarian at a Spanish-language immersion school in Austin, Texas.

Patrick Traynor is an assistant professor in the College of Computing at Georgia Tech, having earned his PhD and MS in computer science and engineering from Pennsylvania State University and his BS in computer science from the University of Richmond. He is a member of the Georgia Tech Information Security Center (GTISC) and a co-director of the Converging Infrastructure Security Laboratory (CISEC). His research focuses primarily on security in cellular networks, particularly the problems that arise as this piece of critical infrastructure converges with the larger Internet. He is also interested in the systems challenges of applied cryptography and security for the Internet, mobile devices, and wireless systems.